# CAULDRON OF TERROR

*To all those murdered by Hamas. And may you rest in peace.*

# CAULDRON OF TERROR

## HAMAS, ISRAEL, AND THE WORLD

### FIVE HUNDRED DAYS IN GAZA

MARK D. SILINSKY

Pen & Sword
MILITARY
AN IMPRINT OF PEN & SWORD BOOKS LTD.
YORKSHIRE – PHILADELPHIA

First published in Great Britain in 2026 by
PEN AND SWORD MILITARY
An imprint of
Pen & Sword Books Limited
Yorkshire – Philadelphia



Print ISBN 978 1 03614 282 7
ePUB ISBN 978 1 03614 284 1
ePDF ISBN 978 1 03614 286 5



A CIP catalogue record for this book is available from the British Library.



Typeset in Times New Roman 10/12.5 by
SJmagic DESIGN SERVICES, India.
Printed and bound in the UK by CPI Group (UK) Ltd.

The Publisher's authorised representative in the EU for product safety is Authorised Rep Compliance Ltd., Ground Floor, 71 Lower Baggot Street, Dublin D02 P593, Ireland.
www.arccompliance.com

*For a complete list of Pen & Sword titles please contact*
PEN & SWORD BOOKS LIMITED
George House, Units 12 & 13, Beevor Street, Off Pontefract Road,
Barnsley, South Yorkshire, S71 1HN, England
E-mail: enquiries@pen-and-sword.co.uk
Website: www.pen-and-sword.co.uk

or

PEN AND SWORD BOOKS
1950 Lawrence Rd, Havertown, PA 19083, USA
E-mail: uspen-and-sword@casematepublishers.com
Website: www.penandswordbooks.com

FSC
www.fsc.org
MIX
Paper | Supporting responsible forestry
FSC® C013604

# Contents

# Table of Figures and Maps

# Chapter 1

# Introduction

## Wars within Wars

They arrived by land and air, catching everyone completely off guard. October 7, 2023, marked the bloodiest day in Israeli history. In the early hours, during a Jewish holiday, several thousand terrorists invaded Israel's southern scrublands from Gaza, aiming to massacre as many people as possible. They attacked over 22 facilities, including a music festival, military installations, and kibbutzim, tossing grenades indiscriminately into gatherings of dancing youth and kindergartens.[1]

Gaza's extensive tunnel system enabled large groups of assailants to maneuver undetected by Israeli security forces. The underground stronghold shielded Hamas from the Israeli Defense Forces' (IDF's) surveillance. The shooters disguised themselves as civilians and positioned non-combatants as lookouts. They also utilized civilian homes, mosques, and medical facilities to conceal their activities. During the pre-operational surveillance, Hamas operatives placed covert signals, such as red sheets hanging from windows or spray-painted slogans, to mark locations on the battlefields. This was meticulously planned. There were immediate comparisons to Pearl Harbor and September 11, 2001. Soon, parallels also emerged regarding the annihilationist bloodlust of the mobile killing units, or Einsatzgruppen, of Nazi Germany. On October 7, the assailants were Hamas operatives and their supporters. It was, by far, the most sophisticated attack to emerge from Gaza.[2]

Attackers moved freely from house to house, spraying gunfire at everyone – men, women, boys, girls, and infants. They also shot pets at random. As rivulets of blood seeped into the soil beneath the fallen, entire families lay dying or dead. Many women and girls were raped, disfigured and then killed.[3] Explained one witness, 'We saw evidence of rape . . . and this was also among grandmothers down to small children.'[4] Many corpses were charred beyond recognition, and the homes of families became embers. Body bags contained entire families – mothers, fathers, grandparents, and small children. Hundreds of glazed-eyed witnesses wandered in stunned silence, trying to grasp what had just happened. Of the 1,195 people killed, 815 were civilians, including 79 foreign nationals. Among them were at least 282 women and 36 children. Palestinian armed groups took 251 civilians and personnel from Israeli security forces hostage and brought them back to Gaza following the attack.[5]

The assailants spray-painted their names and the designations of their Hamas unit outside the victims' homes as trophy signatures and marks of triumph. Many of the attackers videotaped the killing spree with body cameras to capture and later relive the moment they slaughtered entire families. They uploaded the event to social media for everyone to see. Then, along with their captives, they skedaddled to Gaza to await the world's response.[6] As with previous terror campaigns, or Intifadas, Hamas aimed to combine kinetic warfare with a psychological campaign to undermine morale in Israel.[7] The immediate global response was shock. Soon, the world looked for answers. Why did such carnage occur in our time, and what type of war was this?[8] There were different responses.

The day also symbolized national solidarity in Israel, as citizens rushed to the battlefield or opened their homes to those in need. On vacation, Israelis took the earliest flights back home, while others volunteered for reserve duty. Many donated money and welcomed the now-homeless kibbutzniks into their homes.

Hamas' war against Israel is complex and cannot be reduced to a single type of conflict. This war is both revolutionary and global. Hamas seeks to eliminate Israel and establish an Islamist Palestinian state, which defines it as a revolutionary conflict. It is undoubtedly a worldwide struggle. Hamas has supporters among both the Sunni and Shia communities and receives significant support from allies throughout the Middle East and Europe. Iran's Foreign Minister cautioned US leaders that Tehran may retaliate against America if Israel escalates the situation into a war.[9] After the October attack, Iranian spiritual leader Ayatollah Khamenei declared the war in Gaza to be the world's most important issue.[10]

Former US National Security Advisor Jake Sullivan announced that Iran was significantly complicit in the attack and that the United States would increase sanctions against Tehran. The US typically supports Israel, even though the relationship is often tense. In addition to formal diplomacy, various international agencies and non-governmental organizations are deeply involved in the affairs of both Palestinians and Israelis. This conflict poses an existential threat to both Israel and Hamas.

The Palestinian people bear a legacy of suffering, as most are not involved in terrorist activities. Many have lost their lives in the crossfire between various warring factions within Palestinian territory. Some of this conflict arises from the ongoing power struggle among rival Palestinian factions. At the same time, other casualties result from Israel's unintended killings of civilians, along with its deliberate policy of demolishing homes. All of this has tarnished Israel's image worldwide.

## Hamas

The goals and values of Hamas are enshrined in its Charter, issued in 1988. It presents a harsh critique of Israel and world Jewry, referencing *The Protocols of the Elders of Zion* as one of its sources. The Charter is rooted in the principles of the

Muslim Brotherhood, which advocates for establishing a society governed entirely by Islamic principles. It echoes the Brotherhood's slogan, 'Allah is its target, the Prophet is its model, the Koran its Constitution; Jihad is its path, and death for the sake of Allah is the loftiest of its wishes.' Hamas, by its own admission, exists to obliterate Israel. Since 1997, the United States has classified Hamas as a foreign terrorist organization. It is also corrupt.

Some critics of Hamas describe its governance structure as kleptocratic, likening it to an organized criminal syndicate. Many Gazans live in poverty, while some political leaders reside in Qatar, a key patron of Hamas. Khaled Mashaal has misappropriated $4 billion in aid intended for ordinary Gazans and currently lives in a luxury hotel in Doha, far removed from the realities his constituents face on the battlefield. Qatar also hosts other Hamas leaders, some of whom are billionaires.

## The Morning After – 'We are all Hamas'

Why didn't Israeli intelligence anticipate the attack, and why didn't security and defense forces respond promptly? Answers continue to be debated. There is a consensus that many Israelis believed that improving living standards for Arabs reduced their level of violent animosity toward Israel. Many Gazans worked in Israel or benefited from medical care and economic opportunities. Israelis failed to grasp the depth and intensity of the hatred Gazans feel for Israel. And what about the protective wall? Israel's celebrated security barriers proved no more effective than the Maginot Line in May 1940 or Germany's Atlantic Wall in 1944. Israel's hubris is now, indeed, shaken.

Another blow to Israel came from the student solidarity for Hamas that erupted on campuses worldwide. Marches against Israel began almost immediately after the Hamas attack and continued. In startling accusations, student groups labeled Israelis as butchers and Gazans as victims. These accusations were made even before Israel retaliated. Soon, students set up tents on university lawns, and many professors joined in solidarity by providing food to the community encampments.[11] A few comedians found humor in the killing. Asian-American Hans Kim snickered, 'It's a real halal-ocaust over there.'[12]

The clash extended beyond campuses. Around the world, activists marched with placards reading 'From the river to the sea, Palestine will be free,' while others chanted slogans advocating the annihilation of Israel. Pro-Israel demonstrators faced violence, and several incidents made news headlines, including the intimidation of business tycoon Peter Thiel, who found himself trapped inside a debate hall at Cambridge University by students accusing him of complicity in genocide.[13] On city streets and campuses, anti-Israel activists tore down solidarity flyers featuring images of Israelis held captive somewhere in the tunnel labyrinth of Gaza.

Some Hollywood and international celebrities joined the fray. Draped in a keffiyeh, Swedish climate activist Greta Thunberg was arrested in Sweden for violating protest regulations.[14] During street marches in New York City, anti-Israel protesters openly waved Hezbollah and Hamas flags.[15] Those wearing face masks to hide their identities were particularly aggressive and confrontational. Some chased Jewish students from various areas of campus, forcing them to barricade themselves in safe rooms. In Europe, many Jews chose not to wear identifiable religious attire.[16] In Amsterdam, vandals defaced a statue of Anne Frank with red paint. The lettering read 'Gaza.'[17]

## Intersectionality and Triumphalism and Congress

A perplexing intersection of diverse groups exists within the vast anti-Israel coalition, including hard-left activists collaborating with radical Muslims, or Islamists, and militant LGBTQ+ individuals. The gay advocacy group Queers4Palestine shouted, 'Palestine will live forever!' Some feminists downplayed or denied the atrocities, claiming that allegations of rape were Israeli propaganda. Hollywood celebrities, who often advocate for feminist causes, maintained a deafening silence regarding the mass rape of Israeli women. Israeli women activists confided to the left-leaning Israeli newspaper *Haaretz* that they feel betrayed by international feminists who, in their view, abandoned the raped and murdered women of October 7. However, some surprising and encouraging expressions of empathy emerged from traditional critics of Israel. Reverend Al Sharpton issued a strong condemnation of the attack.

Hamas leaders showed no remorse about the attack, with many appearing boastful. Ghazi Hamad, a senior Hamas official, declared that Israel should be annihilated, arguing, 'The existence of Israel is illogical. It is the existence of Israel that causes all this pain, blood, and tears. It is Israel, not us.'[18] Hamas leader Khaled Mashal reveled in the slaughter of the Al-Aqsa Flood, the codename for the October attack, and invited the world to generate a tsunami of support for the operation. He called for a 'media Flood' to spread the Palestinian narrative and a 'legal Flood.' On Capitol Hill, anti-Israel rioters attempted to force their way into a pro-Israel congressman's office but faced resistance.

This anger and angst prompted a response from Congress. Jason Smith, the chair of the House Ways and Means Committee, was among many members of Congress who criticized American universities for their failure to clear student encampments and put an end to the harassment of Jewish students.[19] Congresswoman Elise Stefanik advocated for the Hamas and Other Palestinian Terrorist Groups International Financing Prevention Act to impose significant financial penalties on individuals who support Hamas or other terrorist organizations.[20] This outspoken representative from New York declared before the Israeli Knesset that Hamas should be 'wiped off the face of the earth.'[21]

Other US lawmakers investigated the roles of university presidents in campus disruptions. One hearing was titled 'Calling for Accountability: Stopping Antisemitic College Chaos,' during which Ivy League presidents were questioned about their perceived passivity towards student harassment. Following the highly publicized hearings, some university presidents lost their positions.[22]

## Lawfare

Immediately after the killing, there were expressions of support for Israel and its national tragedy. President Biden stated that Hamas' assault is a 'violation of every code of human morality.'[23] Russian Foreign Minister Sergei Lavrov remarked, 'There is no excuse for the barbarity of October 7.' In July 2024, the new British Labour government's Justice Secretary reaffirmed her earlier statement, 'I unequivocally condemn the despicable actions of Hamas, who targeted innocent Israeli civilians. The hostages must be returned.' It was the worst day of Jewish killings since the Nazis. However, other Western leaders seemed to reward Hamas for its actions. Ireland, Spain, and Norway recognized the 'State of Palestine' shortly after the Hamas attack, and others promised to follow suit.

The International Criminal Court (ICC) addressed the case by establishing a legal and ethical equivalence of criminality between Hamas and the Israeli Defense Forces. Immediately following the attack, critics of Israel initiated lawfare, seeking to harass or stigmatize Israel through national and international courts. The ICC, established to prosecute the most egregious war crimes, issued arrest warrants for both Hamas and Israeli leaders on charges of war crimes and crimes against humanity. The ICC issued warrants for Israeli Defense Minister Yoav Gallant, Prime Minister Benjamin Netanyahu, Hamas chief Yahya Sinwar, Mohammed Al-Masri, the commander-in-chief of Hamas' military wing, and Ismail Haniyeh, head of Hamas' political bureau. This courtroom tactic drew praise from many of Israel's critics but faced condemnation from Alan Dershowitz, who argued that the ICC lacked authority and described the reasoning as absurd. Then-Hizbullah Secretary-General Hassan Nasrallah also criticized the equivalence, rebuking ICC chief prosecutor Karim Khan for his 'equal treatment of the executioner and the victim' and the 'injustice' done to the Hamas leaders. He claimed that only criminals were Israeli.[24]

Lawsuits against Hamas have emerged globally. One case was filed against two prominent anti-Israel groups on American campuses: National Students for Justice in Palestine and American Muslims for Palestine, for conducting information operations on behalf of Hamas. A hostage taken by Hamas has sued a US nonprofit, claiming that the group, People Media Project, publicly advocated for the attack. Students have also initiated legal actions against their universities. New York University settled with Jewish students who alleged that administrators were indifferent to protecting their civil rights, allowing widespread acts of hatred.

In Jerusalem, Israeli lawyers and politicians are considering the legal future. Should there be high-profile trials for captured Hamas conspirators? Would it resemble the iconic Adolf Eichmann trial of 1961? Should there be an international aspect, given that the victims come from various parts of the world? This may echo the Nuremberg trials.

## The War to End All Wars?

What does the future hold for Gazans and Israelis? As of early 2026, the political positions of Israelis and Palestinians have solidified. Many Israelis who were once hopeful that Palestinians could become peaceful, if not always friendly, neighbors now face a bleak outlook. Many Israelis adopt what historian Daniel Pipes refers to as Israel Victory. This policy represents a shift from Israel's historical pattern of concessions and restraint, focusing instead on dismantling Hamas. Under Israeli Victory, any abduction of Israeli citizens or rocket fire from Gaza will provoke immediate and overwhelming retaliation. According to the logic of Israeli Victory, militant Gazans must feel defeated and powerless. Only then can a lasting peace be achieved.

And what about the Palestinians? Many Gazans are reluctant to criticize Hamas openly due to fear of imprisonment or death. Hamas relies on a network of informants in Gaza who report their activities to neighbors. However, credible polls indicate that many Middle Easterners, particularly Gazans, have expressed approval of the killings in October. For many Muslims, the attack represented a battle in a holy war. While many Arab intellectuals championed the emergence of extreme violence as a legitimate response to the struggle against colonialism, others disagreed. An Algerian author remarked that Palestinian leaders are hypocrites who advocate for peace and human dignity yet remain silent or even condone the 'monstrous barbarity' exhibited by Hamas. This viewpoint was echoed by a well-known Egyptian TV host who stated about Palestinians, 'We are defeated, but we convince ourselves that we are victorious. We refuse to face reality. We are living in a delusion.'[25]

Some prominent observers outside of the Middle East cite the October 7 attack as having changed the world. From Harvard Yard, political scientist Stephen Walt speculated that the ongoing, broad peace initiatives aimed at normalizing relations between Saudi Arabia and Israel were derailed. The attack also redirected attention away from Eastern Europe, particularly Ukraine, and China. Now, the world's focus has shifted to the Middle East – Israel, Hamas, and Iran. Some observers argue that the only victor of the attack was Hamas. Although assassinations have diminished Hamas' leadership roles, they have increased its popularity among Palestinians and worldwide. Many external observers of the Middle East feel confused and fatigued by the ongoing violence and long for an end to the war. British Prince William called for 'an end to the fighting' in the Middle East, citing the human cost.[26]

What is the likely face of the future? While many Gazans initially chanted, 'We are all Hamas,' this jingoism faded as the reality of near-total war set in. By the summer of 2024, some Gazans, their faces covered, pleaded with the world on social media, 'Save us from Hamas . . . I appeal to every living conscience to watch. These are traders in our blood. Every day they trade in our blood.'[27]

There are risks associated with criticizing Hamas in the Gaza Strip. One Palestinian, inspired by Viktor Frankl's autobiographical *Man's Search for*

*Meaning*, felt compelled to speak out publicly, and he did. He said, 'I'm Palestinian and firmly stand against this terror. I pray for the safety of my friends, colleagues, their loved ones, and everyone affected.' This led to death threats against him. While more militant Muslims may proclaim that they love death more than life, many Gazans simply want the war to end and care for their families.

There is pressure on Israel from multiple sources to crush Hamas completely. Many Israelis demand that their armed forces root out and destroy Hamas. Still grappling with national trauma, they are shocked by the global lack of empathy. Former Defense Minister Yoav Gallant described Hamas as the ISIS of Gaza, a brutal organization funded and supported by Iran. 'Hamas is ISIS,' he said. 'The ISIS of Gaza will not exist on our borders. The IDF will destroy Hamas. And we will hunt down every last man with the blood of our children on his hands.'[28]

Not all Israelis support this harsh approach to the Palestinians. One Israeli mental health professional worries that the violence will corrupt and emotionally scar both Jews and Arabs. She remarked about her fellow countrymen that the desire for revenge against everyone is dangerous for both Israelis and Palestinians. Despite the killings of October 7, many Israelis still believe that a lasting peace between two states – one Israeli and one Palestinian – is possible.

Was the October 7 attack successful? Did it accomplish its goal of undermining Israeli national confidence and provoking international condemnation of Israel? Or will it serve as a warning to Israel and the world that Middle Eastern terrorism is likely to continue until the perpetrators are removed from the global stage? What impact do external factors, such as the American-Israeli destruction of Iran's nuclear program in June 2025, have on Hamas? Will Iran reduce funding to Hamas, or will it increase military supplies to seek revenge on the United States and Israel? All of this is the subject of the book you are about to read.

## On a Personal Note

An author writing about Hamas and Israel is unlikely to remain neutral. Somewhere in the book, or even before he begins writing, he will choose to support either Israel or Hamas. Many European and Middle Eastern authors have placed the moral responsibility on Israel, citing the devastation caused by IDF. While achieving neutrality may not be necessary and perhaps even impossible, maintaining objectivity is crucial. Therefore, I have included citations from sources across the political spectrum, as well as from newspapers and journals. I hope the reader agrees that I have presented both sides of the conflict.

This manuscript aspires to be more than a mere compilation of facts; it seeks to tell the story of people, including women, men, and children. Some are perpetrators, some are villains, and many are bystanders, inescapably caught in the maelstrom of total war. I have included profiles of the actors in this ongoing drama at the end of each chapter, keeping the detailed profiles separate from the main text to provide readers with additional biographical details without disrupting the flow of each chapter.

The terminology surrounding this war can be confusing. I avoided some terms that are often used imprecisely or misapplied. For example, 'right wing' is often used cavalierly and almost always pejoratively. Readers may find the glossary helpful. Finally, I want to thank Tara Moran, my commissioning editor at Pen and Sword, as well as my copy editor, Stephen Chumbley, both of whom guided several revisions of my drafts. Stephen corrected my typos, and if the book reads well, it is primarily due to his efforts. As usual, my good friend John and my loving wife, Nadia, gave essential suggestions on the content.

For the record, I have been working for the United States Intelligence Community for over 43 years. Nothing in this book reflects the official stance of any agency or department within the United States government. All opinions, as well as errors, expressed in *Cauldron of Terror* are entirely my own.

## Chapter 2

# Hamas – Its Ideology, History, Men, and Women

*Allah is our objective. The Prophet is our leader. The Qur'an is our law. Jihad is our way. Dying in the way of Allah is our highest hope.*
The motto of the Islamic Brotherhood[1]

## What is Hamas?

What is Hamas? Supporters of Hamas see the group as a resistance movement. Conversely, critics and various governments label it a terrorist organization. Others describe it as militant, with some claiming that it operates as both a militant group and a social organization. There is agreement that it is a deeply religious Islamic political entity that has governed the Gaza Strip for nearly 20 years and is dedicated to destroying Israel. The Gaza Strip is about 25 miles long and varies in width from 4 to 7.5 miles, covering an area of 139 square miles. Its estimated population is 2.5 million people. The southern region borders Egypt and includes an extensive network of underground tunnels.

In early 2026, some refer to Hamas as a battered, surviving mini-army. Three years earlier, it had a military academy that provided training in various specializations, including cybersecurity. It also had a naval commando unit within its 40,000-strong military wing. By 2025, these numbers were revised downward after 18 months of relentless bombardment by Israeli forces. Some observers classify Hamas as an Islamist organization. Islamism is a commonly used term to describe a radical interpretation of Islam. It denies Israel's existence and collaborates with countries, specifically Iran and Qatar, as well as organizations hostile to Israel. Adherents aspire to build a society that closely reflects the lives of the first-generation Muslims, whom they consider having lived in the purest era of Islamic existence. Hamas leaders draw inspiration from this generation for a Palestine that is free of Jews and Western influence.

Hamas, an acronym for Harakat al-Muqawama al-Islamiya, or Islamic Resistance Movement, is defined as a terrorist organization, a national liberation group, a religious-social movement, an Islamofascist force, and a counter-colonial entity. The Council on Foreign Relations describes it as a militant offshoot of the Islamic Brotherhood. The group is an extension of the Muslim Brotherhood, which emerged in Egypt in the mid-20th century. The Brotherhood promoted a radical form of Islam, often referred to as Islamism or Jihadism. Hamas' founder, Sheikh Ahmed Yassin, was a Palestinian activist associated with the Muslim Brotherhood. He drafted the Hamas Charter and initiated a campaign of suicide bombings in the 1990s, for which Israel later assassinated him. The United States government has classified Hamas as a terrorist organization.

Yassin (Profile 1 – Chapter 2) founded Hamas in December 1987, establishing it as the Brotherhood's branch in Gaza. A quadriplegic and partially blind cleric, Yassin had been a prominent activist since the 1970s. He created Al-Mujama Al-Islami, a network of religious, educational, and social welfare institutions supported by wealthy donors from the Arab Gulf states. Yassin organized attacks against Israeli targets and positioned Hamas as the political arm of the Brotherhood in December 1987. At that time, he used violence to gain respect among fellow Palestinians and to secure support from Palestinian Islamic Jihad (PIJ), a Gaza-based, Iran-sponsored militant group. Hamas released its first official statement on December 14, 1987, and one year later, in August 1988, it published its organizational Charter through the Islamic Association for Palestine in Chicago. A connection between Hamas and American-based front groups remains.

In the late 1980s, Hamas' overall strategy was to grind down Israel's national morale through persistent and unpredictable acts of homicidal violence. Large-scale killings would also earn Hamas prestige and portray its rival, Fatah, and Yasser Arafat's Palestinian Liberation Organization (PLO), as weak and ineffectual.[2] Ironically, Yassin was backed *initially* by Israeli leaders as an alternative to the PLO. Israeli leaders soon came to regret this support.

Yassin continued his activism, and in 1989, Israel sentenced him to life in prison for ordering the murder of Israeli soldiers. However, he was released in 1997 as part of a prisoner exchange. In 2003, Israel bombed a building where Yassin was present, but he escaped with only minor injuries. His luck ran out in 2004 when Israel targeted and killed him along with seven others in a missile strike. A month later, Israel killed his second-in-command, Abdelaziz Rantisi (Profile 2 – Chapter 2). After declaring war on Hamas on October 7, Israel revitalized its assassination campaign, which continues to this day.

## The Islamic Brotherhood – The Background for Hamas

Hamas' ideological roots trace back to the early 20th century when an Egyptian schoolteacher, Hassan al-Banna (Profile 3 – Chapter 2), founded the al-Ikhwan al-Muslimun, or Islamic Brotherhood, in response to Western influence in the Middle East. Al-Banna aimed to redirect Egyptian society toward a fully Islamic framework. He proposed a gradual strategy instead of a revolutionary one, providing essential services such as education, religious guidance, basic healthcare, and employment opportunities to those in need. The Brothers served as role models for fellow Muslims, earning their trust and loyalty. They achieved significant success.

The Brotherhood's membership grew rapidly in the 1930s and 1940s. The Palestinian branch emerged in 1945, focusing primarily on education and the promotion of faith to establish an Islamic state. Throughout the 1950s, the Brotherhood refrained from violence and did not initiate significant guerrilla operations against Israel during the 1956 Sinai War. Instead, they concentrated on building mosques and attracting new members from various economic and educational backgrounds. One highly educated and literary recruit would rise to become the intellectual force behind the Brotherhood.

Sayyid Qutb (Profile 4 – Chapter 2) was an Egyptian literary critic who embraced radical Islam after visiting the United States in the 1940s. Similar to al-Banna, Qutb aimed to cleanse Egypt and the entire Islamic world of Western influence, which he perceived as corrupt. From his viewpoint, the West had kept the Islamic world in a state of darkness and subservience. Both al-Banna and Qutb, along with Yassin, supported Islamic revivalism. The Brotherhood's philosophy was a critical component of Hamas' statement of principles: its Charter.

## The Hamas Charter of 1988

> [*The 1988 Charter is*] *a frank and open call for genocide, embedded in one of the most thoroughly antisemitic documents you'll read this side of* The Protocols of the Elders of Zion.[3]
>
> Jeffrey Goldberg, *The Atlantic Magazine*

In 1988, Hamas published its Charter, which called for the eradication of the state of Israel and the establishment of an Islamic society in its place.[4] This Charter presents Hamas' perspectives on Islam, Israel, Jews, and the West. It argues that Israel is an artificial intrusion into Islamic holy territory. It is God's land, and only Muslims can own any of it.[5] This 'Zionist tumor' in the land of Islam needs to be cut out. Hamas holds that land from the Jordan River to the Mediterranean Sea is waqf or holy Islamic land and that Muslims must free it from Jews.

The Charter cites passages from the Koran that proclaim Muslims as superior and advocate for a return to their religious roots. It affirms the spiritual and military superiority of Muslims over all other religions. The Charter keeps non-Muslims in a subordinate status, particularly Jews, who are portrayed as villains in Islam's holy liturgy. The Charter quotes al Banna, 'Israel will be established and will stay established until Islam nullifies it as it nullified what was before it.[6]

The Charter states that jihad, or armed struggle against the Jews in Israel, is part of an ongoing war that will continue until the end of time. This is non-negotiable because the war against the Jews is mandated in sacred liturgy. Hamas' current war against Israel is the latest phase in a long conflict that began at the dawn of Islam and will not end until the Jews are destroyed in the end of days.[7] This is conveyed in Article 7 of the Charter, which frames the Palestinian struggle as the latest iteration of the global Islamic struggle against the Jewish people.

Some of the Charter's antisemitism also derives from sources unrelated to Islam.[8] Modern themes in Hamas' literature merge historical claims of anti-Islamic conspiracies with European antisemitism. A prominent source, and one quoted in the Charter, is *The Protocols of the Elders of Zion.*[9] The *Protocols* is a well-documented hoax created by the Russian secret police in the late 19th century.[10] Today, it is widely cited by antisemitic Islamic scholars and intellectuals and, particularly, politicians. The *Protocols* attribute most of the world's serious social toxins and calamities to world Jewry. War and natural phenomena, such as the COVID pandemic, are often unfairly attributed to Jewish conspiracies.[11]

Nine of the Charter's articles contain direct excerpts from the *Protocols*, and their influence is evident in several others.[12] Article 32 and Article 22 are two articles that reference the *Protocols*. Both provide detailed information about Jewish conspiracies and their most poisonous effects on the world. Readers of the Charter are informed that the Jews control the media and capital markets and peddle narcotics, particularly to Muslims. (Table 1 – Chapter 2)

Hamas, along with several Middle Eastern countries, particularly Iran, recirculates and embellishes these themes. A common meme suggests that Jews are the puppeteers of European colonial forces, using them as proxies to control the world's wealth and wage war on Islam. It is claimed that Jews destroyed the Muslim Caliphate, initiated both world wars, and established the Rotary Club and the United Nations as instruments of world control.

## Table 1 – Chapter 2: Key Element of Hamas' Charter

| | | |
|---|---|---|
| 1 | From the preface, quoting Hassan al-Banna | Israel will exist and will continue to exist until Islam obliterates it, just as it has obliterated others before it. |
| 2 | Article 13 | 'There is no solution for the Palestinian question except through jihad. Initiatives, proposals, and international conferences are all a waste of time and vain endeavors.' |
| 3 | Article 28 | Israel, Judaism, and Jews challenge Islam and the Muslim people. '˜Let the cowards never sleep.' |
| 4 | Article 7 | Based on a hadith or saying about killing Jews who hide behind rocks and trees. |
| 5 | Articles 22 and 32 | Restate ghoulish conspiracy theories, most notably the century-old forgery *The Protocols of the Elders of Zion.* |
| 6 | Article 8 | The Hamas slogan, from the 1928 Muslim Brotherhood Charter, which has become the blueprint for Jihadist killers worldwide: 'Allah is its target, the Prophet its model, the Koran its Constitution; Jihad is its path, and death for the sake of Allah is the loftiest of its aspirations.' |

## 2017 Revision

In 2017, Hamas updated its 1988 Charter. The tone was less aggressive and slightly more conciliatory toward Israel. Some observers were skeptical of Hamas' sincerity and considered the revision a questionable makeover. The new version removed promises to kill Jews and suggested that Hamas might temporarily accept Israel's existence within the pre-Six-Day War borders.

A second change in the revised Charter was the distinction between innocuous and acceptable Jews. While the 1988 Charter condemned all Jews, portraying them as unredeemable and sinister, the revision has no argument with Jews who are not 'racist, aggressive, colonial, and expansionist.' Its enemies were limited to Zionists. Additionally, the document did not reference the Muslim Brotherhood. However, many observers of Hamas were confused by the shift toward more ambiguous rhetoric. Many aspects of Hamas' political philosophy remained highly militant.

## Continuing Claims and Grievances

Hamas' Charter and its revisions reveal widespread contempt for Jews and Israel. Additionally, there are more localized issues. Many Palestinians and other Muslims around the world share these grievances. Some of these arguments have fueled the brief, intense conflicts between Hamas and Israel from 2005 to 2025. The status of Muslim control over the Temple Mount remains a contentious issue, as both Judaism and Islam regard it as sacred. The two principal 7th-century shrines are the Dome of the Rock and the Al-Aqsa Mosque.

In the 1920s and 1930s, the Grand Mufti of Jerusalem accused Jews of various criminal ambitions, including the intent to destroy the Temple Mount and build the Third Temple there. He used these accusations to incite massacres against Jews in 1929 in Mandatory Palestine. For decades, claims of a threat to Al-Aqsa gained traction against Jews. After Israel captured Jerusalem in 1967, Al-Aqsa took on renewed significance. Israeli Defense Minister Moshe Dayan (Profile 5 – Chapter 2) allowed Jews to visit the Temple Mount but forbade them from praying there. However, this did not satisfy many Muslims, who demanded nothing less than total control of Jerusalem. The Temple Mount dispute continues.

The mastermind behind the October attack, Mohammed Deif, named it the Al-Aqsa Flood to honor the iconic mosque. In May 2021, he asserted that Israel had violated al-Aqsa by erecting temporary barriers and detaining militants within the mosque. Israel explained that the IDF implemented protective measures to control rioting. Nonetheless, Deif was determined to exact revenge, which he did two and a half years later.[13] 'Today, the rage of Al-Aqsa, the rage of our people and nation, is exploding. Our mujahideen today is your day to make this criminal understand that his time has ended,' said Deif.[14]

## Elements of Western Authoritarian Philosophies

> *Of all the unanswered questions of our time, perhaps the most important is: 'What is Fascism?'*
>
> George Orwell, 'What is Fascism?', 1944[15]

Many Western observers find it challenging to define Hamas' politics, which blend radical Islam with authoritarian and occasionally secular principles. Some ideas are grounded in Sharia, while others unsettlingly echo the authoritarian ideologies of fascism and National Socialism from the 20th century.

Giovanni Gentile, an Italian professor, shaped fascism during World War I under the slogan, 'All within the state; none outside the state; none against the state.' The first fascist movement to rise to power was Mussolini's Blackshirts in Italy in 1922. The term became widely associated with numerous anti-democratic political philosophies of that era. During World War II, the Soviet Union referred to the German military and political systems as fascist enterprises. Hitler respected fascism but constructed National Socialism as a distinct, though related, ideology. Many Islamic intellectuals from the Middle East were drawn to both fascism and National Socialism.

Hamas' political philosophy has its roots in the Islamic Brotherhood, as outlined in its Charter. It also integrates elements of 20th-century European political systems, particularly fascism and National Socialism. In this sense, Hamas' politics bear a close resemblance to those of the Islamic State in Syria and the Sham, or ISIS, as well as other Islamist organizations. British historian Malise Ruthven characterized the authoritarian Muslim governments in the Middle East as being influenced by Islamo-fascism. This term refers to the combination of Islamic and heavily secular authoritarian principles. Both fascism and Islamism are characterized by state control over politics and society, a concept deeply embedded in Hamas' Charter.

## 'Fascism with an Islamic face'[16]

> *. . . we love Adolf Hitler . . . Adolf Hitler was an Arab . . . Eva Braun is also our cousin.'*
>
> Shouts of young males at a rally in Germany, 2017[17]

Islamo-fascism describes a blend of radical Islam and militant authoritarianism. The terms Islamo-fascism and Islamo-Nazism were rarely used until the early 21st century. After the September 2001 attacks in the United States, observers struggled to find suitable words to describe the politics of militant Islamic radicals. Some believed that the term Islamo-fascism was fitting. Then-President George W. Bush compared Islamism to fascism, and the top US Army official in the Middle East, General John Abizaid, drew parallels between the rise of Islamist ideologies and the emergence of fascism in Europe during the 1920s and 1930s. Military historian Victor Davis Hanson emphasized the themes of enforced conformity and submission found in both Islamism and fascism. President Bush called al-Qaida Islamo-fascistic, saying the group's attacks served as 'a stark reminder that this nation is at war with Islamic fascists.' He also claimed that Islamo-fascism is a 'murderous ideology . . . the great challenge of our new century.'[18]

Columbia University Professor Robert Paxton emphasizes that fascism's core includes group identity, superiority, and victimization, which are deeply rooted in Hamas' ideology. Elements of sacred teachings of Islam declare that Muslims are superior to all other groups of men and women and should have greater rights in an Islamic state. There is also a strong sense of victimhood in the Middle East, where Islamic clergy and intellectuals blame Western colonialism for the region's poverty. Hamas, along with other Palestinian groups, has adopted a culture of grievance.

## Fascism and Hamas

At least nine themes are shared between the philosophies of fascism and Hamas. These themes include collective identity, the leadership principle, martial pageantry, mythical atavism and purity, utopian aspirations, severely restricted human rights, hypermasculinity, martyrdom, and a relentless fight against a primary enemy. First, there is the idea of collective identity. In fascist states, a strong sense of unity exists, with individuals absorbed into the collective. In Germany and Japan, this collective identity was racially homogeneous and deeply rooted in an exclusive, often romanticized history and culture. Unlike National Socialist ideology, Italian and Spanish fascism did not focus on racial theory. In Islam, this collective is called the Ummah.

For Hamas, as with the European fascist leaders, the individual has little value. Hamas sees Gazans as tools in the war with Israel and positions them in apartments, hospitals, and mosques that also serve as fire bases. Hamas has buried caches of arms and explosives under kindergartens, schools, hospitals, and playgrounds.[19] This ensures that non-combatants will be killed. Using Gazans as fodder is part of Hamas' information operations because pictures of dead children portray Israel as a baby killer.[20] As for the Muslims who die because of Hamas' grand strategy, they become martyrs.[21] Their family receives status and financial benefits from Hamas and Fatah. The martyrs are guaranteed a place in heaven.

The second common element of Islamism and fascism is the principle of leadership. The leader holds dictatorial or nearly dictatorial power, ruling absolutely either by divine right, as seen in Japan, or through a popular mandate, as in Germany, Italy, and Spain. In Sunni Islam, there is often no clear or established succession process. Traditionally, leaders are appointed by senior clerical figures, while in Iran, leadership is held by senior clerics.

Third, there is martial pageantry, which is an intense celebration of warrior culture. Many countries honor their military and veterans through monuments, songs, sagas, and holidays. During surges of patriotism, especially in times of war, democratic states pay tribute to their militaries with respect. However, the martial pageantry in Mussolini's Italy, Hitler's Germany, and Hirohito's Japan idolizes militarism. The fighting culture of Hamas takes this further, creating a death cult.

Hamas uses visual art to glorify militarism and martyrdom. Graffiti and traditional art encourage assaults on Israel. Former leaders Ibrahim al-Maqadmah and Abdel Aziz al-Rantisi wrote poetry about the martial struggle. Others followed, documenting imprisonment, martyrdom, suffering, and warfare. Occasionally, Hamas' ideology is closely linked to sports organizations, with mosques forming soccer teams. One team's motto was, 'Prepare for the enemy and fight the occupation.' This message is reinforced in Hamas' schools, where kindergarteners wear uniforms and carry toy rifles.

The fourth common element between Hamas' philosophy and fascism is racial or religious atavism. Many authoritarian philosophies of the 20th century draw inspiration from an ancient and idealized period of purity. Rousseau laid the groundwork for communism by imagining a future without private property. National Socialism aimed to recreate a racially pure past by eliminating racial contamination, while Italian fascists reminisced about the glory and grandeur of Rome. Similarly, Hamas strives to emulate a golden age represented by the first generation of Muslims, which Hamas highlights as a model of purity.

The fifth common thread is utopian aspirations, which are not exclusive to fascist or Islamic societies. Medieval Europeans believed they would reach a celestial paradise for living piously. The significance of the afterlife waned with the scientific revolution in the 18th century. Still, some 20th-century authoritarian philosophies embraced utopian visions that gained popularity. Nazis envisioned a purely Aryan Germany ruling over non-Aryan serfs, while communists imagined a future without economic classes. Fascists generally envisioned a muscular utopia where they held uncontested power. For Hamas, the ideal governance model was based on the first generation of Muslims. Their utopia aims to recreate this embellished past.

The sixth element involves significantly restricted individual rights. Western nations limit government interference in citizens' religious practices, employment choices, marriages, and their ability to express political dissent. In contrast, authoritarian regimes provide far fewer liberal rights. In Nazi Germany, the Soviet Union, and fascist Italy, leaders imprisoned or executed those who opposed their often-absolute authoritarian rule.

Hamas similarly governs under the strictest interpretation of Islamic law, alongside elements of secular law. Women are required to cover themselves or risk being beaten or stoned. The police in Gaza enforce gender segregation, and beat and imprison women who advocate for other women. Hamas operatives kill fellow Muslims whom they suspect of collaborating with the Israeli enemy. There is little refuge in Gaza for LGBTQ individuals who face severe persecution and ostracism. Hamas routinely tortures Gazans believed to be gay.

Hypermasculinity is the seventh common trait. In both Islamism and fascism, strong and clear gender roles are stressed. Women are mainly tasked with bearing and raising children. Men are expected to provide financial support, protect their families, and serve as warriors when needed. The visual and musical arts emphasize the muscular warrior class. In many cultures, masculinity is glorified, but hypermasculinity represents an extreme martial ideal.

The eighth element is the focus on the heroic or martyrdom aspect, sometimes associated with hypermasculinity. Most civilizations celebrate their heroes in national stories, honoring and recognizing those who die in battle within their culture. In non-fascist societies, civilians generally see death in combat as an unfortunate necessity that must be faced with dignity. However, death in battle has a different meaning in Hamas culture. Martyrdom is revered as the highest expression of Islamic devotion. Muslims who die fighting against non-Muslims are called shahids. The Koran assures that the shahid will be granted immediate entry into heaven.

For Hamas and other Palestinians, the most revered shahid before Israel's establishment was Shaykh Izz al-Din Ezzedin Qassam, a Syrian who was killed in 1948 during the Arab-Israeli conflict (Profile 6 – Chapter 2). The al-Qassam Brigade is named after him. One of the most celebrated events in Palestinian folklore is the Great Revolt of 1936–1939, which was suppressed by the British and Jews. Despite this, many Palestinians see this event as the start of their armed struggle and honor the Arabs who died during the Revolt as martyrs and heroes.

The ninth characteristic shared by modern authoritarian ideologies is a constant struggle against a specified enemy. For the Nazis, the eternal main enemy was the international Jew. For Stalin-era Soviets, it was either capitalism or counterrevolution. For Hamas, it is also the international Jew. The 1988 Hamas Charter refers to Jews, not Israelis, with murderous contempt and a desire for destruction. The charter's revision in 2017 downplays the deadly hatred toward Jews as a group but states that Zionism remains its unwavering enemy.[22] However, many statements fail to distinguish between Judaism and Zionism.[23] This hatred erupted into butchery on October 7, 2023, and it continues (Table 2 – Chapter 2).

### Table 2 – Chapter 2: Intersections of Fascism, National Socialism and Philosophy of Hamas

| | Fascism and National Socialism | Philosophy of Hamas |
|---|---|---|
| **Collective of Individuals** | Italian fascism and German National Socialism prioritized the nation or racial group over the individual. | Hamas deliberately places its operatives and munitions among civilians. The individual is sacrificed for the collective. |
| **Authoritarian Leadership** | Leaders possess nearly dictatorial power, unlike the liberal model, where leaders govern with the consent of the governed. | Leaders assume and maintain power without the consent of the governed. They often ruthlessly suppress or eliminate threats to their rule. |

*(Cont'd)*

| | Fascism and National Socialism | Philosophy of Hamas |
|---|---|---|
| **Martial Pageantry** | Glorification of the military. | Hamas celebrates the killing and mass murders committed by its paramilitary units. |
| **Racial and Religious Atavism** | Nazis looked to the racially pure, pre-modern times. Italian fascists drew inspiration from the grandeur and power of ancient Rome. | Salutes the first generation of Muslims as the purest. Looks backward to the Golden Age of Muslim supremacy. |
| **Utopic Aspirations** | Nazis looked to a racially pure paradise. Fascism sought an undivided, homogeneous political unity. | Looks forward to the global dominance of Islam. |
| **Restricted Individual Rights** | Very few political or social choices are made without the approval of the authorities. | Persons under Hamas' control are heavily restricted in their behavior. |
| **Hypermasculinity** | Strong separation between sex roles. Men are dominant in society, and women are often relegated to domestic roles. | Males are the dominant partner in a man-woman relationship. Young men are expected to present as muscular and fearless. |
| **Martyrdom** | For fascism and National Socialism, it is an honor to die for the country or race. It grants heroic status. | For Hamas, dying as a martyr brings status to the family of the martyr and financial payments. It gives the martyr an entry into heaven. |
| **Endless Struggle** | Eternal struggle against racial antagonists. A need to purify the racial body. | For Hamas, there is an endless struggle against the existence of Israel. |

## Hamas Comes to Power

Hamas' first leadership generation appeared in the 1980s. In the 1990s, while Yassin was in prison, his deputies managed Hamas' operations. Rantisi, Khaled Mashaal, and Mousa Abu Marzouk led the political wing of Hamas in Gaza, while its military wing was spread across the West Bank. In the early 1990s, Iran and Syria began supporting Hamas as it moved its military and political committees to Damascus. During this time, Hamas focused on building and strengthening its political influence. The assassination of Hamas leaders in 2004 created a power vacuum that was quickly filled. These targeted killings may have unintentionally strengthened Hamas by energizing the group's militant side. Israel now faced a fully militarized Hamas alongside a more adaptable Palestine Liberation Organization.

Hamas' increased prominence attracted financial and military support from Muslim countries that saw it as the stronger competitor in the Muslim fight against Israel. This further boosted grassroots support for Hamas.

Hamas gained political power in 2006 by winning more seats than Fatah and competing secular parties in a Palestinian election. Few expected Hamas to achieve such a major victory. This marked a turning point for Hamas, as it was the first time the organization succeeded in a large-scale election. The following year, it took control of Gaza from Fatah, ending the PLO's long-standing dominance over the Palestinian electorate. Hamas declared that it had not abandoned its goal of destroying Israel. However, Hamas' political language was often inconsistent, sometimes sounding conciliatory toward Israel and other times sounding resolutely aggressive. Israel handed over that land to them in 2006, along with modern greenhouses, barns, and storage facilities for vegetables and orchards with extensive irrigation systems. Then, Gazans destroyed them.

Hamas established a one-party regime in the Gaza Strip, while Fatah governed the West Bank. By the summer of 2007, Hamas controlled most of Gaza, whereas Fatah had formed a separate government in the West Bank. In the 1990s, Yassir Arafat called Hamas a 'bunch of ants.' It seemed that Fatah would indefinitely maintain its monopoly on political control over the Palestinians. A generation later, few in the PLO shared that arrogance. The power of the Palestinians was now divided indefinitely.

## Does Hamas Have Wings?

As Hamas gained political legitimacy in 2006, observers sought to understand its ambitions, capabilities, leadership, and structure. Significant differences existed between Hamas' and Fatah's ruling styles. By 2007 and 2008, Fatah's governance had become more technocratic. One observer, Jonathan Brown (Profile 7 – Chapter 2), opined that responses to Israeli aggression primarily drove Hamas' rule. In his view, Hamas cannot be defined by a single term; it is a multifaceted entity that includes social, political, military, and educational aspects.

The structure of Hamas raises a question: is it a unified political and military entity, or is it composed of several allied organizations or factions? Hamas consists of three main components: a vast network of social organizations, including schools and hospitals, in the West Bank and Gaza Strip; a political division that engages in extensive fundraising; and an armed militia wing, the Izz ad-Din al-Qassam Brigades, which orchestrates suicide bombings.

Yassin claimed that Hamas was a single enterprise. He said its 'wings,' including its military wing, the Izz al-Din al-Qassam Brigades, were fully integrated with the social and political elements. 'We cannot separate the wing from the body. If we do so, the body will not be able to fly. Hamas is one body.'[24] He saw elements as reinforcing themselves with the central goal of destroying Israel.[25] Rantisi explained, 'Hamas's political wing determines overall policy for the movement.'[26]

Long after Yassin's death, Hamas remains unified, and its funds and activities are interconnected. It continues to utilize its charities to finance terrorism operations.[27] Mosques and charities incite, recruit, and provide logistical and operational support for terrorists, and they are places where suicide bombs are made.[28] Hamas and Fatah use schools, orphanages, summer camps, and sports leagues to socialize even the youngest children to aspire to die as martyrs.[29]

## Hamas and Terrorism

Hamas continues to use terror to weaken the resolve of Israelis. Terror remains a key part of a broader strategy focused on diminishing Israeli national morale. Ongoing and unpredictable attacks on civilians are intended to make life in Israel unbearable. This tactic was apparent during the wave of assaults in the Second Intifada, which started in 2000 and lasted four years.

From underground, Hamas' ghost army periodically emerged from a tunnel network to infiltrate Israel, kill indiscriminately, and then quickly retreat underground for cover. Hamas targeted various busy civilian locations, including buses and light rail stops, nightclubs, restaurants, markets, universities, and even a hotel hosting a Passover Seder. They aimed to undermine Israeli morale and devastate the economy by shifting resources from productive sectors to defense. The Intifadas have hurt many parts of the Israeli economy by draining and reallocating resources, and the attacks have led to concessions.

In December 1992, the al-Qassam Brigade killed six Israeli soldiers, prompting the Rabin government to exile suspected terrorists and their supporters. However, Rabin also withdrew some Israelis from Gaza and Jericho, actions that came before the Oslo Accords. Hamas leaders cited Israel's withdrawal from Gaza in 2005 as evidence that terrorism was effective and would continue. Hamas has regarded, and still regards, terrorism as a valuable tactic. The belief that Israel feared Hamas probably helped Hamas' election victory in 2006, one year after the Second Intifada ended.

Kidnapping for prisoner exchanges has compelled Israel to negotiate the release of imprisoned Palestinian operatives. The most notable exchange was the Gilad Shalit deal, in which Israel released 1,000 Palestinian prisoners for one Israeli soldier.[30] An imprisoned female terrorist recommended that Palestinians 'take another Shalit.'[31] On October 7, 2023, Hamas took over 200.

Hamas also kills Israelis to demonstrate to the world that it is highly operational and that its fighters are eager to attack the Israeli enemy. This murderous enthusiasm attracts funding from Muslim nations. Hamas does not rely solely on sympathy to secure foreign support. It kills Israeli citizens, which earns it respect among those hostile to Israel's existence. Iran provides Hamas with material and financial backing. Along with Qatar, Turkey shelters some of Hamas' top leaders and helps fund the organization's activities. Terrorism shows the world, especially Hamas' Islamic benefactors, that it is strong, well-organized, armed, and eager to kill.

Ironically, another reason for using terrorism is the self-inflicted destruction and impoverishment of social infrastructure that it causes. During the First Intifada, Israel demolished the homes of individuals linked to Palestinian terrorism. Media outlets sympathetic to the Palestinians labeled these retaliatory strikes as war crimes through collective punishment. By placing munitions depots and bomb-making facilities near schools or beneath hospitals, Hamas provoked retaliatory or preemptive military strikes. Israel targets these sites and others, which attracts funding from international organizations and various Western countries to rebuild the facilities (see Chapter 8). Some of the funds intended for reconstruction and development are used as planned. Meanwhile, other money is diverted to terrorist operational planning, with much of the revenue ending up in the bank accounts of Hamas leaders living in luxury in Qatar.

The funds are allocated to charities under Hamas' control. In turn, those who receive aid are expected to support Hamas. An Israeli defense official said, 'In the territories, there are no free lunches . . . Those who receive help from the Islamic associations pay with support for' Hamas.'[32] Palestinians who benefit from Hamas charities are expected to allow operatives to use their homes as safehouses, harbor fugitives, and permit Hamas to store weapons on their property.

Some of this money also goes to imprisoned Hamas and Fatah operatives as part of the 'pay-to-slay' agreement. Hamas and the PLO pay millions of dollars each month to terrorists and their families, including those captured after the October 2023 murder.[33]

The motivations for terrorism – political success, affirmation of Hamas' importance, and fundraising – prompted Hamas to launch terror campaigns that went far beyond sporadic, uncoordinated bombings and killings. Each campaign lasted several years and became known as the Intifadas or uprisings. These took place in Gaza and the West Bank and involved both Hamas and Fatah.

## Hamas and the Intifadas

### *First Intifada*

The term 'Intifada' describes large-scale, coordinated, and ongoing Palestinian attacks against Israeli targets over a specific period. The First Intifada started in December 1987 after a collision between a truck driven by an Israeli and a car driven by a Palestinian, which resulted in four Palestinians' deaths. Israeli authorities believed the incident was an accident; however, many Palestinians saw it as revenge. Soon, Palestinian anger broke out in the streets of Gaza and the West Bank, leading to what became known as the First Intifada. Some leaders in the West Bank were surprised, as the PLO's leadership had been exiled to Tunis and had lost some influence over the Palestinian population.

Violent attacks and non-violent protests occurred within the civil administration and schools, led by the Unified Leadership of the Uprising (UNLU). Stone-throwing became more popular during the First Intifada because of its powerful depiction in the media. Photos of children throwing stones at Israeli soldiers and tanks became iconic, boosting public support for Hamas. Gaining media sympathy became a key and effective strategy during the Second Intifada, earning it the nickname 'War of Stones.' Violence decreased around 1993, when Arafat signed the Oslo Accords, a partial peace deal with Israeli Prime Minister Yitzhak Rabin. Hamas rejected the ceasefire and carried out periodic suicide bombings. Seven years later, a new Intifada would begin.

## *Second Intifada – Blood Red Miniature War*

The Second Intifada started in 2000 after Ariel Sharon (Profile 8 – Chapter 2) visited Jerusalem's Temple Mount, a site sacred to both Jews and Muslims. This event triggered widespread protests, demonstrations, and suicide bombings, resulting in nearly 1,000 Israelis being killed or wounded in Palestinian terror attacks. However, Sharon's visit was motivated by years of disappointment and frustration stemming from poor living conditions and deep-seated pessimism. Many believed their lives had not improved since 1993 and felt disillusioned after the failed Camp David summit in July 2000.

One of the most notorious attacks of the Second Intifada was the bombing of a hotel in Netanya, which was the Passover Seder Massacre of March 2002. Thirty, primarily older adults, some of whom had survived the Holocaust, were killed, and dozens were maimed and injured when a Hamas suicide bomber detonated his explosive.[34] Palestinian operatives, Hamas and Fatah, who helped plan the attack, received multiple life sentences.[35] The families of the attackers were awarded hundreds of thousands of dollars.

Other horrific attacks made international headlines because they were especially gruesome. In August 2001, a suicide bomber detonated his device at the Sbarro pizza restaurant in Jerusalem in the early afternoon when pedestrian traffic was at its peak.[36] It killed 16 people, including seven children. Scores of others were maimed and disfigured. One of the injured lay in a coma for 22 years before she died in June 2023. Hamas claimed responsibility for the attack. A female conspirator, who disguised herself as a Jewish tourist to enter the restaurant, bragged about her participation. She was released from prison in a 2011 exchange for Hamas' abducted Israeli soldier, Gilad Shalit.[37]

In April 2003, two British-born operatives of the Al-Aqsa Martyrs Brigade entered Israel from Jordan. One tried to enter Mike's Place, a popular nightclub in Tel Aviv near the United States Embassy.[38] The security guard prevented him from entering the pub, and the bomber detonated himself, killing three people and injuring 55. His accomplice's suicide bomb failed to go off, and drowned attempting to escape.

In response to the attacks, Israeli forces targeted militant strongholds in Bethlehem, Jenin, Nablus, Qalqilya, and Ramallah – areas that had been under Palestinian control for years. The operation uncovered 23 bomb-making facilities. In 2004, Israel assassinated Yassin, and the Second Intifada ended sometime the following year. However, sporadic terrorist attacks continued. In late 2008, Israel launched Operation Cast Lead to weaken Hamas. The outcome was uncertain; Hamas was not defeated and may have even grown stronger after the attack.

Once again, the conflict received significant support from the Palestinian public. However, some observers argue that the Intifada did not succeed. While the suicide bombings stopped, so did the Intifada, without any noticeable gains. As a result, some assessed Hamas' use of terror as a failure since Israel did not surrender.

## *The Third Intifada – The Global Intifada*

The term 'Global Intifada' was created well before the October 2023 attack but became more popular afterward. The term is slang and carries different, nuanced meanings for those who use it. However, the refrain is mostly used as a call for the violent elimination of Israel. Some protests have been peaceful, many have been loud, and some have involved varying levels of violence.[39]

Global Intifada has become a rallying cry at protests worldwide after October 7, 2023. Notable locations include Times Square, the Consulate General of Israel in Manhattan, central London, Harvard University, and Crown Heights, New York, a neighborhood with a large Jewish community. It has been shouted at many American universities. This slogan has been adopted by various anti-Israel activist groups, including Within Our Life. This community group, which identifies as Palestinian-led, organized protests to boycott Israel outside *The New York Times*, Penn Station, Grand Central Station, BlackRock, and Israeli tech companies. At McGill University in Canada, a student protest became tense when campus police dismantled an anti-Israel demonstration. Students shouted, 'F – the dismantling, globalize the intifada.' In Europe, 'Intifada' was a song by a popular Spanish band accusing Israel of genocide against Palestinians, comparing it to the Holocaust. The song was banned in Germany (see Table 3 – Chapter 2).

**Table 3 – Chapter 2: The First and Second Intifadas – Key Elements**

| | Cause | Dates | Results |
|---|---|---|---|
| **First Intifada** | The Intifada began on 9 December 1987 in the Jabalia refugee camp after an Israeli truck driver collided with parked civilian vehicles, killing four Palestinian workers, three of whom were from the refugee camp.[40] | Violence began in 1987 and subsided in 1993, when Arafat signed the Oslo Accords. | Images of Palestinian boys throwing stones became iconic in the media. In contrast to the Second Intifada, this was largely organic and began spontaneously. |
| **Second Intifada** | Ariel Sharon's visit to the Temple Mount and the failure of the Camp David Summit. | September 2000 – February 2005. | The proliferation of suicide bombings began, producing large-scale Israeli fatalities. Hamas was not defeated, and it gained increased international credibility. |

*(Cont'd)*

| | Cause | Dates | Results |
|---|---|---|---|
| **Third Intifada** | This began after the October 2023 attack from Gaza. It is called the Global Intifada and heavily propagandistic. | After October 7, 2023. | High propaganda value globally. |

## Hamas Terrorism Post-October 7, 2023

Israeli security officials expected a repeat of the Intifada suicide bombing campaign, which Hamas' foreign policy adviser, Dr Ahmed Yousef (Profile 9 – Chapter 2), had promised. However, by early 2026, this had not occurred. Several factors contribute to this. It is much more difficult for Hamas to infiltrate Israel. The IDF is on high alert, and the security barriers provide additional protection. Additionally, the IDF recognizes the threat posed by tunnels.

Israeli intelligence has targeted locations controlled by Hamas, including mosque classes, student unions, sports clubs, and other sites used by Hamas for training and recruitment. Hamas has recruited Palestinians not affiliated with the al-Qassam Brigades for logistical and operational support, even instructing suicide bombers to their targets. However, there may not be widespread willingness to volunteer for such missions. A sense of betrayal dampens support for Hamas. Its leaders promised liberation but have only brought devastation, especially after 2023. During both Intifadas, Israel mainly focused on defensive measures, such as border and internal security, while maintaining a defensive stance. Since October 7, Israel has adopted an offensive approach, keeping Hamas' leadership off balance.

The full extent of high-level and systemic corruption has been made clear to the world in recent years.[41] Four of its leaders – Moussa Abu Marzouk, Khaled Meshaal, Ismail Haniyeh, and Yahya Sinwar – embezzled billions of dollars intended for the impoverished people of Gaza, many of whom live in near poverty or destitution.

## Summary

Since its formation, Hamas' main rivals have included Fatah and other factions of the PLO. Since 2007, Hamas has governed Gaza, while Fatah controls the West Bank; both groups aim to eliminate Israel. Hamas is an Islamist organization, whereas Fatah is more secular and nationalist. Hamas continues to promote terrorism and does not recognize Israel, while Fatah pursues negotiations and takes a gradual approach to establishing a Palestinian state.

Hamas uses terror to achieve political goals, secure funding, exert power, and show its influence on other Palestinians and the world as a continuing, vibrant, and deadly force. It deliberately places its weapons among schools, mosques, and hospitals to draw Israeli fire on civilian sites. This is part of its propaganda and information operations. When children are killed or hurt, horrifying images are broadcast worldwide. These images depict Israel as the Goliath and the Palestinians as David.

There have been three Intifadas. In the first two, Hamas emerged intact and, in some ways, even stronger. This is the Third Intifada, and unlike the earlier ones, Israel has vowed to eliminate Hamas. Israel has developed its counterterrorism strategies since the formative days of the Jewish state, which is the subject of Chapter 3.

**Profile 1 – Sheikh Ahmed Yassin**
**Names:** Sheikh Ahmed Yassin
**Nationality:** Palestinian
**Profession:** Islamic spiritual or sheikh and leader of Hamas
**Connection to October 7, 2023:** Charismatic, quadriplegic, and driven, he led Hamas until the IDF assassinated him. He broke his neck as a young boy and used a wheelchair for the rest of his life. Always studious, he studied English at Cairo University and later became a popular teacher in Gaza. He supported war against Israel and was intermittently imprisoned for nearly 10 years in Israeli detention prisons.[42]

Yassin brought Hamas from obscurity to fame and notoriety after splitting from Arafat in 1994, when the Nobel Prize-winning leader of the PLO accepted a two-state solution. Yassin demanded that all Israeli land be surrendered to Palestinians and ordered a wave of suicide bombings. In response, Israel decided to eliminate him.

In March 2004, a drone spotted him being carried to prayer in his wheelchair and targeted him with an invisible laser. Helicopters launched three Hellfire missiles, one of which hit him directly, killing him along with nine others. Many Palestinians idolized him, while Israeli authorities wondered if they had created a martyr who would inspire future generations of Palestinians.[43]
**Current Status:** Dead. Assassinated by the IDF.

**Profile 2 – Abdelaziz Rantisi**
**Names:** Abdelaziz Rantisi
**Nationality:** Palestinian
**Profession:** He described himself as one of the seven founders of Hamas. Generally considered Yassin's most influential aide.
**Connection to October 7, 2023:** He was a dedicated supporter of the Islamic Brotherhood who aimed to establish an Islamic state in Israel. Al-Rantisi rose to prominence in the 1980s and 1990s. Israel arrested him multiple times, with one imprisonment lasting up to two and a half years. He provoked violence and called for the kidnapping of Israelis to secure the release of Palestinian prisoners held in Israel.

Both the Israelis and Yasser Arafat's PA imprisoned him, and he despised both Israel and the PA. He accused the PA of murdering Hamas operatives. In 2003, al-Rantisi survived an Israeli assassination attempt, suffering wounds to his leg,

arm, and chest. However, in 2004, the IDF killed him by firing seven missiles at his car, all of which hit their target.
**Current Status:** Dead.

**Profile 3 – Hassan al-Banna**
**Names:** Hassan al-Banna
**Nationality:** Egyptian
**Profession:** School teacher and Founder of the Islamic Brotherhood
**Connection to October 7, 2023:** The foundational ideology of Hamas is rooted in the teachings and legacy of the Islamic Brotherhood, founded by Hassan al-Banna. He remains one of the group's greatest heroes, along with Abd-al-Aziz al-Rantisi and Ahmad Yassin, whom Israel assassinated. Al-Banna was also assassinated, but by Egyptian police rather than Israelis. He emphasized the importance of education in cultivating generations of pious Muslims. Additionally, he criticized the Westernization of Arab societies elites.[44]

Some Western observers are sympathetic toward the Islamic Brotherhood. Director of National Intelligence James Clapper described the Brothers as 'largely secular.' Professor John Esposito of Georgetown University said that they are a force for democratization and stability in a turbulent Middle East.[45] People in Israel who know about Hamas and al-Banna are less likely to praise them. They point out that al-Banna said, 'Israel will exist[46] and will continue to exist until Islam will obliterate it, just as it obliterated others before it.' Several Arab countries are not interested in the Brotherhood. In 2014, the United Arab Emirates officially labeled the Islamic Brotherhood as a terrorist organization.
**Current Status:** Hamas leaders still highly regard al-Banna. They share his view that the West is corrupt and its values are toxic. However, both Hamas and al-Banna emphasize the importance of using Western technology to carry out their attacks enemies.[47]

**Profile 4 – Sayyid Qutb**
**Names:** Sayyid Qutb
**Nationality:** Egyptian
**Profession:** Literary intellectual; Engine for the Muslim Brotherhood
**Connection to October 7, 2023:** Sayyid Qutb wrote about Americans, Jews, Islam, and much more. He gained a reputation as a literary expert when he was young. He played a key role in launching the career of Naguib Mahfouz, who later won the Nobel Prize for Literature. However, he became disillusioned with the government and the ruling elite in Egypt, which led him to embrace radical Islam. This change happened during his educational trip to the United States, where he became convinced that American culture was both infectious and corrupting. In 1949 and 1950, he attended a small teachers' college in Greeley, Colorado. He disliked everything he experienced, including football, social dances, and dating. He was appalled that Americans had lawns in front of their houses.

He returned to Egypt and became the ideological leader of the Muslim Brotherhood, whose previous leader had been killed in 1949 by Egyptian police. His writings appeal to Hamas, especially because of his numerous references to martyrdom and the promise of a place in heaven for those who die for their belief in Islam.[48]
**Current Status:** In 1966, he was hanged for his involvement in a conspiracy to overthrow Nasser's government. He felt grateful for becoming a martyr and remains a hero in Hamas and much of the Islamic world.[49]

**Profile 5 – Moshe Dayan**
**Names:** Moshe Dayan
**Nationality:** Israeli
**Profession:** Soldier
**Connection to October 7, 2023:** Moshe Dayan is regarded as one of the most distinguished soldiers in Israel's history. Born in 1915, he lived in the country's first kibbutz and, in 1936, joined the Haganah. The British arrested and imprisoned him for a time. In June 1941, he lost his left eye in battle in Lebanon, after which he wore a distinctive eye patch.

He created a doctrine for both conventional and insurgent warfare. His ideas still influence Israel today. Long before he became a legend, he worked under his military mentor, the controversial but effective British officer, Orde Wingate (see Chapter 3), who devised an innovative tactic for hunting and eliminating Arab militants, especially those attacking civilians. Wingate taught and inspired Dayan to lead his men from the front and to strike the enemy where and when it's least expected. He also advised Dayan to respect Arabs who avoided hostilities. Wingate valued intelligence, and both focused on action-oriented soldiers.

Dayan's ambivalent attitude toward the Arab population developed during his service with the British. He took orders from Ode Wingate and was determined to understand Arab customs and ceremonies. While serving in the Wingate-led strike units, he learned to be tough yet respectful toward Arabs in Palestine. In the 1950s, he developed tactics against insurgents that reflected Wingate's methods. He served as an observer in Vietnam in the early 1960s. His crowning achievement was his performance in the 1967 War, which strengthened his reputation. What would he think of the IDF's performance in October 2023? What lessons would he draw? What advice would he give for the future?
**Current Status:** His counterinsurgency ideas remain embedded, though modified, in Israeli doctrine. He is considered a national hero.

**Profile 6 – Shaykh Izz al-Din Ezzedin Qassam**
**Names:** Shaykh Izz al-Din Ezzedin Qassam
**Nationality:** Syrian Province, Ottoman Empire
**Profession:** Preacher, anti-British agitator
**Connection to October 7, 2023:** He had impeccable religious credentials. He memorized large parts of Islam's sacred texts and graduated from al-Azhar

University in Cairo, the most prestigious center for Sunni Islamic studies. He became a militant when Italy invaded Libya in 1911 and organized volunteers, whom he called mujahideen, to fight against the Italians and later the French. He then partnered with Hajj Amin Al-Husseini, the Grand Mufti of Jerusalem, to prevent Jewish immigration to Palestine.

Al-Qassam stressed the moral integrity of his followers. Men should be devout Muslims and generously support the poor. He drew young, impoverished men from the slums of Haifa and gave them a sense of purpose. He organized attack squads called 'Black Hand' to kill British and Jewish personnel. This put him on Britain's most-wanted list. British soldiers chased him and his associates and shot them dead in 1935.

**Current Status:** He remains a martyr to many Arabs. Hamas has honored him by naming a battalion after him.

**Profile 7 – Jonathan Brown of Georgetown**

**Names:** Jonathan Brown

**Nationality:** American

**Profession:** Professor of Middle East Studies at Georgetown University

**Connection to October 7, 2023:** Jonathan Brown, the chair of Georgetown University's Department of Arabic and Islamic Studies, is a notable figure in Middle Eastern academic circles. He is also closely associated with Georgetown's Alwaleed bin Talal School of Global Affairs and the Alwaleed bin Talal School of Muslim-Christian Understanding. He was raised as an Episcopalian but converted to Islam on his 20th birthday. He is Sunni and adheres to the Hanbali school of Islamic jurisprudence.

Brown frequently speaks and presents with credibility at forums worldwide and is not hesitant to express his opinions on social media. In 2024, he tweeted, 'Israeli security forces are lunatics. Israel is insanely racist.'[50] He remarked that Israel has been engaged in a genocidal project for decades. At a Middle East symposium, he said, 'The problem is that the Israeli political creature, the Israeli political establishment, has not told Jews in Israel that they are not allowed to take stuff that doesn't belong to them, and that is, I think, a fundamental problem . . . If you can tell people that your religious belief does not give you the right to take the possessions of someone else.'[51]

His critics are skeptical of his views on Israel, which are prevalent among university students. If Israel is 'genocidal,' why has there been such demand from Palestinians to work there? Do demographic numbers support his theory of coordinated mass murder? His critics also urge him to speak unequivocally about slavery and denounce its modern practice. However, he undoubtedly has his supporters, one of whom is Sami Al-Arian, a former professor at the University of South Florida who was deported. Al-Arian was indicted for violating the Patriot Act. Brown is married to Al-Arian's daughter.

**Current Status:** Full professor at Georgetown University

**Profile 8 – Ariel Sharon 'Bulldozer'**
**Names:** Ariel Sharon
**Nationality:** Israeli
**Profession:** Soldier
**Connection to October 7, 2023:** The 'Bulldozer' was short, wide, and audacious in war. He proved to be a capable and daring soldier, credited with rallying the IDF to victory after facing a tactical defeat early in the October 1973 War.[52] Like Dayan, he was born in Mandate Palestine and became involved in arms at an early age. Throughout his life, he fought in all of Israel's wars, including the War of Independence. Like many Israeli general officers, he played a political role and contributed to the establishment of the Likud Party in 1973.[53] He was a hawk, but he changed when he became Prime Minister in 2001.

He determined that it was too costly to continue occupying Gaza and withdrew all Jews from the Gaza Strip. This decision earned him enemies in Israel but did not earn him friends among Hamas, which now controlled Gaza entirely. Israelis from both sides of the political spectrum criticized his tenure. Left-oriented Neve Gordon wrote, 'Sharon's actions during his tenure as Prime Minister strengthened Hamas.'[54] His fellow Likudniks express harsher criticism of his policy toward Gaza.
**Current Status:** He has a mixed reputation as a Prime Minister, but he is highly respected as a warrior.

**Profile 9 – Dr Ahmed Yousef: 'Hamas is a Charitable Organization'**
**Names:** Ahmed Yousef
**Nationality:** Palestinian
**Profession:** Senior political leader in Hamas. He was particularly influential with Ismail Haniyeh.
**Connection to October 7, 2023:** Ahmed Yousef has been a trusted insider among Hamas leaders. Those outside that inner circle may be confused about his true stance on international relations. With his extensive connections to groups and decision-makers in Europe and the United States, he refers to himself as 'Hamas's gate' to the West.[55] He often presents himself as Hamas's moderate, compassionate face. He explained, 'Hamas is a bulwark in the face of radical and militant ideas and trends.'[56] He argues that Hamas is not a terrorist organization but rather a charitable and social entity.[57]

Yousef founded the United Association for Studies and Research, which operated in the United States from 1989 to 2004. Critics of the association claim that it was linked to Hamas. Yousef argues that Hamas is not a terrorist organization but states that Israel is a terrorist state. However, the US Department of Justice maintains that Hamas is a terrorist organization and has deported non-citizens who assisted Hamas. One of those arrested and facing deportation is Yousef's son-in-law.[58]
**Current Status:** Unknown .

**Profile 10 – Moussa Abu Marzouk**
**Names:** Moussa Abu Marzouk
**Nationality:** Palestinian
**Profession:** He is a founding member of Hamas and Deputy Head of its Political Bureau and a US-based organizer of Hamas activities who was deported after unlawful actions were uncovered. The US Department of the Treasury designated him as a Specially Designated Terrorist in 1995.
**Connection to October 7, 2023:** Moussa Abu Marzouk is a constant contender for leadership of Hamas.[59] For decades, he has served as Hamas' second-in-command. Since helping to establish Hamas, Marzouk has remained dedicated to his goal of destroying Israel. He often issues this call, especially when Israel makes diplomatic progress on the world stage.[60] He is very cozy with Iran and praises the Islamic Republic for its support.[61]

Marzouk lived in the United States for many years. After studying engineering in Cairo during the 1970s, he earned graduate degrees in the US. He held a Green Card and lived in Springfield, Virginia, where he founded the Islamic Association for Palestine. However, American authorities imprisoned and deported him because of his involvement in terrorism. He did not experience poverty abroad; instead, he is a billionaire residing in Qatar alongside other wealthy individuals associated with Hamas.
**Current Status:** Likely living in Qatar and playing a very senior role in Hamas.

# Chapter 3

# Israel, Hamas, and Counterterrorism

*We [Special Operations] tend to take an indirect approach. We can engage without being escalatory or aggressive.*

British Lt Gen Marshall Webb praising Orde Wingate at a naming ceremony for the 77th 'Chindits' Brigade[1]

Israel's ongoing war with Hamas is the latest in a series of conflicts – some large and conventional, like the wars of 1967 and 1973, while others have been shorter and quicker. The only consistent element in Israel's conflict with the Palestinians has been counterterrorism.

Israeli counterterrorism strategy predates the country's founding in 1948 by several decades. Jews worked with the British military to fight Arab terrorists in the 1930s. In the late 1940s, some Jews targeted British symbols of authority to pressure Britain to relax immigration rules and speed up the move toward independence. These early years saw future Israeli leaders developing counterterrorism policies. Core parts of this established doctrine became the basis of Israeli methods for addressing the Palestinian terrorism issue.

The struggle over land ownership in present-day Israel began with a surge of Jewish immigration in the early 20th century, especially after the collapse of the Ottoman Empire. As Jews moved into Mandatory Palestine, attacks by Arabs on Jewish homes, farms, and people increased. Major incidents took place in 1920, 1921, 1929, and 1933. Meanwhile, Jews in the Arab world faced harassment, intimidation, and sometimes being forced out of their homes. Both Arabs and Jews aimed to create independent nations. Arab hopes for political independence were driven by regional nationalism, especially in Egypt, Iraq, and Syria, while many Jews pushed for their homeland.

One of the first large-scale killings occurred in April 1920 when Arabs rampaged through the Jewish quarter of Jerusalem, beating residents, looting stores, and randomly harassing and killing pedestrians. In response, British authorities stepped in to stop the rioting. Jewish leaders formed the Haganah, a developing Jewish self-defense organization. However, it took years before it gained professionalism, a group of capable non-commissioned officers and officers, and expertise with weapons. Initially, the Haganah practiced restraint; however, later, faced with repeated Arab attacks in the 1930s, many leaders promoted pre-emptive strikes.[2]

The deadliest riot in Mandate Palestine occurred in 1929, where Arabs killed 67 Jews. Some highly religious Jews called this attack the 'third destruction,' referring to the two destructions of the Temple in Jerusalem that happened early Judaism.[3]

## The Arab Revolt and Its Legacy for Today

The 1920s and 1930s were decades filled with both hope and despair for Zionists. The Jewish community in Palestine was lively, welcoming Eastern European Jews fleeing the Russian Civil War, the rise of National Socialism, and hardships in their homelands. However, Jews who moved to Palestine did not receive a warm welcome from the Arabs. The influx of Jews angered many Arabs in Mandated Palestine, leading some to organize a widespread boycott. This was followed by harassment and violence against Jews. The first phase of a large-scale rebellion was mainly led by the urban elite, the Higher Arab Committee, which organized the general strike known as the Arab Revolt in 1936. The strike continued despite British intervention. The second phase of the Revolt was marked by increased militancy, as Arabs attacked Jews, Jewish businesses, and British citizens.

The British faced challenges from Arab hit-and-run tactics targeting British and Jewish interests and pursued an unconventional response. They found their solution in Captain Charles 'Orde' Wingate (Profile 1, Chapter 3) and sent him to Palestine in 1936 to suppress the Arab rebellion.[4] The uprising was led by Arab nationalists and some Islamists, involving Arab fellaheen, or peasants.

Unlike many British officers, Wingate supported the Zionist cause. The leaders of the Haganah trusted Wingate and saw him as one of their own. Compact, scrappy, and reclusive, this intelligence officer and gunner earned the nickname 'Wingate of Judea.' Earlier, he studied Arabic and Arab civilization at the School of Oriental Studies in London. He urged the Haganah to break its dependence on the British without hesitation. According to Wingate, the British were not friends of the Jews, and definitely not of the Zionist cause. Initially, he was unimpressed by the poor martial demeanor of the Jews in Palestine, criticizing them for being too passive, patient, and comfortable on their farms. He was determined to instill a fighting spirit in their ranks to confront hostile Arabs. He started by emphasizing physical toughness through extremely long marches with little food and no water.[5]

Wingate founded the Special Night Service (SNS), composed of British and Jewish infantry soldiers. Its main goal was to safeguard farms and oil pipelines from sabotage by Arab forces. Wingate continued the British tradition of deploying irregular units, a characteristic feature of British Special Operations Forces in World War II. These squads were small, never exceeding 200 men, yet they effectively neutralized the Arab threat. They also provided a psychological boost to the growing Jewish community. Wingate's success with the SNS earned him Britain's Distinguished Service Order. His legacy has been passed down through the generations, and his efforts helped create a modern, practical, and self-sufficient army. Moshe Dayan studied directly under Wingate, learning his unconventional tactics and style. Dayan and other platoon commanders gained knowledge of ambushes and nighttime attack techniques. Elements of Wingate's strategies and tactics remain a core part of the IDF's doctrine today and have also influenced US counterinsurgency strategies since September 2001.

## Wingate's Doctrine, Hamas, and the 2023 Attack

Wingate's doctrine of unconventional warfare in Palestine was based on four key pillars: a focus on the population, harsh measures against enemies, extensive intelligence, and the ability to seize and hold the initiative. First, his doctrine prioritized a population-centered approach that included efforts to protect civilians not involved with militants. This strategy resembled what the United States attempted in Vietnam and Afghanistan, where it proved to be considerably less effective. The idea behind this population-focused strategy was that killing civilians would be counterproductive and could create more militants. Angry and alienated citizens are more likely to support terrorist groups. Wingate influenced Dayan, who, many years later, would adopt a more conciliatory attitude toward non-hostile Arab populations to win their respect and support for cooperation.[6]

After the October 1973 War, many strategists criticized Dayan for focusing on a population-centric approach, which many Palestinians viewed as a weakness. A similar observation arose 50 years later when Hamas launched attacks on multiple fronts. This population-centric strategy continued to influence Israeli policymaking in the 21st century. From the introduction of the Oslo Accords in 1993 until October 2023, Israel aimed to integrate Palestinians into its economy. According to this plan, as stakeholders in Israeli prosperity, Palestinians would be less likely to attack the state. Israel was hesitant to strike locations where militants operated because these sites were often near civilians, fearing mass casualties. Hamas exploited this by placing weapons depots in kindergartens, mosques, and hospitals, making it more difficult for Israel to protect noncombatants from harm.

A second aspect of Wingate's doctrine was the harsh and sometimes brutal treatment of militants. This severity allowed the SNS to maintain control at night. Israel's first Prime Minister, David Ben-Gurion, acknowledged that Wingate's methods were incorporated into the IDF's doctrine. In the 21st century, Wingate's strategy of harsh treatment of enemy forces has been reflected in Israel's targeted assassinations, house demolitions, and administrative detention. During Hamas' early years, its leaders feared that an Israeli missile could kill them and their families at any moment. After the October 2023 attack, some critics argued that Israel had become more lenient over time. From this perspective, Hamas' junior and mid-level operatives, collaborators, militant rhetoricians, clerics, and recruiters no longer feared or respected the IDF.

A third element of his strategy emphasized the importance of strategic and tactical intelligence. Strategic intelligence involved a thorough understanding of Arab social structures, leadership, clan affiliations, customs, ceremonies, and military capabilities. Wingate highlighted the importance of regional and cultural knowledge among his officers. He learned Hebrew and expected his officers to master local languages while becoming familiar with the customs, ceremonies, and beliefs of the local population.

He also highlighted the importance of current and actionable tactical intelligence. Key tactical questions include: Where are weapons stored, and will they be used soon? What planning and tactics is the enemy likely to adopt? Wingate built a network of Arab informants to gather information on the intentions and dispositions of hostile Arabs. Israel faced heavy criticism for its lack of preparedness on October 7, 2023, and for neglecting to use the harsh retaliatory measures Wingate advocated in the 1930s.

A fourth element of Wingate's doctrine was seizing the initiative, which required Jews to leave the safety of their settlements to confront their Arab enemies. Jewish Palestinians would decide the timing, location, type, and scale of the attack to keep the enemy off balance and unable to predict the next move. This was one of the first missions for the night squads in 1937 and 1938 that were tasked with finding, eliminating, and destroying Arab fighters hiding in the hills of Galilee. Arabs attacked Jewish villages, stole livestock, and set fire to trees and crops. They ambushed British patrols and Jewish motor convoys while extorting local Arab villagers. Wingate revamped the counterinsurgency strategy by emphasizing surprise, stealth, and unpredictability in his nighttime attacks. His innovative approach to doctrine and strategy is still celebrated, with Israelis calling him 'friend,' or 'haver' in Hebrew. However, the events of October 7 raised questions about how much the IDF had strayed from Wingate's core principles.

## Jewish Terrorism in Mandated Palestine

Both Jews and Arabs engaged in acts of terrorism in Mandate Palestine. From the mid-1940s through the War of Independence, Jewish terrorists targeted British and Arab targets. Four Zionist insurgent groups – the Haganah, as mentioned earlier, along with the Palmach, Irgun, and Lehi – were responsible for most of these attacks.

The Haganah, a self-defense group that started in 1920 and was professionalized by Orde Wingate, grew over the years to around 27,000 members by 1947. In the late 1930s, parts of the Haganah worked with the British to suppress the Arab Revolt. By the early 1940s, Europe had become a death zone for Jews. As historian Yehuda Bauer said, these were the crisis years. Jews in Palestine needed to help the

British fight the Nazis. But British policy limited Jewish immigration to Palestine. Jewish leaders stayed determined to challenge both Arabs and the British.

The Irgun originated from the Haganah. In April 1937, dissatisfied Haganah leaders broke away to form an independent group called Irgun Zvai Leumi be Erez Israel, commonly known as the Irgun. Another faction was Lehi, also called the Stern Gang, which split from the Irgun in 1940. More radical than both the Haganah and the Irgun, it was founded by Avraham Stern (Profile 2 – Chapter 3), a scholar, intellectual, and tactician who saw the British as the main enemy of Zionism. Finally, the Palmach, or strike force, served as an elite fighting unit under Haganah's control. Established in May 1941, it included about 2,000 men and women. The Palmach's goal was to carry out hit-and-run operations against the British to pressure them into releasing Jews who entered Palestine illegally. The most notorious Jewish terrorist attack was the bombing of the King David Hotel, carried out by the Haganah.[7]

Observers of the Middle East debate how effective the Jewish terrorist campaign was. The British withdrew from Palestine, but records show they planned to leave soon after the Nazis were defeated. They did not leave under terms favorable to Zionism. Maybe terrorism sped up the British withdrawal, or maybe it didn't. In the ethical debate about Jewish terrorism in the 1940s, Jews mainly targeted military and diplomatic officials, symbols of British prestige, and Britain's immigration policies. Still, many civilians lost their lives because of Jewish terrorists. After independence, security and intelligence units from before independence were either disbanded or merged into the IDF. Haganah leaders learned from Wingate about how important intelligence is, which was used for both defensive and offensive operations.

## Palestinian Terrorism – From Israeli Independence to Hamas

The Israeli victory in 1948 brought independence but did not provide lasting security. Arab terrorism began before Israeli independence and continued after this victory. The issues of refugee settlement and population resettlement remained a festering wound in the Middle East. Historians disagree on the number of Arabs who either left Israel voluntarily or involuntarily. The Palestinian refugee problem has never been resolved. Gaza became overwhelmed with Arab refugees, and the prewar population of 100,000 doubled. According to historian Benny Morris, the Palestinian refugee issue would shape the still-popular narrative of the tormented Palestinian. It served as a metaphor for the biblical passage of David facing off against the Israeli Goliath.[8] None of this alleviated the destitution of the Gaza Strip. Gazans were not offered Egyptian citizenship.[9]

Palestinian terrorism in the 1960s and 1970s attracted worldwide attention and achieved its goal. Palestinian leaders allied with the Soviet Union. After the significant victory in June 1967, Arafat (Profile 3, Chapter 3) aimed to raise the Palestinian cause to an international stage. He used dramatic violence to make headlines globally, supported by Soviet-backed diplomacy. This strategy earned him a Nobel Peace Prize and the international recognition he sought.

Hamas aimed to gain prestige among Palestinians, sought direct support from Iran and Qatar, and received indirect aid from Europe. European assistance could help rebuild homes and restore the economic infrastructure that was either damaged by Israel or left neglected and in poor condition. In its rivalry with Fatah for status and resources, Hamas escalated its terrorist attacks as the 20th century came to an end. In response, Israel employed various tactics, including targeted assassinations, home demolitions, and administrative detention.

## Three Israeli Counterterrorism Tactics

### *Targeted Assassinations and 2004*

Targeted assassination is a long-standing tactic with deep historical roots. In its early days, Israel aimed for vengeance against Nazi war criminals. Before gaining independence, the Irgun and Stern Gang assassinated key political and military leaders. Later, Israel shifted its focus to Middle Eastern terrorists. One scholar estimated that the number of those killed in these acts reaches into the thousands. Several Israeli intelligence agencies carried out these operations over 70 years. The most notable or controversial series of assassinations was the revenge attack for the 1972 Munich Olympics, as depicted, if somewhat dramatized, in print and film.[10]

According to most authoritative accounts, Mossad plans and conducts operations outside of Israel, while Shin Bet operates within Israel. The IDF often coordinates with both agencies and sometimes carries out operations. Israel responded to the outbreak of the Second Intifada in September 2000 by targeting high-level Palestinian terrorists, beginning on November 9, 2000. In Bethlehem, an Israeli Apache helicopter fired a missile, killing a leader who was attempting to establish a Hezbollah cell in the Gaza Strip. The anger from September 11, 2001, made this tactic more acceptable to leaders in the United States, Israel's most significant supporter.[11]

In 2001, Israel publicly announced its strategy of targeted assassination. It began by openly executing terrorist operatives and individuals deemed likely to commit terrorist acts, especially those willing to carry out suicide attacks. That same year, Israel's internal security service, Shin Bet, expanded its kill list to include recruiters, arms suppliers, and smugglers. It also continued targeting lower-level members of Palestinian terrorist groups. In 2003, Israel tried to assassinate Yassin in response to a Hamas attack on a ship in Ashdod, which resulted in 10 deaths and threatened hundreds more.

In 2004, Israeli leaders decided to eliminate Hamas' senior leadership. A Hellfire missile hit its target when it struck Yassin and seven others in Gaza City. The IDF targeted the spiritual leader Rantisi and the political figure Izz al-Din al-Sheikh Khalil, who was killed in Damascus. Later that year, the IDF also killed prominent Hamas political and military leaders Mahmud Zahar, Imad Abbas, and

Adnan al-Ghoul. The year 2004 was violent for Hamas. Twenty years later, Israel would launch airstrikes that killed numerous high-ranking Hamas and Iranian leaders across the Middle East. The IDF eliminated Mohammed Deif (Profile 4 – Chapter 3) in a strike that caused nearly 100 deaths at the blast site. Among those killed that year were Iranian generals attending an event at Iran's consulate in Syria. A drone strike in Beirut targeted an exiled top Hamas official, Saleh Arouri.[12]

Israel faced significant international criticism because of this. Under international law, targeted assassinations fall into gray areas of legality. Some scholars call them extrajudicial executions, which are only lawful when the target poses an immediate threat, like a suicide bomber or an assassin. Others argue from a broader perspective, believing they are legal if the targets are considered combatants. From this view, individuals seen as combatants are considered legitimate targets. Some Western countries, such as the US and Israel, have adopted this broader approach interpretation.[13]

Since their inception and revitalization at the turn of the century, Israeli assassinations have faced numerous challenges. First, there have been significant failures, particularly the 1973 mistaken killing of an innocent Palestinian waiter in Norway and the nearly farcical, botched poisoning attempt on Meshaal. Both incidents damaged the image of the Mossad and that of Benjamin Netanyahu's government (Profile 5 – Chapter 3). Furthermore, there is an ongoing debate regarding the effectiveness of this tactic. Muslim militants often welcome death and become martyrs. Their deaths provide financial benefits to their families and fuel a desire for revenge.

## *Home Demolitions*

In addition to killing Hamas leaders, Israel has punished the families of terrorists, especially suicide bombers. Home destruction as a counterterrorism method predates Israel's independence. In Mandate Palestine, British authorities confiscated and demolished homes connected to terrorism. Israel has used that Wingate-era tactic to respond to the rise of terrorism at the turn of the 21st century.[14] Israel began to destroy homes during the Second Intifada. The residences of families of suicide bombers were prime targets. The demolition of their homes was sometimes timed to coincide with enforced store closures and curfews.[15]

From 2000 to 2005, the IDF destroyed 558 Palestinian homes. Israel stopped this tactic in 2005 as Palestinian terrorism decreased. However, home demolitions resumed in 2014 after a series of Palestinian attacks. Israeli policymakers reasoned that killing individual would-be suicide bombers was necessary but not enough. The suicide bomber is determined to die and believes he will become a martyr with immediate entry to heaven and its rewards. Still, he might reconsider his plans if it seems likely that his family's house will be destroyed. Additionally, if his family or friends learn of his intentions, they might try to stop him or report it to Israeli intelligence, which has happened.

Several human rights organizations in Israel condemn this practice. The Israeli Information Center for Human Rights in the Occupied Territories has labeled it immoral and unlawful. There is substantial debate regarding the costs and benefits of home demolitions, as Israel faces repercussions in international opinion. Images of destroyed homes and grieving Palestinians amplify perceptions of Israeli cruelty. Journalists quickly sought out the now-dispossessed and sorrowful Palestinians for interviews. International human rights organizations have condemned this tactic as a form of collective punishment, which is prohibited by international law. The demolitions have been cited as evidence that Israel has committed war crimes.

### *Administrative Detentions*

According to Amnesty International, administrative detention is a process that holds individuals without trial or charges. For years, many have been interned in various military camps operated by the IDF. Critics of Israel have accused the country of violating international law. The UN has established a global standard in its Convention Against Torture and Other Cruel, Inhuman or Degrading Treatment or Punishment (CAT). In 1991, Israel ratified the CAT. However, detention laws are subject to interpretation by the involved parties, allowing Israelis to assert that they comply with their understanding of the law. The Israelis claim that suspects are brought before a judge within eight days of their arrest, with the judge deciding whether to extend the detention. According to Al Jazeera, approximately 9,500 Palestinians from Gaza and the West Bank were incarcerated in the Israeli prison system as of April 2024.

## Three Wars in Gaza

Hamas remains committed to its 1988 Charter, which seeks nothing less than the destruction of Israel. Although temporary truces exist between Israel and Hamas, they are merely brief moments of calm during which Hamas reorganizes and prepares. The ceasefire following the First Gaza War of 2008–2009, known as Operation Cast Lead, was succeeded by the Second Gaza War of 2014, named Operation Protective Edge, which ultimately led to the ongoing conflict known as the Third Gaza War of 2021, referred to as Operation Guardian of the Walls. In 2021, a skirmish in Jerusalem escalated into a major riot, followed by a series of rocket attacks from Hamas.

### *First Gaza War 2008–2009 – Operation Cast Lead*

On December 27, 2008, Israel launched Operation Cast Lead against Hamas in the Gaza Strip after three years of escalating tensions. Following Hamas' rise to power in Gaza, there was a shaky peace with Israel that lasted for two years. In reaction to Hamas' continuous missile strikes into Israel, Israel consistently monitored traffic to and from Gaza. A lull ensued, and both parties observed a ceasefire negotiated by Egypt.

Hamas established an extensive network of tunnels along the border with Egypt to smuggle weapons, money, and other goods into and out of Gaza. They also excavated additional tunnels to serve as bunkers and traps for abducting IDF personnel and concealing rockets and their launchers. Many entry points are concealed or situated in civilian areas, such as hospitals and residential buildings.

The objectives of Operation Cast Lead aligned with Wingate's doctrine of counterterrorism. Ruthless attacks against Hamas militants aimed to eliminate their capacity and intent to use Gaza as a launchpad for missiles targeting Israel. Israel also adopted a population-centric model. Operation Cast Lead was characterized as a minor, swift war rather than a retaliatory strike.

During the brief conflict, approximately 1,400 Palestinians lost their lives, including around 300 children and hundreds of other unarmed civilians. Extensive areas of Gaza were leveled, and homes were destroyed, leaving thousands homeless and further damaging the already dire economy.

The operation lasted only a few weeks and was intensely contested. Israel adhered to Wingate's principle of fierce fighting against the militant enemy. Human rights NGOs vehemently claimed that Israel betrayed Wingate's second rule of population-centric compassion. Human Rights Watch, which has faced criticism for an anti-Israel bias, raised concerns about what it alleged were at least 12 instances in which the IDF destroyed private homes and businesses without explicit and legitimate military purpose justification. The report maintained that many of these attacks were unnecessary because they occurred as Israel was winding down its operations.[16]

Many post-conflict reports were particularly critical of Israeli tactics and targeting. Amnesty International highlighted indiscriminate attacks with precision weapons that destroyed civilian homes without warning. It is alleged that Israel killed numerous children while they played and slept, along with medical personnel. The crux of Amnesty International's argument rested on the assertion that Israel operated as a *de facto* occupying force. Consequently, it violated the Geneva Convention's laws of war by controlling electricity, water, and telecommunications in Gaza. Israel contended that Hamas used Gaza civilians as 'human shields.' However, the report argued that the civilian victims were visible and posed no threat. Israel vehemently disputed the allegation that it was reckless in its attacks.

Operation Cast Lead brought Israel two years of relative peace. When Hamas or PIJ launched a barrage into Israel, the IDF would respond with proportionate counterstrikes. Although Israel destroyed much of Hamas' missile arsenal and other weaponry, it did not stop the flow of arms into Gaza. Israel never fully closed the Egyptian border, which allowed Iran to send in missiles with significantly longer ranges, some of which struck Tel Aviv. Despite its limitations, Cast Lead upheld peace for over two years. Then came Operation Pillar of Defense.

## *Operation Pillar of Defense – Not Long Enough to be a War*

Low-level exchanges continued until mid-November 2012, when Hamas fired 200 rockets and several mortar rounds into Israel. In response, Israel launched Operation Pillar of Defense, targeting Hamas military chief Ahmed Jabari and conducting strikes on additional targets. Pillar of Defense aimed to destroy missile stockpiles and storage sites, as well as to target Hamas leaders. The presence of Iranian-manufactured Fajr-5 long-range missiles put Tel Aviv within range.

Israel's missile defense improved significantly, but so did Hamas' missile inventory, which it unleashed on Israel in November 2012. Hamas and PIJ fired 1,456 rockets into Israel, striking Tel Aviv. In retaliation, the Israeli Air Force (IAF) targeted over 1,500 sites in Gaza, including rocket launchers, weapon stockpiles, and Hamas government infrastructure. They also killed Ahmed Jabari (Profile 6 – Chapter 3), the commander of Hamas' military wing, who was directly linked to the kidnapping and imprisonment of Gilad Shalit (Profile 7 – Chapter 3).

The results of this operation were inconclusive. The tunneling system remained largely intact. Funding, technology, and hardware for missiles continued to flow in from foreign sources. Israel did not eradicate the source of terror. The IDF claimed that it had severely damaged Hamas' command and control, although the extensive terrorist infrastructure, facilities, and military bases remained. These attacks resulted in numerous Palestinian fatalities not associated with Hamas. Acknowledging the widespread civilian casualties, Israel stated that Hamas had positioned leaders, command headquarters, underground rocket launchers, tools for terrorist activities, control rooms, weapons storage, and production facilities within civilian areas.

Pillar of Defense demonstrated the effectiveness of the Iron Dome defense system. Israeli sources reported an interception rate of 84%. The week-long operation cost Gaza's economy nearly $230 million. The population remained impoverished, while the leaders were wealthy, and there was ample funding available to acquire weapons for the next conflict in 2014. It was not long or lethal enough to be called a war. But it was a bloody conflict.

## *Second Gaza War of 2014 – Operation Protective Edge*

The next conflict was Operation Protective Edge, which began on July 8, 2014, and proved to be more brutal than previous conflicts. Both sides stumbled into the war as the exchanges of gunfire escalated into a full-scale battle. Initially, Hamas kidnapped and murdered several Israeli youths, while militants in Gaza launched a barrage of rocket fire. According to the BBC, between July 8 and August 27, 2,000 Gazans, along with 66 Israeli soldiers and seven civilians in Israel, lost their lives. The IDF reported that 1,000 Palestinians were killed.

Israeli attacks commenced with an air campaign, followed by a ground incursion aimed at uncovering and destroying tunnels utilized by the IDF Golani Brigade. The fighting was intense. Israel accused Hamas of firing rockets at Israeli civilians while using Palestinian civilians as human shields, complicating efforts to avoid civilian casualties. IDF spokespersons asserted that Israel established new high standards in military ethics by warning civilians before attacks through the distribution of leaflets, making phone calls, and sending text messages about impending strikes. The IDF also canceled strikes to prevent unintended casualties. The primary goal of Protective Edge was to eliminate the tunnel system in the Gaza Strip. The IDF concluded that this operation largely achieved its objectives.

## *Third Gaza War of 2021 – Operation Guardian of the Walls*

During the conflict that Hamas called the Sword of Jerusalem and the IDF termed the Guardian of the Walls, two distinct military doctrines collided. Hamas aimed to provoke retaliation from the IDF by launching heavy and indiscriminate rocket fire at Israeli population centers. This strategy was effective, leading Israel to respond with rockets in areas where militants and civilians were present.[17] Israel's Iron Dome intercepted approximately 90% of incoming missiles. Israel held Hamas responsible for civilian casualties, arguing that they intentionally placed civilians alongside militants. The IDF faced criticism in international political circles due to the widespread distribution of photographs showing injured Palestinian women and children. These allegations could also serve as the basis for actions in international courts seeking to hold Israel accountable.[18]

Human rights organizations claimed that Israel's response breached laws designed to protect civilians and their property during wartime, as outlined by international humanitarian law, including the Fourth Geneva Convention of 1949, which focuses on the protection of civilians in conflict situations.

The IDF's primary objective was to eliminate Hamas' missile sites and assembly points. The group fired nearly 3,000 missiles, demonstrating that Hamas and PIJ were well-prepared for the conflict and that their military capabilities had been significantly enhanced compared to earlier Hamas-Israel skirmishes.[19] They could launch more attacks using various missiles that have greater destructive power and a longer range. Located eight miles from the Gaza border, Ashkelon suffered nearly 1,000 rocket strikes, resulting in the deaths of two women and injuries to 295 residents. These attacks coincided with riots happening within Israel. In response to the unrest, Israel went on high alert, closed many schools, reduced flights from Ben Gurion International Airport, and increased street patrols. Operation Guardian of the Walls lasted 11 days and was marked by intense and bloody confrontations.[20]

Hamas studied the war in detail. It tested Iron Dome and determined that it could overwhelm it in the future if it saturated Israel's borders with enough rockets. Hamas also increased its cyber and intelligence capabilities.[21]

The IDF's after-action reports assessed Israel's response to the Hamas attack as adequate. The country's communication systems operated efficiently, swiftly delivering warnings to the public. The Israeli population largely supported the government's heavy-handed tactics, with little doubt that Hamas was the aggressor. The report concluded that the Iron Dome defense system successfully intercepted missiles from Gaza and that the security barrier was robust. While these findings were likely accurate, strategists in 2023 noted that such assessments contributed to a sense of complacency within the IDF. Some referred to this as frozen thinking and argued that this hubris could leave Israel unprepared for the Fourth Gaza War, which would erupt on October 7, 2023.

For years, Israel maintained a mixed and flexible relationship with Hamas, often creating confusion. Its policy included elements of the Wingate doctrine – harsh treatment for terror leaders, combined with generally passive and sometimes benign relations with non-aggressive Palestinians. However, contrary to Wingate's advice, it prioritized defensive measures – the security barrier and Iron Dome – over the proactive and aggressive search-and-destroy missions that Wingate advocated. Wingate's emphasis on strategic and tactical intelligence was utterly absent. Hubris within the upper echelons of the Israeli security establishment blinded them to the ever-growing threat that would erupt on October 7 and shock the world.

Hamas was prepared. The ghost army had trained, moving through the Gaza Metro of tunnels while evading expected attacks. Hamas effectively learned from its rapid conflicts with Israel. It reinforced the tunnel system with blast doors that sealed off sections, protecting them from bombs and drone strikes. By the day of the attack, Hamas assailants could navigate the dark, narrow passages using night-vision goggles. The tunnels served as advanced command-and-control centers and contained extensive storage facilities. Then, it commenced.

Hamas launched an attack at dawn following an artillery barrage. Operation al Aqsa Flood began with torrents of Hamas militants pouring into various points of assault near the Gaza border. Hamas struck 50 years and a day after the surprise attack of the Yom Kippur War and was hit by lightning. The Izz al-Din al-Qassam Brigades, also known as the Qassam Brigades, breached the barrier using tractors, heavy trucks, and explosives. The bloodiest day in the history of Israel had just begun. This would be the fourth war (Table 1 – Chapter 3).

**Table 1 – Chapter 3: Wars and Operations between Hamas and Israel**

| | Reason for Starting the War | Nature of the War | Length | Results |
|---|---|---|---|---|
| **First Gaza War Operation Cast Lead** | Israel attacked after receiving repeated missile fire from Hamas. | Characterized as a minor, rapid conflict rather than a retaliatory strike. | December 27, 2008 – January 18, 2009 | 1,400 Gazans killed. Large areas of Gaza were leveled. This brought Israel two years of relative peace. |
| **Operation Pillar of Defense** | Hamas fired 200 rockets and several mortar rounds into Israel. | In retaliation, the Israeli Air Force targeted over 1,500 sites in Gaza, including rocket launchers, weapons stockpiles, and infrastructure associated with the Hamas government. | November 14–21, 2012 | The results were inconclusive. The tunneling system remained intact. The IDF killed Ahmed Jabari, a Hamas leader, showcasing the effectiveness of the Iron Dome defense system. |

| | Reason for Starting the War | Nature of the War | Length | Results |
|---|---|---|---|---|
| **Second Gaza War of 2014 – Operation Protective Edge** | Both sides stumbled into the war as the exchanges of gunfire escalated into a full-scale battle. | The stated IDF goal was to collapse the tunnel network and end missile attacks. | July 8–August 27, 2014 | Between 1,000 and 2,000 Gazans, 66 Israeli soldiers, and seven civilians died. The IDF concluded that its objectives were reached. However, much of the tunnel system remained. |
| **Third Gaza War of 2021 – Operation Guardian of the Walls** | The IDF retaliated against the missile attack. | Extensive Israeli airstrikes targeted rocket manufacturing sites, command centers, and the tunnel network. | May 6–May 21, 2021 | IDF claimed partial victory. Iron Dome was largely successful. Successful Hamas information operations harmed Israel. |

## Summary

Mandated Palestine was in a state of social, ideological, and religious flux. The British deployed Wingate to restore order and instill military discipline and competence in the Jewish forces, which he successfully accomplished. His unconventional warfare doctrine in Palestine was grounded in four strategic pillars: a population-centric approach, harsh measures against adversaries, robust intelligence, and the seizure and maintenance of the initiative in combat. These concepts were loosely integrated into Israeli doctrine and transmitted through generations.

In all these operations, the IDF aimed to warn civilians near military targets that they could be harmed if they did not evacuate the target zone. In successive small wars, the IDF sought to 'mow down the grass,' which involved periodically attacking military and paramilitary sites in Gaza, focusing on eliminating terrorist leaders. These operations temporarily curtailed Hamas' full capabilities. In the spirit of Orde Wingate, Israel intended to protect uninvolved Gaza civilians by alerting them to impending attacks. Additionally, the Israeli economy offered employment, education, and limited healthcare to these civilians. Simultaneously, the IDF executed intense strikes against terrorists and their supporters. Its tactical targeting intelligence was accurate and timely.

Despite these many successes, they were not sufficient to keep Hamas at bay. Israel's strategic intelligence provided an overly optimistic view of Hamas' intentions and capabilities. Its tactical intelligence failed to predict the timing and location of the attack. Consequently, the invasion on October 7 caught Israel off guard and came as a complete surprise. The fourth Israel-Hamas war had begun.[22]

**Profile 1 – Captain Charles 'Orde' Wingate: Friend**
**Names:** Orde Wingate
**Nationality:** British
**Profession:** Soldier; counterinsurgency specialist[23]
**Connection to October 7, 2023:** Sometimes referred to as the Father of the IDF and occasionally called 'friend,' Jewish Palestinians and contemporary Israelis regard Wingate as one of the most righteous Gentiles of Mandate Palestine. Wingate had a deep affection for the Jewish Palestinians, primarily due to his strong Christian faith and belief that divine providence promised the Holy Land to the Jews. However, many in the British Army felt little affection for the eccentric and sometimes cantankerous officer. Nevertheless, it was impossible to deny the transformation of the ragtag Jewish fighting units into a professional fighting force. With his mission in Palestine accomplished, Wingate began his next mission in Ethiopia.[24] He died at 41 in a plane crash. Wingate is buried in a communal grave with the other victims of the crash.[25]

Wingate's lessons on unconventional warfare were passed down through generations. Young men and boys who trained under him in the 1930s became senior officers in the 1967 and 1973 wars.[26] Churchill regarded him as a genius, admired his eccentricities, and accepted his foibles. David Ben-Gurion speculated that he could have become Israel's first chief of staff had he lived.
**Current Status:** His unwavering support for Zionism and his contributions to guerrilla warfare and counterinsurgency secure him a special place in Israeli history.[27]

**Profile 2 – Yasser Arafat**
**Names:** Yasser Arafat (sometimes spelt Yasir Arafat)
**Nationality:** Egyptian and Palestinian
**Profession:** Founder and chairman of the Palestine Liberation Organization (PLO)
**Connection to October 7, 2023:** In his lifetime, Nobel laureate Yasser Arafat was celebrated as the father of the Palestinian movement. He played a pivotal role in building the PLO and felt at home internationally. He formed alliances in his various temporary homes: Kuwait, Syria, Jordan, Lebanon, Tunisia, and ultimately in parts of the occupied West Bank. Over the years, he experimented with insurgent warfare,

terrorism, and diplomacy. In 1974, he stood before the United Nations holding an olive branch, symbolizing peace, and a gun as a figure of war against Israel.[28]

After the Camp David summit in 2000, Arafat permitted the Hamas military wing to escalate terrorism in Israel, signaling the start of the Second Intifada. In July 2000, Arafat informed the head of the Hamas military wing at that time, 'I have no objection to Hamas taking action.'[29] Arafat funneled weapons to Hamas through an unidentified organization in Gaza, according to a senior Hamas official. Arafat's relationship with Hamas was often fraught. Hamas leaders felt betrayed when Arafat, in a sense, made peace with Israel through the Oslo Accords. They claimed they were invited to promote terrorism within Israel.[30]

**Current Status:** Arafat died in November 2004. With his death, Hamas became stronger among Palestinians, which allowed the organization to seize power in 2007.[31]

**Profile 3 – Avraham Stern: Fascist or Patriot?**

**Names:** Avraham Stern

**Nationality:** Born in Poland; Stateless in Palestine

**Profession:** Leader of the eponymous Jewish terrorist group, the Stern Gang

**Connection to October 7, 2023:** Some called him a proponent of 'Hebrew fascism.' He migrated to Palestine in 1925, at age 25, and studied at the Hebrew University. A trained linguist, he was passionate about reviving Hebrew as a national language. His scholarship and the beauty of his poetry earned him a position at an Italian university. However, following the 1929 Arab riots, he turned to militarism and became an effective organizer.

He grew to despise the British, whom he accused of blocking immigration. He also harbored a strong dislike for Arabs and hoped to expel them all. He broke away from a paramilitary group to form his own terrorist organization.[32] Though most Zionists halted terrorist attacks against the British, Stern made them his primary target.[33] British detectives tracked him down and, in 1942, shot him in his underwear and slippers at home. His successor continued to target British victims, and Jews were accused of collaborating with them.[34]

**Current Status:** This romantic poet and terrorist holds a mixed reputation in Israel. Those on the left do not regard him as a hero, whereas nationalistic Israelis do.

**Profile 4 – Benjamin Netanyahu**

**Names:** Benjamin Netanyahu

**Nationality:** Israeli

**Profession:** Career politician, Prime Minister

**Connection to October 7, 2023:** A global figure for decades, Israeli Prime Minister Benjamin Netanyahu was first elected in 1996, becoming the youngest Prime Minister in history. He is knowledgeable about American politics and holds a degree from the Massachusetts Institute of Technology. A proven leader, he served in an elite military unit. He understands both warfare and politics and is determined to dismantle Hamas to ensure it cannot be rebuilt. 'The IDF is about to use all its force to destroy Hamas' capabilities. We'll strike them to the bitter end and avenge with force this black day they brought on Israel and its people.'[35]

He has made three demands: Hamas must be destroyed, Gaza must be demilitarized, and Palestinian society must be deradicalized. These are the three prerequisites for peace between Israel and its neighbors. The chief prosecutor at the ICC is seeking to arrest him for war crimes. At home, his critics have accused him of supporting Hamas during its early stages. They emphasize that he was the Prime Minister at the time of the attack. The killings occurred on his watch, and he must bear some responsibility for the intelligence failure and lack of preparedness.
**Current Status:** Prime Minister Netanyahu stated that he does not intend to resign anytime soon. He is too busy destroying Hamas. 'Imagine allowing the defeated Nazis in 1945 to rebuild Germany. It's inconceivable. It's ridiculous.'[36]

**Profile 5 – Mohammed Deif: 'Heroic Figure'**
**Names:** Mohammed Deif
**Nationality:** Palestinian
**Profession:** Commander of Hamas' military wing
**Connection to October 7, 2023:** Born in the southern Gaza enclave of Khan Younis, Deif was introduced to the Muslim Brotherhood as a teenager. Hamas would later emerge from the Brotherhood as an offshoot.[37] In the 1980s, he studied science at the Islamic University of Gaza, where he deepened his involvement in radical Islam. He established a theater group called The Returners, reflecting his dream of expelling all Jews from Israel. Deif continued his acting career after joining Hamas, occasionally playing minor roles in propaganda videos.[38] He joined Hamas shortly after its creation in 1987. He was arrested and briefly detained by Israel in 1989. Later, he became a senior member. He organized much of the attack on October 7.[39]

The IDF has repeatedly attempted to kill Deif. One estimate suggests there have been seven attempts, some of which likely cost him the lives and limbs of family members. He remains a shadowy figure, with only three known pictures of him. A spokesperson for Hamas stated in July 2024, 'We say to Netanyahu that Mohammed Deif is listening to you now and mocking your false and empty statements.'[40] Perhaps Deif was laughing at the time. But according to Israeli authorities, he was killed sometime in late July 2024.[41] This was the IDF's eighth attempt. Israeli Defense Minister Yoav Gallant stated that Dief's death 'reflects the reality that Hamas is disintegrating, and that Hamas terrorists may either surrender or face consequences.'[42]
**Current Status:** Dead. The ICC canceled the arrest warrant against Deif when it confirmed his death.[43]

**Profile 6 – Ahmed Jabari: The Commander of Hamas' Military Wing**
**Names:** Ahmed Jabari, also called Abu Mohammad
**Nationality:** Palestinian
**Profession:** Leader of the al-Qassam Brigades

**Connection to October 7, 2023:** He was born in 1960 into a family of radical Islamist activists and studied at the Islamic University of Gaza. As a militant and coordinator, he spent years in and out of Israeli prisons. He rose quickly within Hamas and distinguished himself as a specialist in kidnapping and prisoner exchanges. In 2006, he oversaw and planned the kidnapping of Gilad Shalit.[44] He issued some puzzling commands. In 2011, Israel released him and scores of prisoners convicted of murder, robbery, and drug dealing in a prisoner exchange.[45] Israel often attempted to kill him. In August 2004, the IDF killed his eldest son, brother, and several cousins.

In 2012, the IDF finally succeeded in killing him. Jabari was never popular in Western diplomatic or intellectual circles. A German newspaper expressed a general European view that the killing of the *de facto* commander of Hamas' military wing had tactical benefits for Israel. However, targeted assassinations violate international law. 'But the attack on Ahmed Jabari immediately escalated the conflict and is strategically counterproductive for a government that wants to protect its people.'[46] In response to the attack, Hamas called up operatives and fired 83 rockets into southern regions of Israel.[47]

**Current Status:** Dead.

**Profile 7 – Gilad Shalit: Israeli Captive**

**Names:** Gilad Shalit

**Nationality:** Israeli

**Profession:** Former soldier

**Connection to October 7, 2023:** Israel tightened its control over Gaza after Hamas captured 19-year-old Corporal Gilad Shalit in a bold cross-border raid in June 2006. In response, Israel blocked numerous imports and exports to and from Gaza until he was released. The IDF also launched airstrikes in Gaza. The fate of Corporal Shalit became a national issue. Five years later, Shalit was released in a drastically unbalanced exchange of 1,027 Palestinian prisoners for him. German negotiators helped broker the deal.[48] Upon his release, Shalit underwent surgery to remove shrapnel from his body.

The release was celebrated in Mitzpe Hila's hometown and across Israel. Upon his arrival home, people greeted him with joy and enthusiasm.[49] Some Israelis had become weary of the national drama, calling it the Gilad Shalit reality show.[50] Throughout the ordeal, Israeli citizens remained deeply divided over the price that Israel should pay for one of their own. This division was greatly amplified after October 7, 2023.

Palestinians also celebrated the exchange. Ramallah was adorned with green flags, and people wore Hamas headbands. The exchange enhanced Hamas' prestige in the West Bank and reinforced its international standing.

**Current Status:** Ten years after his release, Shalit got married. During his captivity, he was granted honorary citizenship in Paris, Rome, and New Orleans.

# Chapter 4

# The War of Words – Hamas Versus Israel

*The goal of modern propaganda is no longer to transform opinion but to arouse an active and mythical belief.*

Jacques Ellul, French philosopher

The war in Gaza is fought not only with guns and rockets but also with words. This is a battle of ideas, with combat zones located in classrooms, online, on the streets, in boardrooms, on television, and across social media worldwide.

Modern strategists recognize the importance of shaping public perceptions. Alexander the Great used propaganda to secure victory and maintain his influence. Prussian military theorist Carl von Clausewitz highlighted the significance of morale in a nation's ability to wage war. General Douglas MacArthur emphasized the necessity of public support in military operations. Today, Muslim states and leaders, particularly Qatar among Sunni factions and Iran among Shia groups, utilize influencers like intellectuals, politicians, social media figures, and journalists to shape public opinion. Israel and its proponents also present their viewpoints. Credible Western journalists from both national and independent media outlets attract large audiences (Profile 1 – Chapter 4).

Modern Western militaries define 'information operations' as government-sanctioned psychological activities, military deception, and propaganda aimed at advancing national goals. This definition is based on the Department of Defense's Joint Publication 3-13 in the US. Both Hamas and Israel engage in information operations. 'Disinformation' refers to the dissemination of false information intended to deceive or mislead an audience, typically for political purposes. Disinformation tactics encompass distortion and deception, involving the twisting of facts or the spreading of lies, as well as defamation and misdirection, which include blaming innocent parties.

Perceptions of casualties have been a focal point in the Israel-Hamas war, influencing international support for both sides of the conflict. For decades, Israel has worked to enhance its global image, a task complicated by opposition from a coalition of Arab nations, the international Muslim community, and left-wing commentators who depict Israel as a remnant of colonialism. Conversely, Palestinians are often viewed as freedom fighters. Until recently, Hamas was not widely recognized outside the Middle East and among foreign policy scholars and journalists. However, by mid-October, Hamas gained worldwide notoriety and respect, achieving unprecedented prestige.

Some media outlets in the Middle East have demonstrated strong sympathy for Hamas. For years, Qatar's Al Jazeera has upheld a prestigious reputation as the 'CNN of the Arab world,' serving as an essential tool in the Qatari regime's foreign policy. Al Jazeera portrayed the October 2023 attack as retaliation against the Israeli occupation. After the October 7 attack, Hamas' leaders leveraged their position in Qatar to advance their war objectives. Al Jazeera aired exclusive footage of the October 7 attack, showing Hamas terrorists crossing the border, seizing Israeli military vehicles, taking hostages, and celebrating extensively. Just hours after the attack, Palestinians in Gaza and the West Bank celebrated their victory in the streets. Al Jazeera presenters and journalists have also expressed praise for the attack on their social media accounts.[1]

Throughout the war, Al Jazeera supported Hamas in various ways. The network provided highly sympathetic coverage and frequently interviewed Hamas leaders. Several of the network's journalists were identified as Hamas operatives after the IDF confiscated their laptops. Its operatives identified Israeli individuals and strategically important locations. Al Jazeera's reporters communicated military-related information to Hamas and PIJ, including details about Israel's order of battle, military capabilities, and troop movements. Al Jazeera journalists supplied targeting information for missile strikes. The channel interviewed military analysts, some of whom offered real-time assistance to Hamas.

Foreign powers have taken sides in this conflict. President Trump has remained steadfast in his support for Israel and has consistently condemned Hamas. The American State Department backs this perspective. Other nations have been notably critical of Israel. China expands its global influence in the Middle East through its social media platform TikTok. There is a significant gap between anti-Israel and pro-Israel tweets on social media. One figure indicated a one-to-seven ratio against Israel. An expert explained, 'Israel is losing on TikTok.' On TikTok, pro-Hamas videos outnumber pro-Israel videos by 30 to 1.[2]

TikTok has become one of the most popular applications worldwide and is widely used among children and teenagers. TikTok estimates that as of 2023, it has 37.3 million Gen Z users.[3] Like China, Russia uses messaging to undermine Israel. Several Russian-speaking groups used messaging services to disseminate images and assertions mirroring those of Hamas.[4]

## Themes in Hamas' Information Operations

Hamas is skilled and experienced in propaganda and psychological warfare. Its media operations include satellite and terrestrial broadcasting channels, radio stations, media production companies, and online platforms. Hamas has an extensive international support base made up of like-minded sympathizers. Supporters consist of politicians, journalists, and intellectuals who harbor contempt for Israel and the West, especially the United States.

During the current war, Hamas has shaped its messaging around six major themes: the deliberate targeting of hospitals and schools; the intentional targeting of non-combatants, particularly women and children; Gazans as victims of colonial exploitation – the Green-Red Connection; the David versus Goliath narrative – weak versus strong; good versus evil; and the assertion that anti-Zionism is not antisemitism. These themes are not static or discrete; many overlap. Additionally, they are presented to different audiences. To Western audiences, Hamas is often depicted as a hapless victim under the jackboot of a powerful, racially white, colonial Israel. An example is Al Jazeera's coverage of Gazan Hassan Saad (Profile 2 – Chapter 4). This 38-year-old shares his family's suffering under the weight of IDF attacks. For this audience, Hamas generally downplays overt antisemitism. However, for Middle Eastern audiences, Hamas employs stark and ancient antisemitic imagery and accusations.

### *Deliberate Targeting of Hospitals and Schools*

Since the IDF began targeting Hamas' command and control centers, munitions depots, and sniper concealment points, it has occasionally attacked hospitals and schools. This happens because Hamas deliberately places its personnel, weapons, and communications equipment there. Hamas see this as a double win. The IDF may hesitate to strike these facilities for fear of harming non-combatants. However, if they kill women and children, such images serve as propaganda to reinforce the perception of Israeli inhumanity. For this reason, many hospitals in Gaza serve a dual purpose: treating injuries while also functioning as military centers for Hamas. However, Hamas does not acknowledge these military aspects. One example is the Kamal Adwan Hospital, which has acted as a major Hamas command-and-control center and a sanctuary for hundreds of Hamas militants.[5]

Hamas often exaggerates the number of civilians killed, the circumstances surrounding their deaths, and the level of poverty and hunger in Gaza. Israel has destroyed numerous buildings and displaced many Gazans from their homes as the IDF conducted operations to dismantle Hamas. However, claims of extensive targeting of civilians in major media outlets – BBC, CNN, *The New York Times*, *The Washington Post*, and Al Jazeera – were challenged.[6] An example is the March 23, 2024 Al-Jazeera report alleging that Israeli soldiers raped Palestinian women at Al-Shifa Hospital in Gaza City. The report was revealed to be false.

A prominent example of a false allegation is the attack on the Al-Ahli Hospital on October 17, 2023. The assertion that Israel launched a missile was debunked within hours through Western aerial photography. However, this claim, along with the accompanying photographs, was circulated worldwide, inciting protests. *The New York Times* waited six days before retracting its claim, despite ample evidence available on the first day indicating that Israel was not the perpetrator. Some European leaders delayed their responses for several days. In contrast, other Western leaders swiftly endorsed the accusation of Israeli guilt, despite a lack of evidence. Christiane Amanpour apologized more than a month later after incorrectly suggesting that British-Israeli women, shot at point-blank range by terrorists, were armed and had exchanged fire with the IDF.

Often, established media outlets intentionally fail to report that these facilities performed double duty as staging grounds for terrorist operations. Critics of the British health magazine *The Lancet* claim the magazine overlooks or downplays Hamas' use of hospitals and schools for storing weapons and sheltering militants.[7] *The Lancet* reported that Israel had dug a massive grave, a claim that remains unsubstantiated, and it cited Hamas' casualty counts as accepted facts. Critics argue that the cumulative effect of the magazine's reporting has been to polarize the Israel-Hamas conflict.[8]

It is difficult for many Gazans to protest Hamas' control of the hospital. Mohammed Saqer, the head of nursing at Nasser Hospital in Khan Yunis, publicly pleaded with Hamas not to store arms there. The Palestine Islamic Jihad responded immediately, 'You've crossed the line – be careful. This is your first warning.'[9]

## *Deliberate Targeting of Noncombatants*

Hamas often accuses Israeli personnel of deliberately and consistently targeting non-combatants, a claim echoed by international media outlets. While IDF attacks have resulted in non-combatant deaths, its spokespersons assert that they have exercised due diligence to prevent such casualties. They argue that the ratio of combatant to non-combatant fatalities is impressively humane by any historic standard of warfare. Israeli authorities claim that Hamas repeatedly misrepresents the extent and circumstances of unintentional deaths. According to the plan, a claim will be made so frequently that it becomes unchallenged and accepted as accurate.

Critics have accused Hamas of engaging in creative lying, known as 'tawriya' in Arabic. Hamas uses words and phrases rich in double meanings and obfuscation. While a Hamas spokesperson may not outright lie, they might intentionally mislead the audience. Hamas frequently employs this tactic when discussing fatalities among non-combatants. For instance, the head of the Palestinian Mission to Britain claimed that the IDF deliberately killed a Palestinian woman without justification, referring to the deceased protester as a 'peace activist.' However, the slain woman's organization supported terrorist activities, and its Charter promotes 'armed struggle.' Additionally, she was throwing rocks at the IDF when she was shot. She may have been a peace activist, depending on the definition of the term, but she was not peaceful when she threw rocks. Given the evidence surrounding her death, particularly her rock throwing, it is unlikely that she was entirely blameless.

Hamas also employs the tactic of kitman to mislead the public about war casualties. Kitman is a tactic of omission intended to deceive. A statement may not be false, but crucial facts are omitted, creating a misleading impression for the audience. For instance, according to the Palestinian TV channel Al-Quds Today, in December 2024, the IDF killed five Palestinian journalists in an airstrike. This may be technically accurate, and the five may have been on the TV channel's payroll. However, the IDF claimed that they were also operatives of Palestinian Islamic Jihad (PIJ) posing as journalists. Israeli spokesmen asserted that the five had been placed on the Israeli assassination list after their status was vetted through multiple sources. If Israel's claims are valid, this represents an example of kitman.

### *Victims of Colonial Exploitation – The Green Red Connection*

The Palestine controversy resonates in Western intellectual circles and on university campuses because the left views Israel as a remnant of the colonial era. Placards are carried through Western cities and Ivy League campuses, with students chanting in unison that Palestinians must rule from the 'river to the sea.' Protesters claim that Jews must return to Poland. The vocabulary associated with the Palestinian-Israeli conflict is flexible, employing terms linked to a European imperial past. In the years leading up to the onset of the 2023–2024 war, opponents of Israel accused the state of practicing apartheid. Israel disputes the use of this terminology, along with commonly used terms such as colonialism, settler colonialism, ethnic cleansing, refugee, and genocide.

Perhaps the most provocative and disputed term is genocide. Soon after its creation, the United Nations adopted the Convention on the Prevention and Punishment of the Crime of Genocide. Francesca Albanese, the Special Rapporteur on the Occupied Palestinian Territories (Profile 3 – Chapter 4), issued a report to the UN Human Rights Council accusing Israel of genocide. Albanese has repeatedly compared Israelis to Nazis to lend credibility to the claim that Israel is a genocidal power. Her opponents argue that this charge lacks merit. Israel has neither gas chambers nor mobile killing units targeting civilians, and the population of Gazans has increased, not declined. They assert that this is a highly ineffectual genocide, as the number of Gazans has grown substantially over the decades. In 1950, the population of Gaza was 63,444. In 2025, it is several million.

### *David Versus Goliath – Weak Versus Strong*

Hamas presents Palestinians as a weak yet righteous force standing against a powerful and brutal enemy. This portrayal is sometimes framed as a biblical reference to the story of David and Goliath. This tactic plays on emotions and often aligns with other rhetorical themes, provoking a strong emotional reaction from the audience. Following Israel's actions in October 2023, critics described IDF strikes as indiscriminate, heavy-handed, and genocidal. This reinforces the perception of a brutal Israel, despite the IDF's attempts to minimize civilian casualties.

Critics of Hamas emphasize that these contrasting portrayals – weak Palestine and brutal Israel – are entrenched and that Hamas skillfully employs a blame-the-victim tactic. When evidence of a Hamas attack on an Israeli becomes undeniable, leading critics of Israel argue or imply that Israel deserved the attack. Hamas asserts that all Israeli casualties are part of the formidable Israeli war machine and deserve to die. Leading Palestinian groups have rallied to their countrymen in Gaza. The PA praised the Hamas attack in October 2023 as 'resistance.'[10] Husam Zomlot, the Head of the Palestinian Mission to Britain, blamed Israel as the 'occupying power.'[11] The anti-Israel group IfNotNow announced, 'Their [Jews and non-Jews] blood is on the hands of the Israeli government.'[12]

## *Good Versus Evil*

An information operations theme closely linked to the weak-versus-strong idea is the good-versus-evil theme. This polarized view contrasts the noble Gazan with the evil Israel. From this standpoint, Israel is not only overwhelmingly powerful but also cruel, portraying a cesspool of deceit and corruption. As a result, there can be no negotiation with evil Israel. Israel is demonized, and the conflict is portrayed as polarized. Through this Manichean perspective, Israel appears to lack any redeeming qualities.

These stark and ancient tropes would struggle to gain traction in the United States, and European governments, particularly Germany, would feel compelled to act against those promoting them. Contemporary Western university administrators would be uneasy with their prevalence on campus. For this reason, Hamas' information operations targeting Western audiences avoid overt antisemitism. However, Hamas and its allies, especially Iran, openly disseminate crude antisemitism among Middle Eastern audiences.

Towards the Middle East, Hamas and its online supporters describe Jews as destroyers of civilizations, manipulators of the world's political decision-making, controllers of international finance, and murderers of non-Jews. Jews fabricate claims of the Holocaust to enrich themselves and Israel, pollute Indigenous culture, and start wars for their pleasure and benefit.[13] Some stereotypical images are indistinguishable from their classic European counterparts. Hamas' lurid canards include claims that Jews destroy civilizations, seek control over global political decision-making, manipulate international markets, murder non-Jews for ritualistic blood use, fabricate falsehoods about the Holocaust to enrich themselves and Israel, corrupt indigenous cultures, and instigate wars for financial gain.

## *Anti-Zionism is Not Antisemitism*

Many Western critics of Israel, especially intellectuals and professors, argue that anti-Zionism is distinct from antisemitism. Many supporters and opponents of Israel contend that hostility toward the country does not necessarily stem from a deep-seated hatred of Jews. There is an ongoing debate about when strong anti-Israel sentiments turn into antisemitism.

Jewish critics of Israel are often valued for their ability to deflect accusations of antisemitism. Ilan Pappe (Profile 4 – Chapter 4), an Israeli academic at the University of Exeter, advocates for ostracizing Israel through boycotts. He opposes the very existence of Israel and refers to its war of independence as a Nakba, or disaster. Many critics of Israel frequently reference his works and commentary. He is not alone. Norman Finkelstein (Profile 5 – Chapter 4) has authored over 10 books, including *The Holocaust Industry: Reflections on the Exploitation of Jewish Suffering.*[14] He gives lectures worldwide at universities, activist rallies, churches, and public squares. He has been denied tenure at several universities and is banned from Israel.[15]

The New Historians, also known as Post-Zionist historians, are especially popular among the international left. Many of them are former Israeli citizens or far-left Jews who criticize Israel. British academic Avi Shlaim, a prominent figure in this movement, often appears in international media. He claims that 'Hamas is not a terrorist organization' and 'was elected to power in a free and fair election.'[16]

## *Hamas' Tactics to Implement Information Operations Themes*

To promote these themes, Hamas utilizes various tactics in information operations. Three of these tactics include disinformation, deception, and the manipulation of individuals who are easily influenced. Occasionally, these tactics overlap, making it difficult to draw a clear distinction between them. Israel has also employed some of these tactics.

***Disinformation*:** Disinformation refers to false information typically spread for political purposes. It represents polemical writing instead of a sober and impartial account of significant events. The Soviet Union excelled in disinformation during the Cold War, and the distortion of history remains prevalent in the Middle East dialogue.[17]

Hamas often spreads false and exaggerated information to promote its political goals. It receives support from sympathetic journalists and government-funded media outlets, especially Al Jazeera. For example, international media organizations like the BBC and *The New York Times*, whether intentionally or not, have circulated the misleading claim that Israel deliberately targeted a hospital in Gaza, causing hundreds of deaths. This accusation is without merit. Sometimes, a single piece of content contains multiple types of disinformation. This is clear in the BBC's 2025 documentary, 'Gaza: How to Survive a War Zone.' After a detailed review, the film was found to include staged scenes of Gazan children, portrayed as innocent victims caught in the chaos of ongoing and indiscriminate IDF operations.

The murder polarized the war and overlooked the IDF's efforts to warn Gazans about planned bombings at specific locations. Furthermore, there is no indication that the adolescent boy narrating the film is the son of a Hamas deputy minister. *The Telegraph* pointed out at least five instances in the movie where the Arabic term for 'Jew' – 'Yahud' or 'Yahudy' – was mistranslated as 'Israel' or 'Israeli forces' or omitted entirely. When an independent journalist exposed these inaccuracies, the BBC withdrew the film and apologized for 'unacceptable mistakes.'

***Deception*:** Deception is closely connected to disinformation. It involves lying but often also includes distortion and half-truths. Sometimes, words are used inaccurately or deceptively in the Israel-Hamas conflict until they become part of everyday language. This is takiya, which Westerners often refer to as double-talk. Hamas uses deception to craft a national narrative claiming Israel intentionally, repeatedly, and unnecessarily attacks civilians. They deny placing weapons in schools, hospitals, civilian areas, and mosques to mislead the IDF and to use Gazans as human shields. Mainstream media often collaborates, either directly or indirectly, with Hamas officials to report stories of atrocities that may be inaccurate, false, or greatly exaggerated. While this might not be outright lying, it is still deceptive.

Another example of deception is an Al-Jazeera video showing dead Gazans along a road as victims of deliberate Israeli murder. This claim was false and fits the definition of Kitman, as explained earlier. Israel provided a safe passage south for those civilians, but Hamas blocked their exit so they could be used as human shields.[18]

***Exploiting Gullibility*:** This tactic exploits the gullibility of celebrities, naive intellectuals, and civil society leaders to promote a cause. The derogatory term for this method is 'exploiting useful idiots.' This phrase does not mean those labeled as such are unintelligent; many are accomplished and well-educated. However, many are naive and eager to use their influence for personal gain and prestige. The term became popular in the 1930s when British and American intellectuals praised Stalin's Soviet Union.

In the Hamas-Israel conflict, the term 'useful idiots' refers to opinion makers who uncritically accept Hamas' claims. Western celebrities can have significant influence due to their large social media followings. This is especially true for the French channel France 2 and its popular weekly show, *Quelle Époque!* The host and producer of the show in May 2025 stated that the Gaza Strip 'is Auschwitz, that's it, that's all there is to it.'[19] After facing a barrage of criticism for the hyperbolic analogy, the host retracted his statement and apologized for the offense. However, his comparison had been circulated among his viewers.

A similar situation occurred in June 2025 when *The Washington Post* issued a correction to an unsubstantiated claim that the IDF killed over 30 people near an aid site in Gaza, citing Gaza health officials as its source. After readers and the IDF challenged the allegation, the *Post* recanted, admitting that it had given 'inappropriate weight' to the claim, which originated from Hamas.[20]

An example of an unfounded accusation on social media comes from Alana Hadid, the sister of Bella (Profile 6 – Chapter 4) and Gigi Hadid, who asked, 'Did you know Israel forcibly sterilized Ethiopian Jewish women and then tried to cover it up?' Hadid has nearly 700,000 Instagram followers.[21] There is no truth to this claim, but its widespread circulation likely influenced young followers' opinions, causing further reputational damage to Israel. Sometimes, aid leaders or diplomats intentionally make exaggerated claims, knowing they are false, to support their agenda. This was true with Tom Fletcher, United Nations Under-Secretary-General for Humanitarian Affairs, who stated in May 2025 that 14,000 babies could die within 48 hours in Gaza unless a large amount of aid was immediately delivered.

When challenged with evidence that contradicted the possibility of starvation, Fletcher admitted he was eager to get aid into Gaza and exaggerated the facts to pressure Israel. He publicly expressed regret for making the statement and acknowledged he needed to be more 'precise' when presenting his facts publicly.[22]

Other young influencers with substantial audiences are much more supportive of violence against Israelis and Jews abroad. One such influencer is Guy Christensen, a TikTok personality with over three million followers. After two Israelis were murdered in Washington DC, in May 2025, Christensen wrote, 'I do not condemn the elimination of the Zionist officials who worked at the Israeli embassy last night.'[23] He continued, 'I want to first urge you to support Elias's [the murderer's] actions. 'He is not a terrorist. He's a resistance fighter.' Finally, some exchanges with credible opinion makers are confusing. One example is Leslie Stahl's March 2025 *60 Minutes* interview with freed hostage Keith Siegel. During the interview, Siegel recounted the cruelty inflicted on him and his then-incarcerated wife by his captors. After explaining that he endured 484 days in captivity during which his jailers regularly beat and starved him, Stahl asked Siegel, with a straight face, if Hamas had starved him due to a food shortage. Siegel assured the journalist that there was no lack of food in Hamas' makeshift jails; his captors ate quite well in front of him, with provisions intended for Gaza refugees. The exchange quickly went viral on the internet.[24]

## Israeli Information Operations

Israel also conducts information operations. At the outbreak of the war, Prime Minister Netanyahu stated, 'Victory over these enemies begins with moral clarity . . . with knowing the difference between right and wrong.'[25] Israel conducts both offensive and defensive information operations. Offensive operations use language to promote a cause or issue, while defensive operations aim to prevent opponents from effectively swaying public opinion with their rhetoric. The primary national agency advancing Israel's information operations is Hasbara, a Hebrew term meaning to explain an existing event. Following the October attack, Hasbara began conveying Israel's response to a global audience. In the first week, 43 million viewers accessed the site.

Early in the war, Israel faced a dilemma about whether to allow the world access to the disturbing videos filmed by Hamas during its rampage. Initially, Israeli leaders withheld graphic footage of children being burned alive or shot at close range. After previous atrocities, Israeli officials avoided sharing distressing visuals that could traumatize the victims' loved ones. However, skeptics of Israeli claims demanded verification. In response, the Israeli government released a 47-minute video compilation of clips taken by Hamas to a select group of political leaders, international organizations, diplomats, members of Congress, and journalists. Israel urged social media platforms to remove content that might support or glorify terrorism. They achieved some success, as Human Rights Watch and Meta both removed certain content, with Meta employing AI moderation systems to reduce pro-Hamas material.

## *Four Themes of Israeli Information Operations*

Israel's information operations during the Iron Sword conflict are based on five themes: self-defense, communal interest, hypocrisy, counter-attack, and leveraging pro-Israel support NGOs.[26]

***Self-Defense*:** The first theme is Israel's legal right and national duty to defend itself – a principle shared by all nations. This fundamental right is rooted in tradition and international law. Israel asserts that its survival depends on defeating forces that seek to destroy it. Israel and its advocacy groups circulated images of the attack and interviews with survivors to convince a global audience that eliminating threats from Hamas is essential. The Israeli government's website, which features the horrors of Hamas' October 7 massacre in southern Israel, experienced a surge in online traffic during the week after its launch, according to the IDF. The site has garnered over 43 million views to date.

***Communal Interest*:** A second key theme for Israel is the shared interest among all countries in fighting the global threat from Hamas. Prime Minister Netanyahu stresses that Israel's fight is also America's. While this message doesn't resonate with Middle Eastern and European nations, it does find support in the United States.

***Hamas Hypocrisy*:** The third theme of information operations is hypocrisy. Israel points out the hypocrisy of Hamas leaders, some of whom have lived luxurious lives in Qatar while Gazans suffer from poverty and despair. Even while hiding underground in Gaza, Sinwar had access to showers, multiple bathrooms, and a fully equipped kitchen. His wife was seen carrying a Hermès purse valued at $32,000. Other Hamas leaders also enjoyed comforts in Qatar and now in Turkey. Today, much of Gaza lies in ruins.

Israel also points out leaders from Arab countries – Egyptians, Jordanians, and Syrians – who criticize the IDF for its assaults in Gaza, even though these nations have previously targeted Hamas factions. In 2014, an Egyptian court banned Hamas, calling it a terrorist group. Some of the more sarcastic comments target self-described civil rights groups that support Hamas, even though the group's death sentence for LGBTQ+ individuals still stands. These include Queers for Palestine.

***Countering Disinformation*:** A fourth theme in information operations focuses on countering the disinformation spread by Hamas and Israel's adversaries. Israel invested $7 million in an advertising campaign early in the conflict, receiving additional support from pro-Israel organizations based in the United States. The UNRWA ranks high on Israel's list of disfavored international organizations. Through commercial advertisements and Israel's information initiatives, the goal is to expose and discredit this organization. They emphasize the direct connections between Hamas and UNRWA and have identified UNRWA schools that serve as command centers and weapons storage sites.

In response to the October 2023 attack, the IDF's international communications office has expanded by adding over 200 reservists, media specialists, and linguists. Other units, including the National Public Diplomacy Directorate, have increased their personnel and enhanced their resources. Many Israeli spokespersons aim to connect with younger social media users. For instance, 22-year-old military press officer Masha Michelson (Profile 7 – Chapter 4) stands out on social media, presenting the IDF's case on platforms such as TikTok, Instagram, and X.

Israeli senior officers often appear on television to brief journalists and government officials. IDF spokesman Colonel Jonathan Conricus and Mark Regev promote Israel's stance while disputing Hamas' claims. Yoseph Haddad (Profile 8 – Chapter 4), an Arab-Israeli, is one of Israel's top domestic and international advocates. Several Israeli spokespersons have become celebrities within certain circles, including Avichai Adraee, an IDF officer known in the Middle East for his excellent Arabic skills and deep knowledge of Arab culture. Many see him as highly articulate, and millions have listened to his podcast and debates.

Many Israeli commentators have grown increasingly frustrated in their efforts to counter what they see as unfounded accusations of war crimes and racism. For example, Amnesty International labels Israel as an apartheid state. One commentator asked, 'How can you address the apartheid issue when it doesn't exist?' He and others emphasize that Arabs hold prominent positions in the Knesset, academia, and other respected fields. Arabs are also integrated into the economy, sports, and popular culture. On television and YouTube, Israeli comedians, independent of the government, use sharp one-liners and dark humor to critique Hamas.

An early target of Israeli satire was directed at the throngs of protesters at Columbia University. In the satire a pink-haired, pierced student declared, 'Where everyone is welcome – LGBTQH.' The satirist snickered that the 'H' stands for 'Hamas.' In the skit, a fellow progressive student, draped in a keffiyeh and majoring in queer post-colonial studies, also mockingly voiced her belief in astrology, adding, 'Yeah, I totally support Hamas; it's so trendy right now.' Performed in both Hebrew and English, the skit went viral.

Popular media is chock-full of unsourced material, some of which is likely satire and parody. For example, A young man cradling an AK-47 standing before rubble explains Hamas's participation in Gay Pride Week. Half smiling he says, 'We have a drag show for them. We drag them to roof and then we throw off.' Another keffiyeh clad young man explains to the camera, 'Of course we respect pronouns, especially in our hostage videos.'[27]

### *Partnering With pro-Israel, Non-Israeli Organizations*

Israel is not completely isolated in its propaganda efforts. It has allies among Jewish, Christian, and politically conservative groups. One of these groups is Honest Reporting, a nonprofit organization registered in the United States. Its stated goal is to challenge false claims about Israel and provide tools to fight biased journalism. Honest Reporting debunked the claim that Israel attacked al-Shifa on

December 22, 2023. It reviews reports from major media outlets and publishes its findings on its website.

Another pro-Israel NGO deeply involved in information warfare is UN Watch, led by veteran pro-Israel activist Hillel Neuer (Profile 9 – Chapter 4). Neuer is an activist and investigative journalist who has targeted the controversial UN Special Rapporteur on the Occupied Palestinian Territories. He claims to have uncovered her involvement in financial irregularities. The Christian Broadcast Network is very pro-Israel, engaging in various missions that include humanitarian aid and relief, media evangelism, and defense of the Holy Land.[28]

## Human Rights Organizations

Many NGOs are actively engaged in the Israel-Palestine conflict, with several supporting Palestinian organizations. Human Rights Watch (HRW) and Amnesty International (AI) are two of the most prominent, influential, and well-funded NGOs involved in this conflict. Two organizations are very influential in the war of ideas. The judgments, data, and analysis of these organizations are important in shaping world opinion.

### *Human Rights Watch and Amnesty International*

HRW founded by Robert Bernstein in 1978, has become a highly influential and frequently cited human rights organization. Well-funded, it has prominent representation at the UN and the ICC. The organization presents itself as a non-partisan advocate for human rights; however, critics accuse it of having an anti-Israel bias. It has strongly condemned Israel's military response, labeling it a war crime and characterizing it as 'crimes of apartheid and persecution against Palestinians.' It opined that the Israeli government is using civilians' starvation as a weapon of war in Gaza, which constitutes a war crime. Critics of HRW argue that its leadership has portrayed Israel as the aggressor in the conflict with the Palestinians. They mention Kenneth Roth, who has led the organization for many years. While the NGO acknowledges that Hamas' targeting of Israeli civilians violates the laws of war, it also criticizes the IDF's military response. HRW's Middle East director, Sarah Leah Whitson, states, 'There is simply no legal justification for launching rockets at populated areas.'[29]

AI affirms its independence from all institutions, ideologies, economic interests, and religions. Since Hamas was established, AI has consistently condemned both Israel and Hamas, especially in 2009, 2015, 2017, 2023, and 2024. Over the years, AI has criticized the IDF's extrajudicial killings of Hamas leaders. In 2009, both Israel and Hamas expressed dissatisfaction with an AI report that accused them of war crimes. Hamas denied intentionally using civilians as human shields, while Israel denied deliberately targeting women, children, unarmed paramedics, and ambulances helping the wounded. It also reported incidents of Palestinian women and children being shot at close range by Israelis while fleeing the fighting, as well as attacks on homes where children were playing on roofs. AI called for an immediate ceasefire in Gaza to prevent civilian casualties. AI recommended negotiating a ceasefire to stop the attacks and allow agencies to deliver life-saving medicines and food to the region. AI has urged donors to continue funding UNRWA.[30]

AI has shown hostility toward Israel. In 2022, it declared that Israel has been an apartheid state since its founding. The next year, it claimed that Israel committed genocide. Critics argue that AI fails to clarify that Israel has responded more than acted aggressively in its multiple wars. They accuse AI of ignoring the continuous rocket fire from Gaza over the years. They believe it is too biased to be trustworthy. Additionally, critics question the sources AI relies on when reporting on genocide. They argue that AI has helped create a new definition of 'genocide' specifically for Israel, while also previously developing new definitions of 'apartheid' and 'occupation' solely for Israel.

### *American-Israel Public Affairs Committee*

Several prominent pro-Israel NGOs have significantly influenced the debate in the Middle East within the US. The American Israel Public Affairs Committee, or AIPAC, is the most well-known pro-Israel lobbying organization in the United States and likely worldwide. It is transparent about its mission, which it states on its website: 'building bipartisan support for the US-Israel Relationship.' Its stated goals include 'supporting security assistance to Israel,' 'promoting peace,' and 'countering Iran's aggression and nuclear' weapons. It claims a membership of over 100,000 and makes political contributions to pro-Israel organizations and candidates.[31]

By most accounts, its efforts have played a crucial role in several close Congressional races.[32] This influence has pleased some politicians and observers but has angered others who openly disdain it. Representative Ilhan Omar dislikes the organization and what she calls its extraordinary influence. AIPAC also faces opposition, especially from J Street. J Street describes itself as 'pro-Israel, pro-peace, pro-democracy.' However, J Street has endorsed several politicians who have made anti-Israel remarks. Its founder, Jeremy Ben-Ami (see Profile 11 – Chapter 7), often clashes with AIPAC. Despite this, there are times when they support the same candidate for the same agenda.

### *Students for Justice in Palestine*

> *Intifada! Intifada!*
> *There is only one solution . . .*
> *Intifada, revolution!*
> *Intifada! Intifada!*[33]

Students for Justice in Palestine is the most well-known anti-Israel student organization in the United States, claiming to have a presence on approximately

200 campuses.[34] It is both anti-Israel and anti-American, viewing both nations as colonial enterprises. In September 2024, leaders called for efforts to collapse Israel and the 'American empire.'[35] Its leaders rally their adherents to cancel all 'Zionist events and start an Intifada everywhere.'[36] The founder of SJP, Dr Hatem Bazian explained. 'Our fight for a free Palestine is a fight against racism, against Islamophobia . . .'[37]

SJP leaders praised the actions of Hamas. Its poster for a 'Day of Resistance' featured an image of the paraglider that Hamas terrorists had used to massacre and rape young Israelis at a music festival. They planned many of the 2024 student encampments on US university campuses.[38] SJP members and their supporters regularly disrupt lectures presented by professors and guest speakers. Some also harass students with slurs and threats.[39]

## Summary

The Hamas-Israel propaganda war from 2023 to 2025 shook the world's media landscape. Israel briefly experienced sympathy. However, the relentless global barrage of anti-Israel commentary from various sources effectively overwhelmed Israel's limited resources. As a result, large populations around the world began to see Israel as a pariah state. Israel strives to reclaim the moral high ground, but this remains a challenge. Lastly, false memes in the information war can sometimes be spread unintentionally. Their origins are not always clear, but when they are widely and frequently circulated, they can effectively discredit a nation. This was the case with American comedian Ari Shaffir's (Profile 10 – Chapter 4) assertion that Israeli soldiers are required to kill a kitten during their military training to harden their souls. This claim, like many others surrounding the Hamas-Israel war, is false. No one is permitted to murder cats in Israel.

**Profile 1 – Maha Abuelkas: Voice of France24**
**Name:** Maha Abuelkas
**Nationality:** Likely Palestinian
**Profession:** Journalist
**Connection to October 7, 2023:** Many of her critics accuse her of pretending to be an objective journalist while hiding her sympathies for Hamas and its terrorist actions. With proficiency in several Western languages and fluency in Arabic, she is well regarded in fashionable European intellectual circles. Her critics claim that her claims to objectivity are suspicious and that she secretly supports Hamas. Maha Abuelkas has worked for France 24 since 2013 and regularly reports on events in the Middle East. Her critics emphasize her links to Hamas, citing, for instance, her receiving open praise from Hamas leaders.

As for the October 2023 attack, some of her comments suggest that she placed the blame on 'the Israeli occupation' for 'severe assaults and violations against human rights, land, and sacred sites.'[40] Her supporters argue that she doesn't have

control over her fan base and isn't required to decline any awards she receives. They claim that her reporting differs from that of pro-Israel reporters because she views the situation differently.
**Current Status:** As of this writing, she is still employed by France24.

**Profile 2 – Hassan Saad: 'We Just Want to Live'**
**Name:** Hassan Saad
**Nationality:** Palestinian
**Profession:** Currently an activist to end Israel's attacks
**Connection to October 7, 2023:** Hassan Saad is a simple man who wants to provide for his family. This has become increasingly difficult because of the constant barrage of rockets. He feels anger toward many people, some of whom are Israeli and others Palestinian. He has organized protests in Gaza, demanding an end to the war. He says that his main trigger was receiving an eviction notice. He would have to leave his home.[41] 'The idea of taking to the streets to protest, holding signs that call for an immediate end to the war, was born.'[42]

Many other Gazans share his fatalistic outlook. While many see Israel as the main enemy, others have come to despise Hamas and want it removed from Gaza. In spring 2025, hundreds participated in the largest anti-Hamas protest in Gaza since the war began. They called for Hamas to relinquish power, which was a risky move. One person said that Hamas must step down and listen to the voices of the grieving – the voices rising from beneath the rubble; it is the truest truth voice.'[43] Many of these Gazans, like Hassan Saad, are ordinary people, and in Saad's words, 'We just want to live.'
**Current Status:** Presumed to be alive.

**Profile 3 – Francesca Albanese: 'Wake up'**
**Names:** Francesca Albanese
**Nationality:** Italian
**Profession:** Lawyer of international law specializing in human rights; United Nations Rapporteur for Palestine since 2022
**Connection to October 7, 2023:** As rapporteur for Palestine, the controversial Ms. Albanese serves as an important voice in the Hamas-Israel conflict. Many Palestinians and her supporters praise her for her writing and commentary. She denied that the October attack was antisemitic, framing it as a response to occupation, harassment, and degradation. Hamas appreciated her report on IDF attacks, which she described as criminal and genocidal. Albanese urged Poland and other nations to arrest Prime Minister Netanyahu if he visits. She accused Israel of ignoring Hamas' attempts to exchange prisoners and causing unnecessary civilian casualties.

She is well-known on university campuses in the West. While she is celebrated in hard-left and pro-Palestine circles, she faces criticism from pro-Israel and conservative groups. Some critics call her statements reckless, malicious, and defamatory, pointing to what they see as unfounded claims of Israeli murder and rape based on hearsay. Her critics accuse her of exploiting her status to travel and give lectures around the world. Israel has banned her from entering the country. A minister said, 'The era of Jews being silent is over. If the UN wants to remain relevant, its leaders must publicly disavow the antisemitic words of the special envoy – and fire her 'immediately.'[44]

**Current Status:** In April 2025, the UN Human Rights Council extended Albanese's mandate as rapporteur. She continues to speak internationally and pleads that 'fellow humans' embrace her cause. She pleads that people 'wake up.'[45]

**Profile 4 – Ilan Pappe: 'The Biggest Prison on Earth'**

**Names:** Ilan Pappe

**Nationality:** Born Israeli

**Profession:** Professor at the College of Social Sciences and International Studies at the University of Exeter, United Kingdom; Director of the university's European Centre for Palestine Studies; and Co-Director of the Exeter Centre for Ethno-Political Studies. He is also affiliated with St Anthony's College, Oxford.

**Connection to October 7, 2023:** Israel-born historian Pappe argues that he began to understand the language of the colonized after forming friendships with Palestinians in Israel and formally studying Arabic. His perspective on the ongoing conflict between Hamas and Israel is clear; he describes it as genocidal. It is part of a broader campaign to kill, depopulate, and ethnically cleanse Gaza.

Critics argue that Pape's work lacks objectivity in its historiography and only presents a misleading sense of neutrality when Arabs attack Jews. They accuse him of portraying successive Arab riots, which resulted in many Jewish deaths, as justified reactions to colonial violence. He made these claims in his book, 'The Ethnic Cleansing of Palestine,' which brought him fame. A common theme in his speeches is that Palestine is the world's largest prison. In response to the claim that his work lacks fairness, he said he aims to address the power imbalance on behalf of the 'colonized, occupied, and oppressed Palestinians in the land of Israel.'[46]

**Current Status:** Now in his seventies, Pape is still affiliated with the University of Exeter and serves as a regular, well-respected commentator on Middle East affairs.

**Profile 5 – Norman Finkelstein: 'Heroic Resistance'**

**Names:** Norman Finkelstein

**Nationality:** American

**Profession:** Untenured professor, lecturer, activist, blogger

**Connection to October 7, 2023:** A highly controversial critic of Israel, Norman Finkelstein has authored 10 books about the Middle East, most of which focus on the Palestinian-Israeli conflict. Based on his writings and speeches, he shows strong hostility toward Israel and is outspoken about it. He displays anger on various issues and rages in lecture halls when faced with differing opinions. When an audience member challenged him on his claims of Israeli atrocities, he once barked back, 'My late father was in Auschwitz. My late mother was in Majdanek concentration camp . . . please shut up. I will not be silent when Israel commits its crimes against the Palestinians.' He expressed significant personal animosity toward Alan Dershowitz, a well-known defender of Israel and an academic colleague.

Whether due to his anger management issues or a perceived lack of scholarly merit in his publications, he never received tenure at a university, despite earning a PhD from Princeton. Then, the October 7 Hamas attack thrust him into the spotlight alongside his 13th book, *Gaza: An Inquest Into Its Martyrdom*.[47] He praised Gaza's 'heroic resistance' of October 7.[48]

Many of his critics accuse him of being a pamphleteer who spreads dubious anti-Israel tropes. Some label him a conspiratorial quack, claiming he sees vast conspiracies that do not exist. They mock his theatrical performances on the lecture circuit. Despite this, he has a significant following that seriously supports him.
**Current Status:** Dr Finkelstein is quite popular in anti-Israel and leftist circles. He travels around the world spreading his message about Israeli atrocities. In early 2025, he led a debate at Yale to assert that 'The state of Israel is responsible for genocide.' The motion passed overwhelmingly.

**Profile 6 – Bella Hadid: 'Cakewashing'**
**Names:** Bella Hadid
**Nationality:** American
**Profession:** Supermodel and activist
**Connection to October 7, 2023:** Bella and her sisters, Gigi and Alana, were born to a Palestinian father named Mohammed, whose family moved to the United States when he was a teenager. Mohammed thrived in real estate, and his daughters grew into tall, striking models who gained international fame. They have large followings, and their fashion choices, spending habits, and relationships are often featured in women's and girls' magazines in the West. Among the Hadid sisters, Alana is the most openly anti-Israel, yet she has not yet reached supermodel status and doesn't have the same level of popularity as her sisters.

All three Hadid sisters support Palestine, and Bella is especially outspoken about Israel. In 2021, she participated in a pro-Palestine protest in New York with Dua Lipa, a well-known British singer. However, unlike many young celebrity critics of Israel, she actively speaks out against religious hatred. She condemned fellow celebrity Kanye West's blatant antisemitism. She also blamed Hamas for using violence. 'Regardless of the history of the land, harming women and children and creating terror does not and should not do any good for the Free Palestine,' movement.'[49]

However, her critics question her sincerity and knowledge of the Middle East. She claimed that Hamas operatives made a birthday cake for Israeli hostage Almog Meir and that Israelis treat Palestinians worse than Hamas captors treat Israeli captives.[50] However, Meir and the other captives were severely malnourished. He did not remember a delicious birthday cake. A user on social media called her a 'Hamas groupie dressed up in Chanel.'[51] Other critics snickered at her 'cake' comment and coined the term 'cakewashing.' One suggested it was time for Bella to 'taste the cakes in Gaza.'[52]

**Current Status:** Bella Hadid remains one of the most prominent anti-Israel celebrities of Middle Eastern descent. Another is former adult star Mia Khalifa, who claims Lebanese heritage and is very antagonistic toward Israel. Like the Hadid sisters, she has a large social media following.

**Profile 7 – Masha Michelson: The Face of the IDF**

**Names:** Masha Michelson

**Nationality:** Israeli

**Profession:** Head of IDF International Press

**Connection to October 7, 2023:** Following the October 7 attack, Masha Michelson gained online fame, earning the title 'the Face of the IDF.' At 22, she became a prominent voice for the IDF in discussions and interviews around the world. Her youth and relatable, girl-next-door looks appeal to young people in the West. She plays a key role in Israel's information war and maintains credibility with younger audiences. She explained, 'When you need to address the world (referring to the world of the young), they're more likely to listen to someone who looks like them.'[53]

She faces a daunting task in Israel's information warfare, playing a crucial role. She and her team compete against Palestinian supporters worldwide. Michelson also connects with operators on TikTok, reaching millions of young viewers. She aims to share Israel's perspective on the conflict with American and European college students, many of whom believe that Israel is a colonial project with no rightful place in the Arab world. Her sharp comments have attracted a following, and she remains steadfast. While explaining the IDF's actions in Gaza, she states, 'Hamas has to pay!'[54] She added, 'Unprecedented attacks need an unprecedented response.'[55]

**Current Status:** She continues to advocate for the IDF.

**Profile 8 – Yoseph Haddad**

**Names:** Yoseph Haddad

**Nationality:** Israeli Arab

**Profession:** Journalist, Social media influencer; reservist soldier in the IDF

**Connection to October 7, 2023:** Some see him as the authentic voice of Arab Israelis, while others consider him a traitor to the Palestinian cause. At times, he feels unable to win the information war he faces. Yoseph Haddah is an Israeli influencer who shares the Israeli perspective on the Israeli-Arab conflict. He is the CEO of Together – Vouch For Each Other and was part of a group of pro-Israel figures, including British human rights lawyer Natasha Hausdorff, British-Jewish journalist Jonathan Sacerdote, and a staunch opponent of Hamas, Mosab Hasan Youssef, who defended Israel at a high-profile debate at Oxford. During his trips to London, he wore a long yellow ribbon, symbolizing hope for the release of Israelis hostages.[56]

If Israel is an apartheid state, Haddad remains unaware of it. He jokes, 'Last week, I woke up one morning in my Nazareth home and was astonished to discover I was living under a racist apartheid regime whose only purpose is "the promotion and perpetuation of the superiority of one group of people – the Jews."'[57] Hadad's message is clear: 'We're Arabs from Israel, and we're here to tell you that Hamas is a terrorist organization. Hamas murdered and raped Jews and Arabs from Israel. Don't believe the terrorist sympathizers, and don't believe Hamas supporters.'[58]

His face is well-known throughout Israel, and people often stop him on the street to express their gratitude. A reservist soldier stopped him, smiled, and said, 'I won't have another chance to say this – thank you for everything you do.' A senior citizen shouted, 'God bless you!' This outpouring of appreciation highlights the popularity of his concise autobiography, *Let Me Explain*.[59]

**Current Status:** Popular in Israel but seen as a traitor to many Arabs.

**Profile 9 – Hillel Neuer: Israel's Counterweight in the United Nations**

**Names:** Hillel Neuer

**Nationality:** Canadian born

**Profession:** Director of the NGO UN Watch; international lawyer; essayist

**Connection to October 7, 2023:** Hillel Neuer faces many opponents both within and outside the United Nations. He pushes back against the surge of anti-Israel resolutions from the agency and questions why members are mostly silent about crimes in other countries. For example, he noted that the World Health Organization condemned only one country for violating people's health rights: Israel.

Neuer claims he was barred from speaking at the dais to protest Francesca Albanese's reappointment as special rapporteur. A main villain for Neuer is UNRWA, which he accuses of knowingly participating in the October 7 massacre. He asserts that agency officials regularly call for the murder of Jews and that a Hamas member leads the UNRWA Teachers Union. His battle against Hamas sometimes feels like a world war because it seems much of the world is against him and the state he supports. He has repeatedly accused European NGOs and states of direct and deliberate complicity with UNRWA. Those accused usually deny any such activity, and Neuer then presents evidence to support his claims.

He frequently appears on podcasts and is a regular guest on shows that examine the current conflict in Gaza. European parliamentarians and UN employees are very hostile to him, and many try to avoid him. They see him as a pest. However, he has demonstrated that he and his organization will remain in Europe for the foreseeable future.

He also has his supporters. In 2018, McGill University awarded Neuer an honorary doctorate of laws for his work in advancing human rights and for being 'a voice for those without one.'[60] In September 2016, the City of Chicago declared a Hillel Neuer Day to salute his contributions to 'promote peace, justice and human rights around the world.'[61]

**Current Status:** He resides in Geneva and serves as the director of UN Watch.

**Profile 10 – Ari Shaffir and his Father's Dead Kitten**
**Names:** Ari Shaffir
**Nationality:** American
**Profession:** Comedian
**Connection to October 7, 2023:** The funnyman styles himself after comedian Sam Kinison and makes loud, outrageous claims. Although he may not be among the A-list comedians, Ari Shaffir has garnered a following among younger audiences who appreciate dark humor. He combines jokes with political commentary. For instance, Shaffir snickered at the death of Kobe Bryant, saying, 'Whenever a celebrity dies, it's worse than 9/11.' He occasionally warns his audience, 'Don't bring your mom. It's going to be that kind of show.'[62]And he often delivers.

Raised as an Orthodox Jew in Maryland, Shaffir embraces the lighter side of Judaism. In his special titled 'Jew,' which garnered four million views on YouTube, he discusses the joys and challenges of growing up in a religious family environment. However, his performance on the Joe Rogan show earned some laughs but also drew significant criticism. He claimed that his father, allegedly a commando in the IDF, shared that it was common practice in the IDF for soldiers to raise and nurture kittens only to kill them later. The purpose was to toughen the hearts of Israeli soldiers.

There is no evidence to support this claim. Podcaster Aaron Cohen, who served in Israeli special operations, firmly denies that this ever happened. In Israel, cruelty to animals is illegal and can result in fines and short imprisonment. He is upset that a local comedian would spread a falsehood that could damage the IDF's reputation. Cohen states that it is neither funny nor true.
**Current Status:** Ari Shaffir is still on tour.

## Chapter 5

# Cities of Slaughter

*They came to kill, kill and kill.*

Israeli Maj. Gen. Itai Veruv[1]

*Raise your hands up to the sky, high and strong. Open your eyes, believe, and dance!*

Moran Stella Yanai, held hostage for 54 days, explaining the need for optimism and joy, June 2024

For years, Israel has maintained a complex, flexible, and often ambiguous relationship with Hamas. Its policy included elements of the Wingate doctrine – harsh treatment of terrorist leaders and generally passive, sometimes benign relations with non-aggressive Palestinians. However, in contrast to Wingate's advice, it emphasized defensive measures like the security barrier and Iron Dome over proactive and aggressive search-and-destroy missions that Wingate recommended. Wingate's focus on strategic and tactical intelligence was completely absent. Hubris among the upper ranks of the Israeli security establishment blinded it to the ever-growing threat that would erupt on October 7.

On October 7, 2023, Hamas was ready to launch an attack. The fighters trained by navigating the Gaza Metro tunnel system and avoiding expected assaults. Hamas learned from its past conflicts with Israel. It strengthened the tunnel network with blast doors that secured different sections, protecting them from bombs and drone strikes. By the day of the attack, Hamas operatives could move through the dark, narrow tunnels with night-vision goggles. The tunnels served as advanced command-and-control centers, equipped with extensive storage facilities. Then it began.

After extensive practice, Hamas demonstrated skill in unconventional tactics. The preparations for this day started a decade earlier. In 1987, Hamas operatives descending from hang gliders killed six soldiers and injured at least seven others before they were fatally shot. This event became known as the Night of the Gliders. Nearly 36 years later, Hamas used the tactic on a larger scale.

Operation al-Aqsa Flood began with torrents of militants pouring into multiple points of attack near the Gaza border. Hamas struck 50 years and one day after the surprise attack of the Yom Kippur War, hitting with incredible speed. The Izz al-Din al-Qassam Brigades, known as the Qassam Brigades, breached the barrier using tractors, heavy trucks, and explosives.

In three waves, between 5,000 and 5,600 militants breached the security fence under cover of a barrage of 4,694 rockets and mortars. Just after 6:30 am, the first wave, made up of about 1,500 experienced Hamas operatives, rushed through the fence and headed directly toward towns, kibbutzim, and small military posts. Shortly after, a second wave, consisting of about 2,500 fighters, penetrated deeper into Israel, aiming to attack Be'er Sheva, Ashkelon, and various air force bases.

Some assailants wore fatigues while others dressed as civilians. They emerged from a maze of tunnels and descended via paragliders during their multi-pronged attack. They came out of hiding in plain clothes, sometimes wearing sandals or tracksuits, before firing at Israeli troops, attaching explosives to their vehicles, or launching rockets from civilian areas. Soon, smoke billowed from homes set ablaze, and sirens wailed warnings that the nation was under attack. This marked the worst breach of Israel's defenses in 50 years, and the assailants appeared giddy with killing. They pursued everything within the Gaza Envelope, a settled area next to Gaza. Using various levels of force, they struck at least 19 kibbutzim and five moshavim, which are cooperative communities, as well as the cities of Sderot and Ofakim, along with a hippie-like concert.

To weaken the defenses, Hamas launched waves of rockets against multiple sites. At the same time, fighters used paragliders, motorcycles, and four-wheel-drive vehicles to overwhelm Israeli defenses, invading towns and communities, killing people of different nationalities, and taking dozens of hostages. Iran trained, armed, and funded the group.[2] They killed over 1,200 people at the festival and in nearby kibbutzim and took more than 250 people hostage and back to Gaza to languish as captives somewhere in the underground lairs of Gaza.[3] After a barrage of rockets, assailants broke through barricades at the border and drove down Route 232, carving a deadly path through rural kibbutzim communities.[4] They blocked off the main road from the north and the south.[5] Spreading out and overwhelming the kibbutzim, setting structures on fire, burning, or suffocating people inside. They shot those who ran and tossed grenades into homes and safehouses.

Operational planning had begun two years before the attack. Attack plans found on slain Hamas militants confirm Hamas' mission. The orders read, 'Kill as many people as possible, seize hostages, and quickly move them into the Gaza Strip.' Other documents include detailed maps showing that Hamas intended to kill or take hostage civilians and school children.[6] Manuals included How to Take Captives and offered guidance to Hamas. Another captured document instructed the assailants how to say in Hebrew, 'Take off your pants,' and 'Raise your hands and open your legs.' These instructions would be forced on captured women throughout the day and in their underground empire.[7] There was also a code language that operatives practiced. The code word for the captives was 'diamonds'.

A kibbutznik related how organized and specialized his assailants were. By his account, one group would break into the house and kill those in the safe room. A second group would torch the dwelling, if necessary, and a third group would torture the victims and loot the residence.[8] The attack was well-executed because it had been well-rehearsed.

Militants practiced landing their paragliders while firing weapons. They had been patient and used intelligence to prepare the battlefields. For months, operators sent secret signals warning of minefields and indicating tunnel entrances. Fighters would transport hundreds of hostages away. This tactic had proven effective in earlier operations. They would use them as human shields and bargaining chips. Terrorist groups and criminal enterprises regularly employ this tactic. However, this attack was different because of the number of toddlers and the elderly who were abducted.

## Intelligence Preparation of the Battlefield

Patiently and methodically, Hamas collected intelligence over many years, following traditional tactics mandated in Islam, such as Muruna. By utilizing Muruna, Muslims can better blend into the world of non-believers and gain a deeper understanding of their operational environment. Westerners call this tactic going undercover. Hamas used Muruna to infiltrate kibbutzim and gather intelligence. Posing as guest workers in the Gaza Envelope, they obtained vital information that proved crucial on the day of the attack. Hamas members and strong supporters disguised themselves as journalists to cross Israel's border and, at times, engaged in violence.

Taqiyya is generally defined as a Muslim's effort to conceal their true political beliefs in order to mislead an opponent or rival. It is similar to Muruna but usually concentrates on a person's words rather than their clothing. This tactic has been widely used by Hamas and its supporters, as well as by international organizations. For example, Marwan Al-Ghoul (Profile 1 – Chapter 5), a CBS reporter in the Middle East, presents himself as an objective journalist. He may be. However, his critics challenge this by noting that his Facebook account revealed him asking, 'Are the Jews human like us?'

Some front-line reporters were alerted to the attack. Some journalists were actual members and documented the killing spree as members of Hamas. They gathered at key locations to witness and write highly sympathetic accounts of the day for Hamas. Yousef Masoud (Profile 2 – Chapter 5) of *The New York Times*, who won a George Polk Award for photojournalism, has since been identified as a member of Hamas.

## Supernova Music Festival – 'It was like a family'

Hamas likely wasn't aware of a music festival that celebrated peace and environmentalism. Even the attendees didn't know its location until three days before the event. The initial target was probably a nearby kibbutz, Re'im. However, once Hamas discovered the festival, it became a main target. This festival was called Supernova, also known as the Nova Festival.[9]

They were a gentle, yet slightly wild group who danced all night to the pounding electronic music in a large field near the Gaza border. Approximately 3,000 young Israeli revelers celebrated a Jewish holiday at the open-air Tribe of Nova festival.[10] It was a rave, and young, cheery-faced international attendees came to dance, swirl, laugh, and drink shots. Its trance culture resembled a 21st century Woodstock. 'It's that kind of mentality . . . These are the sweetest people. They would never harm anybody.'[11] Trance culture, which originates from India, promotes yoga and philosophies of international peace. As one devotee explained, 'You're not allowed to bring flags of your own country . . .'[12] They are also environmentally aware and demand that all plastics at the raves be recycled.

Some described the festival as a family gathering. A Tel Aviv bartender offered, 'People prepared for this party for weeks. Everyone knows each other. It was like magic.'[13] Some parents had concerns about their children attending. One mother was anxious about drugs and alcohol, and the scantily clothed attendees.[14] But her daughter assured her, 'Don't worry, I'm just there to dance and have fun.'[15] But not everyone felt completely comfortable. Ukrainian-born Vlada Patapov (Profile 3 – Chapter 5) chose to attend at the last minute, but as she approached the festival, she sensed 'something wasn't right.'[16] She remembered an eerie silence that she feared heralded trouble. Within hours, she would earn the nickname Lady in Red, referencing her red dress as she ran for her life among a panicked crowd. However, things remained calm in the early morning of the seventh. There were stages, stacks of large amplifiers, a camping area, and a makeshift cafeteria. Supernova attracted dancers from around the world, and 16 DJs from various countries spun the electric vinyl. In keeping with the spirit of world peace, no attendee was allowed to bring weapons to the dance. This would prove to be a mistake.[17]

As dawn broke on October 7, the bass-heavy musical beats faded. Some tired dancers were cleaning up trash, taking naps, or chatting. Then, things started to shift and change.[18] In the words of one attendee, 'At 6 a.m., hell started.' From a distance, black dots emerged and gradually grew larger. Rockets rained down on the area, and sirens blared the alarm. However, the sound of the sirens was briefly drowned out by gunfire spraying into the clusters of revelers. Terrorists arrived in vans, trucks, and motorcycles, firing at anything that moved. A survivor explained, 'It happened in an instant . . . They shot from close range, and it was terrible.'[19] Just meters away, a man shouted in Arabic, 'God is great!'[20]

An unstoppable wave of Hamas operatives surged toward the dancers. The sound of automatic weapons alerted one young woman that the enemy was closing in. 'Israeli soldiers don't shoot in an automatic mode,' she recalled. She did not hear any staccato firing in semi-automatic mode, which signaled that the IDF was not returning fire.

A leading Israeli security official who first noticed the attack grabbed the microphone and yelled that the party was over and people should run for their lives.

He lost his life. Some of the dancers were stoned or drunk and could not grasp the urgency of their situation. This was a very Bohemian crowd. However, soon all the dancers, both clear-headed and those high on narcotics, realized something was very wrong, and many fled the scene in their cars if they could reach them. Some of the drivers had been shot and were bleeding out in their vehicles. Others had been hit in their legs and could not operate the cars.[21] It often did not help to be an Arab or a Muslim. Pleading for his life, one Muslim claimed solidarity with his attackers. He stated he was Muslim as well. But Hamas responded, 'No! For us, you're even worse than a Jew!' They shot him.[22]

When they could not escape the oncoming waves of killers, some pretended to be dead, and at least one woman smeared some of the oozing blood from a nearby dead dancer on her face. Sometimes, feigning death proved effective, but often it did not. As the killers approached a target, they watched for any involuntary movements or trembling. When in doubt, they fired, often in their heads.

Some sought shelter in portable toilets, but the terrorists riddled the stalls with bullets. Others fled and took refuge in ditches, scattering in different directions. Some found shelter in the festival's walk-in industrial refrigerator. However, the terrorists ferreted them out and killed them, often laughing while doing so.[23] Many people panicked; others staggered and collapsed, wounded by gunfire. Many of the dancers maintained their composure and lay down on the ground to evade the blast and shrapnel.[24] Others reached their cars, but gunmen were waiting and shot them one by one. A survivor explained, 'We were hiding and running, hiding and running, in an open field – the worst place you could imagine.'[25] Another survivor described a surreal sensation about fleeing through the killing fields. 'It was like in movies. You see all gray, wind in your face, and sound, then you don't hear anything in your ears.'[26]

Hamas-filmed videos include footage of victims in blood-soaked clothing being corralled and herded into vans as hostages. Dancers took refuge when they could. A woman hid in the brush for hours, breathing carefully and trying not to make a sound. She fended off her fear by concentrating on the chortling birds in the brush above her. 'I tried to think of what I was grateful for . . . the birds that were still singing, the sky that was so blue.'[27] It was challenging to flee, but few could escape the screams of the dying and the pleas to God for rescue and mercy.

Furiously searching for escape, the fleers describe the moment as hauntingly cinematic. They were searching for escape routes that did not exist. 'I feel like I was hunted. They tried to kill me. We were helpless.'[28] Some reached out to God, while many turned to their parents, who were far away. When faced with the likelihood of death, others recited a Hebrew prayer that begins with 'The Lord is our God . . . ' One young woman called her father to tell him, 'Dad, they shot me!'[29] A California-born attendee texted his mother, 'I love you,' and 'I'm sorry.'[30] A young man's last known text to his family read, 'We are in a horror movie.' Revelers who managed to flee ran across open farm fields and along dry riverbeds as militants fired at them, trekking several miles to the safety of towns farther away from the border.[31]

When the hunted could fight back, they often did. One example was a man in a sedan who was trying to escape when he saw two assailants on a motorcycle, one of whom was blasting a rifle at the fleeing pedestrians. 'I knew it's either I hit him, or I know I die, or other people die, or somebody will die.'[32] With full force, he drove into the motorcycle. He survived, and the assailants died.[33]

Soon, news spread across the country. Within an hour of the breaking news about the attacks, Israeli Prime Minister Benjamin Netanyahu announced that the state of Israel was officially at war. Immediately, volunteers from all over Israel rushed toward Gaza to confront the invaders and rescue those in danger. Among those who risked everything to help was an Israeli Arab paramedic who ran toward the sounds of gunfire to assist everyone under attack. For the first responders, the full extent of the horror gradually unfolded as they approached the battlegrounds. As they drew closer to the scene, they saw people running toward them in a state of anguish and panic. As they continued to advance, they noticed some dancers limping or crawling from gunshot wounds.

Then came the images of bodies scattered across the fields or resting beside bushes. Individuals were writhing in agony or lying down dead. The scene grew increasingly gruesome as the responders approached a stage and saw the piles of bodies, sometimes next to each other, riddled with bullets. Along the way, responders saw naked or half-naked bodies tied to trees, and sometimes, several corpses were lashed to the same tree. One responder recounted, 'There was a case of a couple who were in an embrace, naked, and tied to a tree. Both had been shot in the chest.'[34]

Soldiers of all ranks and medical workers from various fields reported to Supernova. IDF Major General Yair Golan (Profile 4 – Chapter 5) arrived to transport the wounded safely. As he approached the center of the festival, he witnessed the carnage. 'While I was driving along the road, I suddenly realized the horror when I saw bodies, you know, scattered along the roadway.'[35] A Staten Island-born ambulance driver was enjoying his day off when he received the news and drove straight to Supernova. He was shocked to find his friends and fellow kibbutzniks among those who had been shot. 'I treated people from the kibbutzim, my city, nearby cities, civilians, soldiers, police officers, and attendees of the music festival.'[36]

## *After the Rampage*

When the IDF and first responders arrived at Supernova, most of the attackers had fled, though it would take days to clear the area of Hamas and its threats. The battlefield was quiet, with remnants of the festival scattered haphazardly across the field. They included water bottles, windbreakers, collapsed tents, overturned portable toilets, and paperback books. This scene was somewhat different from other outdoor music festivals. Upon closer scrutiny, however, bullet casings and blood stains littered the ground and stained garments.[37] Then, there were the bullet-marked ticket booths, which served as evidence of the killing.[38]

After Hamas terrorists left with captives, Israeli first responders treated the wounded and dying. Soon after, specialized teams began forensic investigations. Israel's investigation unit, Lahav 433, worked to make sense of the vast amount of evidence and began collecting over 1,500 witness statements.[39] 'The first thing was to identify the victims. People were waiting to hear what happened to their loved ones.'[40]

Supernova had become a crime scene, and members of notable Israeli post-attack organizations were on site to collect bodies and remains.[41] Zaka's mission is to collect bodies under Jewish law and purify them with water for burial.[42] Its members are highly trained, yet they were overwhelmed by the devastation on this date. They had never encountered anything like this before. As a spokesperson for Zaka explained, 'You get dizzy at some point. Some of the bodies are burned. Some are mutilated. Some of the bodies are decapitated. Every house has a story.'[43]

## The Battle for Sderot

Located within one mile of the Gaza border, Sderot was established three years after independence. This small town, with a population of 30,000, attracted Moroccan Jews expelled from their homeland, followed by Romanians and Ethiopians. For many years, it faced rocket attacks from Hamas due to its proximity to Gaza. However, it had never been breached before. Sderot was among the hardest-hit cities during the October 7 massacre and was only cleared of terrorists after hours of close-quarters combat. Bulldozers were used to demolish the police station on top of the remaining terrorists inside.[44]

Many residents were asleep and unprepared for the day's attack. Thirteen senior citizens were waiting by a bus when the attackers arrived and opened fire. They were heading to the Dead Sea to relax in the sun. At 6:30 am, as a massive rocket barrage began targeting the town, their minibus got a flat tire, stranding them by the roadside near a municipal smart shelter. The son of a victim explained, 'They stood no chance. He [his father] was looking forward to a leisurely day at the Dead Sea, hoping to take a break from work.'[45] Nadejad Spravchilov fled Soviet communism to start a new life in Israel. Her life ended on October 7, 2023 (Profile 5 – Chapter 5). The only survivor was the driver. He remembered that the group had taken a picture together. But, reflecting on the 'Five minutes later, everyone in the picture except me and the dog is dead.'[46]

Approximately 50 Hamas operatives invaded the town from three points. They murdered 53 civilians before they were repulsed, some four hours after the fighting started.[47] Most of the fighting ended by 10:30 am. By that time, Israel's soldiers had confined most of the living intruders to the town's police station. Sderot's civilian alert squad was in the city but lacked sufficient weapons or training.

A battle erupted at the police station, turning it into the center of a fierce firefight in the town. Hamas operatives barricaded themselves inside and exchanged gunfire with the IDF outside. After coming under fire, the IDF reduced the station to rubble. Twenty police officers in Sderot lost their lives as Hamas fighters stormed the station. 'They conquered it, for real,' explained a witness, 'they encircled the station. This place was a death trap.'[48]

Coordination between local Israeli forces and the 1,000 IDF troops deployed during the attack was chaotic. Residents were not adequately informed that terrorists had infiltrated and were on a killing spree. They believed they were only under air attack, unaware of the marauding groups of terrorists firing indiscriminately. Several ultra-Orthodox residents of Sderot firmly held to their faith, praying for God's salvation and initially refusing to evacuate their homes by car. It is forbidden for religious Jews to travel by car on the Sabbath. When a soldier saw them walking along the road, he persuaded them to get into his vehicle and go to safety.

A post-attack investigation concluded that many Israeli lives could have been saved if proper warnings had been issued and if the IDF had intervened. The investigation praised the determination of many Israeli defenders but criticized their lack of professionalism. In a harsh after-action report, investigators noted that the right rifles were never issued to the Sderot emergency defense team in August 2022 because of a paperwork dispute between the municipality and the IDF. For years, team members received no training. One survivor expressed the feelings of others when he said his anger and fatalism: 'I'll never return, not now and not in a million years. Sderot is dead to me – I can't even bear to hear the word.'[49] The remains of the station were laid to rest in the Negev wilderness; today, a memorial stands in its place.

## Murder, Rape, and Captivity

> *Some women were raped before they were dead, some raped while injured, and some were already dead when the terrorists raped their lifeless bodies. I desperately wanted to help, but there was nothing I could do.*
>
> Witness S reliving the festival.[50]

By early morning on the day of the attack, it was clear to the IDF that coordinated, large-scale murders were happening across the Gaza envelope. This was not a small-scale attack but a full invasion happening at multiple points. After assessing the scope of the invasion, IDF soldiers responsible for managing the situation were shocked by how heavily armed the enemy appeared. They had also taken positions among civilians, forcing frontline commanders to make impossible decisions about whether to open fire. 'They came in with so much ammo, RPGs, PK machine guns, mortars, grenades,' said a defense official. 'So you could have terrorists in one room firing at the IDF while a family shelters in the next room. It was tough.'[51] The IDF acknowledged its failure during the first 10 hours of Hamas' attack. As the afternoon went on, more soldiers arrived in the area, along with armed civilians eager to help.

The IDF reported that many Israeli soldiers had not been ordered to act but had taken the initiative on their own. Eventually, defensive lines were established near the breached perimeter fence to prevent further terrorist escapes and to eliminate or capture gunmen attempting to re-enter. There were instances of kidnapping, killing, wounding, and rape. Multiple women were assaulted, and numerous men raped various women. Several responders detailed the overwhelming evidence of sexual assault, including broken pelvises, lacerations, and puncture marks on victims ranging from children to seniors.[52] One man remains consumed by the indelible image of an 'angel-faced' young woman fighting off nearly 10 men who took turns raping her as they laughed. When she could no longer keep them at bay, she begged the men to kill her, which they did. The last rapist shot her in the head. Another man hiding in the bushes saw a different woman battling to keep her clothes on. One assailant took a shovel and decapitated her.[53]

Men and women were raped and sexually degraded. An Arabic-speaking Israeli explained that Hamas called him a doll, referring to him as a sex toy.[54] 'They took my clothes off. I could hear them say Yahood, the Arabic word for Jew, and all these words. There were spitting, screaming, and laughter – impossible things. This day brought a new term of terror for many witnesses and victims. Sabaya is a label in Islam that depicts the human spoils of war. It loosely means slave and handmaiden. The Islamic State used the term to describe the Yazidi captives whom they raped repeatedly.[55] On October 7, it was also widely used.

It wasn't just hardened and trained militants who killed and captured Israelis. Israel's defense minister explained that 'dozens' of UN employees participated, often with enthusiasm. One UNRWA teacher crowed, 'I'm inside, I'm inside with the Jews! We have female hostages; I captured one!' At least 30 UNRWA employees were involved. The attackers reveled in a carnival-like atmosphere of butchery. It seemed to be a joyous release of their passions and frustrations. According to their accounts, they were killing in the name of their religion. In one exchange, a preening young killer called to his parents to boast, 'Your son killed Jews . . . Ten with my own hands, Mom!' To which his proud mother responded, 'Oh my son, may God protect you . . .'[56]

Hamas rushed back to Gaza, but not alone. The dead, as well as the living, were carted to Gaza, often as war trophies and pawns for trade. One lifeless, half-naked young woman was filmed in the back of a truck. A man next to her pulled her hair and shouted praises to God. The corpse of another young woman was carried through the streets to the scorn of the living, who mocked her lifeless body and spat on it.[57]

## Kibbutz Alumim 'Black Sabbath'

Supernova served as a collective expression of youthful joy through music, inviting dancers of all faiths and races. It was as secular as Kibbutz Alumim is religious. Kibbutz Alumim opened its doors to the world, particularly South Asia, where

22 Thais and 19 Nepalis worked. Its moniker was 'Ninety-percent paradise and five-percent hell.' Kibbutz Alumim has stood since 1966, and over 50 years later, it remains a lush home to 500 residents, including soldiers, students, and young couples. Most were born in Israel.[58]

Alumim is more religious than other secular kibbutzim that line the near border with Gaza, and on October 6, it was in a festive mood. They celebrated Simchat Torah, and the dancing continued past midnight. However, instead of heading to synagogue the following day, residents were jolted from their beds at 6:29 am as rockets pounded the area near kibbutz.[59]

Alumim residents were accustomed to occasional rocket attacks, which they neither trivialized nor feared obsessively. It was simply part of their lives. One explained, 'We became like robots. On and off. War today, no school. Oh, look, it's 12:30 pm, and the war's over. On and off.'[60] As part of their routine, residents hurried to their reinforced rooms, a process they had repeated many times during exercises and live-fire drills. However, this morning was different. A cascade of Iron Dome missiles traced ribbons in the sky as they intercepted incoming rockets, the majority of which struck their targets.

Then came an eerie, ominous pause, followed by an unprecedented land attack. The kibbutz had two entrances: one locked for the Sabbath, while the other had only a padlock that was shot off. After that, the terrorists stormed the compound. The shelters were designed to protect against bombs but were not intended to defend against a land invasion, which was now underway. Many shelters lacked door locks and were never designed to be lockable; however, they now needed to be secured. Residents improvised by using brooms or belts to keep the doors closed.

The assailants were aware of their mission and the orders they had received. Maps containing detailed instructions and points of attack were found on a dead terrorist. Independent squads would target the armory and war room to immobilize the defenses before attacking unarmed residents. However, the attackers made a significant mistake by attempting to enter the wrong gate, which delayed their assault on the armory.[61] But, roaming bands of killers were hitting their marks, and panic set in among the targets.

Tamara Noy heard from her daughter, 'Mom, how are you two? In Be'eri, it's a disaster, a holocaust.' Noy was sheltered in her safe room, where she remained for hours, listening to shots and screams outside. She could not see the killings happening beyond the walls. Neither could fellow kibbutznik, British-born Esther Marcus (Profile 6 – Chapter 5), who confined herself with her adult children and two babies for 27 hours. 'We turned off the lights, had no food, and some people had to use the safe rooms as bathrooms. The whole time, we heard shooting outside.'[62] She and her family survived. But when she finally stepped out into the sunlight, she learned that her neighbors and friends had been killed.

For those forced to shelter for hours on end, life became torturous. Clustered closely together, families feared the enemy would blast or burn them out. They heard the marauding invaders drawing closer as the nearby popping sounds of rifle fire grew louder. They also endured extremely cramped conditions. Sometimes, the electricity failed, cutting off the air conditioning. The shelter's stale air choked the dwellers who risked opening the door for fresh air.[63] Babies could not be changed, and young children struggled to cope with a danger they could not fully comprehend.

Some were trapped in safe rooms or hiding in small corridors that felt like coffins. They could not leave for fear of being shot, but they needed to drink water, which was unavailable in the room. As they suffered from extreme thirst, they began to drink their urine. One Israeli who was shot and immobilized cried out to others to end his suffering by ending his life. He pleaded for water from others. When that was not possible, he begged, 'Kill me. I can't stand it anymore. Kill me with a knife if you can.'[64]

The 12-member security team, known as Kitat Konenut or KK, was mobilized to establish a defensive line, repel the attackers, and hold the fort until army units arrived in force to assist them. They had practiced extensively and sprang into action, searching for visual clues by following dark crimson footprints left by the assailants and the blood trails of the victims. However, they soon found themselves overwhelmed by the deluge of armed attackers as Hamas fighters flooded in on motorcycles. It was an invasion. Ambulance driver Filad Honwald and his son scoured the area for the wounded, transporting them to a central location for treatment. Despite the odds, the KK managed to fend off most of the invaders.

Alumin was the site of international devastation. The day before, its fields were filled with foreign nationals, particularly Thais and Nepalese, who tended crops and gained firsthand agricultural experience. At least 10 Nepali agriculture students were killed. One Nepali stood out for his bravery. Sheltering shoulder to shoulder with 16 others, a 23-year-old agricultural science student and amateur rapper exhibited heroic behavior that day. He gathered fellow workers to the safety of a nearby kitchen and then tried to rally them. The group slipped back out and rescued the victims. However, before they could move, the militants returned with reinforcements.[65]

People struggled to survive, from the young to the old, from students to professors. Professor of brain science Eitan Okun secured his wife and five children in the safe room and, along with members of the kibbutz alert squad, set out to confront the terrorists who had infiltrated the area kibbutz.[66] His efforts, along with those of the other security team members, prevented what could have been an even more severe incident.[67] The following morning, the surviving 450 residents were relocated to hotels in Netanya.

## Kibbutz Be'eri – Hellscape

*It's like a 9/11 . . . [but] You know everyone who died.*

Kibbutz secretary Alon Pauker.[68]

*They descended from the sky like angels of death.*

Mark Anspach[69]

People from Be'eri sometimes giggled that the kibbutz was so close to the Gaza Strip because, otherwise, it would be too perfect.[70] 'It was a joke, something we used to say because Be'eri is so beautiful,' a resident reminisced.[71] It is as secular as Alumim is religious. Its beauty wilted on October 7, when Be'eri became the most ravaged community from the combined attacks. About 90 terrorists breached the kibbutz's thin defenses and proceeded to murder over 130 people and abduct 25. Postmortem operations revealed that most were killed by gunfire or burned alive in their lives homes.[72]

The kibbutz has a volunteer emergency squad of about 15 people, assigned to protect the community from danger until the army arrives. With an army base just a few minutes away, residents felt confident that rescue would arrive soon. However, they were wrong.

First, the rampaging militants attacked homes with hand grenades, rocket-propelled grenades, RPGs, and gunfire. Then, they set them ablaze, hoping to smoke out families hiding inside. Many were burned alive, and both Arab and Jew would be victims. One victim would recount, 'There were like 12, 11 guys. They fought against 300 terrorists. I was useless. I felt useless . . . They're burning us alive.'[73] One dead Hamas fighter had a notebook with hand-scrawled Quranic verses and orders that read, simply, 'Kill as many people and take as many hostages as possible.' Others were equipped with gas canisters, handcuffs, and thermobaric grenades designed to turn houses into infernos instantly.[74]

## *Death in the Family*

When the first responders entered Be'eri, they found parents and children gunned down in their living rooms, kitchens, and bedrooms. In one house lay the incinerated corpse of what appeared to be a young person. There were many other grim scenes. He noticed an old man reclining in a chair on the porch, a coffee cup perched next to him. But the man was not moving. He had been shot dead.[75] Elsewhere on the kibbutz, three generations of Israelis were killed and later buried together. A 73-year-old grandmother, her 43-year-old son, and her barely 10-month-old granddaughter – three generations of one Israeli family – were killed by Hamas in a single afternoon.

Many parents witnessed the horrific slaying of their spouses and children before their eyes, helpless to intervene. The well-coordinated slaughter unfolded like a live drama, repeated in Be'eri and other kibbutzim. Assailants killed and kidnapped without regard for sex or age. Lifelong kibbutznik Avida Bachar (Profile 7 – Chapter 5) huddled with his family in their safe refuge room.[76] As he lay dying, the teenage boy pleaded, 'Bury me with my surfboard.'[77] His mother, too, would bleed out when a bullet fragment pierced her ribs.[78] Children saw their parents tortured and killed. At Be'eri, a terrorist threw a grenade in a hallway in which a father and his two sons were hiding. The grenade killed the father, and the terrorist led the boys to the kitchen where one boy said, 'Daddy's dead,' and the other begged, 'I want my mom.' The killer responded by opening the refrigerator and asking, 'Is this juice?'[79]

It was a multinational massacre involving some Palestinians who had worked in the Gaza Envelope for years. Hashim al-Birawi spent much of his life in nearby Israeli communities just a few miles from his home. His brother recalled, 'They treated us like family there.' On October 7, this Palestinian was killed too.[80]

People with diverse political beliefs, interests, and nationalities have had their lives ended or shattered. Kibbutzim are often homes to men and women on the liberal left. Seventy-four-year-old Canadian-born peace activist Vivian Silver (Profile 9 – Chapter 5) retired after decades of activism. She was a prominent member of Women Wage Peace, a group that urged Israel to resolve the conflict with the Arabs through negotiation and treaties.[81] She drove Arab patients and their families from Gaza to hospitals in Israel. On October 4, 2023, she marched with Arab women for peace and understanding. That did not protect her from Hamas, which killed her three days later in Be'er Sheva.[82]

Children were shown scant mercy. Honey-blonde, eight-year-old Emily Hand (Profile 10 – Chapter 5) had a sleepover the night before. In the words of her Irish-born father, 'They were having a girly night.'[83] She was abducted and feared dead. Her father confessed he felt relieved when informed she was no longer alive. He affirmed, 'She was dead . . . not in a dark room . . . terrified every minute of every day.' So, death was a blessing.' Emily was shaken but alive and would soon be returned to the loving arms of her family.

By the end of the day, Be'eri had suffered near-total devastation. A young survivor commented, 'There's no kibbutz there anymore. Everything was destroyed.' An on-the-scene IDF major lamented, 'Just like Auschwitz is the symbol of the Holocaust, Be'eri will be the symbol of this pogrom.' An official IDF investigation would later criticize the lack of preparedness and poor coordination among security forces. It also condemned the decision to deploy tank fire into the kibbutz. However, within weeks, many survivors began expressing a desire to return. Some did return, and Avida Bachar, who lost a son, his wife, and a leg, was one of them. More followed his lead.

## Nir Oz

Nir Oz stands at the forefront of desert agriculture technology. As terror unfolded along the Gaza Strip, the kibbutz Nir Oz was affected as well. The emotions of the day – panic, pain, fear, hate, and courage – reverberated throughout the kibbutz, as evidenced by hundreds of recovered texts. Like the attacks at Alumim and Be'eri, the assailants were well-prepared.

As much as any kibbutz, Nir Oz stood naked to the bullets, bombs, and ruthlessness of Hamas. They abducted 80 of the kibbutz's 400 residents, which was one-third of all captives taken that day.[84] As in other kibbutzim, several of the victims at Nir Oz were Holocaust survivors.[85] Many kibbutzniks had gentle hearts, liberal politics, and warm personalities. Elderly Ada Sagi moved to a kibbutz because she was drawn to its principles of 'equality and humanity,' as she put it. Her son remembered that she studied Arabic to communicate more intimately with her Palestinian friends and neighbors.[86] But, much like peace activist Vivian Silver of Be'eri kibbutz, Ada Sagi was killed without mercy.

The assailants sauntered from house to house, boring into the gas pipes and redirecting the flow of gas inward toward the homes. Those trapped inside could either emerge and be shot or captured or risk being burned alive by remaining inside. Eyal Barad (Profile 11 – Chapter 5) witnessed the terrorist attack unfolding on his cell phone. He whisked his family to the dark safe room, where his wife and autistic daughter hid. However, his daughter did not understand that their collective safety required silence, and she was hysterical. Eyal needed to cover her mouth while allowing her to breathe. He resolved, 'We all go, or we all survive.' He found the right adjustment, and they lived. Around 20 Nir Oz residents were killed on Oct. 7, and news of the deaths of some of them in Gaza has started to trickle in. Those seized from the kibbutz ranged in age from 9 months to 85 years at the time they were taken. All were civilians, and more than half were women and children. All 13 Israeli hostages released in the first exchange on Nov. 24 were from Nir Oz, and they bought the freedom of 39 Palestinian prisoners from Israel.[87]

As the day ended, Hamas exfiltrated with hostages, and its leaders were pleased. The level of the carnage far surpassed their expectations, as did their haul of prisoners. They were astonished at the weak performance of Israel's military capabilities. A Hamas leader boasted, 'We were shocked by the colossal collapse [of Israel's army] . . . this army was a paper tiger.'[88]

By dusk on October 7, the IDF had restored calm to most areas affected by the attacks after clearing out pockets of terrorists. Military units and first responders entered the kibbutzim and found dead bodies scattered throughout the compounds. Under closer scrutiny, the surreal sexual violence and torture against both women and men came into focus.[89] They began to count the dead and injured. They tried to estimate the number of captives.

## Nahal Oz IDF Base

The defenses at the Nahal Oz IDF Base collapsed immediately. Hamas took advantage of the shock and confusion, along with the failure of communication security, to massacre soldiers and civilians in the area. Hamas had conducted meticulous surveillance of the base and the kibbutz, monitoring social media posts by the soldiers. By intercepting IDF on-base communications, Hamas discerned the chaotic security measures. Weapons were inadequate, and many soldiers lacked sufficient training. Tanks were parked incorrectly. This intelligence enabled Hamas to overpower the post, killing 53 soldiers and taking 10 hostages. Sixteen of those killed were women who were burned alive. Investigations concluded that Hamas did not need human sources placed directly in Nahal Oz to fully understand the IDF's order of battle and troop disposition. Hamas operatives effectively manipulated social media used by the Israelis, which proved crucial to their victory there.

## Emergency Medicine

On October 7, medical services in Israel faced a day unlike any other since independence. They were overwhelmed by the sheer number of casualties and the various types of injuries they encountered. This day became one of the most significant terror-related mass-casualty incidents (MCI) in history.[90] Calls flooded in from multiple sites along the Gaza envelope. The calls echoed with shock, disbelief, and despair, pleading for immediate relief. From the now-decimated Nova music grounds to citrus groves in neighboring kibbutzim, and to threatened safe rooms, cars, and open fields turned into hell, cries of panic overwhelmed Magen David Adom's (MDA) centers. MDA is Israel's primary emergency medical response organization. This is one of the countless calls on the morning of October 7 that shared a similar tone, wording, and context:

| | |
|---|---|
| Dispatcher | 'MDA, hello.' |
| Caller | 'Listen, they shot at us! My friend is dead in the car. We're both in a ditch. They're shooting here. Can you locate the phone and get here somehow?' |
| Dispatcher | 'Yes. Stay with me on the line, bro.' |
| Caller | 'We left a party in the forest, there was an encounter, they shot at our car, my friend is dead.' |

The dispatcher then attempted to calm the caller's panic and provided instructions on treating his wounds, assuring him that help was on the way.[91] This theme occurred repeatedly throughout that day.

Situated about 25 miles from Gaza, Soroka Medical Center is the hospital that cared for most of the wounded.[92] Within the first 16 hours, the Soroka emergency department treated 680 patients, including 120 who were critically injured. As victims arrived, the hospital discharged at least 100 patients to make room. They activated staff, many of whom were celebrating the joyous Jewish holiday.[93] At 8:00 am on October 7, Soroka declared a Medical Catastrophe Alert (MCA) and mobilized all available medical practitioners.[94] Barzilai Medical Center in Ashkelon, both in the south of the country, took in about 350 casualties.

## Summary

The age of those murdered ranged from 14 hours old to 92 years old. Naama Abu Rashed, a Bedouin Israeli, was shot while still in her mother's womb. She was a fetus, and a bullet plowed through her mother's womb and severed one of her tiny legs. Ninety-two-year-old Moshe Ridler survived the Nazis but not Hamas. A Hamas rocket-propelled grenade killed him in his safe room.[95] Others who were abducted and hauled to the Hamas metro never returned. Some were murdered quickly, and others died of privation slowly. Eden Yerushlaim (Profile 12 – Chapter 5) was starved before she was shot and murdered. She was so thin that her family barely recognized her remains. Hamas took the video trophy shots of their killings and made grindhouse snuff films from them.

The Bibas family also captured the hearts of Israelis. Shiri Biba and her two young children were captured on October 7, where they languished for over 500 days. The children Ariel and baby Kfir were redheaded. The baby was learning to walk. In February 2023, they were returned to Israel. But they had been murdered in Gaza (Profile 13 – Chapter 5).

Some observers showed very little compassion for the Israeli victims of October 7 but were very vocal in condemning Israel. British activist Sarah Wilkinson (Profile 14 – Chapter 5) crossed a rhetorical legal line by, in the view of British authorities, praising the October 7 attack. In response, she was charged with violating the Terrorism Act of 2000.[96]

Hamas' goal that day was to bring about the destruction of the state of Israel by prompting Hezbollah to launch an all-out offensive from Lebanon and ultimately to bring in Iran.[97] That failed, and the momentum immediately shifted to the IDF. Throughout the war and captivity, there were moments of joy. Although many captives returned dead, some came home alive. The families of the prisoners also suffered. Some sank into despair, while others held onto hope. At times, that hope was rewarded, as in the case of a little girl who missed her dog and was sure he was killed. Her dog was abducted by Hamas but was rescued by the IDF and returned to the little girl who cared for it.

**Profile 1 – Marwan Al-Ghoul: CBS's Man in Gaza**
**Names:** Marwan Al-Ghoul
**Nationality:** Palestinian
**Profession:** Journalist for CBS
**Connection to October 7, 2023:** CBS continues to highlight the reporting of Marwan Al-Ghoul, a seasoned Middle Eastern journalist in his sixties. One year after the war started, Al-Ghoul reflected on the shock of the Israeli response. In his narrative, he does not refer to Hamas invaders as 'terrorists' but as 'militants.' However, his critics argue that his reporting lacks objectivity. He enriches one essay with personal reminiscences, noting his father's displacement in 1948, thereby blurring the line between objective journalism and nostalgic commentary. 'He [his father] died . . . without being able to return to his beloved country Palestine.' He lost a brother in 2009 to an Israeli air strike, and his colleagues at CBS have expressed concern for his safety. Fellow CBS correspondent Holly Williams told him, 'We are so worried about you.'[98]

However, others closely following his reporting do not view him as sympathetically. According to the pro-Israel watchdog group Honest Reporting

al-Ghoul has compared to Israelis to Nazis and agreed with a Facebook comment that read Israel Jews are 'by no means . . . human, these are monsters in a human body.'[99] In 2017, Al-Ghoul wrote that Gaza's civilians should join the 'permanent resistance' against Israel. On October 7, 2023, he posted on Facebook, 'Today is not the same as yesterday. The Palestinian issue is at a long crossroads. Oh Allah, we ask you for patience and victory.'[100]
**Current Status:** CBS continues to hold him in high regard. Williams said, 'Marwan is much loved here at CBS News. He's worked with us on and off for more than two decades. He has enriched our reporting when we've traveled to Gaza over the years, and he has helped keep us safe.'[101]

**Profile 2 – Yousef Masoud**
**Name:** Yousef Masoud
**Nationality:** Palestine
**Profession:** Photojournalist
**Connection to October 7, 2023:** Yousef Masoud is an accomplished freelance photojournalist who has received several international awards. According to one award certificate, he won the Cultures of Resistance Award – Palestine for conveying the suffering and tragedy of Palestinians. He occasionally works for *The New York Times* and received the George Polk Award in 2024 for his coverage of the October 7, 2023 attack. The George Polk Award is one of the most prestigious awards in photojournalism. *The New York Times* praised his 'fearless and compassionate work.'[102]

However, one of his employers was sued on the same day he received the Polk Award. The Jewish Advocacy Center filed a lawsuit against the Associated Press because Masoud worked for them, and the suit alleges that Masoud also worked for Hamas.[103] The suit states, 'There is no doubt that AP's photographers participated in the October 7th massacre, and that AP knew, or at the very least should have known, through simple due diligence, that the individuals they were compensating were longstanding Hamas affiliates and full participants in the terrorist attack that they were also involved in documenting.'[104]
**Current Status:** The lawsuit is ongoing.

**Profile 2 – Vlada Patapov: The Lady in Red**
**Name:** Vlada Patapov
**Nationality:** Ukrainian-born Israeli
**Profession:** Fashion industry, Wedding planner
**Background:** Mother of a young girl who emigrated from Ukraine
**Connection to October 7, 2023:** At 25 years old, this panic-stricken mother of a four-year-old daughter became known as the lady in red because of the red shawl draped over her shoulders as she fled from Hamas operatives at the Nova Festival. She recalls that her main motivation for survival was her daughter. The photograph capturing the horror on her face became a global icon. One year after the attack, she participated

with other models in a semi-morbid fashion show to commemorate the tragedy. Part art exhibition and part fashion statement, the show featured women survivors dressed in tattered clothing and smeared with fake blood to symbolize the attack.
**Current Status:** As of late 2024, Patapov was battling post-traumatic stress disorder and survivor's guilt. She explained, 'What happened to me lasted maybe 18 hours, but for many, the pain continues, and I think about the hostages still in Gaza. We must not forget them.'[105] A Western artist paid tribute to her in solidarity with the captured and killed Israelis. Italian artist Alessandro Palombo painted a mural of her in flight. Soon, someone defaced the mural, erasing her head from the painting. Palombo feared that the collective memory of the atrocity was being erased. He added, 'Instead, these images need to be circulated more until they are imprinted and become a warning against the threat of Islamist terrorism and religious intolerance and, in his words, 'fundamentalism.'[106]

**Profile 4 – Major General Yair Golan: 'Two-State Solution'**
**Names:** Yair Golan
**Nationality:** Israeli
**Profession:** Career soldier; general officer, politician
**Connection to October 7, 2023:** Major General Golan's instincts told him something was off that morning. He received a call from his sister around 8:00, informing him that terrorists had heavily attacked an outdoor concert. Although he had no weapon, he raced in the general direction of the Nova festival. As he approached the festival, he saw people running toward him, pleading for help. He then noticed bodies on the ground and had to slow down to ensure he didn't run over them. Like in other battles, Golan acted as a solid, risk-taking soldier.

Golan was drawn to politics at a young age. He distinguished himself as a soldier in Lebanon, the West Bank, and Gaza, rapidly advancing through the ranks of the IDF. He also earned a master's degree in public administration from Harvard. Furthermore, he has found success in progressive Israeli politics. Today, Labor is the smallest faction in the Knesset, reflecting a significant decline from its founding days in Israel.[107]
**Current Status:** Despite witnessing the slaughter, the general still advocates for nurturing warm relations with his Arab neighbors. He refuses to succumb to pessimism regarding the harmonious, albeit sometimes strained, relations with Arabs. He learned this optimism from his father, much of whose family was killed by the Nazis. His father told him, 'We must be optimistic. And I think this is a lesson that led me through my adult life.'[108] He looks forward to assisting in the creation of two states – one for Israel and one for Palestine.

**Profile 5 – Nadejada Spravchilov**
**Names:** Nadejada Spravchilov
**Nationality:** Soviet and then Israeli
**Profession:** Retired chemist

**Connection to October 7, 2023:** Nadejda and her sister, Natalia Tomayev, were part of a tour bus predominantly filled with retired Israelis embarking on a day trip to the Dead Sea early that morning. The bus experienced a flat tire near Sderot and pulled into a bus stop in the city for the driver to repair it. While they waited outside the bus, air raid sirens warning of a rocket attack began to ring out. The bus stop included a bomb shelter with an automated door designed to unlock when sirens sounded; however, it malfunctioned and remained locked. Moments later, a pickup truck carrying Hamas terrorists drove by and opened fire on the group of seniors, killing all 13 of them, including both Nadejda and Natalia; only the driver survived. The rest were shot dead.[109]
**Current Status:** Dead and mourned.

**Profile 6 – Esther Marcus: Resilience!**
**Names:** Esther Marcus
**Nationality:** Israeli, formerly British
**Profession:** Therapist
**Connection to October 7, 2023:** The level-headed kibbutznik, mother, and grandmother, London-born Esther Marcus, survived the Hamas attack on Alumim. She hid with her family – her husband and six others – and endured when many of her neighbors did not. Marcus moved to Israel at 19, served in the IDF as a mental health officer for over two years, and settled in Kibbutz Alumim, where she raised four children. At the kibbutz and in other parts of Israel, she worked with children and adults who experienced emotional trauma. She coaches drama groups and produces plays. She authored 'Colour Red,' a book to help children manage anxiety caused by rocket attacks.

Her expertise and compassion have helped many cope with the trauma of the October attack. She works as a therapist at the Resilience Center of Sderot Negev, assisting national mental health care professionals with the surge in demand and the displacement of around 250,000 people, including Marcus herself, from their homes in both the southern and northern regions.[110]
**Current Status:** Based in the Sedrot Negev Regional Council, the Center provides emotional first aid to thousands of evacuees. Just one month after her family survived the attack, her husband Stevie suffered a heart attack and passed away at the age of 62. According to her account, her loss fueled her desire to help others.[111] Today, she is very active on social media and YouTube. When people ask her why she is determined to live in her kibbutz, she responds, 'Because this is my home.'[112]

**Profile 7 – The Bachar Family: 'I Was Mistaken'**
**Names:** Avida Bachar, Dana Bachar, Carmel Bachar
**Nationality:** Israeli
**Profession:** Kibbutzniks, farmers, child
**Connection to October 7, 2023:** The Bachar family was at home in Kibbutz Be'eri when Hamas launched its invasion. Avida, the father, tried to protect his family.

They escaped to a safe room that shielded them from incoming rockets, but it could not protect them from the loss of their home due to the invasion. His wife, Dana, and 15-year-old son, Carmel, died before Avida's eyes. He was also shot and nearly bled to death. Doctors amputated one of Avida's legs, and he underwent six months of physical rehabilitation therapy. His son Carmel's last words were, 'I want you to bury me with my surfboard.'[113]

Avida's losses and the devastation of Be'eri on October 7 radically changed his views about Palestinians. He was horrified to witness Arab neighbors of all ages and genders pillaging Be'eri and killing and torturing kibbutzniks. His perspective shifted to become much more hawkish, and he grew passionately vengeful.[114] He related, 'I believed in peace with Gaza, but I was mistaken.'[115]

**Current Status:** Bachar promises to return to live in Be'eri. 'Of course, we will return to Be'eri.' His eldest son has returned to the kibbutz and works in the print shop. Avida vows, 'I'm coming home. I'm coming back to my land.' Dana was buried next to Carmel. Someone placed a surfboard on the boy's coffin before he was interred.[116] At the funeral, Avida, who lost a leg, sat in his wheelchair and wept.

**Profile 8 – Sapir Cohen: Soft-Spoken Woman**

**Names:** Sapir Cohen

**Nationality:** Israeli

**Profession:** Software engineer

**Connection to October 7, 2023:** According to her description, she was a shy and withdrawn young woman with a good job as a software engineer and a boyfriend named Sasha, with whom she shared a home. She had a good life in Ramat Gan. However, on October 7, she and four members of Sasha's family were abducted from a kibbutz and taken to Gaza, where she endured suffering for 55 days. She and the others were released, except for Sasha. Like many other captives of Hamas, she faced malnutrition and abuse during her captivity.

Her religious faith was strengthened as she frequently recalled the 27th Psalm, repeating it often: 'The Lord is my light and my salvation; whom shall I fear? The Lord is the strength of my life; of whom shall I be afraid?' She has horrifying memories of other captives and cannot shake the images of them trembling, crying, or withdrawing into themselves. She comforted a young girl by saying that the Gaza tunnels were exciting, encouraging her to view this ordeal as an adventure. Now free, she clings to her faith in God, certain that she endured the cold, damp, bedbugs, hunger, pain, and fear for a reason. 'But it's promised me just one thing – that behind everything that happened there is a purpose. I just thought about that every time. If I need to be in the tunnels, I will be in the tunnels, and I will try to do the best that I can.'[117]

**Current Status:** She thanks God 'for all the angels you sent me to this hell.' The one angel that is still missing is Sasha.[118]

**Profile 9 – Vivian Silver: Peacenik**
**Names:** Vivian Silver
**Nationality:** Canadian-Israeli
**Profession:** Peace advocate and kibbutznik
**Connection to October 7, 2023:** She was born in Winnipeg, Manitoba, and became one of Israel's most celebrated advocates for peace and harmonious relations with Palestinians. By all accounts, she remained faithful to her beliefs throughout her 74 years. As a girl and young woman, she was influenced by the values of the socialist Zionist Habonim youth movement.[119] In Israel, she advanced feminism through her organizing skills. In 1981, she founded the United Kibbutz Movement's Department to Promote Gender Equality and served on a Knesset subcommittee for the Advancement of Women in the Workforce and the Economy.

She fiercely opposed Benjamin Netanyahu's policies in the West Bank and organized Women Wage Peace to advocate for peace. In 2000, she helped establish the Arab-Jewish Center for Equality, Empowerment, and Cooperation. She reached out to Bedouin women in a shared cause against what fellow feminists describe as patriarchy. Her fellow peace activists remember her as a joyful and optimistic woman.[120] One said, 'She had a moral compass that led the direction of many people who followed her.'[121] Another remembered her 'dazzling smile.'[122]

On October 7, she was killed along with over 100 residents of the kibbutz Be'eri. Her son, Zeigen, mourned her loss. Zeigen mused that her heart would have broken over the events of October 7 and their aftermath. 'She worked all her life, you know, to steer us off this course. And in the end, it blew up in her face.'[123]
**Current Status:** Dead. Murdered on October 7, 2023.

**Profile 10 – Emily Hand: 'A Little Angel'**
**Name:** Emily Hand
**Nationality:** Irish, raised in Israel on a kibbutz
**Profession:** Nine-year-old student
**Connection to October 7, 2023:** Emily was at a sleepover at a friend's house on the kibbutz when she, her friend, and her friend's mother were abducted. Initially, their family was told that they had been killed. Her father reminisced that she was a blonde angel and a standout in the kibbutz's dance routines. Upon hearing that she was found dead, he exclaimed in relief that she couldn't be tortured and defiled. 'So death was a blessing, an absolute blessing.' But those who knew her would receive an even more incredible blessing – she was alive, and the full blessing would come upon her release two months later.[124]

Upon Emily's release, Ireland's Prime Minister Leo Varadkar tweeted, 'An innocent child who was lost has now been found and returned.'[125] Emily was not lost; terrorists had abducted her. Israel's Foreign Minister Eli Cohen reacted by stating that Hamas kidnapped Emily and over 30 others, claiming, 'and you are trying to legitimize it. Shame on you!' After hugging her father and the family dog,

Emily asked to listen to a Beyoncé song. However, Emily also learned of a loss: her first mother had passed away from cancer when she was two years old. Now, her father informed her that his wife, Emily's second mother, was murdered on October 7. Emily and Tom are in recovery.[126]
**Current Status:** Father and daughter assumed to be alive and well.

**Profile 11 – Eyal Barad**
**Names:** Eyal Barad
**Nationality:** Israeli
**Profession:** Kibbutznik, engineer, father
**Connection to October 7, 2023:** Forty-year-old Eyal Barad has faced many challenges, particularly with his six-year-old autistic daughter. He lives in a constant state of danger in Nir Oz, which is less than a five-minute drive from Gaza.[127] On October 7, about 700 Hamas operators and camp followers stormed Nir Oz and committed murder, rape, and pillage. First, they set fire to most of the cars to prevent anyone from escaping. Video footage captured joyous expressions as men and boys looted homes and committed murder.

Barad explained, 'I had no gun; I couldn't do anything. I could only stay by the door and listen to what was happening outside. I knew if I opened the door and went out, I'd be dead with my family.'[128] His children wanted to go outside and play, but the 40-year-old engineer explained that they would be in danger if they did. Nevertheless, the entire family survived. He recalls that those involved in the rampage knocked on the door but did not force their way in. He, his wife, and three children survived, but his wife's father did not. He was shot dead that day. In his recollection of that day, Barad describes the carnival-like atmosphere of the killings and looting. He speaks of three types of Gazans who wandered past his home. The first were uniformed combatants armed with assault rifles, sidearms, and grenades. The second group consisted of gunmen wielding weapons but not wearing uniforms. The third group included ordinary Gazans, including children as young as 10, along with many women too.[129]
**Current Status:** Barad is thankful that his family ultimately survived. However, he, like others, feels betrayed by the IDF. 'We trusted the army and the government, but nobody came to help.'[130]

**Profile 12 – Eden Yerushalmi – A Last Hug**
**Name:** Eden Yerushalmi
**Nationality:** Israeli
**Profession:** Pilates Teacher and part-time bartender
**Connection to October 7, 2023**: When Hamas opened fire, Eden Yerushalmi tried to hide, first under a thorny bush and then feigning death with friends who had been shot dead and were lying in a car. But she was caught.[131] Her sister said, 'When her phone died, I said, 'I hope they shoot her, I hope it's quick.'[132] But she was alive, and Hamas released a video of her in August 2023.[133]

Twenty-four-year-old Yerushalmi was held as a hostage under brutal conditions. Her sisters explained that she could barely stand and had no windows or light. The air was foul, and they could only relieve themselves in a bucket in a confined space.[134] She was murdered with five other captives in late August 2024. She was starving when she was shot. Her sister May saw her body after it was returned to Israel. 'We gave her a last hug to say goodbye. She was so thin, we could feel her bones ticking out.'[135] The sisters portrayed Yerushalmi as a friendly and warm person, with May saying: 'The most important thing is that she was a hero, and she survived eleven months in those tunnels.'[136]
**Current Status:** Dead

**Profile 13 – The Bibas Family**
**Name:** Yarden Bibas, Shiri Bibas, Kfir Bibas, Ariel Bibas
**Nationality:** Israeli
**Professions:** Kibbutzniks
**Connection to October 7, 2023:** Four members of the Bibas family were kidnapped. The mother and both children were murdered during captivity. The father, Yarden, attempted to fend off the Hamas attackers, but he and his family were taken. He was released after 484 days, but his wife, Shiri, and their two children, Kfir and Ariel, remained in captivity. Yarden was separated from them and did not know whether they were alive or dead. He then found out that they were murdered.

Hamas returned their bodies to Israeli authorities during a prisoner exchange. However, Shiri's coffin did not hold her body. Instead, it contained the body of another hostage. Earlier, Hamas had claimed that the Bibas family was killed in an Israeli airstrike, but this assertion was proven false. Ariel and Kfir were likely strangled to death while in the custody of a small Palestinian group, Al-Mujahideen.
**Current Status:** In captivity, Yarden endured frequent physical and emotional torment. He was forced to create confessional videotapes. His friends and family raised funds to support his recovery and help him move forward with his life. As of mid-2025, his situation remained torturous. A family member wrote, 'Beyond the unbearable grief, he must rebuild his life from nothing – physically, emotionally, and financially. He has no home or stability, and each day brings new, unexpected challenges.'[137] Buenos Aires, the largest city in Argentina, has a street named 'State of Palestine' renamed 'Bibas Family Street' in honor of the Bibas family.

**Profile 14 – Sarah Wilkinson: 'Incredible Infiltration'**
**Names:** Sarah Wilkinson
**Nationality:** British
**Profession:** Activist and journalist for the MENA Uncensored network, a pro-Palestine media outlet.
**Connection to October 7, 2023:** On October 7, Wilkinson posted that 'Hamas airforce [*sic*] published their incredible infiltration by air into the illegal Israeli settlements in the Gaza envelope.' This was the latest of her pro-Hamas statements

that attracted the attention of British police. Earlier, she expressed doubts about the existence of the Holocaust. Her salute to Hamas regarding the October 7 attack led British police to arrest her. In an early morning raid on her home conducted by the Counter Terrorism Police, officers took her to prison and confiscated electronic devices. While her support for Hamas was not illegal, it is not uncommon in Europe. However, British authorities cited her approval of mass murder as a legal violation. British police referenced provisions of Section 12 of the Terrorism Act of 2000.[138]

Progressive commentators praise the 62-year-old Wilkinson as a dedicated and prolific champion of Palestinians who highlights Israeli war crimes. The World-Wide Socialist Web commended her as a tireless advocate for the non-white underclass, bringing global attention to Israeli war crimes. The MENA Uncensored network considers her one of its own. MENA praised Wilkinson for her support of the cause. Roger Waters of Pink Floyd condemned her arrest, stating that such law enforcement actions against a human rights activist indicate that Britain is becoming a fascist regime.[139]

**Current Status:** Unknown.

# Chapter 6

# The World Takes Note

*It's not a war. It's not a battlefield. You see the babies, the mothers, the fathers in their bedrooms, in their protection rooms, and how the terrorists kill them. It's not a war . . . It's a massacre.*

Gen. Itai Veruv, head of the IDF's Depth Command

As real-time news of the bloodshed filtered into Western media, world leaders expressed shock at the magnitude and depravity of the violence. Then-US Secretary of State Antony Blinken compared the crimes to those of the Islamic State.[1] The secretary enumerated some of the day's horrors. 'Babies desecrated. Young people were burned alive. Women raped. Parents executed in front of their children, children in front of their parents.'[2]

The United States and European nations initially condemned the attack unreservedly. However, many Middle Eastern countries leaned toward neutrality or criticized Israel in their statements. In the second week of October, 44 nations denounced Hamas and its acts of terrorism. Twenty nations expressed solidarity with Israel, while others insisted that Israel immediately cease its attacks on individuals and locations in Gaza. Additionally, countries such as Iraq, Kuwait, Qatar, Saudi Arabia, and Syria placed blame on Israeli leaders for the regional violence. The international support for Israel that emerged in the immediate aftermath of the bloodshed quickly waned.

In Israel, there was widespread demand for both rescue and retaliation. Politicians from all parties agreed that Hamas needed to be eliminated. The attack undermined any diplomatic credibility that Hamas had gained through its relatively low levels of violence in 2022 and 2023. Israelis were taken aback, as Hamas had never engaged in such large-scale slaughter before. This marked the first time Hamas abducted such a significant number of hostages, including both children and the elderly. The wall, intended as a barrier, collapsed immediately, leading to comparisons with Israel's reliance on the Bar-Lev Line of fortifications along the Suez Canal against the Egyptians in 1973 and the Maginot Line, which the French constructed for their defense against the German Panzers.[3] They all failed, including Hitler's vaunted Atlantic Wall on June 6, 1944. So did Israel's security barrier.

Gilad Erdan (Profile 1 – Chapter 6), Israel's Ambassador to the United Nations wore the iconic yellow star that was forced on Jews by the Nazis during their rule.[4] Unlike the more discreet murderers of the German mobile killing units in World War II, Hamas militants joyfully broadcast their killings worldwide. Images of the day's terror were ghastly, and several became iconic. One was the fright-filled expression of Noa Argamani (Profile 2 – Chapter 6) as Hamas grabbed and whisked her away into incarceration on the back of a motorcycle. A friend of Noa said, 'I can't imagine what's going through her at all – screaming in panic on a motorcycle when some scumbags are holding her, and they don't let her go.'[5] Other twisted photos began to populate the Internet. They displayed burned bodies, women stripped naked from the waist down, and nude female corpses tied to bedposts.[6] Israeli soldiers who arrived at the scene were overwhelmed by the visuals. An IDF spokesman commented, 'It was just like Eisenhower when he discovered Bergen-Belsen.'[7]

Israel declared war on Hamas and unleashed aerial firepower that devastated Gaza. Meanwhile, the IDF and other first responders scoured the sites of destruction for surviving terrorists as well as the wounded and deceased victims. Homes were rigged with explosives. Cautiously, IDF reservists began searching for the injured and those in hiding. They were also prepared to flush out any terrorists who might be concealed or who were too injured to move but could still be armed.

It was also a time to settle scores for earlier, more distant crimes. One notable figure was Hamas terrorist Aziz Salha (Profile 3 – Chapter 6), who helped lynch two Israeli soldiers in 2000 to the delight of the audience. He became internationally infamous through a picture that captured him waving his blood-drenched hands after killing the reservists. Israel captured Salha and later released him in exchange, but he continued to engage in terrorist activities with Hamas.[8] No longer. An Israeli air strike killed him in early October 2024. There were other targets.

## On War, On Peace

Shortly after declaring war, Prime Minister Netanyahu outlined Israel's objectives. The IDF would fight until it eradicated Hamas' military and governance capabilities. Hamas must release the hostages, and the IDF needs to ensure that Gaza could no longer pose a significant threat. To achieve these objectives, Israel would indefinitely maintain freedom of movement in Gaza and establish a security zone along its border. It would enforce a strict blockade to prevent the smuggling of weapons.

Individual terrorists armed with rocket-propelled grenades continued to emerge from tunnels, infiltrate Israel, kill civilians, and then retreat to safety in Gaza. For a year, Hamas militants fired rockets into Israel, some launched from southern Gaza, which was designated as a humanitarian zone. This created a dilemma for Israeli operators trying to destroy launch sites while minimizing civilian casualties. Israel needed to ensure that no militant group could launch missile strikes or ground invasions from Gaza.

According to the plan, civilian life in Gaza will change dramatically. Gazans will govern the Strip, but civil servants will be vetted to ensure they have no ties to radical organizations. Israel will also initiate a de-radicalization program and ensure that UNRWA is banned from Gaza. Following demilitarization and de-radicalization, Israel will oversee the rebuilding of critical infrastructure to promote sustainable development. Israel will oppose any attempts by third parties to impose permanent peace on it or recognize an independent Palestinian state. These are Netanyahu's medium- and long-term objectives. For the foreseeable future, Israel will continue to dismantle Hamas into submission.

## Cleaning the Scene – The Debris of the Dead

Israelis rallied to the cause. Humanitarian aid to the affected kibbutzniks poured in from all over Israel almost immediately. Israelis gathered funds and supplies for both soldiers and civilians throughout the country. Many opened their homes to families who had lost their homes and faced the heartbreaking loss of a mother, father, son, daughter, or friend. One resident of Israel, who had lived there for 50 years, remarked that a spirit of kindness had swept the nation.

At the murder sites, medics and volunteers loaded the bodies into vans, hoping to identify and bury them quickly.[9] The killing fields released a lingering stench of death for days. Body bags covered the streets, and the charred remains of once-bustling homes smoldered. An IDF officer noted that for days, his soldiers continued to discover burned bodies. 'Two days ago, we just found, like, a hand of a person. We found the jaw of a person here.'[10] There was a haunting sense around the kibbutzim. It would take weeks before forensics could determine precisely how many people were murdered and who they were.

Like an abandoned movie set scattered with children's toys and props, the now-empty kibbutzim overflowed with remnants of childhood – toys, sports gear, swings, and trampolines. At Be'eri, a burned dwelling with a collapsed treehouse stood next to charred artifacts, including road signs scattered throughout the landscape. More personal and treasured items were carbonized, like VHS tapes that once held family memories meant to be passed down through generations. A Zaka volunteer from Rhode Island was deeply moved by the everyday items she discovered, emphasizing the human aspects of the tragedy. A list of essential items was taped to a family's safe room door, including a toothbrush, a sandwich, and a 'hug from Mom.' The Zaka volunteer who found the list remarked that there was blood all over that taped list.

A lengthy and meticulous forensic effort to identify the bodies and determine the cause of their deaths began, but it proved challenging from the very start. Uncertainty surrounded who was deceased and who had been captured. Some bodies were too severely burned for visual identification. Examiners could match dental and DNA records for Israeli nationals but identifying the remains of murdered foreign nationals posed an even greater challenge. Across the country, lines of Israelis snaked around designated clinics, volunteering DNA samples to aid in identifying the remains of their relatives.

Sometimes soldiers or Zaka operatives tried to puzzle together visuals that might tell a story of how somebody died. There were corpses of young women with their pants pulled down below their knees. Were they raped? An 85-year-old dead man reposed in a large armchair. Was his last moment of life one of passive resistance? 'I'm sitting here. I'll sit here in my chair, all calm, and let them shoot me.' That is how a fellow kibbutznik assessed it.[11]

Many were overwhelmed by the horrific visuals and the pungent smell of death. Many of the approximately 800 volunteers had received only basic training in crime scene analysis. Some were inexperienced and had slept little for several days due to the heavy demands of the situation's workload. They wrapped corpses in body bags, tagging them with the victim's sex and the address where they were found. Escorted by armed soldiers, they moved from house to house and recited a Jewish mourning prayer before loading the bags on a truck.[12] As for the Palestinians, polls taken soon after the attack revealed their continued support for Hamas. In the West Bank, Palestinians became more supportive of Hamas after the attack.[13] This heavy support would not last.

## The Palestinian Authority

Palestinians in both Gaza and the West Bank celebrated the violent outbreak. In the first week following the attack, leaders in the Palestinian Authority stated, 'No Palestinian will condemn the attack. [Hamas and Fatah] will work together in the struggle until [Israel] disappears.'[14] Fatah boasted that its cadre took part, 'We killed [them] . . . and stepped on their heads.'[15] Fatah delighted being allowed to 'Strike the sons of apes and pigs . . . slaughter everyone who is Israeli.'[16]

The PA's media outlet declared that fallen Hamas militants were 'a source of pride, heroism, and honor for the Palestinian people.'[17] Other tributes were more conventional, stating that 'the martyrs' blood will cause victory and holiness to bloom.'[18] Early in the war, in late October 2023, Fatah called for more aggressive and lethal attacks on the Israeli enemy, which it described as 'weaker than cobwebs.' This overconfidence soon dissipated after Israel unleashed its rockets on Gaza. By the time the IDF eliminated the architect of the attack, Yahya Sinwar, in October 2024, any illusions that the IDF resembled 'cobwebs' had long faded.

## A Nation Mourns

Among Israelis, the initial overwhelming trauma began to fade, yet survivors remained tormented. Many were unable to attend the funerals of their friends and family because so many were buried that same day. With hundreds of funerals, mourners had to manage their time effectively. One person lamented his anguish about choosing which of his friends to say goodbye to. Additionally, there was a pervasive fear of further attacks near Gaza. Services held within the rocket range of Gaza remained vulnerable to strikes. Nevertheless, people continued to attend and participate.

Tears streamed down the faces of grieving Israelis. An acclaimed historian, accompanied by an Israeli singer and songwriter, paid tribute to his most cherished creation – his young daughter, whom he lost at Supernova. He was joined by other parents burying their sons and daughters. In their younger days, when they attended funerals, they would share poems and songs about the elders they loved and lost. Today was different. Now, as one explained, 'I am participating in this memorial ceremony for the first time in my life as a mother who lost the most precious thing in life – my daughter.'[19]

A Holocaust survivor recounted the abduction and murder of her grandson. Another grandmother played a recording of her grandson's last known words, which were, 'I'm a little worried, there are terrorists in the kibbutz, but I'm taking care of myself, and you should take care of yourself, too.' He was then kidnapped and vanished into the vast emptiness below Gaza. For these women and others, this was, in their words, 'a second Holocaust.' Many parents experienced guilt and grief – grief over the loss of a child and guilt, however unfounded, for not being able to save them. On the day of the attack, the Israeli government formally declared war.

## Wanderers – A Nation Dispersed

Almost immediately, some 200,000 Israelis were relocated from 105 communities in the missile range of Gaza.[20] Overnight, evacuees found themselves in major cities, rural communities, and tourist destinations, such as Eilat. Some were moved to upscale five-star hotels, including the Orient Hotel in Jerusalem. Many evacuees arrived at their new locations with almost nothing. Teams of social workers and educators worked to normalize life for both adults and children. Israel's economy faced a setback, and tourism came to a halt. However, the decline in tourists opened up hotel rooms for evacuees, and 60,000 were relocated to Eilat, effectively doubling the city's population.[21]

Parents, teachers, and social workers have been working to alleviate the trauma that continues to affect children who could not comprehend what they witnessed or heard on October 7. These vulnerable children panicked quickly. A principal at an elementary school in Sderot recounted the story of students who lost emotional control at the sight of parachutes billowing in the sky. Another attack? The principal managed to calm the children by explaining that the parachutes carried international aid packages being dropped into Gaza. They were not terrorists, and the children were safe.

After a week marked by dizzying relocations and nationwide funerals, many Israelis could pause, reflect, and look toward the future. One of them was Techelet Grabowsky, who described herself as a 'peacenik-kibbutznik' and had dedicated decades to activism, building relationships with her Palestinian neighbors. She now asked, 'Who is the other party we want so desperately to make peace with? They do not want peace; they want to murder us all.'[22] She was not alone in her grim conclusion.

Grassroots solidarity united Israelis from various faiths and degrees of religious commitment. For decades, the ultra-Orthodox community had refrained from military service. However, this changed – if only temporarily – after the October killings when they offered their services for paramilitary activities. Others are increasingly feeling fatalistic about their future in Israel. While the vast majority of Jewish Israelis believe that defeating Hamas is crucial for the country's security, some see no hope at all. They have decided to leave Israel and start new lives in other countries.

## National Questions

### *Question One – How Could This Happen?*

Israel named its war against Hamas Operation Iron Swords, or Iron Swords War, declaring its mission to dismantle Hamas' military power and eliminate its governance. At the same time, a process of national self-reflection began. Israel's lack of preparedness and the failure of early warnings raised numerous questions about the capabilities of the Israeli Intelligence Community, particularly the Israel Military Intelligence Directorate (IMI) and the Israel Security Agency (ISA). Israel's intelligence, which had been monitoring Hamas, made both tactical and strategic analytical errors. It misinterpreted the overarching strategy of Hamas, which the Israeli intelligence and security establishment believed had become more developmental and assimilationist rather than militant. They thought Hamas would patiently and peacefully advocate for Palestinian statehood and international recognition while restraining the hardliners who were calling for continued acts of terror.

For two years leading up to the attack, Hamas maintained a low profile and seemed committed to economic development rather than warfare. However, evidence suggested that Hamas' peaceful rhetoric concealed its preparations for a significant invasion. Israeli officials acquired Hamas' plans for a large-scale attack two years before it was carried out. They had documents, emails, and transcripts of discussions; however, Israeli security leaders dismissed the plans as overly ambitious and beyond Hamas' military capabilities. These operational plans were codenamed Jericho Wall and outlined Hamas' strategies to assault barriers and fortifications, breach the fence, and subsequently flood into Israel.

Some Israelis in elite units believed that this plan warranted serious consideration. A colonel overseeing the Gaza region warned her superiors that this was not 'just a raid on a village.' She correctly pointed out that this situation was preparation for an invasion. She was not alone in her concerns. A soldier familiar with the Jericho Wall noted that Hamas was training and that its tactics suggested a large-scale invasion. Unfortunately, his superiors ignored his warnings. This failure to anticipate the invasion was one of many mistakes made by Israeli security authorities.

Some military teams performed well against superior forces with larger numbers, while others did not. Communication was lacking. The kibbutzniks' supply and variety of weapons were insufficient for the day's challenges, and they lacked the necessary resources. The IDF believed that the border fence was nearly impenetrable, which is why they redirected forces from the border.

The lack of preparedness forced residents to fend for themselves for extended periods during the attack. Additionally, some police officials accused the IDF and Shin Bet of withholding threat information available on October 6 that might have predicted the attack on Supernova. Citizens felt abandoned and demanded a thorough investigation. Israelis overwhelmingly vowed retribution against Hamas, prioritizing the return of the hostages.

Former Mossad director Yossi Cohen (Profile 4 – Chapter 6) admitted that Israel's national strategy was misguided because it assumed that continued economic development in Gaza would reduce the animosity of Gazans toward Israel and its people. He noted that Israel failed to monitor the flow of money sent to Hamas, much of which was used to build tunnels, conduct training, and smuggle weapons in preparation for the October attack.

## *Question Two – Why did They Do it?*

The second national question concerns the enemy's motives. Why did Hamas attack? Why did they murder infants and young children? There are several speculations. Usually, IDF personnel are primary targets, but all Israelis of all ages are considered fair game due to the near-universal conscription policy. Successive fatwas from prominent religious authorities emphasize the Islamic mandate to kill enemies of Islam, making Israelis and Jews prime targets. Today's infants are tomorrow's soldiers.[23]

Ali Barakeh, a senior Hamas official, claimed that it was retaliation against 'Israeli crimes against the Palestinian people in Jerusalem and the West Bank.' He added that the attack aimed to break the blockade of Gaza and force the release of jailed Palestinians. A final reason was to exact revenge for Israel's alleged raid on the Al-Aqsa Mosque, which some consider a dubious charge.[24] In its first public report, Hamas claimed Operation Al-Aqsa Flood was necessary to, in its words, 'end occupation of Palestinian territories.'[25]

Other observers of the Middle East claimed that Hamas needed to justify its existence and demonstrate its relevance to its patrons in the struggle against Israel. Jonathan Panikoff of the Atlantic Council stated, 'this is what they (Hamas) live for . . . what they're trained for, what they want to be doing.'[26] He speculated that unless Hamas acted decisively, it would lose support to other militant organizations, such as PIJ or Fatah. A survey conducted afterward by the Ramallah-based Arab World for Research and Development found that Hamas had reversed its decline in popularity. Hamas learned a valuable lesson after abducting IDF soldier Gilad Shalit in 2006. Five years later, Israel exchanged Shalit for more than 1,000 Palestinian and Arab-Israeli prisoners held by Israel. 'That wasn't lost on Hamas.'[27]

There were fewer clear explanations for the gratuitous torture, rapes, and the celebratory mood of the massacre. The Jewish world had not seen anything like this since the Nazis. This unbounded malice stunned the first responders, who found nails inserted in vaginas and infants and small children without their heads or limbs. People of all ages and entire families were shot, slashed, and burned alive. The gleeful promotion of crimes on social media is not standard in most modern wars.[28]

Hamas may have filmed the mutilation of girls and women and the gang rapes of living and dead men and women to terrorize the Israeli populace.[29] Many observers opined that this behavior reflects the values of Hamas. Israelis were subhuman, evil, and deserved to be treated this way. As for the PA and Hamas, both groups claim that the massacre, as rendered by the media, did not occur. By the accounts of both Palestinian groups, there were some murders, but Israelis committed the killings.[30] Qadura Fares, the director of the PLO Commission of Prisoners' Affairs, said that Israeli claims were lies and that Israelis murdered their civilians and blamed Palestinians.[31]

Four days after the terror attack, Hamas declared that it did not target children and that Western media had spread 'fabricated claims' and 'adopted the Zionist version.' This confused some observers because Hamas had distributed videos of the rape and murder on social media. Hamas later claimed that the civilian victims who were murdered were 'Zionist military and security establishment' and, therefore, "legitimate targets."'[32] The rhetoric continued to be confusing.

## Response From Around the World

Any compassion European diplomatic circles held for Israel quickly diminished after the IDF began targeting sites in Gaza. As Israel struck these locations, international sympathy started to shift toward the Palestinians and, at times, towards Hamas. Almost immediately, diplomats from around the globe called for a ceasefire and criticized Israel for its lack of compliance. Norway, Ireland, and Spain expressed their intentions to recognize a Palestinian state. Support among Americans also began to decline.

The ICC threatened to charge Israel with, in its own words, war crimes and crimes against humanity. The European Union condemned Israel's actions, as did Antonio Guterres, the Secretary-General of the UN General Assembly. Soon, politicians, diplomats, professors, and students began discussing Israel's alleged genocide. In response, Israel's Foreign Ministry argued that the European Union's comments represented a 'dangerous mix of ignorance, hostility, and the legitimization of terrorism.'[33] Israel also criticized the UN and human rights organizations for their inadequate response to the sexual crimes.[34] From Israel's perspective, their statements were insufficient and inappropriate, given the brutality inflicted on both adults and children, regardless of gender.

Anti-Israel activists quickly organized rallies against Israel. Street protests erupted immediately following the October 7 attack. Commentators noted that anti-Israel demonstrations began hours before Israel's military response. Protesters expressed support for Palestinians, particularly favoring Hamas. Progressive groups swiftly allied with anti-Zionists to show solidarity with Hamas' declared goal of eliminating Israel. Underlying animosity toward Israel surfaced globally. Many Muslims worldwide supported Hamas' actions, while others did not. The Global Imams Council (GIC), an international NGO of Muslim religious leaders based in Iraq, stated in English that it 'condemns in the strongest possible terms the barbaric actions of Hamas.'

## *Is Europe Burning?*

> *I want to shove a sharp knife in the throat of every Jew.*
>
> Belgian novelist Herman Brusselmans

Although they may seem like unlikely bedfellows, European leftist politicians and Islamist groups share a common hostility toward Israel. This animosity is partly rooted in long-standing strains of antisemitism and also in anti-colonialism, anti-imperialism, and anti-Americanism. They believe their goals align with the Palestinian cause. In Europe, a dynamic and growing Muslim population is capturing politicians' attention. In some parades, radical Muslim demonstrators have called for the establishment of a caliphate in Europe. This helps explain why anti-Israel rallies across Europe began even before the IDF's retaliatory operations. Protests erupted in several European countries, particularly Germany, Britain, and France, which host the largest Muslim populations on the continent.

European social media displayed support for Hamas and hostility toward Israel. Many posts showed solidarity with Hamas by tweeting, 'Allahu Akbar,' 'Long live Palestine,' and 'Resistance is yours.' There was also snarky schadenfreude at the suffering and deaths of Israeli victims. On the day of the attacks, some Europeans reacted to the graphic images of Israelis being killed by Hamas. 'This is better than Hollywood!' In response to women and girls being raped, some tweeted, 'They had a good time with her, it seems like,'[35] and 'They are just taking her to a party . . . she will be the guest of honor . . . ' (IND-YT2) or 'That's the price paid for being cute.' Another theme was revenge, such as 'Eye for an eye, baby for a baby' or 'Feel the pain of how Israeli massacred Palestinian kids for 70 years.'[36]

Across Europe, marchers called for an immediate, unilateral ceasefire from Israel. Berlin became one of the primary sites for these protests. Crowds of demonstrators holding various placards demanded the complete isolation of Israel and a boycott of German companies that engage with it. One sign read, 'Boycott Siemens, Free Palestine.' Many Germans were disturbed to see Berliners of Middle Eastern descent celebrating the October 7 attack by handing out candies and singing in apparent jubilation over the deaths of so many Israelis. A year later, Berliners chanted 'Allahu Akbar' when Iran launched 180 ballistic missiles toward Tel Aviv. Concerns about rising tensions and awareness of its Nazi past prompted Germany to disperse some of the more raucous anti-Israel marches forcefully. In Austria, vandals defaced a Jewish cemetery with swastikas.

The demonstrations posed a dilemma for Germans attempting to balance the rights of political expression with the need to protect Jewish-owned businesses, including the few remaining kosher restaurants and the Jewish community itself. However, some politicians and law enforcement officials became increasingly concerned about rising antisemitism. Austria, Hungary, and Switzerland banned these protests, but civil libertarians contested the censorship in court.

Like other European countries, Germany experienced a shift in diplomatic rhetoric. Chancellor Scholz (Profile 4 – Chapter 6) pledged unconditional solidarity with Israel shortly after October 7, stating, 'In difficult times, Germany has only one place, and that is by Israel's side.'[37] As the conflict persisted and German streets filled with angry anti-Israel protesters, the situation became increasingly complex. The display of solidarity diminished. Some drew comparisons to the Islamist attack against the United States on September 11, 2001, when Germans rallied behind Americans against the Taliban. However, they eventually grew weary of their military commitment in Afghanistan and withdrew.

Ten months later, the German foreign minister seemed to blame Israel for Hamas' point-blank murder of hostages.[38] Israel twice reprimanded Germany's Ambassador to Jerusalem for anti-Israel activity.[39] Some saw ominous signals in the widespread and elite condemnation of Israel that harkened to a darker past. Opined one observer, 'There is a new German reality for Jews, in which Holocaust memorials are smeared with the words "Jews commit genocide".'[40]

In Britain, the ever-increasing Muslim population has made anti-Israel demonstrations a staple of social protest. However, the rallies in October 2023 took on a more ominous tone, feeling increasingly hostile and threatening. British television host Rachel Riley tweeted video footage of jubilant, Middle Eastern-looking individuals celebrating, embracing one another, and waving the Palestinian flag in London. On October 7, Riley wrote, 'I just passed two cars in West London, driving with Palestinian flags flying from each window, their occupants bouncing up and down in their cars, seemingly celebrating as if they were at a party. Make no mistake, this is a dangerous and terrifying situation.'[41] This time of terror continued, and nearly one year later, a man was arrested in London for screaming, 'I love October 7.' This sentiment was not unique to him.

To protect London's Jewish community, the Mayor of London, Sadiq Khan (Profile 5 – Chapter 6), established a new bus route connecting the two largest Jewish centers, thereby enhancing security for Jews who wear identifiable religious attire. Nevertheless, protests continued regularly. On the first anniversary of the Hamas attack, a woman voiced the sentiments of many when she turned to a video camera, smiled, and shouted, 'We love Hamas.' The video showed others looking at her and chuckling in solidarity. In London, anti-Israel militants from Palestine Action seized a bust of what they believed was Israel's first Prime Minister and smashed it to pieces. They had the wrong man; it was a statue of another popular figure in chemistry, a professor.[42]

France is also home to millions of Muslims and a vibrant radical intelligentsia, often referred to as bourgeois bohemians or bobos. These groups collaborate effectively on Middle Eastern issues. Thousands of individuals regularly wave Palestinian flags and chant, 'Gaza, Paris stands with you,' along with variations of 'From the river to the sea, Palestine will be free.' This reflects an aspiration for Israel to be eliminated and replaced with Palestine. Attacks are not limited to Israelis and their state's symbols. Jewish individuals and businesses, including kosher restaurants, have been marked with slogans like 'Free Palestine.' French Interior Minister Gérald Darmanin has tightened security for identifiable Jewish businesses throughout.[43]

Though continental sentiment seemed to oppose Israel, some Europeans marched against antisemitism. Prime Minister Elisabeth Borne, representatives from various leftist parties, conservatives, centrists from President Emmanuel Macron's party, and even far-right leader Marine Le Pen demonstrated in solidarity with the Jewish community. Nonetheless, many Jews who are anxious about France's future are leaving.[44] The 2023 and 2024 outbursts of anti-Israel and anti-Jewish fury represent the latest incidents across the continent.[45]

## *The United States*

In the United States, self-styled liberal and Muslim civic organizations swiftly and strongly embraced the Palestinian cause. The Party for Socialism and Liberation, the World Workers Party, chapters of the Democratic Socialists for America (DSA), and independent chapters of Black Lives Matter (BLM) were very vocal in their condemnation of Israeli retaliation. Several organizations, such as the DSA, approved the Hamas attacks on Israeli civilians, stating, 'It is not terrorism or antisemitism to fight against this injustice.'[46] The DSA post read, 'Today's events are a direct result of Israel's apartheid regime – a regime that receives billions in funding from the United States,' and added that 'we unequivocally condemn the killing of all civilians,' but claimed the attack was 'not unprovoked.'[47]

BLM made a symbolic reference to the October slaughter. On October 10, the Philadelphia branch displayed an image of a paraglider, directly referencing an airborne element of the attack. Next to the image was the message, 'I stand with Palestine.'[48]

Mosques were filled with anti-Israel sentiment. Although Hamas has been designated as an international terrorist group, some Islamic and hard-left leaders openly support it and its leaders. At a mosque in Bay Ridge, Brooklyn, a speaker at Al-Awda prayed for the souls of the 'honorable and beloved martyrs and freedom fighters, Ismail Haniyeh, Fuad Shukr, rest in peace.'[49] Months after the October attack, speakers at Iran's International Al-Quds Day rally held in Houston, Texas, praised the October 7 attack in front of the Israeli consulate.[50]

Many of these rallies were also anti-American. In September 2024, in Philadelphia, protesters waved Hamas and PFLP flags and carried a banner proclaiming, 'Amerika is the head of the snake.' Some chanted, 'Yahya Sinwar, you make us proud!' and 'Resistance is justified when people are occupied.' The protest's master of ceremonies led the crowd in a chant, 'U.S. imperialist number one terrorist!'[51] Participants in the September 2, 2024, protest chanted 'Flood New York City for Gaza' and rallied in support of Hamas. Rioters defaced statues of President Andrew Jackson and Benjamin Franklin in Washington DC, with the graffiti 'Free Palestine.'[52]

Sometimes, ignorance combines with passion to become pathetically comical. Driven by righteous rage, a woman in New Jersey shouted, 'Free Palestine, this is genocide,' as she yanked Greek flags from the ground in a restaurant, mistaking them for Israeli flags. Some second-wave feminists were disheartened by the lack of empathy shown by leaders in the global women's rights community. Some feminists were alarmingly slow to acknowledge the widespread sexual assaults, torture, and murders of women that day. In November 2023, the United Nations Special Rapporteur on Violence Against Women and Girls, Reem Alsalem (Profile 6, Chapter 6), stated that the evidence 'was 'not solid' enough to criticize Hamas formally.' The UN's Women's Rights Agency took 55 days before condemning Hamas' attack.

## *Universities*

American university campuses were filled with protests. Anti-Israel encampments emerged on campuses across the United States and spread globally. Progressives and Muslims argued that Israel is a colonialist implant and, therefore, has no right to exist. Palestinian leaders appreciated the support from across the Atlantic. Fatah's youth movement, Shabiba, expressed gratitude to students in the United States, particularly at Columbia University. A German exchange student at Georgetown's Walsh School of Foreign Service was taken aback by students chanting, 'We will finish what Hitler started,' and 'Every day is October 7.'

Elite, leafy, liberal universities buzzed with anti-Israel agitation. Students from Harvard, Yale, Columbia, Princeton, Stanford, Pennsylvania, and other prestigious institutions carried placards proclaiming, 'From the river to the sea, Palestine will soon be free,' while expressing their disdain for those living in the 'settler-colonial apartheid state' of Israel. The extensive pro-Hamas protests at Columbia University were not entirely unexpected, as it has long served as a hotbed for anti-Israel activism. At Columbia, Students for Justice in Palestine declared their 'full solidarity' with the 'Palestinian counter-offensive against their settler-colonial oppressor.'

However, the large number of campuses and the intense passion of the students left many feeling shocked. Harvard seized international headlines when 34 student groups blamed Israel entirely for Hamas' attacks. This prompted former Harvard president Larry Summers (Profile 7 – Chapter 6) to lament, 'I am sickened. I cannot fathom the administration's failure to disassociate the university and condemn this statement.'[53] Protest groups assigned tasks to student leaders, many of whom concealed their identities. Numerous students declined to speak with journalists or peers who weren't participating. Those who did respond often delivered scripted statements. Some protesters took on security roles, forcibly removing counter-protesters and security personnel. Other students indiscriminately tore down images of detainees, including some Americans. At the University of Southern California, videos showed students laughing as they ripped posters of hostages from lampposts and tossed them into trash cans.

Pro-Hamas marchers physically confronted Jewish students on various campuses. Some vandalized Jewish student centers, such as Hillel, and bullied students. Jewish students at Cooper Union, a private college in New York City, were confined to a library while pro-Palestine and pro-Hamas protesters pounded on the doors, screamed, and tried to gain entry. Like their southern counterparts, Canadian protesters openly supported Hamas, with some explicitly calling for the murder of Israelis.[54]

Judging by the placards toted by North American protesters, the rallies were often less pro-Palestinian than fiery anti-Israel. Messages on the posters read, 'Israel is a settler colonial occupying state,' 'Gas the Jews,' 'Rape is resistance,' and 'Burn down Tel Aviv, Death to Zionism' are some of the messages. Columbia protestors promised '10,000 more October 7s.'[55]

Many professors felt powerless to speak out. They recognized the underlying animosity towards Israel that sometimes surfaced during protests. However, they were still surprised by what they witnessed. Alumni, too, were astonished by the transformation of their alma maters into something unrecognizable. Worldwide, Israeli academics noted a chilly reception at conferences in 2024. Some described the unsettling feeling as a covert boycott, with their submitted papers rejected and their exclusion from conference venues.

In Gaza, Hamas captors of Israeli and American hostages reveled in the camaraderie they observed on American campuses. Rescued hostage Shlomi Ziv recounted how his Hamas guards taunted him with articles and photographs. The kidnappers boasted that Hamas has infiltrated universities across America and has won the hearts and minds of American youth. They laughed that an entire generation of American students supports the October 7 attack.[56]

## *International Implications*

Iranian universities organized solidarity protests praising the Hamas encampments, complete with chants of 'Death to America!' 'Death to Israel!' and 'Death to the Jewish oppressors!' An Iranian university offered free tuition for students protesting in support of Islamic terrorism. Kayhan, a prominent Iranian regime newspaper, wrote that 'every student from Harvard, MIT, Boston, Columbia, Emerson, Texas, and so forth has become an Iranian student' and celebrated, 'This is what we call exporting the Islamic Revolution!'[57]

Students and non-students answered the call. In May 2025, a far-left anti-Israel activist went to the Jewish Museum in Washington DC, with the intent to kill Zionists. He succeeded. He randomly selected two young Israelis, shot them, surrendered, and bragged about his actions. An eyewitness and Columbia graduate recalled, 'I saw him screaming and then being handcuffed. But what I saw in his eyes, I mean, I went to Columbia for grad school, and I saw the same thing in his eyes as I saw in the eyes of all the protesters at Columbia. Nothing different between him and them.'[58]

Off campus in the West, wearing a Star of David could lead to bullying or physical violence.[59] Amy Schumer and actress Debra Messing wrote, 'We are scared to leave our homes. We feel compelled to hire armed security. We are frightened to post for fear of receiving more suffocating digital hate.'[60] In Europe, it has become more dangerous for Jews to walk the streets in religious clothing than at any time since the fall of the Nazis.[61] One year after the attack, protests at universities continued and spread throughout the West. At Poland's oldest university, located in Krakow near Auschwitz, someone posted a sign proclaiming, 'Jews to the Gas Chambers.' In stunned disbelief, Steven Spielberg remarked, 'I never imagined I would witness such unspeakable barbarity against Jews in my lifetime.'[62] Their world had changed, and conditions were worsening.

## Counterattack on Campus

After 34 Harvard student groups fully blamed Israel for Hamas' attacks, the university's former president, Larry Summers, voiced his disappointment. Additionally, students, alumni, donors, and politicians opposed pro-Hamas activism, urging administrators to protect students and disperse crowds that prevented others from moving freely on campus. Videos showing kufiyah-draped students intimidating and harassing their peers made headlines. Observers highlighted the terrorism-endorsing rhetoric from Students for Justice in Palestine, which may have violated campus policies against threats. It became increasingly difficult for university administrators to dismiss the widespread wave of vitriol or the takeover of their campus by radicals and uninvited guests. Politicians and donors began demanding that action be taken.

Some states actively opposed disorderly conduct, prompting actions from certain officials. In coordination with the chancellor of the state's university system, Florida Governor Ron DeSantis ordered the arrest of disruptive and threatening students, mainly targeting student occupations. Additionally, students gathered to support Israel and their right to move freely across campus without harassment. Chris Summerlin (Profile 8 – Chapter 6), the dean of students at the University of Florida in Gainesville, issued multi-year suspensions to several students to clearly show that the university would not tolerate threatening behavior.

Another example is the counter-protest organized by Günther Jikeli, a German professor and activist against antisemitism. Demonstrators at Indiana University displayed signs like 'Hamas propaganda has no place at Indiana University' and 'Disarm Hamas,' which resonated across the campus, while some students pursued legal action. Young America's Foundation filed a lawsuit against UCLA for blocking a talk by Islam critic Robert Spencer titled 'Everything You Know About Palestine Is Wrong.' UCLA, however, cited security concerns as the reason for limiting the number of attendees. Additionally, Jewish students sued the university for allegedly creating a hostile environment and failing to protect them from harassment and physical harm. The most dramatic response to the anti-Israel rallies on campus came from congressional hearings, where three college presidents testified and clashed with Republican lawmakers. Some observers noted that the presidents' responses to challenging questions were frequently stiff, incomplete, and at times misleading. Two congressmen who were Harvard alumni criticized the performance of their alma mater's president.

Western governments have also intensified their investigations and responses to the college chaos. One year after the attack and numerous college protests, the US and Canadian governments disclosed that the Samidoun Palestinian Prisoner Solidarity Network, or Samidoun, a primary international organizer of anti-Israel rallies, operated as a front organization for the Popular Front for the Liberation of Palestine. They designated Samidoun as a terrorist entity and initiated legal actions against it. This follows similar measures taken by Germany and Israel.

High-profile celebrities have become outspoken. British guitar icon Eric Clapton stated, 'Israel is running the world, Israel is running the show.' Former Pink Floyd rocker Roger Waters (Profile 9 – Chapter 6), a passionate supporter of Boycott, Divest, and Sanctions, vowed to 'fight back' to defend his 'freedom of speech.' While many other left-leaning figures rallied against Israel, some Hollywood stars, including Dr Phil, Bono and U2, Jon Voight, and Sarah Silverman, voiced their support for the Jewish state.

## Women and October 7

Sheryl Sandberg, a former Meta executive and advocate for women's causes, felt betrayed by her feminist allies due to what she perceived as unwarranted skepticism toward numerous Israeli women's claims of being molested and raped on October 7, 2023. She expressed confusion about why women's organizations worldwide have been vocal and persistent in condemning rape as a weapon of war in other conflicts yet have remained silent in response to the mass rape and assault of Israelis women.[63]

Ms Sandberg was not the only women's rights activist puzzled by the slow response from progressive women. Debra Messing, who starred in the TV show *Will and Grace*, strongly condemned the collective silence of American feminists on this issue. She produced a documentary, 'October 8th: The Fight for the Soul of America,' with documentarian Wendy Sachs, which examined the response to the attack within left-leaning communities in the West.

Some French women have accused mainstream feminist organizations in France of failing to condemn the October attack in a meaningful way. Israeli Knesset member Sharren Haskel highlighted the hypocrisy of British feminist groups, asking, 'Where were the feminist organizations in the UK?' Ambassador Deborah Lipstadt, the US Special Envoy to Monitor and Combat Antisemitism, criticized the reluctance of international women's organizations to speak out against the attacks, describing the delay as 'hypocrisy.'[64]

## Searching for Relief

Back in Israel, a nation mourned and struggled. Shortly after the attack, Israel mobilized healthcare professionals and deployed them to sites near Gaza. Kibbutzniks in Be'eri were severely affected, losing over 130 members. Within a day, the survivors were evacuated to a hotel by the Dead Sea for shelter and treatment of their distress. Therapists assisted them in their mourning and conducted individual and group therapy sessions. However, the intense suffering extended well beyond the local kibbutzim.

Many survivors were forced to relocate because their kibbutzim were reduced to ashes. One explained, '[they] have no home to return to. Everything is destroyed, and they have to live with their relatives. Many who have homes feel guilty that their homes were not burned like their neighbors.' This has created a lasting national trauma that persists today.

Nationwide preliminary surveys have revealed increased levels of post-traumatic stress disorder (PTSD), depression, and anxiety. As of mid-2025, approximately three million Israeli adults may be experiencing PTSD or related anxiety disorders. There has been a significant rise in alcohol consumption in a country that usually has low levels of substance abuse, alongside disrupted sleep patterns and increasing emotional distress. Besides the victims and their families, many mental health care providers have also faced emotional pain. Few anticipated the magnitude of the crime or the degree of sadism and depravity the victims endured. This situation has given rise to a new therapeutic landscape.

If their days are filled with anguish, sleep often provides little relief, as victims relive the day's terror in their dreams. Psychologists have studied these dreams as a window into suffering. Common themes in these dreams include helplessness, guilt, rejection, and loss. A year after the attack, nearly 500 volunteer mental health professionals supported the families of those who were killed, injured, or taken hostage.

## Summary

The October murders near Israel's borders shocked the world. They represented one of the most significant security failures in recent times. There is a consensus that Israeli intelligence had enough information about potential attacks to suggest that the

Jericho Wall, a collection of intelligence reports pointing to a rocket attack, highlights security cameras, machine gun positions, and infiltration routes via paragliders and motorcycles. Over a year after hostilities began, the violence persisted.

Israel responded with overwhelming force, launching an unprecedented barrage of munitions at multiple targets. This triggered widespread anti-Israel activism among individuals and groups. Many universities erupted in protests against Israel, and Jewish students expressed concerns about what they saw as a hostile environment on campus. They also voiced disappointment at the indifferent response to aggressive actions. One pro-Palestinian protester summed up a common sentiment when he shouted, 'I am Hamas!' Activists hostile to Israel vandalized businesses owned by Jews or those serving Jewish clients. Someone spray-painted a red triangle on a Jewish-owned bakery in Sydney, Australia, and slipped a note under the door that read 'Be careful.' The red triangle is often used to mark Jewish property.[65]

**Profile 1 – Gilad Erdan: Israeli Voice at the United Nations**
**Names:** Gilad Erdan
**Nationality:** Israeli
**Profession:** Israeli diplomat, Israeli Ambassador to the United Nations, politician
**Connection to October 7, 2023:** This feisty diplomat, a former Knesset member and politician, served as the nation's voice at the UN during a time of intense international scrutiny. He echoed the sentiments of many Israelis when he bellowed in the halls, 'The UN cares nothing for Israeli blood. It is a collaborator with the Nazis of our day. Working to ensure Hamas' survival and even reward them for murder and rape. I have no words.'[66] His works resonated in Israel and among Jews globally.

He was shocked by the outburst of pro-Hamas sentiment on campuses, particularly in the United States. He explained, 'We always knew that Hamas hides in schools. We just didn't realize that it's not only schools in Gaza. It's also Harvard, Columbia, and many elite universities.'[67] He alarmed some Americans when he compared the rise of antisemitism in America's prestigious universities to the ascent of National Socialism among German youth. In August 2024, veteran diplomat Danny Danon succeeded Erdan as UN Ambassador.
**Current Status:** As he stepped down from his position in New York, Prime Minister Netanyahu praised him, saying, 'Ambassador Erdan represented Israel with respect, determination, and strength, and I thank him for that.'[68] His popularity and prestige earned him the position of global president of Magen David Adom.[69]

**Profile 2 – Noa Argamani: 'A part of me remains in Gaza'**
**Names:** Noa Argamani
**Nationality:** Israeli
**Profession:** Unknown
**Connection to October 7, 2023:** Noa Argamani, whom Hamas kidnapped, was rescued by the IDF after eight months of captivity.[70] Since then, Argamani has

become one of the most recognizable faces of those abducted. Hamas captured her and carried her on the back of a motorcycle on October 7, and this was widely reported in the news media.[71] She and other captives had been moved between apartments, not transported through tunnels. She was rarely allowed to leave the apartment or given any relief from the stale air. When she did go outside, she was dressed as an Arab woman.

Tormented by constant fear, she believed she would die four times. The first instance was when Argamani was kidnapped; the second was when she arrived in Gaza and witnessed a lynching; the third occurred during a missile launch by the Israel Air Force; and the fourth took place during the operation that led to her rescue. She added, 'I thought that was it – but I stayed alive.'[72]

Her rescue was cinematic. A helmet camera captured the footage, and the dialogue during the rescue was recorded. Soldiers from the elite Yamam counter-terrorism unit stormed an apartment where the 26-year-old hostage was held. On January 22, 2024, she heard the most welcome words of her life: 'It's the IDF, and we've come to rescue you.' She and three fellow captives were now free, soon to be reunited with their families and countrymen. She was rescued on her father's birthday. Her mother was dying of brain cancer, but she was able to see her daughter.

Some portray her as an impostor and a participant in a Mossad propaganda campaign. Israeli Arab actress Lama Tatour teased, 'This is what a girl that's been in captivity for nine months looks like? Look at her eyebrows, they look better than mine!'[73] Others criticized her for supporting President Donald Trump. She stood beside him in deep gratitude for his support of Israel during his inaugural parade in 2025.[74]

**Profile 3 – Yossi Cohen: 'Straight out of John Le Carre and Ian Fleming'**
**Names:** Yossi Cohen, nicknamed 'The Model'
**Nationality:** Israeli
**Profession:** IDF Chief of Staff and Head of Mossad
**Connection to October 7, 2023:** Nicknamed 'The Model' for his stylish clothes and sharply coiffed hairstyle, General Yossi Cohen stands at the center of Israel's military and intelligence establishment. He served as the chief of the Mossad for five years and indirectly took credit for approving and overseeing operations that killed and injured many Hizballah operatives. He also confidently claimed credit for the explosions at Iran's Natanz nuclear facility in 2020 and another incident in 2021. Furthermore, he is embroiled in a controversy concerning Qatari funding. Additionally, he played a crucial role in negotiating the release of hostages held by Hamas during the ongoing war. The spy-diplomat is also a prominent businessman and has served as the director of Doral Renewables, an Israeli renewable energy company developer.[75]

Some of his critics accuse him of being undiplomatic. According to the British Guardian magazine, the former Mossad chief allegedly engaged in 'threats and intimidation' against the ICC's chief prosecutor, Fatou Bensouda, concerning the

opening of a war crimes investigation against Israel. If he threatened and tried to intimidate her, he was unsuccessful.[76]
**Current Status:** The Model is likely engaged in high-level diplomatic activity.

**Profile 4 – Chapter Six – Chancellor Scholz: Hamas and Nazis**
**Names:** Olaf Scholz
**Nationality:** German
**Profession:** Former chancellor of Germany
**Connection to October 7, 2023:** Former chancellor Scholz faced a dilemma. As the leader of one of the most significant countries in Europe, which has large Muslim and left-leaning domestic constituencies, he found himself in a challenging position when the October 2023 war broke out. As Chancellor of Germany, he was also sensitive to the Nazi legacy and the systemic murder of European Jews. Scholz quickly expressed his solidarity with Israel following the attack. 'Our solidarity with Israel must be clear.' Shortly after Israel responded, Scholz emphasized the need for Israeli restraint.[77]

Germany banned Hamas shortly after the attack. Interior Minister Nancy Faeser promised to stop the 'spread of anti-Israel and anti-Jewish propaganda under the guise of a "solidarity organization" for prisoners.' Nevertheless, German leaders urged Israel to avoid heavy responses to the killings. Scholz insisted that humanitarian aid should be directed into Gaza, despite Israeli claims that much of it is hijacked by Hamas. Israel also provided evidence that aid groups have not halted the transport of weapons into Gaza.[78]

Scholz called for a deal to free hostages held in war-ravaged Gaza, along with a 'longer-lasting ceasefire,' as the warring parties geared up for more talks. 'We need a hostage deal with a longer-lasting ceasefire.'[79] Perhaps his most controversial and confusing comment involved the ICJ warrant for PM Netanyahu's arrest as a war criminal. When asked if Netanyahu would be arrested if he visited Germany, a spokesman for the German government responded with the anodyne, 'We abide by the law at the national, European, and international level. And that is why we are now examining exactly what this means for us regarding its international application.'[80] Many observers did not understand what this meant. However, the leader of Israel was clear about his position. He told Scholz directly, 'Hamas are the new Nazis.'[81]
**Current Status:** Retired.

**Profile 5 – Sadiq Khan: The Mayor's Balancing Act**
**Names:** Sadiq Khan
**Nationality:** British
**Profession:** Mayor of London
**Connection to October 7, 2023:** He is the first Muslim mayor of London. Observers see him as a virtuoso at balancing the often-opposing demands of his many constituents. He is undoubtedly challenged by the Hamas-Israel conflict.

When asked to comment on the war, Khan responded, 'It's an issue of humanity, and I think you've got to show equivalence. I condemn unequivocally the actions of Hamas on October 7 . . . At the same time, I condemn unequivocally the actions of the IDF and [Benjamin] Netanyahu.'[82] Regarding the attacks on Jews, Jewish property, and Jewish houses of worship, the mayor condemns them, as well as the violence occurring during marches on the streets of London. He adds, however, that there is 'no need' for the pro-Palestine marches in London to continue if the ceasefire between Israel and Hamas proves permanent.[83]

His critics accused him, in some respects, of blaming the victims of these attacks. His political opponents describe his response as weak, subtly aligning with Hamas. Parliamentarian Sir Jacob Rees-Mogg said: 'Israel must surely have the right to self-defense. That doesn't make everything Israel does right. However, condemning them unequivocally and equating their actions with the terrorist acts of Hamas is undoubtedly wrong.'[84] Mr Khan has gone beyond Prime Minister Starmer's criticisms of Israel.[85] Other Britons agree with this sentiment, but many disagree and see Israel as the victim and not the aggressor.

**Current Status:** In April 2025, he spoke to fellow Muslims and Londoners at the Muslim Eid festival, thanking them for their protests against the IDF attacks. His critics pointed out that he did not mention the Israeli hostages still incarcerated in Gaza or the murders committed by Hamas.

**Profile 6 – Reem Alsalem**

**Names:** Reem Alsalem

**Nationality:** Jordanian, born in Egypt

**Profession:** United Nations Special Rapporteur on Violence Against Women and Girls

**Connection to October 7, 2023:** Fluent in five languages, Reem Alsalem, a Jordanian national, was born in 1976 in Cairo. She is a dedicated human rights activist and a graduate of both the American University in Cairo and Oxford University, where she earned a master's degree in human rights law. She has worked with the UN for over 17 years as a consultant on gender and human rights.[86]

This lawyer has been busy since October 7, 2023, speaking out about the human rights implications of the war. For years, she has advocated for Palestinian women and girls. The special rapporteur has claimed that they have faced persecution for years. Israel, according to her, has inflicted 'reproductive violence' on Palestinian women, newborns, babies, infants, and children. She accused Israel of 'forced starvation, ethnic cleansing, torture, executions, arbitrary detention, indiscriminate bombardment, and forced displacement; they have also been subjected to reproductive and obstetric violence, sexual violence, and targeted as mothers. Furthermore, they have been targeted in a very gendered manner because they are women.'[87]

However, her critics highlight her relative silence on the violence perpetrated by Hamas against Israeli women and girls. She seemed to pay little attention to the rape, torture, degradation, and murder of these victims. Six weeks after the Hamas attack, she addressed the need to verify and responsibly investigate Israeli claims. Her muted condemnation of the conflict-related sexual violence against Israeli women appeared only at the end of a lengthy statement that primarily discussed the 'assault on Palestinian women's dignity.' The US Ambassador to the UN expressed disappointment that she wielded so little influence regarding Hamas' crimes against Israeli women and children. Where is the universal condemnation? And where is the outrage?[88]

**Current Status:** Employed by the United Nations.

**Profile 7 – Larry Summers and Claudine Gay: Presidents of Harvard**

**Names:** Lawrence Summers and Claudine Gay

**Nationality:** Both American

**Profession:** Scholars and former presidents of Harvard University

**Connection to October 7, 2023:** Lawrence Summers and Claudine Gay were unconventional choices for the presidency of America's most prestigious university, Harvard. Summers was Jewish, while Gay was a Black woman. Both faced challenges they likely did not foresee. Despite his impressive credentials, the wunderkind economist Summers was driven from his presidency after losing the faculty's confidence. As president, he faced criticism for his remarks on components of Affirmative Action and for defending Israel. An earlier president of Harvard claimed Summers was fired for being unable to lead, brought low by personal flaws and style.[89]

Claudine Gay captured national attention during her performance when Republican lawmakers grilled her at the House Committee on Education and the Workforce hearing on 'Holding Campus Leaders Accountable and Confronting Antisemitism.' By most accounts, Claudine Gay did not perform well and seemed evasive. It did not help her that for years, Harvard has required all students to complete a mandatory diversity training session that describes terms like 'fatphobia' as forms of 'violence,' which could result in a student being suspended or expelled. Now it was Gay who was defenestrated. She was not let go because of her nonchalance or antisemitism on campus, but because of her multiple cases of plagiarism.

**Current Status:** Both are still affiliated with Harvard University, although they are no longer in senior leadership roles.

**Profile 8 – Chris Summerlin**

**Names:** Chris Summerlin

**Nationality:** American

**Profession:** Educator and administrator in higher education. Dean of Students at the University of Florida.

**Connection to October 7, 2023:** Some high-level university administrators adopted a lenient approach towards student demonstrators, while others were less accommodating. At the University of Florida, Chris Summerlin overruled administrators who recommended that students arrested for misconduct should be counseled rather than suspended or expelled. Summerlin imposed multi-year suspensions on students arrested for on-campus unlawful conduct.[90] One of the protesters spat on the police officers and was arrested for battery.

Some of the arrested students are appealing to have their punishments overturned. They could have had the charges dropped from their records if they had pleaded guilty, but they refused to do so. One student said, 'We're standing in solidarity with each other and collectively demanding that the state drop the charges against us.'[91] Many faculty members stand behind the arrested individuals, with nearly 100 signing a petition asking Summerlin to reduce the charges. However, other faculty members support Summerlin and have grown weary of the protests. Steve Orlando, a spokesman for the university, stated, 'The University of Florida is not a daycare, and we do not treat protesters like children – they knew the rules, they broke the rules, and they will face the consequences.'[92]

**Current Status:** Summerlin is still employed by the university.

**Profile 9 – Roger Waters: 'Totally out of Proportion'**

**Names:** Roger Waters

**Nationality:** British

**Profession:** Rock star

**Connection to October 7, 2023:** Roger Waters, co-founder of Pink Floyd in 1965, has been advocating for BDS against Israel for many years. He urges fellow celebrities to boycott performing in Israel. He explained, 'To peacefully protest against Israel's racist domestic and foreign policies is not antisemitic.'[93] Waters has an intense animosity towards Israel. Regarding the Hamas attack on October 7, Waters alleged that Israel fabricated reports of rape and the murder of infants. He asserts that there is no evidence of sexual violence by Hamas against women.[94] When Piers Morgan confronted him with evidence, Waters responded, 'Piers, you may or may not be making this up.'[95] He insisted that the Hamas massacre was thrown out of all proportion.'[96] 'Of course I don't condone that, but the thing was totally thrown out of all proportion by the Israelis making up stories about beheading babies.'[97]

Other British rock stars do not agree with Waters, and some have expressed sympathy for the Israelis. When U2's Bono heard about the October 7 killings, he changed the lyrics of his 'Pride (In the Name of Love).' On October 7, 2023, during a performance in Las Vegas, Bono mentioned the Supernova killings in that night's rendition. He sang, 'Early morning, Oct. 7/Sun is rising in the desert sky/ Stars of David, they took your life/They could not take your pride.'[98]

**Current Status:** Waters stands by his version of October 7. He added: 'I have not had a single anti-Semitic thought in my entire life,' and insisted his criticism was of the Israeli government's actions.[99]

## Chapter 7

# Foreign Powers and the Middle East

The war in Gaza involves numerous international players. Both Israel and Hamas rely on foreign nations for resources, arms, and legal support. Major powers display varying and shifting levels of interest in the conflict, and several states have adjusted their diplomatic priorities. For instance, the Soviet Union was a key player in the Middle East for decades; however, Russia's interest in the region has declined in the 21st century. Saudi Arabia, once a significant supporter of various Palestinian terrorist groups, now leans toward the West and has nearly recognized Israel. Turkey, which was secular and aligned with the West for much of the 20th century, has become a vocal critic of Israel and a proponent of Palestinian efforts to achieve statehood.

Many countries have provided financial, developmental, and military aid to Hamas. Monitoring the flow of weapons into Gaza can often be challenging. Hamas' arsenal includes AK-47 assault rifles from China and Russia, as well as rocket-propelled grenades manufactured in North Korea and Bulgaria. Iran trains engineers in Gaza on design and production methods. Numerous Islamic nations, both Shia and Sunni, view the Palestinian issue as a point of ideological and political convergence. Support for the Palestinian cause unites secular, left-leaning parties and governments with Islamic states and organizations.

## The Greater Middle East

### *Qatar*

Qatar is an oil-rich mini-state that wields global influence through propaganda efforts backed by generous funding to both Muslim and Western nations. It has invested heavily in Western universities and sympathetic charities. On the surface, Qatar appears to be a modern, Westernized political player that mediates conflicts and provides humanitarian aid. Qatari leaders have hosted Arab-Israeli talks, despite the country's lack of diplomatic relations with Israel. Some early efforts trace back to 1996, when then-Israeli Prime Minister Shimon Peres visited the country. However, Qatar also supports terrorism and Islamism worldwide. Former

Knesset member Dr Einat Wilf (Profile 1 – Chapter 7) stated, 'Qatar is not our friend; Qatar and Hamas are the same.'

The Islamist terrorist organizations that Qatar supports include the Muslim Brotherhood, Al-Qaeda, the Taliban, Hizbullah, the Al-Nusrah Front/Hayat Tahrir Al-Sham, ISIS, Hamas, the Shia Iranian proxies in Yemen, and the Houthis. In 2017, Saudi Arabia, the United Arab Emirates (UAE), Bahrain, and Egypt declared a boycott of Qatar because of its support for terrorist groups.

Qatar's relationship with Hamas is mercurial. Until November 2024, Qatar was a vocal and generous supporter of Hamas.[1] For years, it funded Hamas' fleet of military ambulances, combat motorcycles, and other combat and equipment munitions. It financed the construction of the Gaza tunnel system.[2] Qatar has supported infrastructure development in Gaza and contributed to the construction of the power plant. For years, Qatar's foreign ministry has funded the salaries of Gaza's civil servants and the humanitarian needs of Palestinian families.[3]

The royal family-owned media outlets, particularly Al Jazeera, have expressed sympathy for Hamas in their reporting on the October 7 attack. In addition to offering favorable coverage, Qatar has long acted as a haven for Hamas' operations and leadership. Sharing common political and religious ideals, Al Jazeera promoted Hamas by featuring sympathetic interviews with leaders, including Ismail Haniyeh. Qatari leaders consistently reassured American political leaders that Qatar was an honest broker in the Hamas-Israeli war. However, then-Secretary of State Antony Blinken cautioned the Gulf state about its close ties to Hamas, whose Doha office served as the primary residence for its self-exiled leader, Ismail Haniyeh, along with other Hamas leaders. Qatar's Prime Minister, Mohammed bin Abdulrahman Al-Thani (Profile 2 – Chapter 7), defended the Hamas office, stating that it was a means of bringing communication to end the conflict.

Late in 2024, Qatar agreed to expel several Hamas leaders from the country. This decision followed the death of American-Israeli hostage Hersh Goldberg-Polin (Profile 3 – Chapter 7) and Hamas' rejection of yet another ceasefire proposal. Additionally, Qatar decreased its financial aid to Hamas.[4]

## *Iran*

> *Dear university students in the United States of America, you are standing on the right side of history. You have now formed a branch of the Resistance Front.*
>
> Iran's Supreme Leader, Ali Khamenei[5]

Iran views Hamas as a front-line fighting force against Israel. Iranian mullahs have found allies among Hamas leaders, despite Iran practicing Shia Islam while Hamas adheres to fundamentalist Sunni Islam. Ismail Haniyeh expressed gratitude for Iranian support and thanked Iran's new president, Masoud Pezeshkian (Profile 4 – Chapter 7), for his nation's ongoing assistance.

During Hamas' formative years in the 1990s, Tehran provided significant financial and military support. Iran supplied military equipment, training, and funding totaling hundreds of millions of dollars. Since then, Tehran has expanded its political and military connections throughout the Middle East. Following the September 2001 attacks, Arab states were hesitant to support Hamas for fear of provoking President Bush and American opinion leaders. However, Iran increased its support, enabling Hamas to strengthen its position in Gaza in 2007 and engage in conflicts with Israel in 2008–09, 2012, and 2014. During the 2021 brief Gaza war, Supreme Leader Khamenei (Profile 5 – Chapter 7) publicly backed Hamas.[6]

Iran's Foreign Minister, Hussein Amirabdollahian, worked with Haniyeh to advance their shared interests in what they both call the 'Axis of Resistance.' This Axis refers to an informal alliance of nations and terrorist groups aimed at eliminating Israel. Hamas representative Khalil al-Haia reiterated his longstanding mutual calls for the destruction of Israel.[7]

Israel accused Iran of extensive involvement in the October attack. Iranian leaders have denied and claimed partial credit for assisting Hamas in its actions. Official Iranian sources indicate that some IRGC leaders were significantly involved in training operatives for the October assault. They asserted that Hamas' offensive was retaliation for the American assassination of senior Iranian commander Qasem Soleimani, who was regarded as an Iranian hero. An Iranian official emphasized that the conflict transcended regional boundaries and was a global concern.

Iran's Supreme Leader, Ayatollah Ali Khamenei (Profile 5 – Chapter 7), denied that any Iranian leader had prior knowledge of the October 7 attack. However, this claim is questionable given the numerous documents seized by the IDF and the close operational ties between Iran and Hamas. As the war escalated, Khamenei vowed to avenge Haniyeh's death. He defended Hamas' actions on October 7, asserting that they were 'correct, logical, and lawful,' considering the Palestinians' right to resist the Israeli occupation of their land. Iran's foreign minister stated that the country was prepared to 'play its part' in securing the release of Israeli hostages and Palestinian convicts.

Avril Haines, the former US Director of National Intelligence, cautioned that Iran has interfered in American domestic politics by promoting political activities, particularly on university campuses. She warned that Iran is funding demonstrations on these campuses. Families of American victims of the Hamas attack on October 7, 2023, are suing Iran for its role in facilitating the massacre.[8]

## *Saudi Arabia*

Saudi Arabia is a leading power in the Arab world and has demonstrated a greater willingness to normalize relations with Israel compared to many other Middle Eastern countries. It actively participates in the League of Arab States (LAS) and the Gulf Cooperation Council (GCC). For years, the royal family of the kingdom has engaged in discreet discussions with Israel regarding security issues, particularly concerning the increasing influence of Iran. In November 2017, a member of

Israel's security cabinet publicly acknowledged that Israel was cultivating ties with Saudi Arabia to help counter Iran. In 2018, Crown Prince Muhammad Bin Salman openly recognized Israel's right to exist. The kingdom endorsed the 2020 Abraham Accords but did not formally join them, facilitating relations among Israel, Bahrain, the United Arab Emirates, and Morocco. Riyadh is widely seen as a likely future participant.

Progress toward diplomatic normalization has stalled after Israel attacked Hamas.[9] By November 2023, Riyadh became openly critical of Israeli attacks and suspended normalization talks. At a summit in Riyadh with Arab and Muslim leaders, including bin Salman, they denounced Israeli actions as genocide. The kingdom has paused US-brokered discussions on recognizing Israel, emphasizing that any normalization deal hinges on the establishment of an independent Palestinian state. Hamas criticized the Saudi-funded Al-Arabiya and Al-Hadath channels for their 'pro-Israel' coverage of the Gaza war.[10]

## The Palestinian Authority

Hamas' rival and occasional partner, the PA, has supported the Hamas attack on October 7 since the beginning of the war. From its inception, the PA has positioned itself as a moderate, Western-leaning government, contrasting with the deeply religious Hamas. It does this to attract funding from Western countries and has been successful. Some of the money it receives is given to families of Palestinian suicide bombers or those killed by the IDF. This practice is referred to as the 'Pay-For-Slay' program, which rewards past actions and promotes terrorist attacks.[11]

The October attack was approved by the PA's senior religious adviser, Mahmoud Al-Habbash, who called it 'legitimate resistance.' His only concern was the cost calculation in Palestinian lives.[12]He mused on the ratio of Palestinians killed to Israelis killed and asked if it was worth the cost.[13] However, by summer 2025, leaders in the PA voiced concern about Hamas' widespread theft of property and food supplies in Gaza. One incident of many reflects the despair of many Gazans who feel completely abandoned and terrorized by Hamas vigilantes. A letter from a young woman cited Hamas' Arrow Unit as roving, self-appointed hunters of collaborators. Part of the note reads: They took them (her brother's group) off the bus, bound them, and shot them, after falsely accusing them of 'collaboration,' and they continued to chase them while they were wounded, up to the entrance of Nasser Hospital, where they shot them again 'and prevented the doctors and staff from treating them.'[14]

## Europe

Many Europeans have maintained negative views of Israel since its founding, with some continuing to harbor intense animosity toward the country. Following World War II, there was initial sympathy for the emerging, struggling Israel. However, as memories of World War II began to fade and after Israel's victory in 1967, the country increasingly came to be perceived as the aggressor. By the 1970s, anti-Israel rhetoric had spread widely across European parliaments, universities, and civil society. By the 2000s, a resurgent political left in European nations further fueled the existing animosity toward Israel.

European states expressed condolences to Israel shortly after the October 2023 attack. Immediately after the attack, both Austria and Slovenia displayed the Israeli flag, as did the mayor of Nice, France's third-largest city. Other European nations offered similar symbols of mourning. However, diplomatic expressions of sympathy quickly diminished after the IDF began its counterattack. Within one week, several states with long-standing animosities toward Israel condemned its military actions, and members of the United Nations initiated a wave of diplomatic criticism against the IDF. There was no doubt about where most European countries stood.

Many European states express a unified stance on various issues related to the ongoing war. They urge both Israel and Hamas to commit to a long-term solution based on two independent states. Some heads of state and prominent diplomats hold both parties accountable for the conflict. Many view Israel as an unwarranted presence in the Middle East. Another area of agreement among European states is that Israel should facilitate the free flow of food and medicine into all of Gaza. They assert that displaced Gazans and their descendants should be allowed to return to their homes.

### *Norway, Ireland, and Spain*

In May 2024, Norway, Ireland, and Spain announced their intention to recognize the state of Palestine. This development did not surprise world capitals. All three countries have stood with Palestine since October 7, and Norway has avoided labeling Hamas as a terrorist organization. In the Republic of Ireland, Sinn Féin, currently the largest party in Northern Ireland, has sustained a decades-long relationship with Hamas. Moreover, senior Spanish officials have shown support for the Palestinian 'right to resist' and for the idea of Palestine 'from the river to the sea.' As of April 2024, nine countries have recognized the state of Palestine.

Palestine's recognition by European countries granted Hamas prestige and a stronger bargaining position in global affairs. Hamas' Political Bureau member Bassem Naim stated, 'We believe this will be a turning point in the international stance on the Palestinian issue.'[15] Hamas welcomed the recognition; however, predictably, Israel and its supporters did not. Foreign Minister Israel Katz (Profile 7 – Chapter 7) remarked that 'History will remember that Spain, Norway, and Ireland chose to award a gold medal to the Hamas murderers and rapists.'[16]

Spain clarified that the decision is 'not against Israel, not in favor of Hamas; it is in favor of peace.'[17] Israel was not convinced and recalled its ambassador to Spain and those from Ireland and Norway. In 2006, Norway welcomed Hamas leaders and established a mutual understanding that Israel was an occupier and oppressor. These ties continue to exist.[18] Norwegian Prime Minister Jonas Gahr Støre (Profile 8 – Chapter 7) stated that a Palestinian state is the only path to peace.[19]

One of the most historically and profoundly anti-Israel countries in Europe is Ireland. Ireland's Taoiseach, or Prime Minister, urged the European Union to impose economic sanctions against Israel. This suggestion followed the Taoiseach's accusation that Israel was seeking revenge on Hamas, less than one month after the IDF began their military operations.[20] Ireland's current president, Michael Higgins, its Prime Minister, Simon Harris, and the Archbishop of Armagh and Primate of All Ireland condemned the IDF's counterattack as 'merciless and disproportionate.'[21] Prime Minister Harris stated that he would likely arrest Israelis if they visited Ireland. Not all Irish politicians support Hamas, and relatively few criticize the organization. Alan Shatter, a former Irish justice and defense minister, condemned his country's recognition of Palestinians for encouraging terrorism.[22]

Most European countries condemned Israel's heavy bombardment of Gaza. The Netherlands' Foreign Minister, Caspar Veldkamp, canceled a planned visit to Israel in protest of IDF attacks. Italy's defense minister stated that Italy would be obliged to arrest Israeli politicians if they visited. Spain has consistently and vocally condemned Israel for years. Spanish Deputy Prime Minister Yolanda Díaz stated, 'Palestine will be free, from the river to the sea.'[23] Spanish Defense Minister Margarita Robles described Israel's military operation in Gaza as a 'true genocide.' After October 2023, Spain increased its funding to Hamas-linked UNRWA.

## *France*

France has maintained an uncertain relationship with its Jewish community and Israel. This ambivalence partly stems from the significant collaboration during World War II. The nation was also divided during the Dreyfus case, which troubled it for years. Jews have been woven into the fabric of French society for centuries. However, since 1967, most French leaders have aligned themselves with Arabs in the Middle East for commercial, cultural, and ideological reasons.

For decades, Paris has sought to engage in dialogue with Hamas, provided that it recognizes Israel. French leaders are still waiting. France has not recognized Hamas as a legitimate political entity and has condemned its terrorist attacks, particularly in 2023. France is a major donor to the Palestinians, typically channeling its aid through UN agencies. The government distinguishes between Palestine and Hamas. In June 2025, President Macron strongly suggested that France would recognize the state of Palestine, following promises by PA President Abbas that he would reform and moderate the policies of the PA.[24]

## *Germany*

*When Gaza burns, Berlin burns.*

Graffiti spray-painted on a torched school in Berlin, 2024[25]

Germans discuss their unique and cautious relationship with Israel in the aftermath of the unprecedented murders committed by the Third Reich. The countries share a puzzling relationship. While current German leaders affirm Israel's right to exist, many Germans perceive Israel as the aggressor in the conflict with Hamas.[26] Berlin does not diplomatically recognize Hamas and has designated it a terrorist organization. Shortly after the 2023 attack, Germany announced a complete ban on Hamas activities within the country, reinforcing its classification as a terrorist group. It remains a significant donor to Palestinians through UN agencies.

According to Germany's domestic intelligence service, Hamas has around 450 members in the country. Their activities include expressions of sympathy, propaganda, and financing and fundraising efforts to support Hamas abroad. The German government has officially banned Samidoun, a group responsible for a celebration in Berlin that commemorated Hamas' October 7 attack on Israel. Interior Minister Faeser emphasized that Germany sent a strong message by banning Hamas and Samidoun, indicating that the country will not engage in any efforts to demonize Israel or harm its interests.[27]

Germany has issued deportation orders for several international students who marched in support of Hamas in March 2025. Authorities argued that the students' support for Hamas poses a public safety threat and revokes their rights to free speech and assembly. In 2022, German intelligence warned of Hamas operatives collecting donations and spreading propaganda. Intelligence discovered Hamas networks in several large German cities. Some Hamas supporters remain quiet, while others are vocal and outspoken when given free rein. One in Hamburg left no doubt as to where he stood. 'I want Adolf Hitler back, that's my opinion. I'm for Hitler, gas the Jews.'[28]

## *Britain*

Among all European countries, the United Kingdom has the closest historical diplomatic and military ties to the disputed territory. Britain governed Mandate Palestine from the post-World War I treaty period until the outbreak of Israel's War of Independence. Most Britons have not sided with Israel in its dispute with the Palestinians, and some political and civil society leaders urge the government to stop arms sales to Israel. Labour members have called for a complete ban on arms deliveries to Israel. This hostility toward Israel is reflected in far-left politicians, including George Galloway (Profile 9 – Chapter 7) and Jeremy Corbyn.

Prime Minister Keir Starmer has delivered mixed messages since the war began. He has occasionally called for a ceasefire while reiterating Israel's right to defend itself against terrorism. He also dismissed the sympathy expressed by other European leaders for Hamas leaders killed by the IDF. However, by mid-2024, his administration seemed to shift its stance on Israel, as Deputy Prime Minister Angela Rayner pledged that the government would recognize the state of Palestine.

When asked whether Britain would arrest and hold for trial Israelis accused of war crimes by the ICC, a spokesperson for Starmer emphasized that he 'respects the independence of the ICC.' However, he stated there is 'no moral equivalence between Israel, a democracy, and Hamas and Lebanese Hezbollah,'[29] which are classified as terrorist organizations. Britain has maintained public ambiguity about how it would implement the arrest warrants if Israeli leaders were to visit the UK.

Foreign Secretary David Lammy announced a partial arms embargo on UK weapons for Israel, including components for fighter planes, helicopters, and drones. This ban was widely seen as a diplomatic gesture to appease Starmer's Labour base and as an act of solidarity with other Europeans who are critical of Israel. In May 2025, Lammy asserted before Parliament that 'Israel's plan is morally unjustifiable, wholly disproportionate and utterly counterproductive.'[30]

## *Central and Eastern Europe*

Several Eastern European countries – Hungary, Poland, and the Czech Republic – have taken strong stands against Hamas, Islamic terrorism, and immigration from the developing world. Among the most vocal leaders is Hungary's Prime Minister Viktor Orbán, who defied the ICC arrest warrants for Netanyahu and Gallant and subsequently withdrew Hungary from the ICC in protest. Orbán has announced that any outward support for Hamas will not be tolerated.[31] 'Hamas flags will not fly in Hungary, and they will not fly.'[32] Orbán refers to Israel as the anchor of the West in the Middle East, and he shares a close and long-standing relationship with Netanyahu.

Poland was home to millions of Jews before the Nazis, leaving an imprint on Polish society and its international relations. Similar to the Hungarian government, the Polish leadership has supported Netanyahu and invited him to march in Poland on the 80th anniversary of the liberation of Auschwitz-Birkenau. He did not have to fear being arrested under the ICC warrant.

The Czech Republic's support for Israel is stronger than that of most Western European countries. According to the Israeli Ambassador to Prague, 'The Czech Republic is probably one of Israel's best friends in Europe.' Referring to the earlier war Operation Guardian of the Walls, Ambassador Daniel Meron observed, 'The Czechs know that Hamas are the bad guys and Israel are the good guys.'[33] Czech leaders rejected efforts within the EU to sever ties with Israeli universities in an act of solidarity with Palestinians.[34]

The Soviet Union played a crucial role in shaping the Palestinian historical narrative as a victimized nation striving to escape the grip of Israeli neo-colonialism. Moscow effectively collaborated with Yasser Arafat in the mid-1960s to portray Israel as an extension of American power in the Middle East, resonating with the international left, the developing world, and the Muslim community. Russia has designated Hamas as a terrorist organization; however, it views Hamas as a credible, legitimate, and popular political force for change in Gaza. Moscow maintains diplomatic contact with Hamas' political wing and facilitates high-level meetings between Hamas leaders and Russian officials. Unlike Western European countries that provide significant charitable aid to Gazans while keeping a diplomatic distance from Hamas, Moscow donates little food or financial assistance but offers rhetorical support for Hamas.

Vladimir Putin, Russia's unpredictable leader, has long allied himself with Hamas and other militant Islamic groups that oppose the United States and Israel. He welcomed senior Hamas and Iranian officials to Moscow. Putin attributed the violence in the Middle East to failures in US diplomacy. Some observers express concern about a growing, loose alliance between Russia, Iran, and Hamas. Osama Hamdan, from the Hamas Political Bureau, noted that Hamas maintains communication with Russia and China as part of a 'resistance axis.' He also stated that the next phase of conflict will focus on resistance efforts in the West Bank.

By Israeli and Serbian accounts, Serbia is Europe's most pro-Israel country. This close relationship rests on a mutual concern about Muslim-based violence and a shared victimization during World War II. President Aleksandar Vučić is an outspoken ally of Israel.[35] In the aftermath of the October 7 Hamas massacres in southern Israel, few world leaders reacted as swiftly and decisively as Vucic. Vucic had Serbia ready to respond. 'On the 8th, in the evening, we got a message from Israel. "We need this and that. We were not absolutely ready, we need it as soon as possible."'[36] Immediately, Vučić agreed to help.

## Asia, Sub-Saharan Africa, South America

### *China, India, South Africa*

China has engaged with Palestinians as part of its diplomatic outreach to developing, non-European nations. Its policy resembles that of Russia. It has supported the PLO and other Palestinian groups opposing Israel. In 1988, China recognized the State of Palestine and does not consider Hamas a terrorist organization. It distinguishes itself from Hamas by advocating for a two-state solution. Beijing has offered its diplomatic services to mediate between Israel and Hamas.

India's foreign policy toward the Middle East is more sympathetic to Israel than that of China. India led the non-aligned movement in the 1960s and 1970s, during which developing nations chose not to side with the United States or the Soviet Union. This policy also supported newly independent countries that were once colonies of European powers. However, this perspective shifted in the 1990s as Israel emerged as a global leader in technology and arms sales. Additionally, since gaining independence, India has grappled with Islamic militancy and separatism. India normalized relations with Israel in January 1992, softening its previously pro-Palestinian stance rhetoric.[37]

Nonetheless, India's stance on the Israel-Hamas conflict aligns with that of most European nations. Israel has the right to exist, but so does Palestine in some form. India supports Palestinians through UNRWA and engages with Palestinian leaders in the PA, albeit not with Hamas.[38]

Various African states maintain differing relations with Hamas and Israel. There is a wide range of awareness and enthusiasm regarding the conflict between Hamas and Israel, and the Middle East often does not take priority for African nations. Some countries have established commercial, particularly agricultural, ties with Israel.

Figure 2.1– Map – Israel, Gaza, and the West Bank.

Cyprus
Paphos
Lemosos
Larnaka
Tartus
Homs
Tadmur
Lebanon
Tripoli
Syria
Ad Nabk
Beirut
B'abda
Zahle
Saida
Douma
Damascus
Nabatiye et Tahta
Al Qunaytirah
Palestine
Haifa
Nazareth
Dar'a
As Suwayda
Irbid
Mediterranean Sea
Al Mafraq
Nablus
Tel Aviv
As Salt
Az Zarqa
Gaza
Ramla
Ramallah
Amman
Jerusalem
Gaza City
Al Khalil
Rashid
Dumyat
An Nabk
Bur Said
Beer Sheva
Al Karak
Alexandria
Kafr el Sheikh
El Arish
El Daba
Damanhur
El Mansura
Israel
El Alamein
At Tafilah
Tanta
Shibin el Kom
Zagazig
Ismaïlia
Benha
Jordan
Ma'an
Giza
Cairo
Suez
Egypt
Al Aqabah
Saudi Arabia
El Faiyum
Gulf of Suez
Beni Suef

Figure 2.3 –Yahaya Sinwar at a Hamas Rally.

Figure 3.1– Remnants of Hamas's Rockets launched into Israel.

Figure 4.1 – Pro-Israel Supporters in New York's Times Square.

Figure 4.2 – Photos of Israeli Hostages.

Figure 5.1 – Nova Festival Memorial Site Near Gaza.

Figure 5.2 – The Gaza Strip and Surroundings.

Figure 5.4 – Israeli Magen David Ambulance.

Figure 5.5 – Territory near Nova Festival.

Figure 6.2 – Remnants of Kibbutz Kfar Aza.

Figure 6.3 – An Israeli family’s home on October 8, 2025.

Figure 6.4 – Anti-Israel protesters in Hollywood, California.

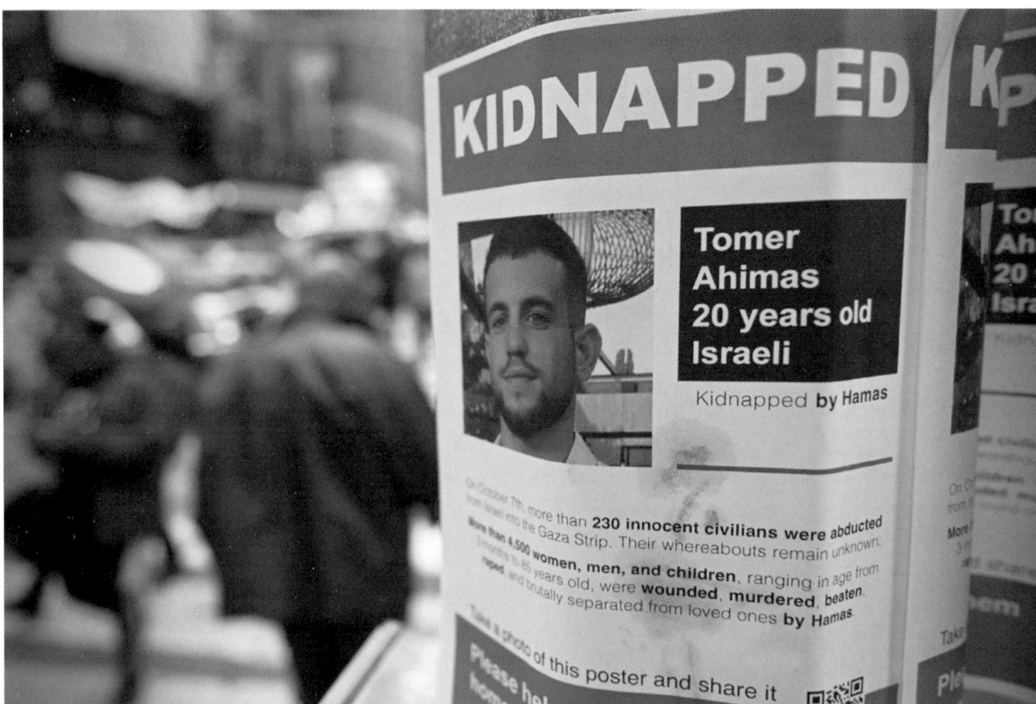


Figure 6.5 – Poster of a kidnapped Israeli placed in Manhattan, New York.

Figure 7.1 – Leaders Benjamin Netanyahu and Donald Trump.

Figure 8.2 – Soldiers and their armor.

Figure 8.3 – Merkava.

*Above*: Figure 8.4 – Map of Gaza Strip.

*Opposite above*: Figure 8.5 – Rubble of Gaza after Israeli Bombardment.

*Opposite below*: Figure 8.6 – War Map in Gaza.

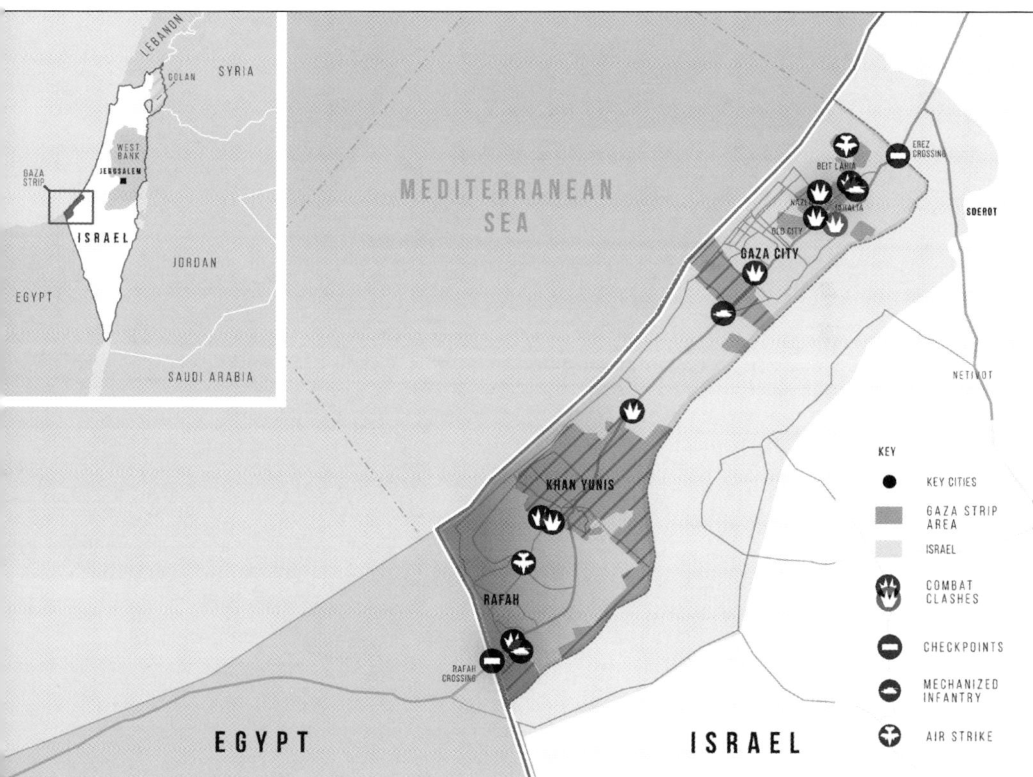
LEBANON
GOLAN
SYRIA
WEST BANK
JERUSALEM
GAZA STRIP
ISRAEL
JORDAN
EGYPT
SAUDI ARABIA
MEDITERRANEAN SEA
EREZ CROSSING
BEIT LAHIA
SDEROT
OLD CITY
GAZA CITY
NETIVOT
KHAN YUNIS
RAFAH
RAFAH CROSSING
EGYPT
ISRAEL
KEY
KEY CITIES
GAZA STRIP AREA
ISRAEL
COMBAT CLASHES
CHECKPOINTS
MECHANIZED INFANTRY
AIR STRIKE

Numerous African nations, especially in Sub-Saharan Africa, quickly condemned Hamas' attacks on Israel, particularly the incident on October 7, 2023 attacks.[39]

The most vocal critic of Israel during Swords of Iron have been South Africa, which has a long history of strong anti-Israel rhetoric. In South Africa, the ruling African National Congress (ANC) has consistently expressed solidarity with the Palestinians, stemming from what it describes as a shared struggle against colonialism and apartheid. The ANC has hosted delegations from Hamas and has also filed a case against Israel at the ICC for committing genocide. One of South Africa's most prominent critics of Israel is Ebrahim Rasool (Profile 10, Chapter 7), who has been declared unwelcome in the United States.

## Argentina

President Javier Milei is a friend of Israel, the Trump administration, and the West. In his first address to the United Nations General Assembly, Milei claimed the organization had veered from its original purpose to pursue human rights.[40] Instead, it has become an enemy of free nations and an apologist for dictatorships. Milei is both a vocal ally of Israel and a friend of Netanyahu. In July 2024, Argentina became the first country in Latin America to classify Hamas as a terrorist group. Milei shares many values with Netanyahu and Trump. Standing before the General Assembly, he accused the United Nations of being 'one of the main proponents of systemic violations of freedom.'[41]

## The United States

*In Gaza, in the Gaza Strip [Israel] has been, um, over the top.*

President Biden[42]

During his presidency, Joseph Biden offered both aid and criticism to Israel. He showed no sympathy for Hamas but urged Israeli leaders to ensure that the IDF limit its strikes to confirmed Hamas targets. He dismissed any accusations that Israel committed genocide, as claimed by the ICC. However, as early as December 2023, he warned Israel that it was losing support due to 'indiscriminate bombing' of the Gaza Strip.[43]

By most accounts, President Biden disapproved of Netanyahu, as did his former employer, President Obama. Biden publicly suggested that Netanyahu was extending the war to benefit his career. Biden criticized the IDF for using excessive force – a term he used repeatedly – but acknowledged Israel's right to destroy Hamas.[44] The Biden administration was inconsistent in its views on governance in the post-Hamas context of Gaza. The White House did not acknowledge any role for Hamas; however, the administration indicated that the PA would likely assume a prominent role. The US provided over $2 billion to Gazans.[45] He promised that aid would continue if inspections confirmed it should reach civilians, rather than Hamas.[46]

Since the onset of the Israel-Hamas war, the US has supplied over 5,000 MK-84 munitions, which are 2,000-pound bombs. For years, the Pentagon has stored weapons in Israel, presumably for US military use. However, it has allowed Israel to reduce some of these supplies during the Gaza conflict. To pressure Israel to ease some of its attacks, Biden deliberately delayed the delivery of both 2,000 and 500-pound bombs to Israel to persuade the IDF not to enter the city of Rafah.[47]

## *Trump Comes to Town – 'Unleash Hell'*

When Donald Trump was reelected, Israel once again had a friend in the White House. In 2017, he recognized Jerusalem as Israel's capital, which made him a hero among many in that country. He also acknowledged Israel's claim to the annexation of the Golan Heights and facilitated the Abraham Accords, securing diplomatic recognition for Israel from key Arab states.

Upon his election in 2024, President Trump rallied behind Israel and assured Prime Minister Netanyahu that he would provide verbal and material support, which he did. He also announced that former Arkansas governor Mike Huckabee (Profile 11 – Chapter 7), an ardent Zionist, would be his Ambassador to Israel. Huckabee frequently visits Israel and guides evangelical Christians. He refuses to use the term 'West Bank,' calling the disputed territory 'Judea and Samaria.'[48]

Trump also aligned American policy towards Iran more closely with Israel's stance. He reversed President Biden's accommodating policies towards Iran, reimposed sanctions, and demanded that Tehran stop and then reverse its nuclear weapons development program. President Trump's domestic policy on terrorism and student visas has differed significantly from President Biden's. The change was immediate and well-publicized. In March 2025, the Justice Department established a task force to investigate Hamas for its October 7, 2023, attack on Israel, as well as potential civil rights violations.[49] The Justice Department charged senior Hamas leaders in connection with the October 7, 2023, attack against Israel, according to court records documents.[50]

The departments of Justice, State, and Homeland Security quickly enhanced their capabilities to investigate, apprehend, and deport individuals who express sympathy for terrorist organizations, including Hamas. Executive orders facilitated the deportation of activists affiliated with or supporting Hamas, particularly student organizers. The Trump administration also enacted executive orders directing federal agencies to fight antisemitism. The State Department canceled the visas of foreign students and subsequently deported them. This issue has faced opposition from civil libertarians who see it as a clear violation of human rights. They cite the case of Moshen Mahdawi from Columbia University, whom they portray as a peace activist (Profile 12 – Chapter 7).

US Director of National Intelligence Tulsi Gabbard (Profile 13 – Chapter 7) warned that 'radical Islamist terrorism' poses the greatest threat to the safety of the American people.[51] President Trump's proposal to relocate Gazans to Egypt and Jordan in response to the ongoing crisis in Gaza has faced significant backlash, particularly from Cairo. Egyptian leaders have categorically rejected the plan, warning that it could destabilize the country economically, politically, and socially.[52]

Senior leaders in the United States and Israel share a common perspective on the Middle East, particularly the urgent threat posed by Iran's nuclear ambitions. Leaders in both nations understand the root causes of regional conflicts, especially in Gaza, Lebanon, and other areas in Syria.[53] Their joint operations against Iran's nuclear installations underscored their common view of the Iranian threat.

## International Organizations

In the broader Israel-Hamas conflict, international organizations play crucial roles in legal battles, financial challenges, weapons procurement, and the struggle for global and public opinion. Political entities, such as the United Nations and the European Union, alongside legal organizations like the International Criminal Court and human rights advocates, are expected to remain significantly involved. Their participation in this conflict, along with that of other groups, is likely to provoke considerable controversy.

### *The United Nations*

> *There is not a UNRWA site, school, mosque, or kindergarten in which we didn't find weapons. None. One hundred percent.*
>
> Col. Elad Shushan, commander of the 646th Reserve Paratroopers Brigade[54]

The UN has been involved in the Israel-Palestinian conflict since Israel's War of Independence. For decades, the UN has passed significantly more critical resolutions against Israel than against any other country. Following the October 2023 attack, it demanded that Israel exercise restraint. When Israel responded with force, UN leaders openly criticized its military actions in Gaza.

The UN established the United Nations Relief and Works Agency (UNRWA) to provide humanitarian assistance to Arabs displaced by the creation of Israel. Although only a limited number of individuals from this population still qualify for aid, UNRWA continues to receive funding.[55] It has 32,000 staff members primarily working in official refugee camps.

UNRWA has maintained a tense relationship with Israel, which has significantly worsened since the war in Gaza began, prompting Israel to call for UNRWA's disbandment repeatedly. Hamas exerts considerable influence within UNRWA, and Israeli intelligence has identified over 100 UNRWA personnel who also act as Hamas terrorists. At least 42 UNRWA employees participated in the attacks on October 7. Hamas terrorists exploited UN resources, including food aid bags, vests, ammunition, and explosives. They utilized UNRWA facilities near the agency's

Gaza City headquarters as command centers, and UNRWA provided an advanced computer network to the group.[56]

For years, UNRWA has funded Palestinian schools. The course content in UNRWA schools is controversial and imbued with nationalistic jingoism, alongside anti-Israel and anti-Semitic themes.[57] Under threats of defunding, UNRWA promised in 2021 to eliminate all hate-filled curricula. However, this has not occurred. In its own words, UNRWA acknowledged that teachers had 'mistakenly' produced and distributed 'offending material.'[58]

On October 7, Hamas positioned itself within schools in Gaza to fire upon Israeli troops. The entrances to their tunnels were notably located near UNRWA schools. Snipers and anti-tank missile operators have been deployed near the windows of UNRWA schools to target Israeli soldiers' armor.[59] Educators associated with Hamas also served as fighters in Hamas' al-Qassam Brigades, the most effective militia within the organization.[60] An Israeli captive who was released testified that a UNRWA teacher kept him in an attic for 50 days. Numerous tunnels connected to UNRWA-funded schools were filled with weapons, leading to a nearly half-mile-long tunnel packed with arms beneath the school. Captured Hamas records indicate that school personnel, including senior leaders, were complicit in Hamas activities.[61]

UNRWA leaders deny any involvement or responsibility. One of the defendants in a lawsuit, UNRWA chief Philippe Lazzarini (Profile 14 – Chapter 7), demanded that Israel stop what he described as defamatory remarks about the agency. Lazzarini emphasized that the agency is vital to international efforts supporting the people of Gaza. He has led the agency since 2020.[62]

Many Gazans rally behind UNRWA and continue to show their support, valuing the aid and job opportunities it provides. However, some Gazans express less appreciation for UNRWA, citing its coordination with Hamas in Gaza. These Gazans argue that UNRWA places its facilities near Hamas' military outposts, while other observers assert that Hamas operatives are diverting funds and supplies meant for UNRWA. Many of them hope that Hamas will leave.

## *European Union*

The European Union's (EU's) position on the Gaza War reflects its long-standing, highly ambivalent stance on the Palestine-Israel conflict. In mid-November 2023, the EU published 'What the EU Stands for on Gaza and the Israeli-Palestinian Conflict.' In the document, there is no explicit condemnation of Hamas as the party that initiated the slaughter. Countries in the EU have divided into different support camps between Israel and Hamas. The EU has generously donated to Palestinians through UNRWA and other agencies. Some investigators in the EU Commission were doubtful that most of the funds were reaching impoverished Palestinians. One commissioner noted that 'Hamas was called, recognized, and acknowledged as a terrorist organization. How was it possible to pour €225 million into a place that a terrorist organization fully controls, and nobody did anything or said anything?'[63]

### *International Criminal Court – Court of Last Resort*

The ICC opened its doors in 2002. It claims to be the world's only independent court established to investigate the most serious offenses, including genocide, war crimes, and crimes against humanity. It has been described as a court of last resort because it adjudicates crimes that sovereign courts will not address.[64] Like many other international organizations, the ICC frequently and vocally addressed the Israel-Palestine conflict. Richard Goldstone, a former judge on South Africa's Constitutional Court, was the first prosecutor at the ICC to investigate military actions during the exchanges between Israel and Hamas (Profile 15 – Chapter 7). Nonetheless, his successors at the ICC would continue to promote the image of Israel as a criminal state subject to sanctions. Indictments and sanctions would follow Israel's response to the October 2023 attacks.

The ICC made headlines by issuing arrest warrants for Israeli Prime Minister Benjamin Netanyahu, Israeli Defense Minister Yoav Gallant, and senior Hamas leaders on charges of war crimes and crimes against humanity. Karim Khan enumerated Israel's actions as 'starvation,' 'willful killing,' and 'extermination and/or murder.' He asserts that Israel's attacks targeted the Palestinian civilian population and constitute war crimes. 'We argue that the alleged crimes against humanity were part of a widespread and systematic assault on the civilian population of Israel by Hamas and other armed groups as dictated by organizational policies.'[65] Khan also repeatedly called for the release of all hostages in Gaza and warned against Israeli military action in Rafah.

Netanyahu responded, 'We will not bow to it.'[66] Gallant scoffed at the indictment, arguing that Israel was lawfully and ethically responding to Hamas, an enemy responsible for atrocities against Israeli children, women, and men. A spokesperson for the French Foreign Ministry pledged to act in accordance with the ICC Statute. Germany's foreign minister asserted that Berlin was 'bound by' the court as a nation that recognizes the institution and respects international law. American leaders immediately criticized the indictment.

President Joe Biden criticized Khan's actions, and many supporters of Israel were disappointed that Western states did not forcefully and openly state that they would not arrest Israeli leaders.[67] The US House of Representatives sanctioned the ICC's indictment of Israel's leaders.[68] The president signed an executive order that penalizes the ICC for engaging in 'illegitimate and baseless actions targeting America and our close ally, Israel.'[69] However, some Israelis are working within the ICC's legal framework. Families of Israeli captives are pursuing a case against Hamas at the ICC. The case against the Hamas leaders includes 'kidnapping, crimes of sexual violence, torture, and other allegations.'[70]

## Summary

In 2023, the world's attention focused on the Gaza Strip. Different countries often viewed the situation in vastly different ways. A broad initial sympathy for Israel faded within days in many nations, some of which began to vocally condemn Israel.

European countries with large, dissatisfied Muslim populations called for a ceasefire from both sides, even as Hamas continued to hold many Israelis hostage. Support for Israel remained in Europe, particularly in Poland, Hungary, and the Czech Republic. In July 2025, 25 countries including Britian, Japan, and a many European countries signed on to a joint statement demanding that the 'war in Gaza must end now.' The document places the onus on Israel to cease military operations immediately.

In South America and Africa, leftist leaders have aligned their countries with the Palestinians, whom they describe as victims of Israeli aggression. The newly elected conservative president of Argentina supports Israel. Under President Trump, America supplied a substantial amount of weapons to Israel and backed it in international forums. Israel has found a strong ally in President Biden, who is committed to the shared cause of defeating Hamas and ensuring that Iran never obtains nuclear weapons. If Orde Wingate had been revered as an ally and 'friend' of Israel in the 20th century, Donald Trump would likely be regarded as its most prominent advocate today.

**Profile 1 – Dr Einat Wilf: 'A Constructive Voice of Reason'**
**Names:** Einat Wilt
**Nationality:** Israeli
**Profession:** Lawyer
**Connection to October 7, 2023:** According to one of her fans, 'Slim and elegant with gorgeous gray-blue eyes, Einat Wilf could easily have been a model.'[71] Perhaps this Harvard and Cambridge graduate once traversed the fashion catwalk part-time. What is certain is that she commanded respect as a foreign policy advisor to Vice Prime Minister Shimon Peres and as a strategic consultant with McKinsey & Company. Dr Wilf is the author of four books on Israel.

Her fans commend her depth of knowledge, patriotism, and mastery of language. She has coined several terms that have gained widespread usage. For example, she is credited with coining the term 'Palestinian placard strategy.' The term refers to the slogans that appear on placards at anti-Israel demonstrations, which she said, 'Is the repetitive, nursery rhyme equation of Israel, with evil.'[72] She argues that Israel is portrayed as the collective Jew, embodying all the evils and social pathologies of the modern state system, including apartheid, white supremacy, and genocide.

She is openly hostile toward Qatar and Hamas, both of which she views as implacable enemies of Israel. 'We are up against an enemy that not only invaded our country and our homes to gleefully murder and mutilate the most peace-loving people in their beds but went on to kidnap hundreds of them to ensure they face no consequences for what they did on October 7.'[73]
**Current Status:** Still serving as an activist for Israel.

**Profile 2 – Sa'oud bin Abd Al-Rahman Al Thani: 'We Are All Hamas!'**
**Names:** Mohammed bin Abdulrahman Al-Thani
**Nationality:** Qatari

**Profession:** Deputy Prime Minister of Qatar; Minister of Defense
**Connection to October 7, 2023:** Despite its small size, Qatar holds significant regional and international importance. It hosts a strategic US air base and a Taliban office, and it has actively engaged in the Hamas-Israel conflict. Deputy Prime Minister Al-Thani, a member of Qatar's ruling Al Thani family, was appointed to this role in November 2024 as part of a cabinet reshuffle. Al-Thani has frequently appeared in the news during various ceasefire negotiations.

Al-Thani declared, 'We don't have a war with Israel.'[74] However, he refers to Israel as 'occupiers,' demands that the Jewish state withdraw from 'the West Bank, Gaza, and the Golan Heights,' and insists that Palestine has its capital in East Jerusalem.[75] In 2014, he tweeted, 'We are all Hamas.' The donations that Qatar has made to Gaza have attracted the attention of Israeli observers. However, some critics point to the enrichment of Hamas leaders and the construction of the tunnel system. Qatar is a key supporter of the Muslim Brotherhood, of which Hamas is an offshoot.[76] Al-Thani also opined that Israel 'controls' the US.[77]
**Current Status:** Serving as both deputy foreign minister and defense minister.

**Profile 3 – Hersh Goldberg-Polin: 'I Love You, and I'm Sorry'**
**Names:** Hersh Goldberg-Polin
**Nationality:** American Israeli
**Profession:** Kibbutznik
**Connection to October 7, 2023:** He was at home in the Georgia mountains, where he had attended summer camp as a boy. Hersh Goldberg-Polin also vacationed there with his family. That is why Camp Ramah Darom held a service in his memory when they learned that Hamas had murdered him after 11 months of captivity. He, like many other young revelers at the Nova festival, was abducted. However, he had time to text a last message of his free will: 'I love you' & 'I'm sorry.'[78]

He lost an arm to shrapnel. Hamas threw a grenade at him and others, and he tried to toss it away. For months, the world outside Gaza did not hear from him. Then, Hamas released a proof-of-life video. For the first time, his family and friends felt hope. Immediately, his parents petitioned for his release and protested. The parents explained that since their son's abduction, 'we live on another planet.'[79] They spoke to UN representatives, Pope Francis, Elon Musk, President Biden, Secretary of State Blinken, and dozens of senators and governors. They relentlessly pursued Israel's ministers and other politicians.[80]

They would never see their son alive. He was murdered in late August 2024 along with five other hostages. Israeli soldiers found their bodies several days after they had been shot. Thousands attended his funeral in Jerusalem. His mother eulogized him in an extended apology. She recalled that his last words were 'I am sorry.' Now it was the mother who apologized. 'If there was something we could have done to save you and we didn't think of it, I beg your forgiveness. We tried so very hard. So deeply and desperately. I'm sorry.'[81]
**Current Status:** Murdered.

**Profile 4 – Masoud Pezeshkian**
**Names:** Masoud Pezeshkian
**Nationality:** Iranian
**Profession:** President of Iran
**Connection to October 7, 2023:** A trained cardiac surgeon, President Pezeshkian has been linked with a more reformist brand of politics in Iran than that exercised by the mullahs. What is certain is his gratitude toward Hamas for bringing the fight to Israel. He explained, 'We appreciate Iran for playing a role in supporting the Palestinian cause. The Iranian leader also praised the Houthis in Yemen for supporting Hamas in Gaza.[82]

As for destroying Iran's nuclear weapon sites, Pezeshkian invited Israel and the United States to try. 'You can target the buildings and locations, but you cannot target those who build them.'[83] He promised to build 1,000 nuclear sites if the US or Israel destroyed 100. Some critics scoff at his threats, dismissing them as mere bluster. One critic compared Pezeshkian to the Madagascar tomato frog, which puffs up to intimidate predators.[84] After the Israeli and American raids on Iran's nuclear sites, Pezeshkian has yet to retaliate.

Nonetheless, Pezeshkian has achieved results from his diplomacy, some of which may be only nominal, while others are likely tangible. He signed a Comprehensive Strategic Partnership Agreement with Russia in early 2025. The specific and practical goal of the agreement is unclear.[85] The obligation to adhere to the principles of the UN and international law is especially important for leaders in Washington DC and Jerusalem. However, these principles and standards are not universally well-defined.
**Current Status:** He remains the president of Iran. He was probably injured in an Israeli bomb attack targeting Iranian leadership.

**Profile 5 – Iran's Supreme Leader Ali Khamenei**
**Names:** Ali Khamenei
**Nationality:** Iranian
**Profession:** Spiritual and *de facto* political leader of Iran
**Connection to October 7, 2023:** He was under constant death watch for years. Many Iranians hoped he would recover, while many others wished he would not. Ayatollah Ali Khamenei, the Supreme Leader of Iran since 1989, remains in office despite the early summer American-Israeli bombing. Now in his nineties, he previously served as president of Iran from 1981 to 1989. Khamenei is the longest-serving head of state in the Middle East and the second-longest-serving Iranian leader of the last century, after Shah Mohammad Reza Pahlavi. He is, by far, the most crucial individual in Iran, controlling the instruments of political, military, religious, and social affairs.[86]

For years, many Shia Muslims and some Sunni Muslims have been waiting for Khamenei's signal to attack Zionist targets worldwide. Khamenei's chief of staff, Mohammad Mohammadi Golpayegani, explained, 'It is obligatory for anyone who can take a step for Palestine to do so.'[87] The supreme leader has given the nod, though

often indirectly, in speeches to anti-Israel activists. He says, 'Once again, children are being killed, homes are being destroyed, and civilians are being displaced. The people must stop this tragedy.'[88] Some of his admirers believe that Muslims do not appreciate Khamenei. In the United States, Michigan imam Usama Abdulghani stated in October 2024, 'It will be a waste and sad, if we only come to appreciate [Khamenei] and take his words as seriously as we should, when he is no longer with us.'[89]
**Current Status:** As of early 2026, the aged mullah is considering leaving Iran to escape a popular uprising.

**Profile 6 – Crown Prince Muhammad Bin Salman**
**Names:** Muhammad Bin Salman
**Nationality:** Saudi
**Profession:** Prince, monarch, diplomat
**Connection to October 7, 2023:** Prince Muhammed was born to King Salman and Fahda bin Falah, the King's third spouse, in 1985. The Prince has a royal lineage and holds a Bachelor of Laws degree from King Saud University. He has broken from earlier generations of Saudi royalty by shifting Saudi foreign policy toward the West. He supports a two-state solution. Unlike many other leaders of Arab countries, he is likely to establish diplomatic relations with Israel. Former Secretary of State Blinken viewed Bin Salman as a key player in securing a long-term ceasefire between Hamas and Israel.[90] According to one source, Salman does not focus on the Palestinian issue as intently as his royal predecessors did.[91] This makes him more flexible in negotiating with Palestinians, Israelis, and Americans.

Critics of Saudi Arabia are skeptical of Bin Salman's overtures, which they claim are merely rhetorical fluff. They contend that Saudi Arabia periodically dangles the prospect of recognizing Israel but never follows through. Additionally, the conditions for diplomatically recognizing Israel and exchanging diplomats are often fuzzy.[92] Salman certainly shares Israel's fear of a nuclear-empowered Iran.[93] It is uncertain how diplomacy will reflect the Israeli-American attacks on Iran's nuclear sites.

Optimists of modernization in Saudi Arabia and the Westernization of its foreign policy emphasize recent progressive changes. Over the past decade, women have become more integrated into the workforce, now serving as police officers, border guards, and law enforcement personnel. This was not the case until Salman assumed office.[94]
**Current Status:** Serving as prince and leader of moderate politics in the Middle East.

**Profile 7 – Israel Katz, Foreign Minister and Defense Minister: All of Gaza?**
**Names:** Israel Katz
**Nationality:** Israeli
**Profession:** Foreign Minister of Israel
**Connection to October 7, 2023:** When Prime Minister Netanyahu dismissed Defense Minister Gallant, he appointed Israel Katz, a loyal Likud member who

has been Minister of Foreign Affairs since 2019. For Katz, Israel's policy in Gaza primarily aims to make every effort to secure the hostages and then destroy Hamas. He adds that Israel's policy also encompasses 'stopping humanitarian aid, which undermines Hamas' control over the population, and creating an infrastructure for the distribution [of aid] through civilian companies in the future.'[95] He is open to resuming humanitarian aid to the Gaza Strip, but only through vetted companies to ensure that food and equipment do not reach Hamas.

His plans for Gaza? For Katz, the future depends on Hamas. The IDF will permanently seize parts of the Gaza Strip if Hamas does not release all the hostages. 'I have instructed the IDF to seize additional areas in Gaza, evacuate the population, and expand security zones around Gaza to protect Israeli communities and IDF soldiers. The more Hamas persists in its refusal to release the hostages, the more territory it will lose, which will be annexed to Israel.'[96]

**Current Status:** Minister of Defense.

**Profile 8 – Norwegian Prime Minister Jonas Gahr Støre**

**Names:** Jonas Gahr Støre

**Nationality:** Norwegian

**Profession:** Prime Minister

**Connection to October 7, 2023:** Jonas Gahr Støre became Prime Minister of Norway in October 2021. He served as Minister of Foreign Affairs in Jens Stoltenberg's second government from 2005 to 2012, and then Minister of Health and Care Services until the change of government in 2013. Before that, he served as State Secretary and Chief of Staff at the Office of the Prime Minister from 2000 to 2001.[97]

Norway brokered the 1992–93 talks between Israel and the PLO, which led to the Oslo Accords that provided for limited Palestinian self-rule. Most observers would agree that these accords have failed to achieve a lasting and comprehensive peace. For years, Norway has turned to Hamas as a suitable and legitimate negotiating partner. As foreign minister, Gahr Støre was among the first Western leaders to recognize Hamas. Norway has also funded the salaries of the PA's public workers and other employees, and this generosity continues.

Gahr Støre has strongly condemned Israel's response to the October 7 attack, criticizing the IDF's actions as disproportionate and in violation of international law. 'International law stipulates that [the reaction] must be proportionate. I believe this limit has been largely exceeded.' In response to proportionality, his critics sarcastically ask, 'How many children should it [Israel] kidnap and hold hostage?'[98]

**Current Status:** Prime Minister of Norway.

**Profile 9 – George Galloway: Gorgeous George and Palestine**

**Names:** George Galloway

**Nationality:** British

**Profession:** Politician

**Connection to October 7, 2023:** As colorful as he is controversial, George Galloway is a veteran British politician who embodies the politics of the alliance between Muslims and left-oriented Westerners. His passion for politics began early and has consistently been rooted in the left side of the political spectrum. On his website, the six-term parliamentarian calls himself a 'freedom fighter . . . honorary Palestinian, Iraqi, Syrian, Egyptian . . . friend of Fidel Castro, Hugo Chavez, Benazir Bhutto, Yasser Arafat, Tariq Aziz. Trembling with indignation at any injustice anywhere.'[99]

He was expelled from the Labour Party in 2003 for encouraging Arabs in Iraq to fire on British troops. He was later dismissed from his job on talk radio due to charges of antisemitism. He has a strong aversion to Israel and Israelis. He dramatically left a debate at Oxford when he was informed that his opponent was an Israeli.[100]

After October 7, he openly denied that many of the reported attacks had occurred. He posted that Hamas did not rape any Israelis and that only one baby died, and that it did so under uncertain circumstances. By Galloway's account, most of those killed were Israeli military personnel. As a parliamentarian for Rochdale, he compared Israel's military offensive in Gaza to the Nazis' actions during the war Holocaust.[101] His repeated denial of Hamas' killings on October 7 confused many of his Israeli critics. They assert that Galloway overlooks the devastation of that day, characterizing some of Hamas' actions as accidents. IDF personnel observed beheaded babies at Kibbutz Beeri on the day of the attack. A reserve colonel said, 'I don't think a baby with its head cut off is an accident, a rocket doesn't do that.'[102]
**Current Status:** Former Member of Parliament; he lost his seat on 30 May 2024.

**Profile 10 – Ebrahim Rasool: Ambassador Non Grata**
**Names:** Ebrahim Rasool
**Nationality:** South African
**Profession:** Diplomat
**Connection to October 7, 2023:** Secretary of State Marco Rubio disapproved of Ambassador Ebrahim Rasool's record, politics, and biography. For Rubio and other senior US leaders, Rasool exemplified much of what they considered toxic about the South African government. Rasool hosted senior Hamas operatives and praised Yassin as 'one of the greatest inspirations.'[103] Haniyeh gave Rasool a signed keffiyeh, which he accepted as a gift. He urged South Africa to prosecute Israel for genocide at the ICC. Secretary Rubio labeled him an anti-white racist and an antisemite. Rasool stated that South Africa was under attack because it serves as a historical antidote to supremacism.

He grew up in South Africa, where he was identified as 'colored.' This stigma fostered a sensitivity to racial prejudice and an awareness of social justice. He served as the Ambassador to the United States from 2010 to 2015, during Barack Obama's presidency, who also had mixed heritage with half-white ancestry. By all accounts, the two enjoyed each other's company.[104]

Secretary Rubio held no warm feelings for Rasool. He called the South African 'a race-baiting politician who hates America.' He added, 'We have nothing to discuss with him, and so he is considered persona non grata.'[105] He returned to South Africa with his wife shortly after he was declared *persona non grata* in March 2025. He wistfully said, 'We bid farewell to the US with no regrets, it is what it is.'[106]

**Current Status:** Unknown. Not residing in the United States.

**Profile 11 – Ambassador Mike Huckabee: At Home With a Chosen People and a Chosen Place**

**Names:** Mike Huckabee

**Nationality:** American

**Profession:** Former governor of Arkansas, current US Ambassador to Israel.

**Connection to October 7:** Ambassador Mike Huckabee found his spiritual home when he assumed his role in Jerusalem as the American Ambassador to Israel. He has long been one of America's most vocal and passionate advocates for Israel, both on television and in civil society. The former governor of Arkansas hosted a talk show on the Fox News Network from 2008 to 2015. In 2017, he transitioned to a Christian-based broadcast television network. He briefly ran against Donald Trump in 2016. After dropping out of the presidential race, he became a loyal supporter of President Trump.

Huckabee's love for Israel stems from his deep religious faith, which has led him to visit the country over 100 times. His critics argue that he is insensitive and at times oblivious to the rights and suffering of Palestinians. In response, he has asserted that there is no such thing as a Palestinian. Regarding Hamas, the ambassador does not believe the organization can engage in honorable negotiations. The ambassador declared Israel 'a chosen place for a chosen people.'[107] He identified the Israel-Hamas struggle as a vertical battle between heaven and hell, between good and evil, between light and darkness. Prime Minister Netanyahu is pleased to have the former governor as his ambassador. Netanyahu said, 'This is a great day for the Israeli-American alliance.'[108]

**Current Status:** US Ambassador to Israel

**Profile 12 – Mohsen Mahdawi: Activist Poet**

**Names:** Mohsen Mahdawi

**Nationality:** Palestinian

**Profession:** Graduate student, proclaimed anti-fascist and peace worker

**Connection to October 7:** Many young Americans and self-proclaimed civil libertarians view Palestine-born Mohsen Mahdawi as a victim of the Trump administration's alleged campaign against fundamental freedoms in the United

States. Mahdawi identifies as a peace worker. At 34, he is an undergraduate at Columbia's School of General Studies and previously earned a bachelor's degree in computer engineering from Birzeit University. Now divorced, he was married to a US citizen for several years.[109] He claims to be a Buddhist and to practice nonviolence.

His detractors are uncertain about his status as a Gandhi-like peace activist. Several point to an alleged incident in the summer of 2015 when a gun shop informed Vermont police that Mr. Mahdawi had visited the store twice, expressing interest in learning more about firearms and purchasing a sniper rifle and automatic weapons to take back to Palestine and kill Jews there.[110] Though Mahdawi denied saying any such thing, he could not dismiss a poem he wrote and posted on social media saluting a terrorist who was responsible for a massacre in Israel in 1978, which left 38 Israelis dead, including many children.[111] His detention by immigration authorities in Vermont brought him national attention. His support for tent encampments at Columbia and promotion of Hamas resulted in a deportation order.

**Current Status:** Several judges blocked the deportation order. He is still in the United States.

**Profile 13 – Tulsi Gabbard: Director of National Intelligence**
**Names:** Tulsi Gabbard
**Nationality:** American
**Profession:** Career soldier, politician, and civil servant
**Connection to October 7, 2023:** Gabbard, a military veteran, criticized the Biden administration for not providing enough support to Israel since October 7. She has been vocal against Islamic terrorism and has shown strong support for the Jewish state, including during a speech at a Christians United for Israel conference. Over the years, her stance on the Middle East has evolved. Previously, she voted against a House resolution condemning the December 2016 United Nations Security Council Resolution opposing Israeli settlements. In 2019, she declined to condemn Rep. Ilhan Omar for antisemitic comments. Nonetheless, Gabbard has clearly stated her opposition to the BDS movement and voted for anti-BDS legislation. In 2020, she even supported Bernie Sanders, a harsh critic of Israel, for President.

This starkly contrasts with today's Tulsi Gabbard. The former Democrat has attended rallies for Donald Trump. By 2022, she had shifted further to the right. In October 2024, she stood by Donald Trump at a rally and announced her decision to join the Republican Party. She described the Democratic Party as 'unrecognizable' from what it had been 20 years before and attacked the 'elitist cabal of warmongers' and 'woke ideologue' in the party. All this attracted her to Donald Trump, and Donald Trump was attracted to her.

**Current Status:** Serving as director of national intelligence.

**Profile 14 – Philippe Lazzarini: 'I'm shocked. Shocked!'**
**Names:** Philippe Lazzarini
**Nationality:** Swiss
**Profession:** Lazzarini was appointed Under-Secretary-General of the United Nations and Commissioner-General of UNRWA in April 2020.
**Connection to October 7, 2023:** For over 30 years, Philippe Lazzarini held senior positions in the UN and the private sector. On October 7, he became the leader of UNRWA. His tenure was controversial. He met repeatedly with senior Hamas officials. According to a report published by UN Watch, senior UN officials, including Lazzarini, spoke of 'cooperation' in their partnership with Hamas. The report noted that Lazzarini continued to meet with senior Hamas officials within a month of the 2023 attack.[112]

Nonetheless, Lazzarini repeatedly denied being aware that UNRWA personnel participated in any hostile acts toward Israel. Some observers of the Middle East were not convinced that he was as uninformed as he claimed. When Israeli leaders proved that a Palestinian school principal was also the head of Hamas' Lebanon branch, Lazzarini identified him as a 'successful teacher and excellent [school] principal.'[113]

His organization certainly alienated Israel and the Trump administration. Israel defenestrated the organization from the country, and the United States cut support. Lazzarini calls this a challenge. The UN agency for Palestinian refugees said Thursday that while an Israeli ban has not yet been lifted, Lazzarini called the loss of US support 'a challenge,' but stated the agency is appealing to Gulf Arab countries and other donors to increase their contributions. He described his agency as the target of a 'massive disinformation campaign' with a politically motivated objective of dismantling it completely.[114]
**Current Status:** Unknown.

**Profile 15 – Richard Goldstone and his Report**
**Names:** Richard Goldstone
**Nationality:** South African
**Profession:** Lawyer
**Connection to October 7, 2023:** He was born and raised in South Africa and claims to have fought against the former apartheid system of racial separation at an early age. He trained as a lawyer and advanced through the legal ranks to serve on the highest courts, having been nominated by Nelson Mandela. His prestige and outspoken commitment to multiracialism drew the attention of the UN, leading to his request to conduct a fact-finding mission on the Gaza conflict in 2009. The completed project was called The Goldstone Report, which concluded that both Palestinians and Israelis committed war crimes. Regarding Israel, Goldstone stated, 'The (IDF) operations were in furtherance of an overall policy aimed at punishing the Gaza population…'[115] Neither Hamas nor Israel was pleased with the report's findings. Israel condemned the report as a broadside against the country

that would hinder its ability to fight terrorism. Hamas resented some conclusions that attributed a significant portion of the responsibility to them.

In February 2010, Alejandro Wolff, the US deputy representative to the United Nations, criticized the report for its bland perspective on the asymmetrical nature of the Gaza conflict, in which Hamas deliberately targeted civilians. The US Congress voted 344 to 36 to condemn the report upon its release. Two years later, Goldstone retracted many of his conclusions, especially the allegations that the IDF intentionally targeted civilians as a matter of policy. One of his critics, Melanie Phillips, called his *mea culpa* 'What self-serving rubbish.' She argued that there was ample evidence that Israel took precautions against killing civilians.[116]

**Current Status:** Unknown.

## Chapter 8

# War Aims and Strategies

*Hamas has only one agenda: to destroy Israel and to murder Jews.*

United States Secretary of
State Antony Blinken[1]

Before October 7, 2023, there was neither war nor peace between Israel and Hamas in Gaza. When the war began, Hamas was prepared, while Israel was not. The shock of the attack's scope, intensity, geographic dispersion, and brutality compelled the IDF to recalibrate its tactics and strategy. Israel faced a conflict unlike any it had fought before. The IDF would encounter asymmetric urban tactics, utilizing tunnels, human shields, and deception against Israel's technological superiority. However, the IDF's objective in the initial onslaught was to repel the invaders and to understand the enemy's intentions and capabilities.

Countries outside the Middle East heightened their military readiness as the war began. The United States deployed an aircraft carrier and additional warships to the Mediterranean and sent emergency supplies of weapons to Israel. Washington expressed solidarity with Israel and warned Iran against using proxies in the region. On October 10, President Biden cautioned, 'To any country, any organization, anyone thinking of taking advantage of this situation, I have one word. Don't. Don't.'[2] The Houthis in Yemen and Hezbollah in Lebanon targeted Israeli and Western interests by launching drones and missiles at commercial shipping sites.

## Hamas' Wars: Goals and Strategies

Hamas head of Political Bureau Khaled Meshaal (Profile 1 – Chapter 8) publicized Hamas' five 'fronts' – the military, popular, financial, political, and media fronts – for Hamas' campaign against Israel.[3] Hamas had five basic goals at the outbreak of the war. They were to kill as many people as possible; to abduct hostages and carry them to Gaza; to break Israel's will to prosecute the war aggressively; to replenish Hamas' leadership and the ranks of the cadre as they were depleted; and to harness and hold international support.

## *Goal 1: Kill, Kill, Kill*

The primary immediate mission of the Hamas invaders was to kill and capture Israelis. On the day of the attack, Hamas' leader of the military wing, Muhammad Deif, implored his fellow Gazans, 'If you do not have a gun, take up your cleaver, hatchet, axe, Molotov cocktail, truck, bulldozer or car ... use them.'[4] Meshaal encouraged suicide attacks, calling them martyrdom operations. They listened; some Gazans did just that. Hamas' indiscriminate killing on October 7 harkened back to the darkest days of Nazi killing units. One observer coined the term kinocide to refer to the intention of mass murder of entire families.[5]

When being interrogated, some days after his capture by the IDF, a Hamas captive explained his mission on October 7:

| | |
|---|---|
| 'Investigator | 'But what was the goal?' |
| Prisoner | 'To kill' |
| Investigator | 'To kill whom?' |
| Prisoner | 'Everyone who was in the room.' |
| Investigator | 'What does that mean?' |
| Prisoner | 'Women, children, everyone. Anyone who was in the house.'[6] |

### Results

On October 7, Hamas executed a tactical surprise and carried out unprecedented slaughter in Israel. Israeli defense authorities at various levels failed to anticipate, engage, and repel the invaders for many hours, allowing for relentless, multi-site, large-scale killing. Caught in a whirlwind of passion, Gazan boys and some girls marched into Israel to participate in the killing and pillaging.

However, Palestinians in the West Bank did not participate in the killing, nor did Hezbollah immediately launch a major attack. The anticipated multi-front, multi-organizational mass invasion that was supposed to inundate Israeli cities and slaughter their residents ultimately failed to materialize. This may have been due to Hamas not coordinating with its PA counterparts for operational security reasons. It could also stem from a lack of enthusiasm beyond Hamas to engage in a murder spree, given the absence of clear, tangible outcomes beyond killing. The prospect of Israeli retribution might have deterred many Palestinians, as their homes would likely be destroyed, and participants could face imprisonment. The widely and jubilantly publicized simultaneous killing of Jewish communities certainly pleased many Palestinians.

While the October 7 killing never presented an existential threat to the Israeli nation, it was, by far, the bloodiest day in Israel's history. It was also the largest and most horrific mass murder of Jews since 1945. In terms of raw carnage and suffering, it was successful. But this did not translate into a mass uprising. It also united Israel to exact revenge and to take preventive measures. It may have eviscerated the kibbutznik-peacenik contingent that had been active and effective in Israeli politics. It will likely haunt Israel for years.

## *Goal 2 – Abduct and Exploit*

The second goal was to capture as many Israelis as possible and use them as hostages. Sinwar emphasized that Hamas' abductees must be kept alive because 'they are an important card' for securing the release of Hamas captives held in Israel. Hamas learned this from past abductions, one being a widely publicized incident. In June 2006, Hamas militants infiltrated Israel and took Gilad Shalit, an IDF soldier, hostage. In 2011, Shalit was exchanged for 1,027 Palestinian prisoners. A senior Israeli intelligence official described the exchange as 'one of the most asymmetrical incidents in recent memory.' It established a precedent.

A key Hamas doctrinal guide is the eight-page 'The Warrior's Guide: Jihadi Version.' This guide contains information about the IDF's order of battle and provides detailed instructions for abducting Israeli hostages. These instructions include using verbal threats and techniques for tackling and incapacitating hostages.[7]

Since the abduction on October 7, Israel has exchanged Hamas detainees for Israeli and foreign captives held by Hamas.[8] The exchange negotiations were a joint effort of Qatar, Egypt, and the United States. The Israeli hostages include infants, the elderly, Israeli soldiers, and civilians.[9] Israel paused its attack in November 2023 in exchange for the release of at least fifty hostages.[10] The negotiations for hostage release were long and arduous. They continued until some hostages were released, while others were tortured for months, murdered, or rescued – a few experienced good luck. An IDF elite unit stumbled upon Bedouin Qaid Farhan Alkadi (Profile 2 – Chapter 8) during a rescue operation.[11] At other times, Hamas shot captives when their rescue seemed imminent. This occurred on September 1, 2024, when Hamas shot six captives dead at point-blank range. Hamas issued instructions that if guards believed IDF rescue forces were closing in, they should shoot the hostages.[12]

### Results

Hamas operatives abducted hostages. The primary reason was to exchange them for imprisoned Palestinians, as had occurred years earlier with Gilad Shalit. However, there were secondary motives. One method of punishing Israel involved inflicting suffering on both Israeli captives and the nation. Captors impose physical and emotional trauma on their prisoners. They broadcast the grief and despair of captive adults and children to the world, allowing friends, parents, loved ones, and national leaders to witness their prolonged and acute pain.

Hamas secured the release of many Palestinian prisoners through exchanges. Hamas' daring and successful efforts to free its personnel from Israeli prisons demonstrated to both current members and potential recruits that it would not abandon them if they were imprisoned. The secondary motive for kidnapping Israelis was to inflict suffering on the Israeli nation. The hostages were not considered prisoners of war under the rules of the Geneva Conventions. They faced starvation, beating, sexual assault, degradation, and sometimes murder fueled by hatred.

Captive children were forced to watch films of the October 7 killings. Jailers told the children that Israel no longer exists and that their parents were dead.[13] A former hostage recounted, 'It was forbidden to cry or to laugh or to talk loudly . . . You can't teach a four-year-old child to cry silently.'[14] Conditions for girls and women are barbaric. Many have been victims of multiple rapes by different assailants.'[15]

Many prisoners experienced powerlessness. It was challenging to find any relief during their incarceration. An Israeli grandfather explained that humor was a form of salvation for those in captivity. He related that in the darkened tunnels, famished and often paralyzed with fear and pain, 'Humor saved us.'[16] Some captives remained unbroken during their captivity and grew stronger.[17] One young woman learned Arabic and cleverly observed and imitated the behavior of her captors. Her composure and connection with Hamas jailers kept her alive, and she aided fellow captives.[18] Other released captives never fully recovered. Hamas achieved victory by securing a disproportionately large number of Palestinians convicted of terrorist-related offenses. They also inflicted emotional pain on the Israeli nation, which was their intent. An Israeli Nobel laureate opined that the terms of the hostage exchange are preposterous (Profile 3 – Chapter 8).

## *Goal 3 – Break Israel's National Morale*

The third goal was to break Israel's national will to continue fighting. Both Hamas and Israeli leaders anticipated a prolonged conflict. Strategists also recognized that Hamas would escalate the violence to undermine Israel's national morale and tarnish its image globally. Hamas sought to fracture Israel's resolve to persist in the war through attrition. They used information operations to engage leftist elements within Israeli society and the international community. Almost immediately following the IDF's counterattack, many Israelis voiced strong protests against the heavy bombardment of Gaza. A significant number were concerned that attacks on Hamas would endanger Israeli hostages. Subsequently, other Israelis aligned with international organizations and described Israel's response as wildly disproportionate.

However, the nation remained united primarily in the goal of destroying Hamas and making every reasonable effort to secure the captives' return. This sentiment was captured by the words of a front-line officer, who said, 'Today in Israel, there is no right-wing, no left-wing, no Haredim. Just Jews.'[19] This harmony persisted throughout much of the war, although many Israelis urged the government to prioritize the hostages' return.

Some Israelis have sharply criticized their country's response to the 2023 attack. Some advocate for rebuilding homes and social infrastructure in Gaza that the IDF destroyed. However, this viewpoint does not represent the prevailing sentiment among Israelis. Many former Israeli peaceniks quickly lost faith in a two-state solution and became very skeptical of negotiations with Gazans.

## *Goal 4 – Keep the Ranks Replenished*

Hamas hindered the IDF's advance in close-quarter combat by setting up booby traps. Military analyst Seth Frantzman speculated that Hamas has persisted because the IDF never defeated Hamas' forces in central Gaza or Gaza City. When Hamas lost units, it rebuilt them. When it lost commanders, it replaced them with new ones. Over the years, Hamas has lost many leaders, including Yassin, al-Rantisi, and Salah Shehadeh. PIJ has also faced leadership losses. Losing fighters and commanders is a recurring pattern. This occurred during the earlier mini-war with Israel. In the May 2021 war, the IDF claimed to have eliminated 25 top Hamas commanders and recruits from a pool of around 300,000 young men. They are accustomed to Israel's airstrikes and moving among the rubble.[20]

### Results

Hamas has considerable experience in rebuilding its ranks and equipment stockpiles during and after minor conflicts. By June 2024, Hamas had lost nearly half of its forces during eight months of warfare and began utilizing hit-and-run tactics. According to US sources, the number of fighters decreased to between 9,000 and 12,000, down from 20,000 to 25,000 before October 2023. However, Hamas managed to restore some of its capabilities. Despite the relentless bombardment by the IDF, Hamas was able to regain some of its military capacities by early 2025. This enabled it to maintain its strategy of attrition while retaining its captives.

## *Goal 5 – Harness International Solidarity*

Hamas acted swiftly to garner global support. Meshaal was excited about the extensive international backing for Hamas that emerged. He emphasized the need for financial assistance and expressed hopes of forming an Arab and Muslim alliance with support from Russia and China. What neither Hamas nor the world could have foreseen was the significant backing Hamas received from college students in the West.

Hamas and its benefactors, particularly Qatar, were strategically positioned to influence the coverage of events in Gaza. Quickly, major media outlets, along with niche hard-left or Islamist websites and journalists, depicted Gazans as beleaguered victims of Israeli aggression. Soon, the term genocide was disseminated in the media, at the UN, on university campuses, and throughout the globe.

### Results

Many Gazans were initially excited about the October 7 attack, and support for Hamas grew quickly. Assessing Hamas' popularity among Gazans is difficult because many were relocated multiple times during the conflict, making accurate polling hard. Some surveys showed limited or mixed support for Hamas and its actions, while others indicated ongoing backing throughout the struggle. Many Gazans united behind Hamas on the day of the killings and for months afterward.

Most Gazans saw killing as a form of resistance. However, as the death toll and destruction of towns and city centers increased, many Gazans began to reconsider. A Gazan lawyer explained, 'This isn't resistance. This is insanity.'[21]

The international Green-Red Coalition, a loose alliance of Muslims and leftist activists, overwhelmingly rallied against Israel. Israel has lost its moral standing, however tenuous it was, among many European churches.[22] Alongside Norway and Spain, Ireland continues to stand out as particularly anti-Israel. It joined South Africa and several other nations in accusing Israel of genocide. In response, the Israeli government has closed its embassy borders.

By summer 2025, the waves of anti-Israel student protests at US universities had receded. President Trump informed campus activists, faculty, and administrators that foreign students on visas could face deportation if they promoted Hamas in the United States. Columbia University remained at the center of campus controversies. Much of this Columbia-Hamas controversy escalated when US immigration officials arrested Mahmoud Khalil (Profile 4 – Chapter 8), a Palestinian graduate student at Columbia, for his role in the student takeover of buildings during the protests[23] (see Table 1 – Chapter 8).

**Table 1 – Chapter 8: The Five Goals of Hamas**

| | | Purpose | Action Taken | Results |
|---|---|---|---|---|
| 1 | **Kill Indiscriminately** | Terrorize Israel; exact collective revenge on Israelis and those who support the state; prompt an uprising of Palestinians in the West Bank; release pent-up anger of Hamas cadre and some Gazans; prove to the world that Hamas is an active and lethal force. | Along multiple lines of attack and slaughter, Hamas units killed men, women, children, and household pets indiscriminately. | October 7 was the most lethal day in Jewish history after the fall of Nazi Germany. |
| 2 | **Abduct and Incarcerate Israelis** | To serve as bargaining chips for gaining concessions from Israel, such as the release of imprisoned Hamas operatives. | Hamas operatives forced people onto moving vehicles, while others marched them across the border into Gaza. | Hamas captured and imprisoned 251 individuals, including Israeli civilians, soldiers, and foreign nationals. |

*(Cont'd)*

| | | Purpose | Action Taken | Results |
|---|---|---|---|---|
| 3 | **Break Israel's Morale** | To create discord among Israel's parties and factions. | Partner with Hezbollah, PIJ, and the Houthis to overwhelm Israel. Collaborate with leaders in European civil society to bring an end to the IDF's attack. | Israel's national morale remained strong. There were some internal divisions, but most Israelis support the government's military actions against Gaza. |
| 4 | **Keep the Ranks Replenished** | To ensure a transparent chain of command, adequate leadership, and sufficient recruits to continue fighting. | Hamas built a pool of vetted, tested, and loyal personnel to move into senior leadership positions. Hamas had anticipated a heavy response from Israel and prepared to bring recruits into action quickly. | The IDF devastated the ranks of Hamas' leadership and cadre. They were replaced. |
| 5 | **Harness International Solidarity** | To influence media coverage that leads to changes in policies regarding international relations. To isolate Israel and to shift focus away from the Hamas attacks on October 7. | Collaborate with sympathetic journalists and media outlets. Present their case to NGOs and international organizations. Advocate for their case at universities students. | Overall, it was largely successful. Immediately following the October 7 attack, protests in solidarity with Gazans erupted and continued around the world. |

## Israel's War – Israel's Goals

From the outset of hostilities, Israel had five goals. They were to stop the invasion, repatriate the hostages, destroy Hamas cadre and infrastructure, assassinate Hamas leaders, and control Gaza.

## *Goal 1 – Stop the Invasion*

On October 7, the initial responders to the scene were local civilians. While the response was chaotic, it was also courageous. They seized available firearms and rushed toward the sounds of screams and gunfire to confront the threat. A second wave of responders included law enforcement officers and counterterrorism soldiers. Simultaneously, the IDF launched helicopter strikes within Israeli territory against the terrorists. However, it took as long as 8 to 12 hours for the IDF to dislodge Hamas invaders at some of the 30 locations.

The IDF regained control of the ground within 72 hours and conducted clearance operations for three days, eliminating the remaining pockets of resistance. Although some infiltrators remained in Israeli territory for up to three weeks, they were not considered operationally significant after the first five days.

### Results

Though it was late in the day for many scenes of slaughter, the IDF halted the invasion by the end of October 7. By the following day, the IDF was cleaning up pools of Hamas operatives who were trapped in Israel. However, the long delays in deploying forces to the slaughter centers proved to be fatal mistakes. On October 8, 2023, Israel targeted multiple sites across Gaza. At the same time, it mobilized 300,000 reservists as Israeli society adjusted to the new war. Colleges and universities in Israel postponed the start of classes and converted their dormitories into housing for reservists or shelters for those displaced by the conflict. The next day, Israel blockaded parts of Gaza and evacuated nearly 60,000 Israelis from towns near the border. Before launching the land operation, the IDF conducted aerial reconnaissance and precision airstrikes. By the morning of October 9, it had attacked 653 Hamas sites. The invasion was halted, and the Gaza envelope was secured.

## *Goal 2 – Secure the Return of the Hostages*

From the outset of the war, securing the release of hostages became a priority for Israel. Israel achieved their release, but as of mid-June 2025, 74 were murdered or died in captivity. However, this came at a significant cost. Many of the hostages faced humiliation during televised exchanges.[24] In early 2025, the hostage deliveries devolved into a cinematic spectacle, humiliating for the Israeli captives and their families. Armed Hamas fighters orchestrated theatrical ceremonies, parading captives onto stages while music blared in the background. During a gruesome ceremony, masked Hamas members presented the captives with release certificates. Hamas fighters stood at attention in front of a banner proclaiming that 'Nazi Zionism Will Not Win.' The prisoners were released, marking the conclusion of the performance. All of this was designed to serve as a national humiliation.

**Results**

Israel retrieved most of the captives at a significant cost. Many died in captivity. Some were slowly tortured and killed, and some were suddenly murdered. Some were exchanged for imprisoned Palestinian murderers. Many of the released hostages continue to suffer. Some could not escape their emotional demons, and several have taken their lives. The Israeli Health Ministry stated that it does not know how many survivors of the October 7 atrocities have died by suicide.[25] Sometimes the loss is overwhelming for the parents of children who died on October 7 or in captivity. This was true for Vladislav Bongart, who lost his daughter, Sofia (Profile 5 – Chapter 8).

## *Goal 3: Destroy Hamas' Cadre and Infrastructure*

> *If you want peace, destroy Hamas. If you want security, destroy Hamas. If you want a future for Israel, the Palestinians, the Middle East, destroy Hamas.*
>
> Israeli Prime Minister Benjamin Netanyahu[26]

In its earlier small wars with Hamas, Israel vowed to eliminate the group's terror infrastructure but fell short of that goal. Early in Iron Swords, senior Israeli leaders assured the nation and the international community that they would not falter in this conflict. Israel's Minister of Finance, Bezalel Smotrich, promised that Israel would destroy Gaza and completely obliterate Hamas' terror infrastructure in the area of operations. The Israeli-approved plan, Operation Gideon's Chariot, would likely involve 'the conquest of the Gaza Strip and the holding of the territories.'[27]

Before the war began, Israel provided Gaza with most of its energy needs. However, Israel quickly halted those supplies after declaring war on Hamas and imposed a complete temporary siege on Gaza. Soon after, Israel allowed essential supplies to enter Gaza, but only after the IDF inspected them. Israel denied any claims of trying to starve Gazans or that any Gazans were starving. It further asserted that it did not violate international law, emphasizing that its operation aimed to prevent Hamas from regrouping. Israel also stated that aid convoys were hijacked and that supplies were stolen because the UN would not allow all Israeli soldiers to safeguard the aid convoys.

The IDF has devastated much of Gaza, resulting in over 43,000 deaths, according to the Gaza Health Ministry, and displacing 1.9 million people – 90% of the population. These figures are fiercely contested, but the overall extent of destruction is clear. Photography, especially aerial photography, reveals the complete devastation of Gaza. Israel and its supporters defend the destruction and loss of life as unfortunate consequences of a righteous war during which Israel followed established rules of engagement. Meanwhile, Israel's critics label it genocide.

An estimated 1.7 million Gazans, accounting for 77% of the population, were displaced between October 2023 and mid-2025. Conditions were often harsh, with many crammed into overcrowded UN-run shelters. Skin diseases and diarrhea are widespread. Health care in Gaza, never robust by any standard, deteriorated sharply after October 7. Even in one of the few hospitals that remained operational throughout much of the war, the Gaza Health Ministry hospital in Rafah, medical conditions worsened as patients periodically slept in corridors and were crowded together in wards. Some observers assert that patients are malnourished. Israel responded that Hamas frequently stole medical supplies from international donors and sold them on the black market. Organized crime rings operated freely throughout the Strip.

The number of casualties on both sides has been contested. Israel claims that Hamas leadership has intentionally and significantly inflated the number of Gazans killed or injured by the IDF to portray Israel as deliberately targeting innocent people. These Israelis assert that the Gaza Ministry of Health has overstated casualty data by including natural deaths and failing to distinguish between civilian and combat casualties. The ministry estimates that more than 44,000 people have been killed since Israel launched its military response to the October 7 Hamas attacks. Israel disputes these figures and accuses the Gaza Ministry of Health of exaggerating the death toll to depict Israel as a genocidal nation-state. Israel contends that most of the Gazans killed were men aged 15 to 45 and that they were Hamas members.

### *Goal 4 – Assassinate Hamas Leaders*

Another priority was the assassination of Hamas leaders, which began immediately. Israel has a storied history of targeted assassination. Even before Israel was founded, Jewish terrorists killed European diplomats and British soldiers during the British administration of Mandated Palestine. In the 1960s, Israel sent letter bombs to target scientists helping Egypt develop rockets.[28] After the 1972 Munich Olympics massacre, Golda Meir ordered Mossad to pursue and kill those involved in the attack. Israel assassinated several of Iran's top nuclear scientists.[29]

One of the early high-profile killings of a senior Hamas leader was Yahya Ayyash, a high-ranking military commander known as 'the Engineer' for pioneering suicide bombings in the 1990s. He was killed in 1996 by a miniature bomb hidden in a mobile phone, planted by an Israeli agent, which exploded when Ayyash answered an incoming call. The following year, Israeli agents attempted to assassinate Khaled Meshaal by injecting him with poison on a street near his office in Jordan. However, the operation was unsuccessful, and Jordanian police arrested the would-be Israeli assassins. An outraged King Hussein threatened to sever relations with Israel unless it handed over the antidote.

The ethics and efficacy of targeted assassinations continue to spark intense debate. For many years, the United States criticized Israel's extrajudicial killings. However, following the terrorist attacks of September 2001, American military and security agencies collaborated with allies to locate and eliminate terrorists. Some world leaders and opinion makers oppose these assassinations, even against notorious terrorists like Osama bin Laden, arguing that such actions are never justifiable under international law. Nonetheless, Israel declared its intention to eliminate Hamas leaders and has remained true to its word.

Some killings are less sensational, while others are puzzling. This was the case with the Aljama family, who were widely respected as pious and prominent members of the Gazan community (Profile 6 – Chapter 8). While people knew they had connections to Hamas, neighbors claimed to be unaware of the extent of those ties. When Israeli forces stormed the Aljama's building, they found Almog Meir Jan, Andrey Kozlov, and Shlomi Ziv, hostages who had been captured from the Nova music festival on October 7, cowering in the building's darkness.[30]

**Results**

There has also been an ongoing discussion about the effectiveness of selective assassination. Assassinations often serve purposes that extend beyond merely eliminating a single target. These purposes include revenge, boosting national morale, deterrence, and undermining collective leadership. Israelis were largely supportive of assassinating Hamas figures after October 7. The wanton and joyous slaughter by Hamas, along with the seeming approval from many Gazans, fueled Israel's demand for retribution. There was national satisfaction with the assassination of the killer of Shani Louk, the young woman whose body was paraded in the streets of Gaza City in the back of a pickup truck on October 7.

For years, several prominent Hamas leaders have resided outside Gaza due to security concerns. Many of them have also accumulated immense wealth, siphoning billions of dollars from international donations. While there are more challenging targets, they are not entirely beyond the IDF's reach. The IDF has tracked down and eliminated numerous leaders, some of whom are listed in Appendix D – Selected Key Assassinations of Hamas Leaders.

## *Goal 5 – Control Gaza*

The long-term goal for Israel, as stated by Prime Minister Benjamin Netanyahu, is the total defeat and elimination of Hamas. Israel's stated objectives also include destroying Hamas' infrastructure, particularly its extensive network of tunnels. Nevertheless, according to Israeli media, Hamas' tunnel network remains operational, although estimates of how much of it is still intact vary significantly.

According to the plan, once Hamas is eliminated, civilians in Gaza will play a crucial role in civil society and public administration. Israel would implement decisive measures to deradicalize schools, mosques, and media outlets. Additionally, it will prevent UNRWA from operating in Gaza, replacing its efforts with those of other aid organizations that are not affiliated with extremist groups. Reconstruction would be funded by countries that have not supported Hamas. However, before Gaza can be free of terrorist elements, there might be a year of intense fighting in the streets, tunnels, and homes.

**Results**

Many Gazans have endured prolonged trauma during the war. Hamas' hubris of October 7 faded soon after the IDF struck the Gaza Strip. While many Gazans supported Hamas throughout most of the war, some grew weary of the fear and misery, yearning for the relative prosperity they enjoyed before 2023. Gaza was never wealthy by Western standards, but its economy and living standards improved. The unemployment rate decreased in 2022 and 2023, and Gaza enjoyed near-record exports. There was a sense of optimism. In 2023, 18,000 Gazans held day jobs in Israel, with plans to expand the program to include tens of thousands of new participants from Gaza. Gazans requiring advanced medical care were brought to Israeli hospitals for treatment.

Many observers are skeptical that Israel committed genocide and asked why Israel would warn Gazans that their dwellings would be bombed before they struck them. What explains the many millions of warning leaflets and robocalls? Why did Israel facilitate the transfer of humanitarian aid into Gaza if its purpose was mass murder?[31] A review conducted by the UK Lawyers for Israel and other advocacy organizations and think tanks cast doubt on the claims of starvation and malnutrition.

By summer 2025, the IDF began revising elements of its strategy in Gaza. It began by bypassing Hamas leaders to partner cautiously with local clan chieftains.[32] Armed clans are reasserting themselves in the Gaza Strip and are battling with Hamas leaders for power and resources. There are seven powerful clans in Gaza.[33]

**Table 2 – Chapter 8: The Five Goals of Israel**

| | | Purpose | Action Taken | Results? |
|---|---|---|---|---|
| 1 | **Stop the Invasion** | Stop Hamas' push towards major cities and repel the invasion. | The IDF directed all available forces toward the Gaza Envelope and unleashed artillery and air power on October 8. | The IDF halted the invasion by the close of October 7. Cleared the Gaza envelope in days. |
| 2 | **Secure the Return of the Hostages** | To return hostages to their families and homes. To eliminate the issue of hostages as a bargaining tactic for Hamas. | Deployed specialized military units to rescue them and negotiated the release of Hamas and Hamas-affiliated captives in Israel. | Partial success and partial failure. The known hostages have been returned but many were murdered in captivity and some were lost in friendly fire. |

*(Cont'd)*

| | | Purpose | Action Taken | Results? |
|---|---|---|---|---|
| 3 | **Destroy Hamas' Cadre and Infrastructure** | To destroy Hamas' ability to reconstitute itself and build its military capability. | The IDF launched Operation Swords of Iron – relentless attacks on personnel, facilities, and residences. | As of 2026, the IDF has killed between 30,000 and 60,000 Gazans, though the numbers are disputed. It displaced nearly 90% of the population at some point. |
| 4 | **Assassinate Hamas Leaders** | To make it difficult for Hamas to control activities. | Unrelenting assassinations of Hamas leaders and those suspected of being in the pipeline. | As of July 2025, it has killed dozens of Hamas senior leaders. The IDF reduced the ability of senior leaders to command, control, and communicate. |
| 5 | **Control Gaza** | Control all entry points. Remove Hamas leaders who may attempt to rebuild Hamas. | Clear and hold strategic points in Gaza. Eliminate Hamas' leaders. | To be determined. |

## The Nature of the War – Strategy, Tactics, and Orders of Battle

### *Israel*

Israel's doctrine synchronized air support with ground and armored units, showcasing considerable flexibility and innovation. The IDF segments the urban battlefield into four dimensions. The first dimension is the sky above Gaza. The second consists of high-rise buildings that provide vantage points for reconnaissance and sniper fire. The third is the complex maze of Gaza's streets, filled with roads and alleys. The fourth dimension includes the subterranean tunnel system, which contains command and control centers, living quarters, and weapons storage facilities. IDF forces were poised to assert dominance across all four dimensions, commencing with an aerial assault. The IDF's tactics evolved in response to Hamas' strategic adjustments.

Israel's use of force is guided by the Purity of Arms ethos, traceable to the principles of Orde Wingate. Purity of Arms is a policy that mandates using force to kill only when necessary. This principle is rooted in Jewish and international law and is formalized in a doctrinal statement. IDF servicemen and servicewomen must ensure they do not cause unnecessary harm to the enemy, which requires exercising self-control in combat. Israel's strategy significantly differed from Hamas'. The IDF aimed to eliminate Hamas in Gaza and prevent additional forces from entering the conflict. The IDF recognized this as its longest, most costly, and deadliest engagement.

## Air War – Death from Above

Hamas understood that shortly after fighting began, Israel's air assets would target positions in Gaza. They aimed to disable as many Israeli aircraft as possible in the early moments of the attack. On October 7, Hamas launched 4,500 rockets and mortar shells at Israeli Air Force bases in the Negev and near Tel Aviv. They sought to saturate the bases to bring down the aircraft. Hamas planned to invade the Tel Nof Base, about 45 miles north of the Strip, with three waves of attack using 10 pickup trucks equipped with weapons. However, the trucks were destroyed by UAVs and ground forces, while the aircraft remained intact. Like the IDF's ground troops, Israel's air assets were unexpectedly unprepared. Additionally, many pilots lacked sufficient training.

The Air Force had not conducted ground invasion exercises from Gaza in recent years. However, Israeli aircraft soon took to the skies and launched a relentless series of strikes. The number of targets hit by the Air Force in the first four months surpassed more than double the daily average of targets struck in 2014 during fifty days of war. In the eleven-day conflict in May 2021, Israel targeted approximately 1,500 sites, reflecting a significantly lower per-day average. The Air Force has been relentless in its attacks on senior Hamas leaders and has reduced large parts of Gaza to ruins. This has also drawn international and Israeli criticism. In spring 2025, nearly 1,000 Air Force veterans signed a letter calling on Israel to end the war. The letter did not suggest that Israeli servicemen and women should not serve in protest.[34]

## City Fighting – 'Attacking the Heart and Guts'[35]

When Iron Swords started in earnest, it hit like a whirlwind. After softening targets with air-launched attacks, the IDF raided Gaza using tanks, infantry, and armored bulldozers. Early in the fighting, Israel imposed a near-total communications blackout on the Strip. The IDF began bombing targets and initiated minor ground incursions in the north through night raids. Soon after, the IDF commenced armored probing operations on the outskirts of Gaza City. Urban fighting had begun.

Attacking defended cities has been one of the most challenging and potentially costly military operations, as reflected in the ancient Chinese text *The Art of War*. It recognizes the difficulties of seizing cities and cautions its readers that the lowest realization of warfare is to assault a fortified city. Historically, urban warfare has been brutal, bloody, and at times prolonged. In the 20th century, monuments in Stalingrad, Berlin, Manila, and Kharkov stand as testaments to the fierce street-by-street and often hand-to-hand fighting. City fighting provides advantages for the defender due to numerous physical barriers and obstacles that an invader must overcome. Defenders are familiar with the terrain and structures, enabling them to effectively conceal themselves within a building and, in the case of Gaza, to hide and navigate an extensive tunnel system.

As IDF leaders predicted, the war evolved into a prolonged, slow-moving urban conflict in the streets and underground tunnels. Hamas operatives were highly skilled at disguising themselves as civilians. The group employed children and older men and women as lookouts to assist in ambushing Israeli soldiers and civilians. Some homes served as makeshift prisons for Israeli captives. From below ground, Hamas' army quickly emerged from a maze of tunnels – often armed with rocket-propelled grenades – to strike at Israeli soldiers before swiftly retreating to their subterranean stronghold. At times, they blended in with civilians.

Israeli forces had to navigate narrow streets while dodging fire from high-rise buildings. There was a constant threat of Hamas operatives appearing from piles of rubble scattered throughout the cities. Many standing structures contained booby traps, prompting IDF operators to adjust their tactics early in the war. IDF strategists learned valuable lessons from previous battles with Hamas.

## Underground Warfare – Tunnels and Shelter

Tunnels serve various purposes in warfare. References to tunneling can be found in the Bible, the US Civil War, and World War I, reflecting their significance in military history. Hamas constructed its first tunnels in the 1980s to smuggle materials from Egypt. Its first documented tunnel attack from the Gaza Strip occurred in 1989. After Israel's withdrawal in 2005, Hamas began channeling aid funds and materials to rebuild tunnels and other military structures. Operatives evaluated the effectiveness of the tunnels.

In July 2014, several infiltrations near the Israeli villages of Sufa and Nir-Am, as well as the Israeli security post Nahal Oz, resulted in the deaths of 11 IDF soldiers, although Hamas also suffered casualties. In a separate incident in 2013, Hamas fighters disguised as IDF members killed two soldiers after ambushing an army patrol car. Additionally, Hamas effectively used its tunnel network to abduct Gilad Shalit in 2006.

All of this was preparation for October 7. Shortly after the war started, the IDF found civilian and militant facilities inside the tunnels. The walls and floors were made of concrete slabs, with some ceilings reaching up to 10 feet high. The tunnels had bathrooms, living quarters, offices, and power supplies. When IDF soldiers entered Gaza, they encountered Hamas operatives scattered throughout the area. Hamas used schools, hospitals, and mosques to hide operatives and store weapons. At one hospital alone, the IDF captured 100 suspected terrorists along with weapons, cash, and intelligence materials. Hamas used ambulances to move its operatives and to seize food meant for Gaza residents. The PA acknowledged that Hamas turned hospitals into military interrogation centers.

Operatives found refuge within the tunnels, protected from IDF surveillance while securely storing weapons and munitions. Hamas could use these tunnels for ambushes during Israeli ground operations in Gaza. They were likened to the German trenches in World War I, which had more permanence than the French or British trenches. IDF Col. Liron Betito, commander of Givati Brigade, opined that the 'center of gravity is the tunnels.' He added that unless the tunnels collapse, the area cannot be controlled. 'This way, [Hamas] will have no choice but to either die inside [the tunnel] or to come outside.'[36]

In response to the sophistication of the subterranean structures, the IDF revised its counter-tunnel tactics. Before October 2023, IDF field commanders evacuated civilians from areas and bombed suspected tunnel sites. This tactic proved ineffective for the IDF because Hamas operators relocated to tunnel shafts that remained undamaged. Hamas then launched attacks from these locations. With this method, the IDF was unable to collapse a sufficient length of tunnels, which spanned 300 miles.

The IDF developed a new counter-tunnel doctrine and tactics nine years after Operation Protective Edge. Within Israel, the IDF replicated Hamas tunnels for soldiers to train in the dark. Detecting tunnel locations is difficult. The IDF used ground-penetrating radar and precision bombs in a tactic called 'kinetic drilling.' Israel's Air Force bombed deep into the ground to destroy the tunnels. It often failed because the munitions couldn't reach close enough to the tunnels to cause them to collapse.

IDF special operators learned to maneuver proficiently underground. The IDF anticipated the need to clear and destroy the tunnel network. In previous wars and skirmishes, IDF personnel avoided fighting in tunnels, many of which were booby-trapped. Drones cannot effectively monitor tunnel activity, and GPS signals are often unreliable in such environments.[37] Israel's technological advantage falters in the underground maze of concrete.[38]

When Israel invaded Gaza, the IDF found miles of tunnels throughout Gaza. The IDF discovered a Hamas command tunnel running under the UNRWA headquarters in Gaza.[39] More notable examples are Gaza-located hospitals that Hamas used for military purposes. They used it extensively, and Israeli forces needed to clear out.[40]

IDF soldiers uncovering hostages in the Gaza underground encountered numerous surprises. In September 2024, nearly a year after the war began, a joint Israeli-American rescue operation freed a 21-year-old Yazidi woman who had been in captivity for over 10 years. The Yazidi religious minority, primarily located in Iraq and Syria, was targeted and killed by the Islamic State in 2014. Abducted at the age of 11 and freed at 21, Fawiza Amin Sido (Profile 7 – Chapter 8) was finally reunited with her family in Jordan.

By the end of 2023, the first IDF soldiers entered the tunnels equipped with infrared vision and advanced navigation tools. Another innovation involved lowering cameras into the tunnels that were connected to explosives, which could be detonated when a terrorist approached. The IDF's canine unit includes dogs trained for various tasks, such as search-and-rescue operations and explosives detection, including bomb detection. Some canines are specifically trained to engage enemies in the tunnels.

The IDF has established a specialized engineering brigade focused on underground tunnel operations. They worked closely with US Army engineers to develop effective technologies and tactics. The Yahalom unit is fully equipped with the necessary tools and strategies to perform a wide range of underground warfare tasks, from detecting, securing, and mapping tunnels and bunkers to exploiting, clearing, neutralizing, and destroying them. The IDF also runs a strong military working dog program, the Oketz unit, which includes dogs trained for operations in subterranean environments.[41] The individual primarily responsible for detecting, studying, and dismantling the extensive network of underground tunnels built by Hamas in Gaza is Maj Gen. Dan Goldfus (Profile 8 – Chapter 8).

**Armored Warfare**

The IDF's armored corps led ground operations in October 2023 as a standard tactic. In late October, IDF armor acted as the battle trailblazer into Hamas' positions after initial hit-and-run raids. IDF armor units advanced into northern Gaza from multiple directions, encircled Gaza City, and severed maritime lines of communication.[42]

By mid-October, Israel began deploying tanks into Gaza. The IDF launched a shaping operation with the Merkava Mark IV, one of the world's most advanced tanks. The Mark IV carries four soldiers on its back, who conduct reconnaissance by fire. Israel's indigenous Merkava tank, featuring a distinctive wedge-shaped turret, boasts multi-layered protection consisting of composite plates and reactive armor. Additionally, it is equipped with the Trophy system, which uses radar and optical sensors to detect incoming missiles and rockets.[43] The Trophy system enabled IDF tanks to breach Hamas' lines of defense.[44]

The IDF used the D9 armored bulldozer, nicknamed 'Doobi', to clear the path for troops. 'Doobi,' which means 'teddy bear' in Hebrew, weighs 60 tons, stands 13 feet tall, and is nearly 15 feet wide. It features armor, a large front dozer blade, and a bulletproof cockpit that protects a two-person crew from snipers.[45] The Doobi clears obstacles, rubble, and booby traps ahead of advancing troops and has been used in previous urban operations. However, the Doobi is susceptible to explosively formed projectiles and mines buried in the road, as well as rocket-propelled grenades fired from rooftops.[46]

## Major Battles of the War

### *The Battles for Rafah*

Rafah has existed for thousands of years. The Canaanites called it Rafah, a name familiar to the ancient Egyptians and Romans.[47] It has served as a gateway for invasions for centuries and retains military significance today. Three historically significant battles took place in Rafah. The first occurred in January 1917, pitting the British against the Turks. The second took place during Israel's War of Independence. The third happened in spring 2024 when the IDF advanced into Rafah to eliminate Hamas, which had regrouped there.[48]

The Rafah border crossing with Egypt is one of two corridors through which supplies enter the Gaza Strip. Netanyahu stressed that seizing it would be a significant step toward destroying Gaza.[49] Because of its strategic location, Rafah became the center of the 'tunnel industry.' Hamas built the tunnels, operated the trafficking of goods between Egypt and Gaza, collected tolls, and trained operatives to navigate the twists and turns of the underground network.

In May 2024, Hamas began a three-month operation to remove its fighters from Rafah, resulting in the deaths of up to 1,000 Hamas fighters and the capture of hundreds.[50] It was controversial from the beginning. The living conditions were squalid, and because Hamas fighters dispersed among the civilian population, noncombatants remained vulnerable. A middle-aged refugee in Rafah said in early May 2024 that the IDF has 'gone crazy; tanks are firing shells, and smoke bombs are covering the skies.'[51] PA President Abbas called the Israeli occupation a threat to the peace. Saudi Arabia warned of a 'humanitarian catastrophe' if the plan went ahead.[52] Rafah is the last organizational stronghold of Hamas.

In mid-September 2024, the IDF announced that it had destroyed Hamas' main fighting unit, the Rafah Brigade. The brigade's four battalions were eliminated, and the IDF secured operational control over Rafah. The IDF revealed the full extent of the tunnel network, which contained separate but interconnected tunnels in the Philadelphi Corridor, linking Egypt to Rafah.[53]

The Rafah Brigade was destroyed, and much of Rafah suffered the same fate. Before the attack, Rafah sheltered over one million people at different times. Many had moved there temporarily to escape the fighting in the north. By autumn 2024, it was mainly in ruins. Most blackened homes had their walls and windows blown out. Few civilians walked the streets of what had become a ghost town. Most of the agricultural land, power grid, water and sewage facilities, as well as municipal buildings, were destroyed.[54] The IDF returned to Rafah in April 2025, following the collapse of ceasefire negotiations. Observers referred to this as 'flattening the ruins.'[55] The IDF explained that it needs to create 'buffer zones' around Gaza's edges, including all of Rafah.

## *Gaza City*

Very early in the war, the IDF attacked Gaza City. Israel divided the Gaza Strip in half, claiming this would make it harder for Hamas to control the area. Israeli forces have advanced deeper into Gaza City in their assault on Hamas in the northern Gaza Strip. However, they faced resistance from militant hit-and-run attacks originating from underground tunnels.[56]

The Israeli military released footage of a tunnel network in Gaza City, which it claimed provided Hamas' senior leadership and operatives with a covert passage through the enclave. The military stated that tunnel shafts were discovered in the residences and offices of senior Hamas officials, enabling clandestine descents via elevators and stairs that allowed for both escapes and extended stays. The central Gaza City complex was connected to nodes from which Hamas leaders could emerge above ground and obtain protected passage to other areas of Gaza.

According to the UN, 'Gaza is the hungriest place on Earth.[57] Many landmarks no longer exist. Rashad al-Shawa Cultural Center, which hosted a meeting between former US President Bill Clinton and former Palestinian President Yasser Arafat in 1988. The Center also included a library and a theater.[58] It contained a theater, a grand hall, a public library, a printing press, and a cultural salon. It was described as the gem of Gaza City. Now, that gem lies in ruins. It was destroyed by Israeli bombardment.[59]

## *Operation Gideon's Chariots*

In mid-May 2025, the IDF launched Operation Gideon's Chariots as the second major operation in the war against Hamas. Operation Gideon's Chariots draws on its biblical roots and resonates deeply. This operation evokes imagery of the great biblical warrior Gideon, who led forces to defeat the more powerful Midianites. The hero Gideon demonstrated military acumen, outmaneuvering his enemy. He trapped them and sent them into retreat.[60]

The offensive followed a week of aerial bombardment by the Israeli Air Force, which targeted over 670 sites linked to the Hamas terrorist organization across the coastal enclave. According to the IDF, the airstrikes aimed to disrupt Hamas' military readiness and support ground forces. Targets hit included weapons depots, terrorist operatives, underground infrastructure, and anti-tank missile launch sites. Israeli troops on the ground have reportedly killed dozens of terrorists, destroyed both above-ground and underground terror infrastructure, and are now taking control of key strategic areas of the Strip.[61]

The campaign is divided into three phases. First, the IDF will take control of Gaza and secure the area. Second, Israel will move Gaza's civilians to designated 'sterile' zones in the southwest while screening for Hamas operatives. The IDF will maintain control of the territory to prevent Hamas from reentering. Ultimately, the IDF will be responsible for managing and distributing humanitarian aid.[62] Implement information operations to persuade Gazans that avoiding Hamas and building lasting relationships is in their best interest for development.[63]

This plan alarmed European countries, with several claiming it was similar to ethnic cleansing. European nations issued a joint statement in May 2025 expressing 'grave concern' and opposition to the planned IDF military operations in the Gaza Strip. Luxembourg's Prime Minister Luc Frieden said, 'Whether in Gaza, Ukraine, or other conflicts, international law and the protection of civilians must be applied universally.'[64]

## Other Killings

Israel's death list is extensive and constantly changing. Selective assassinations remain a central tactic in Operation Gideon's Chariots. Names are removed from that death list, but others are added as intelligence verifies their involvement in crimes. Some of those on the list are prominent Hamas leaders, while others are less well-known but significantly implicated in the October 7 attack. For instance, Mohammed Hassan Mohammed Awad (Profile 9 – Chapter 8) was a planner of the attack and was likely personally involved in the murder of the Bibas family. The IDF and Shin Bet killed him in April 2025.[65]

Hamas and its supporters continued to target Israeli interests worldwide. Zvi Kogan, a rabbi who operated a kosher supermarket in Dubai, was murdered in Abu Dhabi (Profile 10 – Chapter 8). The UAE's interior ministry announced that three suspects had been arrested in connection with the murder but did not provide additional details. Kogan, a prominent figure representing Israel's growing presence in the UAE, had also served in the elite Givati unit of the Israeli military. Israeli security experts suspected that there was a strong Iranian connection.

The IDF openly kills Hamas leaders, but so does Hamas. Hamas also kills its own. Hamas' 'Arrow' unit, Wahdat Sahm, carries out on-site executions against Gazans accused of collaborating with Israel. The murders are usually gruesome and sometimes cinematic. In a statement circulating online, the unit broadcast 'the limbs of 13 thieves and people who incite chaos and anarchy will be amputated and their legs will be shot.'[66]

Israel's 2023–2025 conflict with Hamas was unprecedented. Previous large-scale wars focused on battles that prioritized maneuver, speed, and overwhelming firepower. In the 1967 war, Israel acted swiftly and was well-prepared. In the 1973 war, Egypt initially gained the upper hand but was ultimately thwarted by Israel's tactics and superior weaponry. The conflict with Hamas was prolonged, costly, grueling, and historically deadly. Despite Israel's technical superiority and the military abilities of its pilots and soldiers, the IDF lacked the strategic advantage it had in earlier conflicts.

## Summary

On the day of the attack, Hamas was prepared, while Israel was unprepared. Hamas had five goals: to kill as many people and pets as possible; to abduct hostages and transport them to Gaza; to break Israel's will to wage war aggressively; to replenish their leadership and the ranks of the cadre as they were depleted; and to harness and maintain international support. Israel also had five goals, though they were strikingly different. These included stopping the invasion, repatriating the hostages, destroying Hamas cadre and infrastructure, assassinating Hamas leaders, and controlling Gaza. As Israel predicted, the war was long, slow-moving, and painful for both sides. The successes and failures of both sides in that war are the subject of Chapter 10.

**Profile 1 – Khaled Meshaal: Living Martyr**
**Name:** Khaled Meshaal
**Nationality:** Palestinian
**Profession:** Former head of Hamas' political wing since 1996. Today, he is likely the leader of Hamas in exile.
**Connection to October 7, 2023:** He earned a bachelor's degree in physics and taught science in Kuwait for years. By mid-adolescence, he was drawn to the Muslim Brotherhood and the cause of Palestinian nationalism. Soon after, Yasin founded Hamas, and Meshaal opened a branch in Kuwait. He, along with 300,000 other Palestinians, had overstayed their welcome and was subsequently deported. From there, he moved to Damascus, then to Doha, and finally to Amman.

While living in Amman during the 1990s, Meshaal directed Hamas' suicide bombings in Israel. In response, Prime Minister Netanyahu targeted him for assassination. However, Israeli operatives botched the job. Israeli agents approached Meshaal on the street in Amman and injected a slow-acting poison into one of his ears. They aimed accurately, but one of his bodyguards tackled the would-be assassins. The failed operation quickly escalated into an international incident, prompting President Clinton to urge Netanyahu to save Meshaal. Netanyahu intervened and provided an antidote that jolted Meshaal from his coma and saved his life. This incident bolstered Meshaal's image and earned him the title of the 'living martyr.' There is no evidence that this near-death experience diminished his energy.

He was closely involved in planning and launching the October 7 attack. For weeks after the killing spree, he gloated that the attack catapulted Hamas and the Palestinian cause to the center of global attention. 'There is no change in Hamas' strategy, and what happened on 7 October is completely within Hamas' strategy. The ones who kill women and children, mothers and fathers, are Israelis.'[67]
**Current Status:** Some call him a 'living martyr' due to Israel's failed attempts to kill him.[68] Living in Qatar, he is assumed to be active in Hamas' operations.

**Profile 2 – Bedouin Qaid Farhan Alkadi**
**Name:** Qaid Farhan Alkadi
**Nationality:** Bedouin
**Profession:** Worker on Kibbutz Magen
**Connection to October 7, 2023:** A well-known member of the Bedouin community in Israel, Qaid Farhan Alkandi, was captured and taken to Gaza, where he has been held for over 300 days. He had a large family, with 11 children, including one born in 2023. A Hamas operative shot him in the leg before his capture. Later, Hamas medical staff removed the bullet from his leg without anesthesia. He then endured intense pain, compounded by slow starvation. He also witnessed fellow captives

die before him. Regarding hygiene, he was allowed to bathe only once a month and could not distinguish day from night.

Then, Israeli naval commandos found him while scouring the tunnels. After 10 months of war, he was discovered almost by chance. The commandos had a hunch that some captives were close by. Alkandi heard footsteps and then the sound of men speaking Hebrew. When the soldiers saw him, Alkandi was grinning. The unexpected rescue boosted morale in Israel and provided great photo opportunities. Alkandi was weakened by hunger and taken to a hospital where his very large family embraced him.[69]

**Current Status:** Unknown.

**Profile 3 – Aumann's Game Theory**

**Name:** Yisrael (Robert) Aumann

**Nationality:** Israeli

**Profession:** Economist, mathematician

**Connection to October 7, 2023:** He escaped Germany with his family in 1938, always staying one step ahead of the Nazis. After arriving in America, he attended a Jewish religious school and later went to MIT, where he earned a Ph.D. in mathematics. His dissertation focused on knot theory, which prepared him to study game theory. Very comfortable in the world of ideas, he helped rabbis analyze Talmudic issues, especially those related to inheritance, where his equations proved effective. Much of his life centered around his family. He moved to Israel with his wife and five children; however, his eldest son was tragically killed in the 1982 Lebanon War.

After receiving numerous prestigious awards, he shared the Nobel Prize in 2005 with Thomas Schelling. His esteemed reputation and recognized wisdom gave him a respected voice on the subject of hostage exchanges. He argues that the current terms violate the principles of game theory. He suggested that Israel should release prisoners convicted of crimes against Arabs. He stated that the current terms of trade also make no sense. 'We are releasing terrorists who have killed dozens of people, which is very bad because after their release, they will kidnap and kill many more Jews than the number of hostages. This is obvious. I don't know what the logic is in this.'[70]

He criticizes the Gilad Schalit (sometimes spelled Shalit) exchange, claiming it set a precedent and directly caused the October 7 attack. 'I am glad that Gilad Schalit is now living a normal life, but I am not happy about the thousands of people who were killed as a direct result of the October 7th massacre, which was a direct result of the Shalit deal. I am not willing to have another such thing happen.'[71]

**Current Status:** He is in his late nineties.

**Profile 4 – Mahmoud Khalil: Prison and Bedbugs!**

**Names:** Mahmoud Khalil

**Nationality:** Syrian/Palestinian

**Profession:** Former graduate student

**Connection to October 7, 2023:** This activist likely never anticipated the level of attention he would receive following his protests at Columbia University. Mahmoud Khalil was among the leaders of the prestigious university's demonstrations against Israel. In early March 2025, he was detained by federal authorities and informed that his green card was being revoked. The Department of Homeland Security explained that he violated his status by 'activities aligned to Hamas, a designated terrorist organization.'[72]

His central role in the student takeover of campus buildings is not disputed. He served as a student negotiator. Soon after his detention, he was whisked to a federal immigration detention facility in central Louisiana. His incarceration set off civil liberties disputes and yet further protests at Columbia. Khalil pines, 'For decades, anti-Palestinian racism has driven efforts to expand US laws and practices that are used to repress Palestinians, Arab Americans, and other communities violently. That is precisely why I am being targeted.'[73]

Secretary of State Rubio dismissed it entirely. He explained, 'We are reviewing the visa status of the trespassers and vandals who took over Columbia University's library. Pro-Hamas thugs are no longer welcome in our great nation.'[74] He has both supporters and opponents. He has certainly experienced a decline in his standard of living, and he was dissatisfied with the conditions at the detention center in Elizabeth, New Jersey. His lawyers argued that the facilities there were inadequate. Kahlil added, 'I did not hear anyone mention bedbugs.'[75]

**Current Status:** His legal case is under review by federal courts.

**Profile 5 – Vladislav Bongart: Red, Red Roses**

**Names:** Vladislav Bongart

**Nationality:** Born in Ukraine, Israeli national

**Profession:** Former profession unknown

**Connection to October 7, 2023:** Vladislav and Anna immigrated to Israel from Ukraine in 2006, when their daughter Sofia was four years old. They lived in a small town near Galilee and were very frugal. They had another daughter named Evelina. Their family was close-knit and loving.[76] Sofia had just completed her military service. The soft-spoken and respectful girl had many friends. Sofia and her dad created TikTok videos together.[77] They were close.

But she was killed along with her best friend at the Nova festival on October 7. They were hiding in a bomb shelter when Hamas found them and threw grenades inside. Then, Hamas opened fire on the survivors. Vladislav Bongart never recovered from his loss. Sofia loved red roses, and he often placed one on her white grave. He kept the pain to himself, where it swelled. Eventually, he could no longer bear it. His wife, Anna, described the guilt he felt for not being able to help their daughter. She said, 'We put on a mask and carried our pain. But Vladislav never shared what he was going through.' So, he killed himself.

**Current Status:** Anna mourns her firstborn daughter and husband. She cherishes the memories of life in Israel before the Black Sabbath. Life is tough for her and her family today. She reminisces, 'We immigrated to Israel, brought another child into the family, and even managed to save money, allowing us to buy an apartment. Now, I have to provide for our home.'[78]

**Profile 6 – The Aljama Family: Widely Respected**
**Names**: Ahmed Aljamal and Abdallah Alijamal
**Nationality:** Palestinian/Gazan
**Profession:** Ahmed was a physician deeply involved in a mosque. His son, Abdallah, nicknamed 'Chubby Cheeks,' was a journalist who wrote for the US-based online publication *The Palestine Chronicle.*
**Connection to October 7, 2023:** Family members were devout and connected to Hamas. They used their home in Nuseirat to hold Israeli hostages captive. Abdallah Aljamal was a Hamas operative who captured Almog Meir Jan, Andrey Kozlov, and Shlomi Ziv. The IDF killed both Ahmed and his son Abdallah during the rescue of three Israeli captives in June 2024. The Aljamal family name continues to carry prestige in Gaza. They were known as pious and prominent members of the community. While people acknowledged their connections to Hamas, neighbors say few knew how deep those ties ran.[79]

But many Gazans view the father and son as martyrs. Al Jazeera quickly stated that it never had an association with Abdallah, and *The Palestine Chronicle* rejected the claim that Abdallah was a captor of the hostages.[80] The IDF confirmed that he was heavily involved in numerous Hamas operations. IDF spokespersons added, 'This is further proof that the Hamas terrorist organization uses the civilian population as a human shield.'[81]
**Current Status:** Father and son are both dead.

**Profile 7 – Fawiza Amin Sido**
**Name:** Fawiza Amin Sido
**Nationality:** Iraqi-born, largely stateless
**Profession:** Released captive
**Connection to October 7, 2023:** Yazidi Fawzia Amin Sido was just 11 years old when she and her siblings were taken by ISIS from their village in northern Iraq in 2014. She endured starvation for four days before being given meat and rice. Their captors told them that the meat they were eating was for Yazidi babies. Then, her nightmare persisted for 10 years as she was sold into slavery.[82]

While her two brothers were sent to a camp to be indoctrinated and trained as child soldiers, Fawzia was subjected to sexual slavery and abuse. After over a year in captivity in Iraq, she was transported to Syria, where a Palestinian ISIS fighter enslaved her. She was forced into marriage and gave birth to two daughters. She was prevented from speaking her native language and needed to learn Arabic.[83]

As a Yazidi, she endured harsh treatment. She was freed at the age of 21 when IDF soldiers found her in the Gaza warren of tunnels.[84] Hamas claims that this story is a lie and that she came voluntarily to Turkey, Egypt, and Gaza. Hamas maintains that they treated her with respect and provided her with a private space room.
**Current Status:** She returned to Baghdad to rejoin her family members.

**Profile 8 – Major General Daniel Goldfus: Destroyer of Tunnels**
**Name:** Daniel Goldfus
**Nationality:** Israeli
**Profession:** Soldier, Major General, and theoretician of armored warfare
**Connection to October 7, 2023:** The IDF is the world's most experienced army in tunnel fighting. It has a complete brigade-sized trained and equipped for subterranean warfare.[85] The leader of Division 98 is Daniel Goldfus, who was born in South Africa. He is celebrated as a hero of the Israeli victory in Khan Yunis and is the nation's foremost expert in tunnel warfare. He developed his expertise both diligently and creatively, transforming this tunnel division into a unique and elite force.

One reason the South African-Israeli attained positions such as IDF chief, IDF deputy chief, and IDF intelligence chief is his status not only as the hero of Hamas' defeat in Khan Yunis but also as the general who dismantled the terrorist group's tunnel network. He led the first modern army to conduct large-scale, full-unit invasions while navigating through the Hamas tunnel system. Goldfus emphasizes stealth and works closely with Shin Bet and IDF intelligence sources during operations. He trained his soldiers to move silently in the tunnels, ensuring Hamas forces remain unaware of their presence underground. After extensive training, his soldiers can move through the underground tunnels with the speed and agility of surface troops. A West Point strategist stated that this skill is 'unlike any other military in modern history.'[86]
**Current Status:** Commander of Division 98.

**Profile 9 – Mohammed Hassan Mohammed Awad**
**Names:** Mohammed Hassan Mohammed Awad
**Nationality:** Palestinian
**Profession:** Senior commander in the Palestinian Mujahideen group.
**Connection to October 7, 2023:** He was affiliated with Hamas but not a member of it. Awad was a senior leader in the Palestinian Mujahideen Movement, also known as the 'Mujahideen Brigades.'[87] Infiltrated Kibbutz Nir Oz on October 7, 2023, in the wake of the Hamas-led assault on Israel's western Negev, and oversaw the abduction of the Bibas family, the IDF said.[88] He was also likely involved in the kidnapping of American citizens Gad Haggai and Judi Weinstein.[89]

According to a statement from the IDF, Awad led multiple attacks on Nir Oz and actively recruited terrorists in the West Bank and Israel. He utilized these recruits to plan and carry out assaults on Israeli civilians and security forces. In his role within

the terrorist organization, Awad consistently recruited operatives in the West Bank and Israel, employing them to strategize and execute attacks against Israelis until his death in April 2025. This all concluded when the IDF killed him in April 2024.
**Current Status:** Dead.

**Profile 10 – Rabbi Zvi Kogan**
**Name:** Rabbi Zvi Kogan
**Nationality:** Dual citizen – Israeli-Moldovan
**Profession:** Rabbi and kosher restaurateur
**Connection to October 7, 2023:** Emirati authorities have discovered the body of Rabbi Zvi Kogan, an emissary to Abu Dhabi Chabad.[90] Ultra-orthodox Rabbi Kogan, 28, ran a kosher grocery store in Dubai that attracted Israelis after the two countries established relations in 2020. He was part of the growing optimism that emerged following the signing of the Abraham Accords. However, many Jews faced vulnerabilities in Dubai, making Rabbi Kogan a target for Iranian operatives. He was murdered in November 2024, and his body was found in Abu Dhabi after his abandoned car was discovered an hour away from his home.[91] Many observers of the Middle East believe that Iran sponsored the killing. A UAE court has sentenced three people to death for the rabbi's murder, while a fourth accomplice received a life sentence.[92] The convicted murderers are Uzbek.

Since the establishment of Iran's revolutionary Islamic regime in 1979, Iranian leaders have consistently reiterated their goals of destroying Israel. The country also harbors antisemitic sentiments and has sponsored antisemitic organizations' propaganda.[93] In contrast, the UAE has exchanged diplomatic officials with Israel and welcomed its citizens to visit and live there.
**Current Status:** The rabbi was buried in Israel. The condemned men will face a firing squad, which is used by the UAE for execution.[94]

# Chapter 9

# Afterward – Vivisection

*Happy October 7th, everyone!*

Swarthmore College Students for Justice in Palestine, November 2024[1]

*Victory, victory!! They entered Gaza alive, but today, they are leaving in coffins!*

A Gaza woman, referring to the captured Israeli hostages who died in internment.[2]

When a ceasefire was announced in January 2025, Hamas published the 'Victory Statement' anthem. This anthem declared, 'The pride in the resistance is as firm as mountains, and the determination intensifies under the flames.'[3] A Hamas leader claimed that Gazans were 'a model of patience, steadfastness, and Jihad.' He celebrated the return of Gazans from the south to the north as evidence of Hamas' victory. Hamas leaders boasted that they expelled Israel. However, their jubilation was premature. Wars often end permanently when one of the combatant parties concedes to the other that it lacks the will and resources to continue. This has not happened as of early 2026. There is still some fighting.

As of this writing, it is too early to determine the full extent of victory or defeat for either warring party. As the North Vietnamese communists prepared to conquer Vietnam in 1973, political scientist Chalmers Johnson authored a book titled *Autopsy on People's War*. He mused that a more appropriate title might have been Vivisection on People's War because the war may not be over. Today, the Hamas-Israel conflict simmers. Therefore, this discussion is not an autopsy of Hamas but a vivisection. Israel has devastated much of Hamas' military capabilities, but remnants of the group remain alive and threatening. Swords of Iron and Gideon's Chariot were the latest in a series of wars and mini-wars between Jews and Palestinians in the continually contested land. If Hamas is not destroyed, will it be the last war? Will the next war be more brutal?

## Judgment in Jerusalem

Although it is too early to perform a full post-mortem on the war, comprehensive Israeli investigations have examined the causes of strategic and tactical failures on October 7. Almost immediately after the attack, Prime Minister Netanyahu assured his fellow citizens that he would conduct a thorough investigation into the nation's defenses that had failed that day. Six hundred days later, several investigations have been launched, varying in scope, credibility, rigor, and objectivity.

In February 2025, the IDF acknowledged what it characterized as its 'historic failure.' The IDF report on its performance left little doubt about the military's culpability in the debacle. Titled Complete Failure, the report criticized military leaders for not recognizing Hamas' intent to attack Israel. Israeli leaders and left-leaning Israeli intellectuals believed that Hamas focused on sustained economic development and self-rule in Gaza. This central delusion shaped Israeli strategy, explaining why border protection was so weak and easily breached. The report concluded that Hamas had planned the assault for seven years and had thoroughly misled Israeli military, intelligence, and political leaders.

The military misjudged Hamas' war plans and capabilities. The IDF predicted that Hamas could launch an invasion at up to eight border points. However, Hamas could potentially attack from 60 different routes. Additionally, the IDF misinterpreted indications and warnings in the hour before the attack. The fundamental operational plan for a mass assault was developed in November 2016, followed by tactical planning. Despite this, Israeli military leaders remained unconvinced that Hamas aimed for a full-scale war. The report included an apology.

There were numerous other reports. Kibbutzim analyzed the failures and successes of their security units, as did police and military forces. Unit 8200, the signals intelligence unit, was found negligent regarding the radio traffic from the Gaza Strip. Some analysts stopped monitoring the handheld radios of Hamas operatives in Gaza about a year before the onslaught because it was deemed a misplaced effort. All the while, Hamas was patient, strategic, and burning with purpose.

Another report has introduced a new term into the lexicon of terrorism. The Civil Commission on the October 7th attack released a critical report in January 2025 titled 'Kinocide: The Weaponization of Families,' detailing the crimes committed by Hamas against women and children. Its key findings illustrate the systematic and widespread targeting of families to terrorize and emotionally scar both them and the Israeli nation. The report defined kinocide as destroying entire families to lower national morale.

But Hamas also failed disastrously. While it achieved short-term tactical success, Hamas' operational plan to incite a unified Arab war against Israel fell flat. Palestinians living in the West Bank remained passive. Hezbollah was incapacitated and could not inflict effective, long-term damage. Israel's two-million-strong Arab minority did not rally to Hamas; they did not wave Hamas flags or participate in riots. The Jewish-Muslim fabric of Israel did not fray as Hamas hoped. It stayed strong.

## Aftermath Abroad

On American campuses, on the Arab street, and in cities around the world, anti-Israel activists continue to chant 'Globalize the Intifada.' Many people have acted on that call. In May 2025, an American named Elias Rodriguez (Profile 1 – Chapter 9) murdered a young Israeli couple while standing outside the Capital Jewish Museum in Washington DC. As he shot them dead, he shouted solidarity with Palestine. His death chants proclaiming Israel as a colonial nation of settlers resonate throughout the world, as does his charge of Israeli genocide. Some American progressives on TikTok celebrated the murder, and on Iranian television, a host declared that Rodriguez sent 'two Zionist dogs to Hell.'

Activists still march, and superrich activists fund these marches. One of the loudest and richest enemies of both Israel and the United States is Fergie Chambers (Profile 2 – Chapter 9).[4] While Fergie generously funds anti-Israel activities, other activists continue to commit violent crimes. In June 2025, in a Colorado suburb, Egyptian Mohamed Sabry Soliman threw Molotov cocktails into a rally of supporters of the remaining Israeli hostages. He set aflame eight victims, including an 88-year-old Holocaust survivor. Some of the injuries were serious.[5] He recorded a video before firebombing a pro-Israel protest in Boulder, declaring that Jihad is more beloved than his family and that Allah is greater than Zionists and America.[6]

Aggressive, intersectional rallies continue to take place across the West. A prominent example is the June 2025 Los Angeles riots, where many participants wore kaffiyehs. The street marches protested President Trump's deportation policies, which mainly targeted Central Americans living in the US unlawfully. Some observers were puzzled by the attire, but one explanation is that the kaffiyehs symbolize resistance to both the US and Israel, seen by the left as colonial powers.

Elsewhere in the West, many people watched Greta Thunberg's Freedom Flotilla in June 2025 (Profile 3 – Chapter 9). Thunberg, ever dramatic, skippered the *Madleen*, which was carrying relief supplies bound for Gaza. Some observers watched the yacht's journey with sympathy, while others saw it as a self-indulgent publicity stunt. Israel did not accept it. Naval commandos boarded the boat, removed the 12 passengers, and offered them turkey sandwiches. Greta received the sandwich but declined to watch a film, which was a montage of videos taken by Hamas during its murder spree in October 7.[7]

## Israel Today – White Butterflies

As the war was winding down, freed Israeli captives reflected on their trauma and looked to the future. Freed Israeli hostage Noa Argamani held a Return to Life party after her rescue by IDF special forces. She proclaimed, 'We must appreciate every day of our lives.' She became a fierce advocate for the release of the still-captive hostages. Another young woman showcased her strength and artistic talent to the world at the Eurovision 2025 contest (Profile 4 – Chapter 9). By most outward appearances, she and a few others have largely recovered.

A young British-Israeli woman held hostage by Hamas for 15 months said her physical scars represent 'freedom, hope, and strength.' She underwent surgery for injuries sustained during the October 7 attacks. Emily Damari was shot in the hand, blindfolded, and abducted. After release, she announced, 'I have fully embraced my hand, my pain, and my scars. To me, they represent freedom, hope, and strength.'[8] She noted that her hand would never fully recover and described the 'intense pain' she suffered for a year and a half following an operation in Gaza.[9] Today, she is functional and emotionally sturdy, but many of her fellow former captives remain fragile.[10]

Other captives remain near-suicidal. Ben Shimon, a survivor of the massacre, explained, 'I am practically unable to do anything. I had to get a dog to help me survive daily.'[11] He cannot shake the visual and auditory memories of children being burned alive and screaming for their parents. Wrecked by nightmares that transport them back to October 7, many suffer from survivor's guilt and struggle to answer the question – why was I spared and not them?

Even battle-hardened soldiers experience deep emotional pain from their experiences. The combat involved soldiers running over both dead and living terrorists. One Israeli soldier said that he can no longer eat meat because it triggers images of the scenes he saw from his bulldozer. Complaints arose about the difficulties, especially the bureaucratic hurdles, that survivors faced in having their post-traumatic stress disorder recognized and in getting the necessary care.

For some Israelis, their lost ones still exist in memory and visit them in their dreams. Some connect with their lost loved ones through nature's metaphors. When Irene Shavit sees a white butterfly, she feels she is with her murdered fiancé, Netta. When they would walk together, Irene would say, 'Look, a white butterfly; it's a sign that today's going to be a good day.'[12] Today, Netta comes to her when she sees a white butterfly. 'I know . . . I know with all my heart that he's here with me.'[13] Paulina Belenki visits her murdered father in her dreams. Thirteen years old on October 7, 2023, she thinks about him daily, and at night, she meets with him in her dreams. 'He tells me that he is proud of what I am doing. I dreamed that he, like, came to us and hugged us and told us that this was a drill.'[14]

## Remembrance – October 7 in Art

Memories of Black Sabbath will forever haunt Israel. Some Israelis attempted to capture the tragic day through art. One exhibit recreated the atmosphere of the Nova festival by displaying artifacts found at the scene. The 'Moment Music Stood Still' exhibit begins with videos of young people dancing to pulsing beats, then shifts to scenes of panic. Visitors then proceed to the next scene, where the murder unfolds. The displayed items include the DJ's stage, handbags, remnants of cars, clothing, torn tents, and bathroom stalls riddled with bullets. The artists debated how graphic the violence should be in the exhibition to convey the tragedy and terror of that event day effectively.[15]

Former captive Andrei Kozlov uses painting as a catharsis from the trauma and misery of his eight-month incarceration, during which he saw only darkness. Most of his pictures have the theme of despair and captivity. But he sees elements of joy in his art. He stressed that it is not about darkness but about hope.[16] 'It was a chapter in my life, and I'm thankful and grateful that I got out of there, but I'm not stuck on it. I don't want to always be the "former hostage who was rescued."'[17]

In Israel, memorials appeared almost immediately. At first, most were temporary displays created by family and friends honoring their loved ones or those who had been captured. Other memorials were more carefully arranged, featuring music and photographs at the festival grounds. In this tribute, a single DJ plays electronic music for rows of poster-board pictures showing the faces of the 364 young people who died and those who were abducted. These images showed brothers, sons, daughters, sisters, and parents. Two brothers who survived the ordeal returned to the memorial. One explained that Nova had become sacred ground for him. When he returned, he found himself crying for the first time since the attack. He said that the music brought tears that had been building up since that day's horror.

The fear haunts much of the country. There is no apparent, easy resolution. Israel's Ambassador to the UK, Tzipi Hotovely, explained a new national fear. Israeli ambassador, 'We, as Israelis, have been through terror attacks in our coffee shops, on our buses, on our streets, but never in the past did we feel like our houses were not safe.' This is their new vulnerability: the feeling that you cannot protect your own children . . . I think that October 7th was a watershed moment . . . all across Israel. No one can say in Israel that he's the same person after.'[18] Israel had changed.

## A New Day Will Rise

How successful were the information operations launched by Hamas against Israel? They certainly generated considerable international attention and coordination. Numerous protests and boycotts occurred, but some heated rhetoric may have backfired. Large groups of masked students at prestigious American universities demanded that the world listen to them, and the world did. However, aside from ideological allies, much of their audience remained unconvinced that Israel was uniquely evil. In response to campus intimidation, members of Congress held hearings on antisemitism. University presidents seemed to wilt under the scrutiny of Republican and Democratic representatives who demanded clear and direct answers. Their robotic, sometimes stuttering responses embarrassed the universities, leading to their dismissal. Many alumni were pleased to see them go.

There is a divide between the Western elite and the public regarding the Israel-Hamas wars. This divide is evident in surveys and anecdotal evidence. One example is Eurovision 2025, mentioned earlier. Protesters heckled the Israeli participant, Yuval Raphael, while European policymakers and public intellectuals called for her to be banned from performing. None of these actions was effective. Some of the judges did not give Ms Raphael high scores. However, when European audience members were able to vote anonymously, they awarded Israel first place. Her song was 'A New Day Will Rise.'

European elites, particularly policymakers, have curtailed weapons sales to Israel. However, much of this action is symbolic, likely intended to appease the Leftist and Muslim coalition in certain countries. These threats are expected to make Israel increasingly self-reliant regarding its defense needs and to enhance its arms exports. Israel currently ranks among the world's top 10 leading arms exporters, with arms deals playing a significant role in its foreign policy.[19]

## Gaza Today and Tomorrow

Much of Gaza today lies in ruins. Approximately 90% of the population has been displaced, and over 92% of the roads are damaged or destroyed. Nearly 85% of healthcare facilities are no longer functional. The Gaza Health Ministry claims that over 50,000 Gazans have been killed, although this figure is disputed. There is no precise count of how many of the fatalities were civilians or children. Over 120,000 Palestinians have likely been wounded in Gaza. Other numbers are more accurate; since October 7, 2023, Hamas has fired 10,000 rockets into Israel. Since then, 887 Israeli soldiers have been killed. The number of Israelis displaced by the attacks exceeds 75,500.

Hamas is facing a severe financial crisis. Funds and goods from Iran, once smuggled in through Syria, have significantly decreased. Furthermore, Hamas is struggling to seize and resell humanitarian aid intended for those in need in Gaza. All of this complicates life for both Hamas operatives and everyday citizens. Many young people in Gaza want to leave. They are weary of being used as human shields and frustrated with the ongoing war. According to unofficial data, about 250,000 young individuals have left Gaza since 2007, primarily due to economic conditions. A survey indicated that 44% of young people in Gaza have considered emigrating. The unemployment rate in Gaza has soared to 80%. Just like homes, businesses also lie in ruins.[20]

President Trump suggested relocating Gazans and transforming the crater-ridden coastal enclave into a beachfront tourist destination. His proposed removal and development plan lacked details, and some of his remarks might have been made in jest. Hamas condemned President Trump's proposal as absurd; however, many did not completely dismiss it. Historian Andrew Roberts (Profile 5 – Chapter 9) notes the mass and quick expulsion of German ethnic groups from the Czech Sudetenland. Similarly, the Soviet Union expelled over three million German speakers from Silesia and other areas east of the Oder and Neisse rivers, where they had a long-standing presence. In the years right after World War II, these Germans received little sympathy from non-Germans. Most Allied countries saw this as the consequence of war inflicted on the nation that started the conflict. Some observers cite the post-World War II population exchange as a reason to relocate Gazans to other Arab countries.

## One Man's Opinion

These are my views. The failure of Israeli intelligence to anticipate and respond effectively to the attack will remain a topic of debate for a long time. In my view, revisiting Orde Wingate's doctrine, which was highly effective in combating Arab terrorism during the Palestine Mandate in the 1930s, is advantageous. How was Hamas able to execute such a successful surprise attack? Several factors contributed to this.

By the turn of the millennium, the IDF had significantly strayed from the core principles of the Wingate model presented earlier in this manuscript. Wingate sought sustained victory in the 1930s. However, during the Israel-Hamas conflict, there was neither war nor peace. Israel adopted an ambiguous policy toward Hamas that proved inadequate in deterring it from violence. Some members of the Israeli elite feared that if the IDF eliminated Hamas, a more violent group might take its place. After October 7, it became difficult to envision a group more inclined toward violent actions or more committed to Israel's annihilation than Hamas.

The Israeli strategy was responsive, employing targeted assassinations, home demolitions, and large-scale administrative detention. It was neither preventive nor consistently harsh, and it was not effective war fighting. From 2006 to 2023, Israel was careful to avoid destroying population centers in Gaza whenever possible. Some within Israel's security establishment referred to the practice as 'mowing the lawn,' alluding to the periodic retaliations for Hamas-initiated killings. This approach reduced civilian casualties but conveyed a message that Israel would not respond massively and lethally. The initial optimism faded as Hamas unleashed waves of missiles into Israeli towns and cities.

Israel utilized administrative detention to isolate terrorists and vulnerable youth from the general population. Although the detentions were at times severe, there is no evidence indicating widespread torture as historically defined. Home demolitions took place; however, residents received prior notice.

Many Hamas prisoners received light sentences for serious crimes, while some were released in unequal exchanges, like the 1,000-for-1 Shalit swap. During their imprisonment, they had access to meals and medical care. Some detentions were harsh, while others were more lenient. Israel's policy of detaining Palestinian militants has been inconsistent and confusing. Although it may have deterred certain Hamas operatives, it emboldened their leadership to launch attacks in 2023. Israel did not fully recognize the growing threat that developed over time. The shift toward comprehensive jihad began in 2017 when Sinwar, who received treatment for brain cancer in an Israeli hospital, and Deif led Hamas.

Israel's strategic perspective on a future war with Hamas was flawed. The country relied on advanced technology to maintain a strong defensive position. The defense establishment and Prime Minister Netanyahu focused on making it 'small and smart.' An impenetrable physical barrier would reduce the need for manpower, allowing soldiers to be available for other patrols. The high-tech barrier along the Gaza Strip included cameras, sensors, patrol dogs, and concrete. It was impressive but ineffective.

Israeli intelligence failed catastrophically. The October 7 attack represented a strategic rather than tactical failure. Israel possessed precise order-of-battle intelligence for targeting purposes. Overhead imagery, intelligence, and signals intelligence covered much of the Gaza Strip. The IDF eliminated many of the group's top leaders. Furthermore, there was adequate tactical intelligence indicating that Hamas was likely to launch a full-scale invasion and mass slaughter. Despite these successes in Israel's signals and human intelligence, they did not convert into strategic intelligence success.

Israeli authorities did not foresee Hamas' intention to launch a grandiose and multi-pronged attack aimed at slaughtering thousands. This strategic failure resembled the October 1973 surprise attack by Egypt on Israel. Among senior Israeli leaders, there was a significant lack of urgency. In 1973, Israeli officials did not believe Egypt would dare to risk another defeat. These leaders dismissed warnings from signals intelligence officers that the calm was unsettling. Fifty years later, Israeli leaders clung to the delusion that Hamas had made peace with Israel due to their improving living conditions. A single failure did not cause the catastrophe; rather, a combination of tactical and strategic errors in intelligence and policy enabled Hamas to carry out a successful attack.

Regarding the morality of Israel's conduct during the war, reasonable people hold differing opinions. These discussions were explored in Chapters 7 and 8. I maintain, contrary to many claims of war crimes, that Israel has conducted the war as humanely as could reasonably be expected. No nation capable of responding to the unprovoked attack on October 7 would refrain from launching a significant counteroffensive. While they may kill many civilians, Hamas deliberately used them as human shields and placed their munitions and fighters within homes, mosques, schools, and hospitals.

Israel has the right to block aid to Gaza, including humanitarian assistance, if it has valid reasons to believe that such support will be diverted by Hamas, a designated terrorist group, to further its war efforts. Under international law, Israel cannot intentionally starve civilians. While I see no evidence that Israel deliberately starved civilians, there have been significant delays in supplying food. Israel must ensure that Hamas does not receive any food, medicine, or clothing intended for civilians.

Did anything constructive result from the October 7 attack? Yes, it was not entirely catastrophic. First, it shattered the illusion that Hamas was a cooperative and agreeable partner in pursuing long-term peace. Throughout modern history, there have been bloody and pivotal incidents that alerted the world to dangers that cannot be ignored. Pogroms, or outbreaks of localized murderous rage against Jewish populations, have occurred repeatedly. One of the most notorious incidents was the Kishinev riot in April 1903, which resulted in 49 deaths and over 500 injuries. This atrocity was widely publicized in the West, especially in the United States. In Russia, Tolstoy and Gorky spoke out. Many Russian Jews realized they had no future in that country and chose to emigrate.

Another pivotal marker in history was the November 1938 German rioting, which destroyed 7,000 businesses and most synagogues. Kristallnacht marked the end of German-Jewish civilization. Similarly, the well-planned and highly publicized October 7 attack alerted many observers in the Middle East to the need for Israel to revise its strategy regarding Hamas.

The attack also clarified people's positions on the broader Israeli-Palestinian conflict. Much like a flare illuminating the night's darkness, the outpouring of contempt for Israel on campuses and streets worldwide revealed exactly where the activists stood. Alumni could hardly recognize the quads of their alma maters, now filled with tent encampments as students demanded an end to Israel. Shocking imagery prompted congressional investigations, which in turn attracted large audiences.

Israel, equipped with American weapon systems and munitions, has eradicated Iranian proxy forces in the Middle East, particularly in Syria, Lebanon, and Yemen. It has also diminished Iran's air defense systems, creating opportunities for more effective strikes on its nuclear facilities. Much of Iran's nuclear program is entombed in mountains of soil and rubble. From the perspective of Israeli and Western interests, the Middle East is a safer region today than it was before October 2023.

## Recommendations

These are my recommendations to prevent a repeat of the October 2023 attack:

*Hamas delenda est* – Hamas must be destroyed. First, Hamas must be destroyed. It cannot be reformed or allowed to reconstitute or recast itself. President Franklin Roosevelt promised to exact 'unconditional surrender' from the Axis. He announced, 'We shall not settle for less than total victory.' In this spirit, Israel must eliminate Hamas, and its operators should also feel defeated. After World War I, many Germans argued that they had never been defeated. German leaders in the 1920s and 1930s claimed socialists and Jews had betrayed them. In contrast, Germans in May 1945 felt powerless, at the mercy of their Allied conquerors. That spring, they faced hunger, homelessness, humiliation, and fear for the future. The red flag over the Reichstag symbolized the total ruin of Nazi Germany. Its leadership, military capabilities, and philosophy were exhausted, and the German will to fight was completely depleted. Hamas must feel defeated and too fearful to carry out terrorist attacks.

US Defense Secretary Lloyd Austin warned that the war in Gaza can only be won by protecting civilians, stating that 'the center of gravity is the civilian population.' He adds that otherwise, Israel risks replacing 'a tactical victory with a strategic defeat.' I agree that civilians are the center of gravity, but that center of gravity must recognize that it is not in its interest to attack Israel.

Israel must also propose a humanitarian alternative for the people of Gaza to prevent revanchist Islamists from filling the leadership vacuum. Gazans should be given a vision of a future free from militancy that provides hope for prosperity. An international reconstruction and development plan is crucial. Although this will be challenging, it is essential and achievable if Hamas is no longer in power. Currently, families scrounge for food when Hamas controls distribution. Sometimes, Hamas shoots them or amputates their limbs.[21] Western donors can assist in rebuilding Gaza by addressing the fundamental needs of Palestinians following Hamas' elimination.

Another lesson from World War II is the vital importance of publicly prosecuting war crimes worldwide. Hamas murdered over 40 Americans and abducted 30 more individuals. Perpetrators are subject to war crimes statutes, and the trials could resemble the Nuremberg War Crimes Trials of 1946. There may be three separate trials: the primary trials focusing on Hamas leaders, attack planners, financiers, and commanders of the death squads; another trial might concentrate on the main perpetrators, similar to the Einsatzgruppen trials (Profile 6 – Chapter 9), who were units of German police murdering Jews in the field; and a third trial would involve facilitators of international operations, including those who secured funds from foreign sources and knowingly collaborated with NGOs, particularly UNRWA, connected to the October 7 killings.

Finally, liberal powers should officially unite their efforts to counter the rise of militant Islam. They could form an alliance called the League of Democracies. This alliance would serve as a coalition of like-minded democratic nations dedicated to promoting liberal laws and the fundamental freedoms essential in shaping the evolving Western tradition. The League would welcome countries of all faiths and invite nations with large Muslim populations that support democratic principles.

## 'I love you' and 'I'm Sorry'

October 7 was an unprecedented day in the Hamas-Israel conflict. It marked a remarkable, albeit brief, victory for Hamas. At the Nova festival and in kibbutz communities in the Gaza envelope, Sderot, and other targeted areas, Israelis and others were completely unprepared. In the haunting moments when victims realized they were facing death or capture, they often expressed their love and sorrow. The victims lamented that they might never see their friends or family again. Their loved ones felt deep anguish, unable to help them. They conveyed their affection for each other whenever possible, through words or text messages. Many prayed. At Nova, shortly after the music was drowned out by gunfire, a young Israeli began reciting the Shema prayer. Beside him were Bedouins who had been working at the event. In Arabic, they started reciting their religious prayers.[22]

A young woman who became a widow that day asked if it was possible to extract sperm from her deceased husband, Yahav. If so, she might see his features in their child's face. Yahav would not be entirely lost. When asked if, miraculously, she could activate some magic lever and become someone else who hadn't experienced her loss, this woman firmly said, 'No! I would rather live through this pain 1000 times.'[23] Today, many Israelis and Palestinians are rebuilding their lives. Countless individuals have permanently lost their homes, as well as loved ones and friends. Despite this, they continue to strive for renewal. One young Israeli said, 'There is no such thing as giving up. Even when you see the end, even when you're sure that it's over, don't give up. Never, ever, ever give up.'[24]

**Profile 1 – Elias Rodriguez: 'I Did This for Gaza'**
**Names:** Elias Rodriguez
**Nationality:** American
**Profession:** Activist, history researcher
**Connection to October 7, 2023:** Elias Rodriguez was considered unremarkable by most accounts. An American Latino from a large city, he held a liberal arts degree and was actively involved in social causes. He was of average height and weight for a 31-year-old man. However, he harbored a homicidal rage against Israel, repeatedly accusing it of committing genocide and other crimes against humanity. He traveled to the Jewish Museum in Washington DC, where he waited to target individuals he believed were Jewish. He found two victims and shot them. After killing the two, Rodriguez stumbled into the building, seemingly in shock. People rushed over to comfort him, unaware that he was the shooter. One asked, 'Are you OK? Were you shot? What happened?' He then confessed, realizing he would be taken into custody.

Court documents indicate that during the police interrogation, Rodriguez expressed admiration for the actions of Aaron Bushnell, a former Air Force member who set himself on fire in front of the Israeli Embassy in February 2024. Rodriguez reportedly described this individual's actions as courageous and referred to him as a 'martyr.'

As for the young victims, Yaron Lischinsky and Sarah Milgrim grew up in different parts of the world, but their paths crossed in Israel. Lischinsky was raised in Germany, while Milgrim was raised in Kansas. They met in Washington DC, where their loving eyes locked onto each other at the Israeli embassy. One embassy staff member described it as 'the cutest love story . . . like a poster for a Netflix rom-com.' The hopeful Lischinsky bought a ring for Milgrim and planned to propose within weeks. Yechiel Leiter, Israel's Ambassador to the US, remembered them by saying, 'They were a beautiful couple.' So, why did Rodriguez kill them? In his words, 'I did this for Gaza.'[25]
**Current Status:** In prison, facing a possible death sentence, he has supporters. A fervent anti-Israel group applauded his crime as an act of 'love.'[26]

**Profile 2 – Fergie Chambers: Fortunate Son**
**Names:** James Cox Chambers Jr or Fergie Cox
**Nationality:** American
**Profession:** Left-wing Activist
**Connection to October 7, 2023:** Fergie Chambers stands at the crossroads of left-wing activism, Palestinian nationalism, and nearly unimaginable wealth. He has an impressive pedigree and political lineage. His family has been involved in national-level politics, with his grandmother serving as an ambassador. They were mainstream Democrats and some Republicans. One was a Democratic presidential candidate in 1920. Fergie became a rebel, a radical, and an outspoken communist. He is also a significant funder of radical causes, often dressing the part in a black hoodie and a kaffiyeh.[27]

He sees himself as a 'professional revolutionary.' I define success as the dissolution of the United States government and ending the U.S. empire.'[28] He is undeniably a wealthy revolutionary, having inherited a $250 million share of family assets from the Cox media empire. He has disowned his relatives, who, in turn, have disowned him. He now allocates money to combat Israel and Zionism. He believes 'Israel does not have the right to exist.' He funds several Palestinian action groups, some of which are tied to anti-Israel vandalism.

He has called on US Secretary of State Antony Blinken to be hanged 'for crimes against humanity' and tweeted that 'If you are not unequivocally for the total annihilation of Israel, your soul is rotten.'[29] Now in his late thirties, he is paying the legal fees for members of Palestine Action, an activist group that targets Israeli defense contractors. 'I chant death to America every day. Imperialism is the death of humanity.'[30] He was in and out of drug rehabilitation centers and mental hospitals starting before he was a teenager.[31]
**Current Status:** In early 2024, he began exploring a connection to Islam. He mentioned considering converting to the religion.

**Profile 3 – The World of Greta Thunberg**
**Names:** Greta Thunberg
**Nationality:** American
**Profession:** Activist
**Connection to October 7, 2023:** With monikers including the Swedish Nightingale and the less complementary Selfie Queen, Greta Thunberg has been a staple on the activist left for years. Her initial issue was climate change, which she embraced as a teenager. For reasons uncertain, her activism propelled her to international fame. As a teenager, she had a three-episode series on the US Public Broadcast System in which she challenged world leaders about their role in climate change.[32] In 2019, she yelled in the UN, ' How dare you? You have stolen my dreams and my childhood with your empty words?'[33]

She developed a penchant for getting herself arrested in the many protests, despite being repeatedly warned. From climate activism to anti-Israel agitation, she is often loud and angry, wearing a black-and-white keffiyeh shawl draped over her shoulders.[34] She protested against Israeli participation in the 2025 Eurovision.[35] She expanded her repertoire to include topical issues of global social justice. This included Palestine. Then, she set sail for Gaza to feed the hungry.[36] Some asked why she didn't take her Freedom Flotilla to an African country where people are far more hungry or take her efforts to Ukraine.[37] When Israel announced it would intercept her vessel, South Carolina Senator Lindsey Graham wrote, 'Hope Greta and her friends can swim!'[38]

Greta and her friends were never tested. The Israeli Navy escorted them off the boat, fed them, and requested that they watch a film on October 7, 2023. They took the sandwiches but declined to watch the movie.

**Current Status:** Deported from Israel and back in Europe.

**Profile 4 – Yuval Raphael: A Song for Israel, Europe and the World**

**Names**: Yuval Raphael

**Nationality:** Israeli

**Profession:** Singer

**Connection to October 7, 2023:** She was Israel's choice to represent the country in the Eurovision 2025 contest, which took place in Basel, Switzerland. She entered Israel's national television competition with little prior experience, yet secured first place, earning her a spot at the international competition in Basel. Yuval Raphael sang about a trauma that united her country. She survived the October 7 terrorist attack on the Nova Music Festival by hiding in a roadside shelter. To stay alive, she played dead, lying beneath the murdered bodies of her friends. She confronted her trauma through song.

She returned to Switzerland, where she had lived as a child. By 2025, her world had changed. She also faced challenges in Basel, which she anticipated. Some protesters yelled at her with spittle-flecked hate and accusations of apartheid. She had prepared to sing despite a chorus of boos from the audience. The group Basel 4 Palestine promised to prevent the 'Zionist apartheid state from using the (contest) to spread its genocidal propaganda and 'artwash' its crimes.'[39] Israeli officials decided to limit Raphael's media time for fear someone might try to kill her.[40]

During her performance, two British activists attempted to storm the stage, while others shouted anti-Israel slurs. They were detained. None of this hounding, booing, or spittle-flecked hate deterred the young chanteuse. She conceded that it was 'scary at times, even uncomfortable, but it makes me keep reminding myself why I'm here and my agenda, which is spreading as much love as I can and bringing pride to my country.'[41] Neither were her Eurovision fans deterred from supporting her. Yuval came in second, winning the public vote. Austria's JJ won first place. He was excited about his future and Eurovision's future. JJ said, 'I hope the competition next year will take place in Vienna – without Israel.'[42] As for the European Broadcasting Union, they removed Yuval Raphael from their official

album compilation video, despite her strong finish. Although her performance earned second place among Eurovision voters, she was not featured in the official video. She doesn't exist.[43]
**Current Status:** Unknown. Probably enjoying her fame.

**Profile 5 – Lord Roberts: 'An Evil Crime Against Humanity'**
**Names**: Andrew Roberts
**Nationality:** British
**Profession:** Historian and public intellectual
**Connection to October 7, 2023:** 'I'm a Gentile. I'm not a politician,' explained Andrew Roberts, an acclaimed British historian and member of the House of Lords. However, he felt morally compelled to lead an investigation into the October 7 killings, which he views as a pivotal moment in contemporary history. Driven by concerns about the distortion of history, he wanted to help ensure that the memory of the massacre would not be erased by time. 'I thought that the best way of dealing with that is to have a historically impeccable, intellectually robust report full of evidence from all sorts of sources that will prove for all time that yes, this monstrous event did take place.'[44]

He chaired the UK-Israel All-Party Parliamentary Group's comprehensive study, which aims to map out a timeline of the attack and present verified data about the planning, mission, execution, and consequences of the Hamas invasion. Lord Roberts was deeply involved in the project and, by his account, had nightmares. However, he has no regrets. This document will exist forever as a weapon against denial. 'In future generations, when people come up and say, 'Oh, it never happened . . .,' they will whack this 319-page report down on the table, with all of the endless footnotes and facts, and evidence and witness statements, that shows beyond any doubt whatsoever that one of the most evil crimes against humanity did indeed take place on October 7, 2023.'[45]
**Current Status:** Actively writing history and speaking publicly about international relations.

**Profile 6 – Benjamin Ferencz's Einsatzgruppen Trials -Models for Israel?**
**Names**: Benjamin Ferencz
**Nationality:** American
**Profession:** Lawyer, Prosecutor
**Connection to October 7, 2023:** Born in Transylvania in 1920, Ben Ferencz grew up in Manhattan. He graduated from Harvard Law School in 1943 and soon after served as an artillery officer under Patton. At the subsequent Nuremberg War Trials, he excelled while still in his twenties, becoming a leading war crimes investigator after previously witnessing the sites of the killings. Years later, he reflected, 'Camps like Buchenwald, Mauthausen, and Dachau are vividly imprinted in my mind's eye. Even today, when I close my eyes, I witness a deadly vision I can never forget.'[46]

He also prosecuted the 'roving task forces' called Einsatzgruppen, whose mission was to kill Jews, Roma, communists, and some intellectuals. The press called this the greatest murder trial in history. Ferencz fought for compensation for the victims and demanded harsh sentences for the leaders of the killing squads. He was successful. Of the 24 tried, most received death penalties or life sentences, some of which were commuted. His trial, along with the other Nuremberg Trials, became pivotal markers in international jurisprudence.

**Status Today:** He passed away at the age of 103. But years earlier, he partnered with the United States Holocaust Memorial Museum to establish the Ferencz International Justice Initiative to demand justice for war crimes.

## Appendix A

# Glossary

**Al-Aqsa Flood or Operation Al-Aqsa Flood** – Hamas' attack on October 7, 2023, in Israel.

**al-Ikhwan al-Muslimun or Islamic Brotherhood** – Founded in 1928, the organization aims to promote Islam and counter Westernization in Egypt.

**Al-Mujama Al-Islami** – A network of religious, educational, and social welfare institutions backed by wealthy donors from the Arab Gulf states

**Antisemitism** – Antisemitism is a specific perception of Jews that can lead to hatred against them. Rhetorical and physical expressions of antisemitism target both Jewish and non-Jewish individuals, their property, as well as Jewish community organizations and places of worship.

**Caliphate** – The political and religious state of Muslims that existed from the death of Muhammad until the formal dissolution of the Caliphate in the 20th century.

**Center of Gravity** – As used by Carl von Clausewitz, the enemy's center of gravity is his 'source of strength.'[1]

**Civil Society** – Covers the political decision-making processes involving individuals and the government, as well as trade, religious, educational, environmental, and various non-governmental organizations.

**Clandestine** – Any activity or operation sponsored or conducted by government departments or agencies aimed at ensuring secrecy and concealment.

**D9 or Doobie** – IDF Caterpillar D9 Armored Bulldozer. Doobie is a teddy bear in Hebrew.

**Deception means** – Methods, resources, and techniques that can communicate information to the deception target.

**Disinformation** – False information designed to mislead an audience.

**Eitan** – An advanced 8x8 wheeled armored personnel carrier.

**Fascism** – Originally, an Italian philosophy exalted a nation or race and concentrated national power in the hands of autocratic rulers. Typically, harsh and unforgiving laws dominated all aspects of society.

**Fatwa** – A religious ruling typically issued by an authoritative Islamic source.

**Gaza Strip** – It is approximately 25 miles long and ranges from four to seven and a half miles wide, covering 139 square miles. Its estimated population is 2.5 million people. The southern region borders Egypt and features an extensive network of underground tunnels.

**Goldstone Report** – The UN fact-finding mission on the Gaza conflict was released in September 2009. It was written by South African jurist Richard Goldstone, who later retracted it.

**Green-Red Axis** – A coalition of left-oriented non-Muslim and Muslim activist organizations in civil society focuses on government decision-making. Common themes include multiculturalism, skepticism towards democracy, capitalism, anti-Americanism, and anti-Zionism.

**Guerrilla Force** – A group of irregulars, mainly indigenous personnel, organized in military formations to carry out military and paramilitary operations in enemy-controlled, hostile, or denied territory.

**Haganah** – Zionist paramilitary group that operated in Mandate Palestine from 1920 to 1948.

**Hamas** – Harakat al-Muqawama al-Islamiya, or Islamic Resistance Movement, is characterized as a terrorist organization, a national liberation group, a religious-social movement, an Islamofascist force, and a counter-colonial entity.

**Hamas Charter of 1988** – Hamas' founding document and statement of principle.

**Hamas Charter Revised in 2017** – The tone was less aggressive, and the content was more conciliatory towards Israel.

**Hasbara** – Israel's public diplomacy office. Designed to counter criticism.

**Hezbollah** – Sometimes spelled Hizbollah or Hizballah, it is an Iranian-sponsored, Lebanon-based Shia militant group that is considered a terrorist organization by the US government.

**How to Take Captives** – Hamas manual on how to capture hostages.

**Information Operations (IO)** – The integrated use of core capabilities such as electronic warfare, computer network operations, psychological operations, military deception, and operations security, along with specified supporting and related capabilities, seeks to influence, disrupt, corrupt, or usurp adversarial human and automated decision-making while safeguarding our own.

**Intellectuals** – Individuals whose products are ideas include, but are not limited to, professors, journalists, social activists, and critics.

**International Criminal Court (ICC)** – Located in The Hague, the ICC investigates, prosecutes, and tries individuals accused of violating international law.

**Intersectionality** – The intersection of feminist, leftist, Islamist, and progressive politics.

**Intifada** – The term 'Intifada' refers to large-scale, coordinated, and persistent Palestinian attacks against Israeli targets during a specific period.

**First Intifada** – A series of deadly attacks occurred from December 1987 to 1993.

**Second Intifada** – The Second Intifada erupted in 2000 following Ariel Sharon's visit to Jerusalem's Temple Mount. This triggering incident sparked widespread protests, demonstrations, and suicide bombings, resulting in nearly 1,000 Israelis being killed or injured in Palestinian terror attacks.

**Global Intifada** – A slang term describing a worldwide anti-Israel and anti-Western struggle. Sometimes called the Third Intifada.

**Irgun** – A Zionist paramilitary organization operated in Mandate Palestine from 1933 to 1948.

**Iron Dome** – Israeli missile defense system.

**Irregular Warfare** – A violent struggle between state and non-state actors for legitimacy and influence over the relevant population.

**Islamism** – Refers to political Islam and is rooted in Islamic law. The conflict with Western norms and laws encompasses the requirement that non-Muslims must acknowledge a subordinate religious, political, and social status while under Muslim rule; the inferior status of women; the prohibition of homosexuality; the death penalty for apostasy; and various other laws. The term 'Islamism' was popularized by Daniel Pipes, a Middle East scholar.

**Islamic Revolutionary Guard Corps (IRGC)** – Sepāh e Pāsdārān e Enqelāb e Eslāmi. Sometimes called Pasdaran or Sepah. In this manuscript, the IRGC is usually referred to as the Guards.

**Islamic State in the Sham (ISIS)** – Also known as the Islamic State in the Levant, the Caliphate, Daesh, and the Islamic State, this radical Islamic organization has been active since 2014, under the leadership of Abu Bakr al-Baghdadi.

**Islamic World** – Muslims view this as the land where Muslims are in the majority and where Sharia is practiced. The term sometimes refers to areas in Western countries with significant Muslim populations. Some Muslims contend that any territory that has been under Muslim rule will always be part of the Muslim world. These territories include Israel, Spain, large parts of India, the Balkans, and various other regions across the globe.

**Islamofascism** – A militarized, political, expansionistic, and aggressive expression of Islam.

**Islamophobia** – A term often used to describe an irrational fear or dislike of Islam. Others see the term as a misleading neologism aimed at stigmatizing critics of Islam.

**Israel Military Intelligence Directorate (IMI)** or Aman – The central military intelligence organization of the IDF.

**Israel Security Agency (ISA)** – Also called Shin bet or Shabak internal, it is Israel's security service.

**Israeli Defense Forces** – Military forces of the State of Israel.

**The Izz al-Din al-Qassam Brigades, known as the Qassam Brigades** – A paramilitary unit in Hamas that breached the barrier using tractors, heavy trucks, and explosives on October 7.

**Jericho Wall** – The roughly 40-page Israeli intelligence document predicting the events of October 7, 2023 attack.

**Jihad and Jihadism** – Jihad has several meanings. It can refer to the internal struggle to become a more devout Muslim. Generally, it signifies a military campaign aimed at protecting the Muslim community or expanding its territory.

**Jihadist** – In the context of this book, the term refers to a militant Muslim or a Muslim who advocates violence against non-Muslims for political purposes. It is also known as an Islamist.

**Jihadist attack** – Also known as an Islamist attack, this term refers to an attack that includes at least one of three elements: the attacker claims the act was committed for Islam; an Islamist organization acknowledges the attacker as acting in solidarity with its cause; or a Western intelligence or security agency associates the individual with a domestic, external, or international Islamist agenda organization.

**Kitman** – Lying by omission. An example is when Muslim apologists quote only a fragment of verse 5:32 (that if anyone kills 'it shall be as if he had killed all mankind').

**Lahav 433** – A specialized felony unit of the Israeli police.

**Lawfare** – Employing laws, the legal system, and the threat of lawsuits as a weapon of war.

**Liberalism** – A Western political philosophy that emphasizes autonomy, political and economic freedom, limited governance, and a belief in progress.

**Mandate Palestine** – A geographical entity that was formerly part of the Ottoman Empire and was administered by Britain from 1920 to 1948.

**Merkava Mark IV** – Israel's main state-of-the-art battle tank.

**Mike's Place attack** – On April 30, 2003, a suicide attack occurred at Mike's Place, a beachfront bar in Tel Aviv, Israel, killing three Israelis and wounding 30 others.

**Multiculturalism** – The existence of numerous distinct, at times conflicting, cultures within a single country.

**Muruna** – 'Blending in' by setting aside certain practices of Islam or Sharia to promote others.

**Night of the Gliders** – The 1987 Hamas attack involved hang gliders.

**Operation Cast Lead** – Three-week conflict from December 27, 2008, to January 18, 2009, mainly in the Gaza Strip and southern Israel.

**Operation Gideon's Chariot** – Israel's operation beginning in May 2025 to destroy Hamas.

**Operation Protective Edge** – IDF's military campaign in the Gaza Strip lasted 50 days, from July 8 to August 26, 2014.

**Operation Sword of Jerusalem or Operation Guardian of the Walls** – IDF military campaign in the Gaza Strip from May 10 to May 21, 2021.

**Oslo Accords** – A controversial and disputed agreement between Israel and the PLO held in Norway that was intended to bring peace between Israel and the Palestinians.

**Palestine Liberation Organization (PLO)** – An umbrella organization that represents Palestinians, founded in 1964 under the leadership of Yasser Arafat.

**Palestinian Authority** – Palestinian governing body that administers parts of the West Bank.

**Palestinian Islamic Jihad (PIJ)** – An Iran-sponsored militant group based in Gaza

**Palmach** – The elite Haganah force in Mandated Palestine was incorporated into the IDF after Israeli independence.

**'Peacenik-kibbutznik'** – A slang insider term that describes an optimistic view held by some kibbutzniks about Israeli-Arab relations.

***Protocols of the Elders of Zion*** – The enduring antisemitic hoax claims to prove the existence of international Jewish conspiracies.

**Purity of Arms** – Israel's code of military ethics guides the behavior of its combatants.

**Salafism** – A fundamentalist school of Sunni Islam aiming to restore all aspects of society to the era of the early Muslims.

**Sbarro Pizza attack** – A suicide bomb attack occurred in Jerusalem on August 9, 2001, killing 16 civilians, including seven children.

**Sharia** – Islamic law.

**Simchat Torah** – A Jewish holiday that celebrates the reading of the Torah.

**Special Night Squads** – Jewish night attack units were established by Orde Wingate to suppress the Arab revolt of the mid-1930s.

**Strategy** – Using all tools of power to accomplish a military or political goal.

**Tactics** – Actions undertaken as part of a strategy. Tactics implement strategy into action.

**Taqiyya** – Deceiving to further or safeguard Islam.

**Tawriya** – Deliberately crafting a misleading impression.

**Terror(ism)** – The use of violence or the threat of violence by non-state actors to achieve political aims is often described as a form of psychological warfare.

**Traitor** – A person who has knowingly disclosed state secrets or shifted allegiance to a foreign power without proper authorization.

**UK Lawyers for Israel** – A prominent pro-Israel legal organization.

**Uma** – World community of Muslims.

**Unit 8200** – Israeli intelligence unit of the IDF that collects signal intelligence.

**United Nations Relief and Works Agency (UNRWA)** – The UN created UNRWA in 1949 to provide direct aid to Palestinians.

**Useful Idiots** – A slang term that derogatorily refers to gullible celebrities manipulated by authoritarian propagandists.

**Wahdat Sahm** – Hamas' the 'Arrow' unit conducts on-site executions of Gazans accused of collaborating with Israel.

**The West** – Originally, it referred to all land west of Persia. Today, it denotes democratic and secular states in Europe, the United States, Japan, Israel, Australia, New Zealand, and others.

**Women Wage Peace** – An organization of Israeli and Arab women working together to create lasting peace in the Middle East.

**Yahalom Unit** – Elite combat engineering unit of the IDF.

**Zaka** – Israel's leading nonprofit organization for rescue and recovery.

## Appendix B

# Orders of Battle

### Israel Defense Forces (IDF)

The IDF is a highly organized conventional military with a clear command structure and multiple branches. Its order of battle includes a mix of active and reserve forces, and it is known for its advanced technology and training.

**Branches:** Six – Israeli Ground Forces; Israeli Air Force; Israeli Navy; Computer Service Directorate; Technological and Logistics Directorate; Military Intelligence Directorate.
**Armed Forces:** There are approximately 170,000 active-duty personnel (130,000 Ground Forces; 10,000 Naval; 30,000 Air Force) (2023).
**Infantry Corps:** The backbone of the ground forces, responsible for direct combat. Key brigades include:

- **Golani Brigade (1st Infantry Brigade):** It is known for its toughness and long history of fierce combat. Considered one of the most important and storied brigades, it was formed under Ben-Gurion's leadership in 1948.
- **Paratroopers Brigade (35th Paratroopers Brigade):** Elite airborne infantry. This was the first paratrooper unit in the IDF, established in September 1948. It is highly selective and has a distinct dress.
- **Givati Brigade (84th Infantry Brigade):** Specializes in urban warfare. Its soldiers combat terrorism in the Gaza Strip.
- **Nahal Brigade (933rd Infantry Brigade):** It was established in 1982, during the First Lebanon War, to augment manpower. The brigade conducted operations in Lebanon, the Gaza Strip, and the West Bank.
- **Kfir Brigade (900th Infantry Brigade):** Specializes in counter-terrorism and urban combat.

**Armored Corps:** Operates Israel's main battle tanks, primarily the Merkava series. Key brigades include:
**Artillery Corps:** Provides fire support to ground units, operating various artillery systems.

**Combat Engineering Corps:** Handles tasks such as breaching obstacles, demolitions, mine clearance, and tunnel warfare, often with specialized units like Yahalom.
**Combat Intelligence Collection Corps:** Gathers intelligence on the battlefield, often operating close to enemy lines.

These corps are integrated into larger divisions that can operate across different commands (Northern, Central, Southern, Home Front).

**Active and Reserve Forces**

The IDF employs a unique system blending active-duty personnel (conscripts and career soldiers) with a robust reserve force.

- **Active Duty:** While smaller than some other conventional militaries, the active-duty component serves as the core and provides immediate response capabilities. Conscription is mandatory for most Jewish and Druze men and women, as well as for Circassian men.
- **Reserve Forces:** This is the core of the IDF's manpower. After completing mandatory service, soldiers usually move on to the reserve rolls and often serve with the same units. These reservists can be activated quickly during conflicts, greatly increasing the IDF's combat strength. Many of the most elite combat units depend heavily on reservists, who provide valuable experience and maturity. The IDF's ability to quickly mobilize hundreds of thousands of reservists is a key strategic advantage asset.

**Air Force:** Operates a wide variety of fighter jets, transport planes, helicopters, and UAVs. It also includes air defense commands equipped with systems like Iron Dome, David's Sling, and Patriot.
**Navy:** Consists of various flotillas, patrol squadrons, and special forces units like Shayetet 13 (naval commandos).
**Elite:** Highly trained units:

- **Sayeret Matkal:** This is an intelligence-gathering unit that conducts deep reconnaissance behind enemy lines to obtain strategic intelligence. Sayeret Matkal is also responsible for counter-terrorism and hostage rescue beyond Israel's borders.[1]
- **Shayetet 13:** A marine commando unit operating at sea, on land, and in the air, engaged in a variety of daring and specialized activities. It conducts operations including targeting of enemy maritime infrastructure and gathering high-quality intelligence on the enemy operations.
- **The Shaldag Unit:** 'Kingfisher' is a special forces unit under the command of the Israeli Air Force. It is considered one of the most elite units in the IDF. Most of its operations are classified and remain unknown to the public. The unit was established in 1974 after the Yom Kippur War. Initially, it

operated as a reserve company of the Sayeret Matkal Commando Brigade. Just a few years later, it developed into an operational unit directly under the Israeli Air Force.

- **Unit 669:** Israel's Air Force tactical rescue unit assists downed pilots. This unit specializes in aerial rescue missions for both soldiers and civilians, regardless of location or conditions. It also participates in searches for missing soldiers.
- **Maglan:** The Maglan unit (212) is a commando unit that operates in deep enemy territory to attack and destroy specific targets and gather intelligence. Established in June 1986, it specializes in anti-tank warfare and utilizes advanced weapons. It is part of the Commando Brigade.
- **Duvdevan:** The Duvdevan Unit (217) was formed in June 1986 to focus on security incidents in the West Bank, especially in heavily populated civilian areas.
- **Yahalom (combat engineering):** A specialized unit of the Combat Engineering Corps focuses on underground and concealed terror tunnels. It also handles hazardous ammunition and weapons.

## Hamas

Hamas' military wing, the Izz al-Din al-Qassam Brigades, operates as a non-state actor with a more decentralized and adaptable structure, often employing guerrilla warfare tactics. Although it has established hierarchies, its exact composition and deployment are less transparent than those of a conventional army.

**Key Components and Capabilities:**

- **Structure:** The al-Qassam Brigades are structured into regional brigades and battalions throughout the Gaza Strip (e.g., North Brigade, Gaza Brigade, Central Brigade, Khan Younis Brigade, Rafah Brigade), with subunits down to the squad level. They are designed for resilience and continuity of command, even in the face of leadership losses.
- **Personnel:** Estimates of Hamas' fighting force prior to October 2023 ranged between 20,000 and 30,000 fighters.
- **Weaponry and Tactics:**
    - Rockets and Mortars: Possesses a diverse arsenal of short, medium, and long-range rockets, many of which are produced domestically. They also use mortars.
    - Tunnels: An extensive and sophisticated network of tunnels beneath Gaza is crucial for concealing personnel and weapons, facilitating movement, and launching attacks.
    - Small Arms and Anti-Tank Weapons: Utilizes small arms, RPGs, and anti-tank guided missiles.

  - Drones: Employs drones, including kamikaze drones.
  - Improvised Explosive Devices (IEDs): Increasingly rely on explosives for ambushes and targeting Israeli forces.
  - Guerrilla Warfare: Focuses on asymmetric attacks, hit-and-run operations, and ambushes to counter the IDF's superior conventional power.
  - Naval Commandos: Has a limited naval commando capability for infiltration.
- **Training and Support:** Receives training and material assistance, particularly from Iran and some of its allies like Hezbollah.
- **Areas of Operation:** Primarily based in the Gaza Strip but also maintains a presence in the West Bank and some regional countries.

Hamas' 'order of battle' is fluid and often adapts to increases or decreases in personnel and weapons.

## Appendix C

# Israel's Intelligence Structure

## Key Roles and Missions of Aman, Mossad, and Shin Bet

**Aman's Mission:** Aman's main mission is to provide the Israeli government and IDF with intelligence indications and warnings, conduct analytical studies for national security, and carry out tasks to defend the nation. This includes a broad range of responsibilities:

- **Strategic and Tactical Intelligence:** Analyzes military and political developments in the region, especially those involving hostile nations and terrorist groups. This includes intelligence estimates and orders of battle analysis.
- **Warning Against Threats:** Issues indicators and warnings of impending attacks.
- **Intelligence Collection:** Gathers overt and covert intelligence.
- **Analysis and Assessment:** Processes raw intelligence and analyzes it to create finished intelligence.
- **Information Security and Counterintelligence:** Safeguards Israel's classified information and performs counterintelligence operations.
- **Technological Development:** Constantly enhancing new systems and tools for intelligence tracking, collection, and analysis.

**Aman's Units:**

- **Unit 8200 (Signal Intelligence – SIGINT):** This is Aman's largest and most renowned unit, responsible for collecting and decrypting signal intelligence. It is frequently compared to the National Security Agency (NSA) in the United States.
- **Unit 504 (Human Intelligence – HUMINT):** Responsible for collecting intelligence through human sources and agents.
- **Unit 9900 (Visual Intelligence):** Deals with the collection and analysis of visual intelligence, including aerial images and satellite reconnaissance.

- **Research Department (Hativat Hamehkar):** This unit serves as the national assessor of intelligence, analyzing information from all sources within Aman and the wider intelligence community to form tactical, strategic, and operative assessments.
- **Unit 81 (Secret Technology):** Involved in the development of advanced and often clandestine technological solutions for intelligence operations.
- **Sayeret Matkal (General Staff Reconnaissance Unit):** While sometimes regarded as part of Aman's professional jurisdiction, this elite special forces unit conducts deep reconnaissance and counter-terrorism operations, often providing direct intelligence support to high-level missions.
- **Military Censor:** Part of Aman's information security branch, responsible for pre-publication censorship on security-related matters.

**Place in the Israeli Intelligence Community:** Aman is one of the three main pillars of the Israeli Intelligence Community, alongside:

- **Mossad (The Institute for Intelligence and Special Operations):** Primarily responsible for gathering foreign intelligence, conducting covert operations, and executing counter-terrorism efforts outside Israel's borders.
- **Shin Bet (Israel Security Agency or Shabak):** Responsible for internal security, counter-terrorism, and counterintelligence within Israel and the Palestinian territories.

## Appendix D

# Assassinations – 'Dead Men Walking'

Soon after the October 2023 attack, Israel ramped up its assassinations of Hamas leaders. Listed below are some of the important leaders who have been killed.

### Ismail Haniyeh

On October 7, 2023, Israel targeted Hamas leader Ismail Haniyeh for assassination. In July of the following year, they carried out the plan. The 62-year-old leader of Hamas' political bureau was killed in Iran. Haniyeh, who was based in Qatar and had been elected Hamas' political chief in 2017, died in a pre-dawn strike on his residence while visiting the Iranian capital for President Pezeshkian's swearing-in ceremony.[1] Although Haniyeh was likely not directly or significantly involved in executing and planning the October attack, he was undeniably complicit. In 2003, Haniyeh and the founder of Hamas, Sheikh Ahmad Yassin, survived an assassination attempt together, escaping from a house targeted by an Israeli aircraft. Yassin was killed a year later.

Like several other senior Hamas leaders, he lived in luxury in Qatar, with his fortune estimated at $4 billion. Haniyeh earned a degree in Arabic literature before joining Hamas in 1988. In the late 1980s and early 1990s, he spent several years in Israeli prisons after Israeli authorities accused him of operating the group's security wing. He returned to Gaza in 1993 and was appointed as the dean of the Islamic University of Gaza.[2]

A veteran of Hamas, Haniyeh joined the organization at its founding and served as an aide to Ahmad Yassin. According to his daughter-in-law, Haniyeh expressed, 'I would love to be martyred in Allah's Cause and then get resurrected and martyred again . . . ' His assassination led to Sinwar becoming the leader of Hamas. Three of Haniyeh's sons and four of their children were killed in an Israeli drone strike that targeted their car at the al-Shati refugee camp. His killing triggered calls for revenge and raised questions about the ongoing viability of such negotiations. Following the assassination, Iran observed three days of national mourning in Tehran, the country's capital. Iran promised to exact revenge.[3]

Yahya Sinwar masterminded the October attack, openly boasting about its success and the slaughter that followed. Born in 1964 in a refugee camp in Gaza, he was just five years old when Israel took Gaza from Egypt, growing up in an environment filled with resentment and anger. He moved up the ranks of Hamas, earning a reputation as a hardliner and relentless organizer. He never wavered from his unwavering goal of destroying Israel. However, it was Israel that killed him.

After Israel killed Haniyeh, Sinwar became the group's leader. Lebanon's Hezbollah praised his appointment. Unsurprisingly, Israel placed him at the top of its death list. His death carried a grim irony: he was killed on the first day of the Jewish festival of Sukkot. During that same holiday, one year earlier, he had initiated the October 7 massacre. Unlike the well-planned assassinations of other Hamas leaders, Sinwar's killing was accidental; he was slain by ordinary Israeli soldiers using tanks from the IDF's Gaza division. Sinwar's possessions included a fake passport listing his alias as an employee of UNRWA. Foreign Minister Israel Katz announced, 'Mass murderer Yahya Sinwar, who was responsible for the massacre and atrocities of October 7, was killed today by IDF soldiers.'[4]

## Mohammed Deif

In July 2024, the IDF killed Mohammed Deif, who was the head of Hamas' al-Qassam Brigades. Deif had been on Israel's death list for decades.[5] According to the IDF, Deif orchestrated Hamas rocket attacks and tunnel construction, facilitating highly trained fighters' infiltration of Israel.[6]

Dief's *nom de guerre* was 'Guest' because he escaped IDF targeting by regularly shifting his residence.[7] For years, only three publicly known photographs of him existed. He appeared more sincere than other Hamas leaders because he lived in Gaza with his family and had his children educated there.[8] He joined Hamas in the late 1980s and rose rapidly through the organization's ranks. As Hamas' chief strategist, he masterminded the suicide bombing campaign and expanded the tunnel network.[9] He organized suicide bombing attacks in the 1990s.

He was appointed head of the Izz el-Deen al-Qassam Brigades in 2002. One of his early achievements as a leader was applying lessons from the Second Intifada in the early 2000s. He masterminded the construction of underground tunnels, allowing Hamas fighters to launch incursions into Israeli territory from Gaza. He also emphasized the extensive use of rockets. His lifestyle and persona helped enhance his image as a man of the people. Unlike other Hamas leaders, he lived in Gaza with his family.

Earlier and often, Dief had been fortunate. He held another moniker – the cat with nine lives – because he escaped persistent Israeli missile strikes aimed at him. One of these attacks killed his wife and likely injured one of his children. However, he could not survive a missile strike in July 2024 that killed him and others. The spokesman for the al-Qassam Brigades, the military wing of Hamas, rued, 'We mourn our great people, the martyrdom of the Chief of Staff of the al-Qassam Brigades, Mohammed Deif.'[10]

## Marwan Issa – The Strategic Mind of Hamas

Marwan Issa, 58, was Deif's right-hand man until an Israeli airstrike took his life in March 2024. As a primary target for Nili, a special unit established by Shin Bet, Israel's internal security service, and the Mossad intelligence agency, he was high on a list of members responsible for the October 7 attacks. He served as the deputy commander-in-chief of Hamas' military wing. Like Deif, Issa survived multiple assassination attempts, including one in 2006. His tendency to stay out of the public eye earned him the nickname 'Shadow Man.' His facial features remained unknown to the public until 2011, when he appeared in a group photo taken during a prisoner exchange between Israel and Hamas that he helped organize. Mr. Issa was also classified as a Specially Designated Global Terrorist (SDGT) by the United States in 2019. Israel identified him as one of the three top Hamas leaders who planned the October attack and believed he had commanded military operations since then.[11]

## Saleh al-Arouri

Saleh al-Arouri was a prominent strategist for Hamas and one of its most skilled tacticians, facilitating the flow of money and weapons to operatives in the Gaza Strip and across the Middle East. In 2017, he was appointed Deputy Chairman of the Hamas Political Bureau. He was regarded as one of the group's key political leaders until his death on January 2, 2024, due to an Israeli strike in Beirut, Lebanon. At 57, he was a founding member of Hamas' military wing – the Ezz el-Din al-Qassam Brigades – and played a key role in planning the Al-Aqsa Storm. Al-Arouri mainly led the al-Qassam Brigades' military operations in the West Bank. He was imprisoned in Israel from 1995 to 2010, after which he was deported Syria.[12]

In 2015, Arouri was designated a Specially Designated Global Terrorist (SDGT) by the US government, which banned American citizens from engaging in any financial transactions with him. Three years later, the US State Department offered a $5 million bounty for his capture or killing. Mossad identified him as Hamas' *de facto* Ambassador to Iran and Hezbollah, placing him in a key role to strengthen Hamas' military capabilities with the support of foreign backers.

## Abd al-Hadi Sabah

Abd al-Hadi Sabah was killed in a targeted drone strike in Khan Yunis, southern Gaza. He led the infiltration into Kibbutz Nir Oz on October 7. Sabah, a Nukhba Platoon Commander in Hamas' Western Khan Yunis Battalion, was reportedly instrumental in orchestrating the attack on Kibbutz Nir Oz on October 7, 2023, which resulted in widespread casualties. The IDF emphasized that Sabah was not only a key figure in the October 7 attack but had also been involved in numerous terrorist activities against IDF forces over the years. The agencies noted that Sabah was hiding in a shelter within the designated humanitarian area in Khan Yunis, southern Gaza.[13]

## Jamila al Shanti

Jamila Al-Shanti, the first woman elected to the Hamas political bureau, was the widow of Hamas co-founder Aziz al-Rantisi. In 2006, she was elected to the Legislative Council for the Hamas Change and Reform bloc. She earned a doctorate in educational administration in 2013 from the UAE, and that same year Al-Shanti was appointed Minister of Women by the Hamas government governing the Gaza Strip She was elected to the politburo in 2021 and established the Hamas women's wing. Additionally, she served as a faculty member at the Islamic University. She was killed in an Israeli airstrike on Gaza City in October 2023.[14]

## Ibrahim Biari

Ibrahim Biari, the commander of the Jabaliya Battalion responsible for operations in Northern Gaza, played a role in the October 7 attack. He was involved in a 2004 terrorist attack that resulted in the deaths of 13 Israelis. The IDF killed him in an airstrike in October 2023, claiming that Biari had a significant role in the Hamas attack. The strike on the Jabaliya refugee camp was said to have claimed the lives of 50 others. For two decades, he orchestrated rocket attacks on Israeli military and civilian targets.

## Ali Qadhi

The IDF killed Ali Qadhi, a company commander in the Nukhba unit, in a drone strike after the Shin Bet and the Military Intelligence Directorate identified him. According to the IDF, Qadhi was imprisoned by Israel in 2005 for the kidnapping and murder of Israeli civilians, and he was released to the Gaza Strip as part of the 2011 Gilad Shalit prisoner exchange.

## Muhammad Shaheen

The IDF killed senior Hamas official Muhammad Shaheen in a drone strike in southern Lebanon as part of a joint operation between the IDF and Shin Bet. Shaheen was the head of operations for Hamas in Lebanon, where he planned terror attacks against Israeli citizens both within Israeli territory and during international travel. The IDF reported that Shaheen was heavily involved in directing rocket attacks against Israel and received funding directly from Iran to carry out these operations. They claimed that Shaheen 'was a significant source of knowledge within the terrorist organization and was responsible for various terrorist attacks and rocket launches targeting Israeli civilians throughout the war.'

## Muhammad Sinwar

Mohammed Sinwar was the younger brother of Yahya, who was the leader of Hamas in Gaza from 2017 until his assassination by the Israel Defense Forces in October last year. Yahya masterminded the pogrom of October 7, 2023. Mohammed succeeded him following his death.

# Notes

## Chapter 1: Introduction

1. Selján, Péter, 'The October 7 Hamas Attack: A Preliminary Assessment of the Israeli Intelligence, Military and Policy Failures,' *Academic and Applied Research in Military and Public Management Science*, 2024-04, Vol. 23 (1), pp. 81–98.
2. Seddon, Sean and Palumbo, Daniele, 'How Hamas Staged Israel Lightning Assault No One Thought Possible,' *BBC*, October 8, 2023, https://www.bbc.com/news/world-middle-east-67046750
3. Ellis, R. Evan, 'Implications of the Israel-Hamas War for the Global Strategic Environment,' *Strategic Studies Institute*, US Army War College, November 7, 2023, p. 1.
4. Marks Eglash, Ruth, 'At The Army Base Where Israel Identifies Its Dead: "They Went From House To House Burning Family After Family,"' *Fox News*, October 30, 2023.
5. Israeli dual nationals, Palestinian citizens of Israel, Palestinians from Gaza, and foreign workers, including Chinese, Filipino, Nepali, Sri Lankan, and Thai nationals, and at least one national each from Cambodia, Canada, Eritrea, Germany, Mexico, Sudan, Tanzania, and the United Kingdom.
6. Estrin, Daniel; Abu Bakr Bashir; Balaban, Samantha; Harbage, Claire, 'New Details Emerge About The Hamas-Led Attackers Who Massacred Israelis,' *National Public Radio*, October 27, 2023, https://www.npr.org/2023/10/27/1208836319/israel-hamas-islamic-jihad-militants-videos-details
7. Weimann, G. & Weimann-Saks, D. (2024), 'Coping With Hamas's Psychological Warfare During The Gaza War'. *Studies in Conflict & Terrorism*, 1–20. https://doi.org/10.1080/1057610X.2024.2327669
8. Selján, Péter, 'The October 7 Hamas Attack: A Preliminary Assessment of the Israeli Intelligence, Military and Policy Failures,' *Academic and Applied Research in Military and Public Management Science*, 2024-04, Vol. 23 (1), pp. 81–98.
9. 'Iran Warns the US Won't Be Spared If Israel-Hamas War Spreads.' *Bloomberg.com*, 10/26/2023, Business, Wadhams, Nick https://www.tehrantimes.com/news/501392/Gaza-still-Islamic-world-s-number-one-issue-Leader

10. 'Ayatollah Khamenei: "Gaza Still Islamic World's Number One Issue",' *Tehran Times*, July 21, 2024.
11. At Columbia University, some protesters shouted, 'We are all Hamas.' At McGill demonstrators called for globalizing the Intifada. High schools, too, were scenes of anti-Israel protest and student walkouts, which concerned students and their parents. Source: Israel-Hamas War Poses Tough Questions For K-12 Leaders, Too. By Walsh, Mark, Education Week, 02774232, 5/29/2024, Vol. 43, Issue 27, p. 1. https://web.p.ebscohost.com/ehost/detail/detail?vid=5&sid=ab4764b8-8e57-4e88-9d8c-783c337f5779%40redis&bdata=JnNpdGU9ZWhvc3QtbGl2ZQ%3d%3d#AN=177530010&db=f5h
12. 'Asian-American Comic Hans Kim Mocks October 7 Massacre,' *Jerusalem Post*, November 10, 2023.
13. Zelber, Ariel, 'Peter Thiel Was Trapped Inside Cambridge University Debate Hall By Anti-Israel Protesters,' *New York Post*, May 9, 2024, https://nypost.com/2024/05/09/business/peter-thiel-was-trapped-at-cambridge-university-by-anti-israel-protesters/
14. 'Climate activist Greta Thunberg arrested at Eurovision pro-Palestinian protest,' *Jerusalem Post*, May 11, 2024, https://www.jpost.com/breaking-news/article-800826
15. Starr, Michael, 'Hezbollah, Hamas Terror Banners Flew Openly At NYC Pro-Palestinian Protest,' *Jerusalem Post*, June 30, 2024, https://www.jpost.com/bds-threat/article
16. Anti-Israel agitators in Berlin threw a Molotov cocktail into a public building before spray-painting on its walls, 'Free Hamas' and 'Warning Berlin, we'll burn it down.' Source: Brooke, Thomas, '"If Gaza burns, Berlin burns!" — Town Hall Set On Fire By Anti-Israel Vandals,' *Remix News*, May 9, 2024, https://rmx.news/article/if-gaza-burns-berlin-burns-town-hall-set-on-fire-by-anti-israel-vandals/
17. Starr, Michael, 'Amsterdam Anne Frank statue defaced with "Gaza" graffiti,' *Jerusalem Post*, July 9, 2024, https://www.jihadwatch.org/2024/07/amsterdam-anne-frank-statue-vandalized-with-red-paint-reading-gaza
18. 'Hamas Official Ghazi Hamad: We Will Repeat The October 7 Attack, Time And Again, Until Israel Is Annihilated; We Are Victims – Everything We Do Is Justified,' *MEMRI*, #10592, October 24, 2023, https://www.memri.org/tv/hamas-official-ghazi-hamad-we-will-repeat-october-seven-until-israel-annihilated-victims-everything-we-do-justified
19. Chairman Smith said, 'To say I am disgusted by statements of support for Hamas that we've seen in recent days is an understatement. Celebrating, excusing, or downplaying the horrific rape, torture, and murder of innocent people is the same thing as supporting violence or even calling for it. Releasing such statements, or failing to condemn them, is unforgivable and runs counter to our values as a nation.' Source Lenkowsky, Leslie, 'Terrorism And Tax Advantages Universities And Anti-Israel Groups May Find Their Nonprofit

Status Under Scrutiny,' *Wall Street Journal*, November 5, 2023, p. 1. https://www.wsj.com/articles/terrorism-and-tax-advantages-nonprofit-education-dark-money-hamas-6f649015; 'University administrators, for example, have weaponized their institutions to attack speech and free inquiry as "violence," yet fail to condemn actual violence that threatens our way of life, all while their institutions enjoy lucrative federal tax-exempt status.' Source: Jason Smith, United States House Committee on Ways and Means Chairman, https://gop-waysandmeans.house.gov/chairman-smith-slams-tax-exempt-universities-and-student-groups-support-of-hamas/; and Lenkowsky, Leslie, 'Terrorism And Tax Advantages Universities And Anti-Israel Groups May Find Their Nonprofit Status Under Scrutiny', *Wall Street Journal*, November 5, 2023, p. 1. https://www.wsj.com/articles/terrorism-and-tax-advantages-nonprofit-education-dark-money-hamas-6f649015

20. Stefanik Supports Passage of the Hamas and Other Palestinian Terrorist Groups International Financing Prevention Act Enforcing Sanctions on Any Foreign State Supporting Iranian-backed Terrorists, *Elise Stefanik Homepage*, November 1, 2023, https://stefanik.house.gov/2023/11/stefanik-supports-passage-of-the-hamas-and-other-palestinian-terrorist-groups-international-financing-prevention-act-enforcing-sanctions-on-any-foreign-state-supporting-iranian-backed-terrorists
21. Graef, Aileen and Lotz, Avery, 'Stefanik calls for wiping Hamas "off the face of the Earth" and touts Trump policies in a speech to Israeli Knesset,' *CNN*, May 19, 2024, https://www.cnn.com/2024/05/19/politics/stefanik-israel-speech-biden-trump/index.html.
22. Dion, J. Pierre, '"You Will Be Held Accountable": US Congress Questions University Presidents Over Pro-Hamas Encampments,' *Algemeiner*, May 23, 2024, https://www.algemeiner.com/2024/05/23/us-congress-questions-university-presidents-pro-hamas-encampments/
23. Cassidy, Ernst, 'Booker Urge President Biden to Do Everything in His Power to Rescue American Hostages,' Webpage Senator Bill Cassidy, October 18, 2023,
24. World reacts to ICC prosecutor seeking Israel, Hamas arrest warrants,' *Al Jazeera*, May 21, 2024, https://www.aljazeera.com/news/2024/5/20/world-reacts-to-icc-prosecutor-seeking-israel-hamas-arrest-warrants
25. 'Western media shuns the truth tellers on Gaza,' *The Australian*, January 26, 2025.
26. Kurtz, Judy, 'Prince William Says, "Too Many Have Been Killed" in Israel-Hamas War, Calls for Fighting To End,' *Hill.* 2/21/2024, Vol. 31, Issue 12, p. 23-23. 1/3p https://web.p.ebscohost.com/ehost/detail/detail?vid=35&sid=ab4764b8-8e57-4e88-9d8c-783c337f5779%40redis&bdata=JnNpdGU9ZWhvc3QtbGl2ZQ%3d%3d#db=f5h&AN=175552352
27. 'Save us from Hamas . . . I appeal to every living conscience to watch. These are traders in our blood. Every day they trade in our blood,' *Jerusalem Post*, August 10, 2024, https://www.jpost.com/israel-hamas-war/article-814116

28. 'Showing Explicit Video of Hamas Crimes, Gallant Tells NATO: "2023 is Not 1943",' *The Times of Israel*, October 12, 2023, https://montgomerycollege.idm.oclc.org/login?url=https://www.proquest.com/newspapers/showing-explicit-video-hamas-crimes-gallant-tells/docview/2876165013/se-2.

## Chapter 2: Hamas – Its Ideology, History, Men, and Women

1. Musallam, Adnan A. *From Secularism to Jihad: Sayyid Qutb and the Foundations of Radical Islamism* (New York: Praeger Publishers, 2005), p. 18.
2. Robinson, Kali, 'What Is Hamas?,' *Council of Foreign Relations*, Accessed June 23, 2024, https://www.cfr.org/communities
3. Eshman, Rob, 'The Truth Of Hamas Is In Its Charter, A Founding Document Extolls The Killing Of Every Jew,' *The Forward*, October 10, 2023, https://forward.com/opinion/564190/hamas-charter-truth/
4. In its words, the Charter 'is anchored in religious principles of holiness, divinity, and eternity, with no option for amendment. Source: Mishal, Shaul and Sela, Avraham, *The Palestinian Hamas; Vision, Violence, and Coexistence* (New York: Columbia University Press, 2000), p. 45.
5. On the Hamas concept that Palestine is waqf land, see the Hamas Charter, Chapter 3, especially Article 11. Source – Stern, Eliyahu Dr, '"The Protocols Of The Elders Of Zion" In The Hamas Charter: Islamization Of Western Antisemitism And Its Integration Into The Jihad Against The Jews,' *MEMRI*, Palestinians | Inquiry & Analysis Series No. 1748, February 26, 2024, p. 1. https://www.memri.org/reports/protocols-elders-zion-hamas-charter-islamization-western-antisemitism-and-its-integration#_edn1q
6. Muhammad Maqdsi, trans., 'Charter of the Islamic Resistance Movement (Hamas) of Palestine,' *Journal of Palestine Studies* 4 (1993), p. 122; Gruber, Shai, 'Hamas: Pragmatic Ideology, al Nakhalah,' *The Fletcher School of International Law and Diplomacy*, Spring 2007, p. 1. https://ciaotest.cc.columbia.edu/olj/aln/aln_spring07/aln_spring07e.pdf
7. Stern, Eliyahu Dr, '"The Protocols Of The Elders Of Zion" In The Hamas Charter: Islamization Of Western Antisemitism And Its Integration Into The Jihad Against The Jews,' *MEMRI*, Palestinians | Inquiry & Analysis Series No. 1748, February 26, 2024, p. 1. https://www.memri.org/reports/protocols-elders-zion-hamas-charter-islamization-western-antisemitism-and-its-integration#_edn1; one valuable quotation of Mohammed is, 'The hour of judgment shall not come until the Muslims fight the Jews and kill them, so that the Jews hide behind trees and stones, and each tree and stone will say: "Oh Muslim, oh servant of Allah, there is a Jew behind me, come and kill him," except for the Gharqad tree, for it is the tree of the Jews.' This is quoted in the Hamas Charter. Source: 'The Hamas Charter – The Ideology Behind The Massacre October 23, 2023,' *MEMRI*, Palestinians | Special Dispatch No. 10897, p. 1; https://www.memri.org/reports/hamas-charter-

%E2%80%93-ideology-behind-massacre; Stern, Eliyahu 'The Hadith Of The Stones And The Trees – About The Muslims Killing The Jews Ahead Of The End of Days – In The Hamas Charter And In A Publication Of The Hamas-Affiliated Palestine Scholars Association, Palestinians,'.*Inquiry & Analysis Series* No. 1745, February 15, 2024, p. 1; https://www.memri.org/reports/hadith-stones-and-trees-%E2%80%93-about-muslims-killing-jews-ahead-end-days-%E2%80%93-hamas-charter-and#_edn5

8. Stern, Eliyahu Dr, '"The Protocols Of The Elders Of Zion" In The Hamas Charter: Islamization Of Western Antisemitism And Its Integration Into The Jihad Against The Jews,' *MEMRI*, Palestinians | Inquiry & Analysis Series No. 1748, February 26, 2024, p. 1. https://www.memri.org/reports/protocols-elders-zion-hamas-charter-islamization-western-antisemitism-and-its-integration#_edn1
9. On a text published by the Hamas-associated Palestine Scholars Association promising that the annihilation of the Jews is imminent, and on the possibility that it shows the influence of ISIS on Hamas, see *MEMRI* Inquiry & Analysis No. 1745 – The Hadith Of The Stones And The Trees – About The Muslims Killing The Jews Ahead Of The End of Days – In The Hamas Charter And In A Publication Of The Hamas-Affiliated Palestine Scholars Association – February 15, 2024.
10. The *Protocols* was translated into many languages and proclaims that Jews are the source of most international pathologies. The goal of the Jews is to conquer the world. Jews create wars and coups, corrupt indigenous culture, steal money, run prostitution rings, and control international finance. See late Judge Hadassa Ben-Itto's *The Lie that Wouldn't Die – One Hundred Years of The Protocols of the Elders of Zion* (Dvir, Tel Aviv, 1998 (Hebrew)), pp. 24–9, and an updated edition from 2005, Hadassa Ben-Itto, *The Lie that Wouldn't Die – The Protocols of the Elders of Zion* (Vallentine Mitchel, London, 2020), pp. 9–15.
11. 'The Protocols Of The Elders Of Zion In The Arab And Muslim World,' *MEMRI*, April 21, 2023, Inquiry & Analysis Series No. 1689, pg 1. https://www.memri.org/reports/protocols-elders-zion-arab-and-muslim-world
12. The nine articles containing direct excerpts from the *Protocols* are: 7, 16, 17, 22, 25, 28, 30, 32, 36. Other articles in which the *Protocols*' influence is particularly evident are: 15, 27, 29, 35. Source: Stern.
13. Samia Nakhoul, Samia and Bassam, Laila, 'Who is Mohammed Deif, the Hamas commander behind the attack on Israel?' *Reuters*, October 11, 2023, https://www.reuters.com/world/middle-east/how-secretive-Hamas-commander-masterminded-attack-Israel-2023-10-10/
14. 'How a Secretive Hamas Commander Masterminded Raid on Israel, *Dawn*, June 5, 2025, https://epaper.dawn.com/DetailImage.php?StoryImage=12_10_2023_011_002

15. Orwell, George, 'What is Fascism?' *Tribune*, 1944, http://orwell.ru/library/articles/As_I_Please/english/efasc
16. Hitchens, Christopher, 'Defending Islamofascism. It's a valid term. Here's why,' *Slate Magazine*, October 22, 2007, https://slate.com/news-and-politics/2007/10/defending-the-term-islamofascism.html
17. 'German Culture-Enrichers Say: '"We Love Adolf Hitler",' *Gates of Vienna*, September 12, 2017, http://gatesofvienna.net/
18. 'President Discusses War on Terror at National Endowment for Democracy,' *The White House*, October 6, 2005, https://georgewbush-whitehouse.archives.gov/news/releases/2005/10/20051006-3.html
19. Watson, Dale L., FBI, 'Holy Land Foundation for Relief and Development, International Emergency Economic Powers Act, Action Memorandum,' memorandum to R. Richard Newcomb, director of the Office of Foreign Assets Control, US Department of the Treasury, November 5, 2001.
20. Strozier, C.B. (2024), 'The apocalyptic aims of Hamas,' *Psychoanalysis, Self and Context* 19(1), p. 3.
21. Saarnivaara, Minna, 'Suicide Campaigns as a Strategic Choice: The Case of Hamas,' *Policing: A Journal of Policy and Practice,* Volume 2, Issue 4, 2008, p. 23 Published: January 1, 2008. https://doi.org/10.1080/24720038.2023.2292052
22. The Hamas covenant states that Hamas does not seek war with the Jews but instead 'wages a struggle against the Zionists who occupy Palestine.' The slaughter of Jews, many of whom were peace activists, in October has proven otherwise. Source: Holocaust comparisons are overused – but in the case of Hamas' October 7 attack on Israel, they may reflect more than just the emotional response of a traumatized people. Source: *Moderate Voice*, 12/8/2023, https://web.p.ebscohost.com/ehost/detail/detail?vid=13&sid=b84877ba-6f62-4eae-a5ff-20e634b8f82d%40redis&bdata=JnNpdGU9ZWhvc3QtbGl2ZQ%3d%3d#AN=174098550&db=pwh
23. Litvak, Meir, 'The Antisemitism of Hamas,' *Palestine-Israel Journal of Politics, Economics & Culture*, 2005, Vol 12, Issue 2/3, p. 41.
24. 'Yassin Sees Israel "Eliminated" Within 25 Years,' *Reuters*, May 27, 1998.
25. Margolin, Devorah and Levitt, Matthew, 'The Road to October 7: Hamas' Long Game, Clarified,' *CTC Sentinel*, October/November 2023, p. 1.
26. 'The [Hamas] political leadership has freed the hand of the ['Izz ad-Din al-Qassam] brigades to do whatever they want against the brothers of monkeys and pigs [i.e., Jews].' Source: Levitt, Matthew, 'Hamas From The Cradle To The Grave,' *Middle East Quarterly* Winter 2004, p. 3. https://www.meforum.org/582/hamas-from-cradle-to-grave
27. Pan, Esther, 'Middle East: The Assassination of Sheik Yassin,' *Council on Foreign Relations*, accessed July 7, 2024, p. 1, https://www.cfr.org/backgrounder/middle-east-assassination-sheik-yassin#chapter-title-0-1; David Aufhauser, testimony before US House Committee on Financial Services, *Subcommittee*

*on Oversight and Investigations*, September 24, 2003, at http://www.treas.gov/press/releases/js758.htm.

28. It asserted, 'The political leadership of Hamas directs its terrorist networks just as they oversee their other activities.' Source: 'U.S. Designates Five Charities Funding Hamas and Six Senior Hamas Leaders as Terrorist Entities,' Office of Public Affairs, *Department of the Treasury,* August 22, 2003, at http://www.ustreas.gov/press/releases/js672.htm.
29. 35. Aufhauser, David. Testimony before the US House Committee on Financial Services, Subcommittee on Oversight and Investigations, September 24, 2003, at http://www.treas.gov/press/releases/js758.htm.
30. Margolin, Devorah and Levitt, Matthew, 'The Road to October 7: Hamas' Long Game, Clarified,' *CTC Sentinel*, October/November 2023, p. 1.
31. Reich, Walter, 'Saving Shalit, Encouraging Terror,' *The New York Times*, October 18, 2011, https://www.nytimes.com/2011/10/18/opinion/saving-a-soldier-encouraging-terror.html
32. Levitt, Mathew, 'Teaching Terror: How Hamas Radicalizes Palestinian Society,' *The Washington Institute for Near East Policy*, February 12, 2017, https://www.washingtoninstitute.org/policy-analysis/teaching-terror-how-hamas-radicalizes-palestinian-society
33. Kredo, Adam, 'Palestinian Government Paying $16 Mil a Month to Imprisoned Terrorists, Including Hamas Fighters, Watchdog Finds,' *Washington Free Beacon*, July 23, 2024, https://freebeacon.com/israel/palestinian-government-paying-16-mil-a-month-to-imprisoned-terrorists-including-hamas-fighters-watchdog-finds/
34. 'Israeli Missions around the World, A Palestinian "gift" for Passover-Official Palestinian promotion of terrorism,' *Foreign Policy*, August 4, 2011; https://embassies.gov.il/MFA/FOREIGNPOLICY/Terrorism/Palestinian/Pages/Palestinian_gift_for_Passover_8-Apr-2011.aspx
35. Hirsch, Maurice, '20 years on, PA still glorifies the perpetrators of the Passover Seder Massacre,' *JNS*, March 27, 2022, https://www.jns.org/20-years-on-pa-still-glorifies-the-perpetrators-of-the-passover-seder-massacre/
36. 'Individuals Charged in Connection with 2001 Terrorist Attack in Jerusalem that Resulted in the Death of Americans'. Washington: *Federal Information & News Dispatch*, LLC, 2017, https://montgomerycollege.idm.oclc.org/login?url=https://www.proquest.com/reports/individual-charged-connection-with-2001-terrorist/docview/1876880858/se-2.
37. 'Israel releases list of Palestinian prisoners to be swapped'. *CNN*, October 16, 2011. Archived from the original on March 4, 2016. Retrieved October 16, 2011.
38. 'Mideast: Tel Aviv Suicide Bomber Kills Three, Wounds 26 – Israel Radio.' *BBC Monitoring Middle East* – Political, April 30, 2003. 1, https://montgomerycollege.idm.oclc.org/login?url=https://www.proquest.com/wire-feeds/mideast-tel-aviv-suicide-bomber-kills-three/docview/451065081/se-2.

39. 'What Does "Globalize the Intifada" mean and How Can it Lead to Targeting Jews with Violence,' *AJC*, December 4, 2023, https://www.ajc.org/news/what-does-globalize-the-intifada-mean-and-how-can-it-lead-to-targeting-jews-with-violence
40. Omer-Man, Michael, 'The accident that sparked an Intifada,' *The Jerusalem Post*, 4 December 2011. Retrieved 3 September 2011.
41. 'While Hamas Hoards Gaza's Resources, Civilians Face Humanitarian Crisis,' *The Times of Israel*, Nov 04, 2023, https://montgomerycollege.idm.oclc.org/login?url=https://www.proquest.com/newspapers/while-hamas-hoards-gaza-s-resources-civilians/docview/2887360964/se-2
42. Bevan, Matt and Parry, Yasmin, 'Ahmed Yassin was a quadriplegic refugee who ran a charity. How did he end up founding Hamas?,' *ABC Australia*, October 20, 2023, https://www.abc.net.au/news/2023-10-21/the-disabled-refugee-who-founded-hamas/102993128
43. Ibid.
44. Burton, Guy, 'Hamas and Its Vision of Development,' *Third World Quarterly* 33, no. 3 (2012): 535-537. http://www.jstor.org/stable/41507185.
45. Farahat, Cynthia, 'The Muslim Brotherhood, Fountain of Islamist Violence,' *Middle East Quarterly*, March 2017: Global Issues (accessed April 5, 2025). https://link-gale-com.montgomerycollege.idm.oclc.org/apps/doc/A500259780/GIC?u=rock77357&sid=summon&xid=94e73578.
46. The Covenant of the Islamic Resistance Movement, Hamas Covenant 1988, *The Avalon Project*, Yale Law School, Accessed July 20 2025.https://avalon.law.yale.edu/21st_century/hamas.asp
47. Czornik, Katarzyna, 'E-Jihad or the Way Islamic Fundamentalists Utilize Digital and ICT Progress,' *Journal for the Study of Religions and Ideologies* 23, no. 67 (Spring, 2024), pp. 95–108, https://montgomerycollege.idm.oclc.org/login?url=https://www.proquest.com/scholarly-journals/e-jihad-way-islamic-fundamentalists-utilize/docview/3045626228/se-2.
48. Zelkovitz, Ido, 'Islamic Discourse and Armed Resistance: Fatah's Strategic use of Islam in the Palestinian Struggle 1970–1982,' *Religions* 16, no. 3 (2025): 298, https://montgomerycollege.idm.oclc.org/login?url=https://www.proquest.com/scholarly-journals/islamic-discourse-armed-resistance-fatah-s/docview/3182173825/se-2.
49. Shepard, William E., 'Sayyid Qutb's Doctrine of Jahiliyya,' *International Journal of Middle East Studies* 35, no. 4 (11, 2003): 521-45, https://montgomerycollege.idm.oclc.org/login?url=https://www.proquest.com/scholarly-journals/sayyid-qutbs-doctrine-jahiliyya/docview/195593321/se-2.
50. [55] Al Tahhan, Zena, ' Israeli security forces are lunatics. Israel is insanely racist,' *Al Jazeera*, June 27, 2016, https://www.aljazeera.com/features/2016/6/27/israels-stop-and-frisk-law-blatant-racism
51. Cohen, Haley, 'Georgetown University under the microscope as White House scrutinizes campus antisemitism,' *Jewish Insider*, March 28, 2025.

52. Freedman, Robert O., 'Ariel Sharon: the evolution of a security hawk,' *Midstream*, May-June 2004, 4+. Gale In Context: College (accessed April 13, 2025). https://link-gale-com.montgomerycollege.idm.oclc.org/apps/doc/A118542847/CSIC?u=rock77357&sid=summon&xid=a7bf625
53. Aronoff, Yael S., 'From Warfare to Withdrawal: The Legacy of Ariel Sharon,' *Israel Studies* (Bloomington, Ind.), 2010-06, Vol.15 (2), pp. 149–51.
54. Neve, Gordon. 'Hamas: Sharon's Legacy?' *In these Times*, 02, 2006. 15, https://montgomerycollege.idm.oclc.org/login?url=https://www.proquest.com/magazines/hamas-sharons-legacy/docview/195855179/se-2.
55. 'Former Hamas official speaks out – Al-Monitor: the Pulse of the Middle East,' *Al-Monitor*, 20 May 2015. Retrieved 5 January 2016.
56. 'Hamas Is the Key,' *Haaretz*, September 21, 2007.
57. Yousef, Ahmed, 'Hamas Is a Charitable Organization,' *Middle East Quarterly*, spring 1998, Volume 5, Number 2.
58. *Al Jazeera* English – *Al Jazeera* Media Network: 'Who are the Students Trump Wants to Deport?,' Singer Island: *Newstex*, 2025, https://montgomerycollege.idm.oclc.org/login?url=https://www.proquest.com/blogs-podcasts-websites/al-jazeera-english-media-network-who-are-students/docview/3181699559/se-2.
59. 'Hamas to Appoint Abu Marzouk as Chief: Sources,' *Xinhua News Agency – CEIS*, Oct 24, 2012, https://montgomerycollege.idm.oclc.org/login?url=https://www.proquest.com/wire-feeds/hamas-appoint-abu-marzouk-as-chief-sources/docview/1114968389/se-2.
60. 'Abu Marzouk: Hamas Will Never Recognize Israel,' *Palestine News Network (PNN)*, September 2, 2016. https://montgomerycollege.idm.oclc.org/login?url=https://www.proquest.com/wire-feeds/abu-marzouk-hamas-will-never-recognize-israel/docview/1816353309/se-2.
61. 'Abu Marzouk Lauds Iran's Long-Term Support for Hamas,' *FARS News Agency*, Dec 23, 2014. , https://montgomerycollege.idm.oclc.org/login?url=https://www.proquest.com/wire-feeds/abu-marzouk-lauds-irans-long-term-support-hamas/docview/1639736594/se-2.

## Chapter 3: Israel, Hamas, and Counterterrorism

1. MacAskill, Ewen, 'UK Army Creating New Unit Trained in Using Social Media To Engage in Psychological Warfare,' EUL2015013151790887, London *Guardian*, January 31, 2015.
2. One of those determined to take a more aggressive stance was Menachem Begin, who would later become a leader in another militant group, the Irgun, and then a Nobel Laureate and Prime Minister of Israel. Willis, Richard, 'The Hebrew Insurgency,' *History Today*, 00182753, June 2022, Vol. 72, Issue 6, Page 1.
3. Michels, Tony, 'The Pogroms in Palestine (1929),' *Jewish Radicals: A Documentary Reader* (New York, USA: New York University Press, 2012), pp. 298–9.

4. Boot, Max, 'What Wingate Wrought; The astonishing raids of a Special Operations pioneer in Palestine, Abyssinia, and Burma,' *The Weekly Standard*, vol. 18, no. 16, 31 Dec. 2012. Gale In Context: U.S. History, link.gale.com/apps/doc/A314270103/UHIC?u=rock77357&sid=summon&xid=6cfd33e2. Accessed 5 Apr. 2025.
5. Knight, J. (2011), 'Securing Zion? Policing in British Palestine, 1917–39,' *European Review of History: Revue Européenne d'histoire*, 18(4), pp. 540–3. https://doiorg.montgomerycollege.idm.oclc.org/10.1080/13507486.2011.590283
6. Shamir, E. (2012), 'From Retaliation to Open Bridges: Moshe Dayan's Evolving Approach toward the Population in Counterinsurgency,' *Civil Wars*, 14(1), pp. 63–79. https://doiorg.montgomerycollege.idm.oclc.org/10.1080/13698249.2012.654682
7. Barker, James, 'The Bombing Of The King David Hotel,' *History Today*, 07, 2006. 50, https://montgomerycollege.idm.oclc.org/login?url=https://www.proquest.com/magazines/bombing-king-david-hotel/docview/202819347/se-2.
8. Sarnoff, Michael, 'Gamal Abdel Nasser's Cynical Use of the Palestinian Cause,' *Mosaic*, June 2021. Accessed August 4, 2024, https://mosaicmagazine.com/picks/history-ideas/2021/06/gamal-abdel-nassers-cynical-use-of-the-palestinian-cause/. Initially, Nasser did not champion terrorism, but that changed after a failed Israel attack in Egypt in the mid-1950s. Source: Leonard Weiss, 'The Lavon Affair: How a False-Flag Operation Led to War and the Israeli Bomb,' *Bulletin of the Atomic Scientists*, July 2013, pp. 58–68.
9. Sarnoff, Michael, 'Nasser and the Palestinians,' *Middle East Quarterly*, Volume 23, Summer 2021, Number 3, p. 1. https://www.meforum.org/62399/nasser-and-the-palestinians
10. Luft, Gal, 'The Logic of Israel's Targeted Killing,' *Middle East Quarterly*, Vol. 10, No. 1, Winter 2003, pp. 3–13. https://www.meforum.org/515/the-logic-of-israels-targeted-killing
11. Eiland, G. (2010), 'The IDF in the Second Intifada,' *Strategic Assessment*, 13(3), pp. 27–37.
12. Beaumont, Peter. 'Senior Hamas Figure Saleh Al-Arouri Killed in Lebanon.' London (UK): *Guardian* News & Media Limited, 2024, https://montgomerycollege.idm.oclc.org/login?url=https://www.proquest.com/blogs-podcasts-websites/senior-hamas-figure-saleh-al-arouri-killed/docview/2908818301/se-2.
13. Kretzmer, David, 'Targeted Killing of Suspected Terrorists: Extrajudicial Executions or Legitimate Means of Defence?,' *The European Journal of International Law*, Vol. 16 no.2, p. 171. The United States and Britain assassinated men and women whom they considered combatants. Targets included American and British citizens connected with al Qaeda and the Islamic State.

14. British authorities could confiscate or destroy 'any house, structure or land . . . the inhabitants of which he is satisfied to have committed . . . any offense against these Regulations involving violence.' Source: Schwartz, Yishai, 'Israel Destroys Homes to Deter Terrorists. A New Study Says It Works — But Is It Moral?,' *New Republic*, December 8, 2014, p. 1, https://newrepublic.com/article/120506/study-israels-home-demolitions-policy-works-it-moral
15. Maye, Diane L., 'Measures Of Effectiveness Israeli Counterterrorism Strategies And Tactics During The Al-Aqsa Intifada,' Master's Thesis, Naval Postgraduate School, 2006–09, p. 39, accessed August 10, 2024, https://core.ac.uk/download/pdf/36696298.pdf
16. Because of the limited number of cases examined, we cannot claim that the incidents examined in this report are representative of a broader pattern but instead address them because they are troubling. Further inquiry is required to determine whether they were part of a broader policy or practice. Source: '"I Lost Everything" Israel's Unlawful Destruction of Property during Operation Cast Lead,' *Human Rights Watch*, May 13, 2010.
17. Kuperwasser, Yossi, 'How Israel can Solve its Gaza Problem,' *Middle East Quarterly*, vol. 30, no. 3, 2023, pp. 1–9. https://montgomerycollege.idm.oclc.org/login?url=https://www.proquest.com/scholarly-journals/how-israel-can-solve-gaza-problem/docview/2825572528/se-2.
18. Ahronheim, Anna, 'Operation Guardian of the Walls: Targeting Hamas Terror, Behind the Scenes: Behind the Scenes of Targeting Hamas Terror Targets,' *The Jerusalem Post*, June 3, 2021, https://www.jpost.com/arab-israeli-conflict/gaza-news/op-guardian-of-the-walls-behind-the-scenes-of-targeting-hamas-terror-669989
19. Judah, Ari G., 'Hamas Hits Central Israel with Unprecedented Rocket Fire; Woman Killed,' *The Times of Israel*, May 11, 2021. International Newsstream Collection, https://montgomerycollege.idm.oclc.org/login?url=https://www.proquest.com/newspapers/hamas-hits-central-israel-with-unprecedented/docview/2525092202/se-2.
20. Ibid.
21. Frantzman, Seth J., *The October 7 War – Israel's Battle for Security in Gaza*, Wicked Son Publications, 2024, p. 34.
22. Bowen, Jeremy, 'Israelis, United In Shock, Rally Behind War to Punish Hamas,' *BBC*, October 9, 2023.
23. Mead, P.W., 'Orde Wingate and the Official Historians,' *Journal of Contemporary History* 14, no. 1 (1979): 55, https://montgomerycollege.idm.oclc.org/login?url=https://www.proquest.com/scholarly-journals/orde-wingate-official-historians/docview/1297370300/se-2.
24. Fearn, Nicholas, 'Books: The Man Who Would Be Joshua: Nicholas Fearn Looks at the Eccentric Life and Ruthless Tactics of Major General Orde Charles Wingate, Leader of the `Gideon Force': [FINAL Edition], *The Independent,* March 5, 2000, 55, https://montgomerycollege.idm.oclc.org/login?url=

https://www.proquest.com/newspapers/books-man-who-would-be-joshua-nicholas-fearn/docview/311699320/se-2.
25. Kuttler, Hillel, '75 Years After His Death, Why Orde Wingate Remains a Hero in Israel,' *The Times of Israel*, March 23, 2019. https://montgomerycollege.idm.oclc.org/login?url=https://www.proquest.com/newspapers/75-years-after-his-death-why-orde-wingate-remains/docview/2195763825/se-2.
26. Jacob, Albert, 'Uncomfortable Thoughts about an Uncomfortable Situation,' *The Jerusalem Report*, August 12, 2024. 20, https://montgomerycollege.idm.oclc.org/login?url=https://www.proquest.com/magazines/uncomfortable-thoughts-about-situation/docview/3099754722/se-2.
27. Evans, George, 'The Eccentric Hero: Orde Wingate,' Contemporary Review, 10, 2000, p. 247, https://montgomerycollege.idm.oclc.org/login?url=https://www.proquest.com/magazines/eccentric-hero-orde-wingate/docview/204777162/se-2.
28. Ross, Dennis, 'Yasir Arafat,' *Foreign Policy*, No. 131 (Jul. – Aug., 2002), pp. 18, https://www.jstor.org/stable/3183413
29. Halevi, Jonathan D., 'A Clear Answer to an Old Debate: Arafat Colluded with Hamas Against Israel at the Height of the Oslo Years,' *Jerusalem Center for Security and Foreign Affairs*, Vol 15, No 2, January 15, 2015.
30. Perry, Dan, 'Hamas leader: Arafat urged attacks on Israel,' *NBC News*, September 30, 2010, https://www.nbcnews.com/id/wbna39446327
31. El Amraoui, Ahmed, 'The two sides of Yasser Arafat,' *Al Jazeera,* July 3, 2012, https://www.aljazeera.com/news/2012/7/3/the-two-sides-of-yasser-arafat.
32. Barker, James, 'The Bombing Of The King David Hotel,' *History Today*, 07, 2006. 50, https://montgomerycollege.idm.oclc.org/login?url=https://www.proquest.com/magazines/bombing-king-david-hotel/docview/202819347/se-2.
33. 'Making of a martyr; Palestine under the mandate,' *The Economist*, May 3, 2014, 74(US). Gale In Context: Opposing Viewpoints (accessed April 12, 2025). https://link-gale-com.montgomerycollege.idm.oclc.org/apps/doc/A366615946/OVIC?u=rock77357&sid=summon&xid=484da6c1.
34. Shindler, Colin, 'Book Review: Stern Gang's Lineage of Terror.' *The Guardian* (pre-1997 Fulltext), 05 Oct., 1995, pp. 002. International Newsstream Collection, https://montgomerycollege.idm.oclc.org/login?url=https://www.proquest.com/newspapers/book-review-stern-gangs-lineage-terror/docview/295012761/se-2.
35. 'Israel army to "use all force to destroy Hamas": Netanyahu' (2023, Oct 07), *AFP International*, Text Wire in English, https://montgomerycollege.idm.oclc.org/login?url=https://www.proquest.com/wire-feeds/israel-army-use-all-force-destroy-hamas-netanyahu/docview/2873801807/se-2
36. 'Netanyahu: Hamas staying in Gaza is like Nazis rebuilding after WWII,' *DPA International* (English) September 27, 2024, https://montgomerycollege.idm.oclc.org/login?url=https://www.proquest.com/wire-feeds/netanyahu-hamas-staying-gaza-is-like-nazis/docview/3110296088/se-2

37. 'Mohammed Deif, the Hamas Leader Who Survived at Least Seven Israeli Assassination Attempts,' *Haaretz*, July 14, 2024. https://montgomerycollege.idm.oclc.org/login?url=https://www.proquest.com/newspapers/mohammed-deif-hamas-leader-who-survived-at-least/docview/3079948191/se-2.
38. Raghavan, S., 'Mohammed Deif, The Shadowy Figure Who Heads Hamas' Military Wing' (Posted 03:45:09): Mohammed Deif. WP Company LLC d/b/a, *The Washington Post*, August 3, 2014.
39. Nakhoul, Samia and Laila Bassam, 'How a Secretive Commander Masterminded the Attack: Mohammed Deif has Survived Seven Assassination Attempts, Rarely Speaks and Never Appears in Public,' *The Irish Times*, October 12, 2023. 8,
40. 'Mohammed Deif Listening, Mocking Netanyahu's Empty Claims: Hamas Leader,' *Press TV*. From Global Security, July 14, 2021, https://www.globalsecurity.org/military/library/news/2024/07/mil-240714-presstv07.htm
41. Shotter, James and Andrew England, 'Israel Says it Killed Hamas Military Commander Mohammed Deif,' *Financial Times*, August 1, 2024, https://www.ft.com/content/93c51627-e87f-470c-a00b-f7f5c51f158f
42. Ibid.
43. Ohrenstein, Ariela, 'ICC Cancels Arrest Warrant for Hamas Leader Mohammed Deif,' *Jerusalem Post*, February 27, 2025, https://www.jpost.com/middle-east/article-844016
44. 'Hamas Official in Cairo for Talks on Shalit: Report,' *Xinhua News Agency* – CEIS, June 3, 2011, https://montgomerycollege.idm.oclc.org/login?url=https://www.proquest.com/wire-feeds/hamas-official-cairo-talks-on-shalit-report/docview/870304055/se-2.
45. 'Israeli-Palestinian Prisoner Exchange A Humanitarian Breakthrough,' *United Nations,* October 18, 2011, https://news.un.org/en/story/2011/10/392002.
46. 'German Papers See Israeli Assault on Hamas as Strategically Counterproductive.' BBC Monitoring European, Nov 17, 2012, https://montgomerycollege.idm.oclc.org/login?url=https://www.proquest.com/wire-feeds/german-papers-see-israeli-assault-on-hamas-as/docview/1158835823/se-2.
47. 'Israel Air Strikes Continue After Death of Hamas Military Chief Ahmed Jabari,' *Israel Faxx*, November 15, 2012.
48. Christa, Case Bryant, 'Gilad Shalit Deal: German Mediator Delivers Israel Offer to Hamas: The German Intelligence Official Reportedly Mediating a Prisoner Exchange to Bring Home Israeli Soldier Gilad Shalit had Previous Success with an Israel-Hezbollah Swap in 2008,' *The Christian Science Monitor* (1908-), December 23, 2009. 2
49. Sheth, Sonam and Spirlet, Thibault, 'The Last Time Hamas Released A Hostage, It Took 5 Years For Him To Be Freed,' *Business Insider*, October 17, 2023, https://www.businessinsider.com/hamas-hostage-gilad-shalit-release-took-5-years-2023-10

50. Zirulnick, Ariel, 'Israel Frets Over Gilad Shalit Deal as National Euphoria Fades: The Gilad Shalit Deal has Set a Dangerous Precedent for Prisoner Exchanges and Weakened the Palestinian Authority, Say Some Israeli Officials,' *The Christian Science Monitor* (1908-), Oct 24, 2011. 2, https://montgomerycollege.idm.oclc.org/login?url=https://www.proquest.com/historical-newspapers/israel-frets-over-gilad-shalit-deal-as-national/docview/3056068282/se-2.

## Chapter 4: The War of Words – Hamas Versus Israel

1. Presenters Rawaa Augé and Tamer Almisshal justified the attack, with Almisshal writing: 'Gaza manufactures victory and honor for its homeland and nation.' Presenter Ahmad Mansour shared a video showing Hamas breaching the border fence with a bulldozer in preparation for its invasion of Israel, as well as a video showing Hamas operatives dragging two Israeli soldiers on the ground, which he called an 'historic picture.' Source: 'Presenters, Reporters From Qatar's Al-Jazeera Praise Hamas Attack, Celebrate Israel's Disaster,' *MEMRI* Special Dispatch No. 10879, October 17, 2023.
2. Benaroya, Raphael, 'Information warfare: A strategic imperative for Israel,' *The Times of Israel*, December 4, 2023, https://blogs.timesofisrael.com/information-warfare-a-strategic-imperative-for-israel/
3. Weimann, Gabriel and Natalie Masri, 'TikTok's Spiral of Antisemitism,' *Journalism and Media* 2, no. 4 (2021): 697, https://cris.haifa.ac.il/en/publications/tiktoks-spiral-of-antisemitism
4. Myers, Steven Lee and Frenkel, Sheera, 'In a Worldwide War of Words, Russia, China and Iran Back Hamas,' *New York Times* (website), November 3, 2023, https://www.nytimes.com/2023/11/03/technology/israel-hamas-information-war.html
5. '"His disguise was a façade": How IDF revealed identities, Hamas's plans in hospital – N12,' *Jerusalem Post*, January 4, 2025, https://www.jpost.com/middle-east/article-836040
6. 'Going too easy on Gaza: Israeli right rage after PS5 sells for NIS 700 in Gaza,' *Jerusalem Post*, September 15, 2024, https://www.jpost.com/breaking-news/article-820220
7. 'Hospitals Are Protected In War. But The Safeguard Is Not Absolute,' *National Public Radio* accessed January 15, 2024 https://www.npr.org/2023/11/10/1212073968/israel-gaza-hamas-war-crimes-hospitals; Reis, S.P., and Wald, H.S. 'The Hamas Massacre Of October 7, 2023, And Its Aftermath, Medical Crimes,' and *The Lancet* Commission Report On Medicine, Nazism, And The Holocaust,' *Isr J Health Policy Res* 13, 19 (2024). https://doi.org/10.1186/s13584-024-00608-w
8. Marmon, Shoshana, Daniella M. Schwartz, and Hedy S. Wald, 'A Disingenuous One-Sided Challenge on the Hamas–Israel Conflict,' *The Lancet* 404 (10448)

(July 13, 2024). 124. doi:https://doi.org/10.1016/S0140-6736(24)01253-4. https://montgomerycollege.idm.oclc.org/login?url=https://www.proquest.com/scholarly-journals/disingenuous-one-sided-challenge-on-hamas-israel/docview/3078937819/se-2.

9. Benson, Pesach, 'Gaza Hospital Chief Faces Threats for Urging Terrorists to Leave Medical Center,' *The Press Service of Israel* (TPS-IL), April 14, 2025, https://israel.com/health/gaza-hospital-chief-faces-threats-for-urging-terrorists-to-leave-medical-center/
10. Zilberdik, Nan Jacques, 'Palestinian Authority Leaders Deny October 7 Massacre Took Place,' *Algemeiner*, December 15, 2023, https://www.algemeiner.com/2023/12/15/palestinian-authority-leaders-deny-october-7-massacre-took-place/; Douglass-William, Christine, 'Netanyahu responds to Palestinian Authority's claim that Israel, not Hamas, carried out October 7 massacre,' *Jihad Watch*, November 20, 2023, https://www.jihadwatch.org/2023/11/netanyahu-responds-to-palestinian-authoritys-claim-that-israel-not-hamas-carried-out-october-7-massacre.
11. Adam, Levick, 'Sky News Presenter Fails To Challenge Husam Zomlot's Lies,' *CAMERA*, September 8, 2024:
12. 'I wouldn't say they've taken Hamas's side,' said Dov Waxman, director of Israel studies at UCLA. 'But I would say they've laid the blame for the terrorist attack squarely on Israel.' Eva Borgwardt, IfNotNow's political director, said that the organization did not intend to avoid condemning Hamas. Source: Rosenfeld, Arno, 'Meet the Jews defending Hamas,' *Forward*, October 9, 2023, https://forward.com/news/563870/meet-the-jews-defending-hamas
13. Many of these themes overlap and embellish each other. For example, an Iranian broadcast might claim the Rothschilds pay Israeli soldiers to remove Palestinian children's eyes to sell them on the international market. This draws a spin on blood libel, national destruction, ill-gotten financial profit, and inhumanity. Bernard Lewis referred to this trend of recycling European stories as 'Islamization of antisemitism.' Source: Sachs, Susan, 'Hateful Images of Jews Are Embedded In Islamic Popular Culture,' *New York Times*, Late Edition (East Coast); New York, N.Y. April 27, 2002: B.9.
14. Norman G. Finkelstein, Biography, *Webpage*, Accessed September 10, 2020, http://normanfinkelstein.com/biography/
15. Katz, Yaakov, 'American Israel critic denied entry to country,' *The Jerusalem Post*, May 25, 2008, https://www.jpost.com/Israel/American-Israel-critic-denied-entry-to-country; 'He has also said "Israel has come out of the bowels of hell," is "a satanic state," and compared its actions to those of Genghis Khan.' The most admired Jew in the whole history of antisemitism.' Edward Alexander, professor emeritus of English, University of Washington, referring to Norman Finkelstein. Source: 'The most admired Jew in the whole history of antisemitism,' Norman G. Finkelstein Homepage, Quote attributed to Edward

Alexander, February 25, 2006, http://normanfinkelstein.com/2006/02/25/the-most-admired-jew-in-the-whole-history-of-antisemitism/

16. Shalim, Avi, 'Lessons of the conflict in Gaza,' *Al Jazeera*, August 9, 2014, https://www.aljazeera.com/opinions/2014/8/9/lessons-of-the-conflict-in-gaza
17. For example, a recent Irish children's textbook claims that Jesus was born in a country called Palestine. In fact, the name Palestine was not in use at the time. Source: Lidor, Canaan, 'Irish textbooks say Jesus was from "Palestine," downplay Auschwitz,' *JN*, November 5, 2024, https://www.jns.org/irish-textbooks-say-jesus-was-from-palestine-downplay-auschwitz/
18. The IDF exhorted the civilian population to move southward, spreading pamphlets, using loudspeakers, and making tens of thousands of phone calls to Gaza residents. In one of these phone calls, the IDF officer was told that Hamas militants were preventing them from leaving their homes, were blocking the main Salah Al-Din highway leading to the south and were even opening fire on Gaza residents who were trying to go. 'Hamas wanted Gazans to remain so that more of them might be killed by Israeli bombs, thus giving Hamas a propaganda bonanza. Only Israel cares about the well-being of Gaza's civilians.' Source: Kraiem, Leon, 'UN Report Claims Israel Is Committing Genocide In Gaza, Calls For Arms Embargo,' *Jerusalem Post*, March 25, 2024. A UN report offered a similar fallacy. 'Safe areas' did indeed become 'unsafe' as the IDF targets changed. Still, in every case, the IDF warned Gazans to move, and then move again, to stay safe. Source: Kraiem, Leon, 'UN Report Claims Israel Is Committing Genocide In Gaza, Call For Arms Embargo,' *Jerusalem Post*, March 25, 2024.
19. Lempkowicz, Yossi, 'French TV Producer Slammed For Saying "Gaza Is Auschwitz,' *European Jewish Press*, May 16, 2025
20. '*Washington Post* retracts Gaza aid report, says it failed to meet "fairness standards,"' *Jerusalem Post*, June 4, 2025, https://www.jpost.com/israel-news/defense-news/article-856456
21. Starr, Michael, 'Hadid, Alana, Israel Not Haven For Jews Because It Sterilized Ethiopian Jews,' *Jerusalem Post*, January 5, 2025, https://www.jpost.com/diaspora/antisemitism/article-836206
22. *Jerusalem Post* Staff, 'UN Aid Chief Admits Starving Gazan Baby Claim Was Amid "Desperation" To Let Aid In,' *Jerusalem Post*, May 30, 2025, https://www.yahoo.com/news/un-aid-chief-regrets-claim-083446468.html
23. Sale, Ben, 'Pro-Palestinian Tiktoker With 3.4m Followers, Endorses Murder Of Israeli Embassy Employees,' *JTA*, May 24, 2025, https://www.timesofisrael.com/popular-pro-palestinian-tiktok-influencer-endorses-murder-of-israeli-embassy-staffers/
24. Hoffman, Gil. 'Why the "60 Minutes" Segment with Freed Hostages Fell Short,' *The Jerusalem Post*, April 4, 2025, https://www.jpost.com/opinion/article-848737

25. Netanyahu, Benjamin, 'The Battle of Civilization,' *WSJ Opinion*, October 30, 2023, https://www.wsj.com/opinion/the-battle-of-civilization-in-gaza-israel-hamas-
26. These four points were offered in Prince Williams Odera Oguejiofor's 'The Role of Social Media in Shaping Narratives and Perceptions in the Israeli-Gaza Conflict that Escalated on October 2023,' *International Journal of Academic Multidisciplinary Research (IJAMR)*, ISSN: 2643-9670 , Vol. 8, Issue April 4, 2024, Pages: 75 and 76, https://www.researchgate.net/profile/Princewilliams-Oguejiofor/publication/380734520_
27. These skits appeared on YouTube and do not appear to be easily sourced. They are almost certainly satirical but this author has no evidence it was produced or funded by any Israeli organization. It may be a comedian unconnected with Israel or pro-Israel organizations placed this on the Internet as a spoof.
28. CBN – *The Christian Broadcast Network*, Accessed April 17, 2025, https://cbn.com/ministries
29. 'Gaza: Palestinian Rockets Unlawfully Targeted Israeli Civilians,' *Human Rights Watch*, December 24, 2012, https://www.hrw.org/news/2012/12/24/gaza-palestinian-rockets-unlawfully-targeted-israeli-civilians
30. 'Amnesty International Urges Donors to Reverse Decision to Halt Funding for UN Agency for Palestinian Refugees,' *Anadolu Agency*, January 30, 2024.
31. Overby, Peter, 'Unpacking What The American Israel Public Affairs Committee Does,' *National Public Radio,* February 23, 2019, https://www.npr.org/2019/02/13/694463816/unpacking-what-the-american-israel-public-affairs-committee-does
32. Tusak, Corey, 'AIPAC-backed candidates win big in US elections, strengthening pro-Israel presence in Congress,' *The Jerusalem Post*, November 7, 2024, https://www.jpost.com/diaspora/article-828009
33. 'Gaza Solidarity Rally in Times Square: We Will Start an Intifada in Every Classroom, Every College Campus; We Will Shut Down Every Zionist Event; Israel Has No Right to Exist; Palestinian Resistance Is Not Terrorism,' *MEMRI TV* #7628, November 15, 2019, https://www.memri.org/tv/times-square-gaza-solidarity-rally-intifada-revolution-every-college-campus-shut-down-zionists-israel-no-right
34. Pierre, Dion J., '"Eradicate America": Students for Justice in Palestine Calls for "Total Collapse" of the US,' *Algemeiner*, September 5, 2024.
35. Ibid.
36. 'Gaza Solidarity Rally in Times Square: We Will Start an Intifada in Every Classroom, Every College Campus; We Will Shut Down Every Zionist Event; Israel Has No Right to Exist; Palestinian Resistance Is Not Terrorism," *MEMRI*, November 15, 2019, https://www.memri.org/tv/times-square-gaza-solidarity-rally-intifada-revolution-every-college-campus-shut-down-zionists-israel-no-right
37. Ibid.

38. 'Students for Justice in Palestine,' *Anti-Defamation League*, Accessed April 26, 2025, https://www.adl.org/resources/backgrounder/students-justice-palestine-sjp
39. Shapiro, Danielle, 'Was Called an "Inbred Swine" at Princeton Last Night,' *The Free Press*, April 8, 2025, https://www.thefp.com/p/anti-israel-princeton-protest
40. There is a photo of her being honored by Hamas spokesperson Fawzi Barhoum and Taher al-Nunu the advisor to former Hamas leader Ismail Haniyeh. In another post, Abuelkas laments the death of an *Al Jazeera* 'reporter' Ismail Al-Ghoul (left), a Hamas terrorist who participated in the October 7 massacre in southern Israel. Source: 'Exposés Journalist or Mouthpiece? Hamas Shared Anti-Israeli Message by France24 Correspondent,' *Honest Reporting*, October 18, 2024, https://honestreporting.com/journalist-or-mouthpiece-hamas-shared-anti-israeli-message-by-france24-correspondent/
41. Humaid, Maram, 'Voices from Gaza: Protests demand an end to war and suffering,' *Al Jazeera*, March 28, 2025, https://www.aljazeera.com/news/2025/3/28/voices-from-gaza-protests-demand-an-end-to-war-and-suffering
42. Ibid.
43. Ibid.
44. '"Antisemitic" UN Special Rapporteur Francesca Albanese banned from Israel – officials,' *Jerusalem Post*, February 12, 2024, https://www.jpost.com/breaking-news/article-786519
45. 'UN Rapporteur Calls on all to "wake up" regarding Gaza,' *Anadolu Agency: AA*, July 03, 2024.
46. Brownfeld, Allan, 'Examining "Ten Myths about Israel", by Ilan Pappe,' *Mondoweiss*, January 24, 2018, https://mondoweiss.net/2018/01/examining-myths-israel/
47. 'Norman Finkelstein's Long Crusade. A Cantankerous Israel Critic Takes A Rare Turn In The Limelight,' *New York Magazine*, December 5, 2023, https://nymag.com/intelligencer/article/norman-finkelstein-israel-palestine-scholar-profile.html
48. Ibid.
49. 'Everything Gigi and Bella Hadid Have Said on Israeli-Palestinian Conflict,' *Newsweek*, October 11, 2023, https://www.newsweek.com/everything-gigi-bella-hadid-said-israeli-palestinian-conflict-1833692
50. https://www.dailymail.co.uk/news/article-13525955/Bella-Hadid-Hamas-birthday-cake-Instagram-music-video-Gaza-Calling.html
51. Anderson, Natasha, 'Bella Hadid Called Out For "Hamas Birthday Cake" Post On Instagram As Supermodel Prepares To Star In Music Video Titled Gaza Is Calling,' *Daily Mail*, June 13, 2024, https://www.dailymail.co.uk/news/article-13525955/Bella-Hadid-Hamas-birthday-cake-Instagram-music-video-Gaza-Calling.html

52. Ibid.
53. Cortellessa, Eric,' Inside the Israel-Hamas Information War,' *Time Magazine*, December 22, 2023, https://time.com/6549544/israel-and-hamas-the-media-war/
54. https://www.facebook.com/reel/2060313827640891https://ejpress.org/hamas-must-me-removed-says-israeli-expert/
55. Lempkowitz, Yossi, 'Hamas Must Be Removed, Says Israeli Expert,' *European Jewish Press*, October 9, 2023.
56. 'Israeli influencer speaks up for Gaza hostages on London Underground,' *New York Post*, April 4, 2025, https://nypost.com/2025/04/04/world-news/israeli-influencer-speaks-up-for-gaza-hostages-on-london-underground/.
57. Haddad, Yoseph, 'What apartheid?,' *Israel Hayom*, January 17, 2021. https://www.israelhayom.com/opinions/what-apartheid-2/
58. 'Israeli influencer speaks up for Gaza hostages on London Underground,' *Jewish News Syndicate*, April 4, 2025, https://nypost.com/2025/04/04/world-news/israeli-influencer-speaks-up-for-gaza-hostages-on-london-underground/
59. Friedman, Ami, '"I Destroy Their Narrative": Israel's Renowned Arab Advocate,' *Israel Hayom*, January 9, 2025, https://www.israelhayom.com/2025/01/09/i-destroy-their-narrative-israels-renowned-arab-advocate/
60. Neuer, Hillel, UN Watch homepage, Accessed June 6, 2025, *UN Watch*, https://unwatch.org/home/hillelneuer/
61. Ibid.
62. 'Ari Shaffir, controversial comic who ripped Kobe Bryant, returns to Spokane,' *The Spokesman-Review*, September 23, 2021.

## Chapter 5: Cities of Slaughter

1. Da Silva, Chantal and Sanchez, Raf, 'Death And Heartbreak At Every Turn In Kibbutz Near Gaza That Was Ambushed By Hamas,' *NBC*, October 11, 2023, https://www.nbcnews.com/news/world/death-heartbreak-every-turn-kibbutz-gaza-was-ambushed-hamas-rcna119975
2. There was no indication that Tehran directed or authorized the Oct. 7 attack. Source: Nakhoul, Samia , 'How Hamas Secretly Built A "Mini Army" To Fight Israel,' *Reuters*, October 16, 2023, https://www.reuters.com/world/middle-east/how-hamas-secretly-built-mini-army-fight-israel-2023-10-13/
3. Lisbona, Natalie, 'Of October 7 Describes Horrific Gang Rape By Hamas And How They Slaughtered People Around Him,' *Daily Mail*, July 28, 2024, https://www.dailymail.co.uk/news/article-13675485/Male-victim-October-7-describes-horrific-gang-rape-Hamas.html
4. Hamas militants killed civilians at Kerem Shalom, Sufa, Magen, Ofakim, Re'im Be'eri, Karni crossing, Nahal Oz, Kfar Aza, Sderot, Erez Crossing, Netiv HaAsar, Zikim Beach. Militants also randomly struck at civilians and police official near Gaza and infamously at a music festival. Some of the points of

attack were devastated with many dwellings burnt to ground and people killed, wounded, raped or captured. Other points received less damage and carnage.

5. Mackintosh, Eliza, et al, 'How A Rave Celebrating Life Turned Into A Frenzied Massacre Hamas Attackers Choked Off Avenues Of Escape From The Nova Music Festival, Swarming The Site And Killing People Hiding In Bomb Shelters, Video Analysis And Survivor Testimony Reveals,' *CNN*, October 14, 2023, https://www.cnn.com/interactive/2023/10/middleeast/hamas-music-festival-attack-investigation-cmd-intl/
6. Schecter, Anna, 'Top Secret Hamas Documents Show That Terrorists Intentionally Targeted Elementary Schools And A Youth Center,' *NBC News*, October 13, 2023, https://www.nbcnews.com/news/investigations/top-secret-hamas-documents-show-terrorists-intentionally-targeted-elem-rcna120310
7. Schecter, Anna, 'Their Bodies Tell Their Stories. They're Not Alive To Speak For Themselves,' *NBC News*, December 5, 2023, https://www.nbcnews.com/news/world/hamas-rape-israeli-women-oct-7-rcna128221
8. Lefkovits, Etgar, 'Be'eri farmer who lost his wife, son and leg on Oct. 7 returns to his fields,' *JNS*, April 17, 2024, https://www.jns.org/beeri-farmer-who-lost-his-wife-son-and-leg-on-oct-7-returns-to-his-fields/\
9. 'Hamas Had Not Planned To Attack Music Festival, Israeli Report Says,' *Aljazeera*, November 18, 2023, https://www.aljazeera.com/news/2023/11/18/hamas-had-not-planned-to-attack-israel-music-festival-israeli-report-says
10. Debre, Isabel, and Biesecker, Michael, 'Israeli Survivors Recount Terror At Music Festival, Where Hamas Militants Killed At Least 260,' *Associated Press*, October 9, 2023, https://apnews.com/article/israel-palestinians-gaza-hamas-music-festival-6a55aae2375944f10ecc4c52d05f2ffe; 'Tal Shimony Survived the Hamas Attack on the Nova Music Festival: Hear Her Story of Courage, Resilience, and Remembrance,' *AJC – Global Voice*, February 1, 2024, https://www.ajc.org/news/podcast/tal-shimony-survived-the-hamas-attack-on-the-nova-music-festival-hear-her-story-of-courage
11. Browne, David, Dillon, Nancy, and Grow, Kory, 'They Wanted to Dance in Peace. And They Got Slaughtered, *Rolling Stone*, October 15, 2023, https://www.rollingstone.com/music/music-features/hamas-israel-nova-music-festival-massacre-1234854306/
12. 'Tal Shimony Survived the Hamas Attack on the Nova Music Festival: Hear Her Story of Courage, Resilience, and Remembrance,' *AJC – Global Voice*, February 1, 2024, https://www.ajc.org/news/podcast/tal-shimony-survived-the-hamas-attack-on-the-nova-music-festival-hear-her-story-of-courage
13. Browne, David, Dillon, Nancy, and Grow, Kory, 'They Wanted to Dance in Peace. And They Got Slaughtered,' *Rolling Stone*, October 15, 2023, https://www.rollingstone.com/music/music-features/hamas-israel-nova-music-festival-massacre-1234854306/
14. Sherwood, Harriet, 'How The Hamas Attack On The Supernova Festival In Israel Unfolded,' *The Guardian*, October 9, 2024. https://www.theguardian.

com/world/2023/oct/09/how-the-hamas-attack-on-the-supernova-festival-in-israel-unfolded

15. Ibid.
16. Kessler, Jacob, 'Nova Festival survivor pictured running through desert lays bare her escape from Hamas,' *Daily Express*, December 12, 2023. https://www.msn.com/en-us/news/world/nova-festival-survivor-pictured-running-through-desert-lays-bare-her-escape-from-hamas/ar-AA1labrX
17. Browne, David, Dillon, Nancy, and Grow, Kory, 'They Wanted to Dance in Peace. And They Got Slaughtered,' *Rolling Stone*, October 15, 2023, https://www.rollingstone.com/music/music-features/hamas-israel-nova-music-festival-massacre-1234854306/
18. Debre, Isabel, and Biesecker, Michael, 'Israeli Survivors Recount Terror At Music Festival, Where Hamas Militants Killed At Least 260,' *Associated Press*, October 9, 2023.
19. Sherwood, Harriet, 'How the Hamas attack on the Supernova festival in Israel unfolded,' *The Guardian*, October 9, 2024, https://www.theguardian.com/world/2023/oct/09/how-the-hamas-attack-on-the-supernova-festival-in-israel-unfolded
20. Debre, Isabel, and Biesecker, Michael, 'Israeli Survivors Recount Terror At Music Festival, Where Hamas Militants Killed At Least 260,' *Associated Press*, October 9, 2023
21. https://www.cnn.com/interactive/2023/10/middleeast/hamas-music-festival-attack-investigation-cmd-intl/
22. Agmon, Yair and Mevorach, Oriya, *One Day in October – Forty Heroes, Forty Stories*, The Toby Press, 2024, p. 75.
23. Browne, David, Dillon, Nancy, and Grow, Kory, 'They Wanted to Dance in Peace. And They Got Slaughtered,' *Rolling Stone*, October 15, 2023, https://www.rollingstone.com/music/music-features/hamas-israel-nova-music-festival-massacre-1234854306/
24. Gordon, Anna, '"I Was Saved by a Miracle." A Survivor Recounts the Horror of the Hamas Attack on Israel's Supernova Festival,' *Time*, October 9, 2023, https://time.com/6321984/escaping-hamas-supernova-festival-diary/
25. Debre, Isabel, and Biesecker, Michael, 'Israeli Survivors Recount Terror At Music Festival, Where Hamas Militants Killed At Least 260,' *Associated Press*, October 9, 2023.
26. Browne, David, Dillon, Nancy, and Grow, Kory, 'They Wanted to Dance in Peace. And They Got Slaughtered,' *Rolling Stone*, October 15, 2023, https://www.rollingstone.com/music/music-features/hamas-israel-nova-music-festival-massacre-1234854306/
27. Debre, Isabel, and Biesecker, Michael, 'Israeli Survivors Recount Terror At Music Festival, Where Hamas Militants Killed At Least 260,' *Associated Press*, October 9, 2023.

28. Browne, David, Dillon, Nancy, and Grow, Kory, 'They Wanted to Dance in Peace. And They Got Slaughtered,' *Rolling Stone*, October 15, 2023, https://www.rollingstone.com/music/music-features/hamas-israel-nova-music-festival-massacre-1234854306/
29. She and her brother were abducted by the terrorists and released in late November as part of the hostage deal. Source: Tenoria, Rich, 'Documentary on October 7 Supernova festival massacre makes US debut,' *The Times of Israel*, February 23, 2024, https://www.timesofisrael.com/documentary-on-october-7-supernova-festival-massacre-makes-us-debut/?__cf_chl_tk=9r2XyQ5xrUsnYK7FYlSyi2Vmi4W13ui9vL1Ouj5I8vU-1723301684-0.0.1.1-3945
30. Browne, David, Dillon, Nancy, and Grow, Kory, 'They Wanted to Dance in Peace. And They Got Slaughtered,' *Rolling Stone*, October 15, 2023, https://www.rollingstone.com/music/music-features/hamas-israel-nova-music-festival-massacre-1234854306/
31. Mackintosh, Eliza, et al, 'How A Rave Celebrating Life Turned Into A Frenzied Massacre Hamas Attackers Choked Off Avenues Of Escape From The Nova Music Festival, Swarming The Site And Killing People Hiding In Bomb Shelters, Video Analysis And Survivor Testimony Reveals,' *CNN*, October 14, 2023, https://www.cnn.com/interactive/2023/10/middleeast/hamas-music-festival-attack-investigation-cmd-intl/
32. '"I Knew It's Either I Hit Him Or I Die": Re'im Rave Survivor Recounts Daring Decision,' *The Times of Israel*, October 15, 2023, https://www.timesofisrael.com/i-knew-its-either-i-hit-him-or-i-die-reim-rave-survivor-recounts-daring-decision/
33. Alon Bernstein, Alon and McNeil, Sam, 'A Music Festival Survivor Fleeing The Attack, A Pair Of Hamas Militants And A Deadly Decision,' *Associated Press*, October 13, 2023, https://apnews.com/article/israel-palestinians-gaza-hamas-airstrikes-festival-survivors-5b5dc4eb87be8d7b51dceff1c9f906fd
34. In his testimony to the Association, Davidian said he had seen more than five bodies that had been mutilated 'in intimate places… their organs were cut off, damaged. There was blood from the groin . . . There were also shots to the breasts.'
35. Lim, Megan, 'This Israeli general saw the horror of the Hamas attack. Now, he's urging optimism,' *National Public Radio*, November 8, 2023, /www.kuow.org/stories/this-israeli-general-saw-the-horror-of-the-hamas-attack-now-he-s-urging-optimism
36. Bashinsky, Ruth, 'Israeli-American Paramedic On The Front Line Of Hamas Terror Attack Describes How Three Of His Colleagues Were Slaughtered As They Tried To Save Jewish Villagers And Festival-Goers,' *Daily Mail*, October 21, 2023, https://www.dailymail.co.uk/news/article-12641573/Israeli-American-paramedic-Hamas-terror-attack-Jewish-villagers-festival-goers.html

37. Browne, David, Dillon, Nancy, and Grow, Kory, 'They Wanted to Dance in Peace. And They Got Slaughtered,' *Rolling Stone*, October 15, 2023, https://www.rollingstone.com/music/music-features/hamas-israel-nova-music-festival-massacre-1234854306/
38. Bernstein, Alon and Mcneil, Sam; 'A Music Festival Survivor Fleeing The Attack, A Pair Of Hamas Militants And A Deadly Decision,' *Associated Press*, October 13, 2023, https://apnews.com/article/israel-palestinians-gaza-hamas-airstrikes-festival-survivors-5b5dc4eb87be8d7b51dceff1c9f906fd
39. McKernan, Bethan,' Evidence Points To Systematic Use Of Rape And Sexual Violence By Hamas On 7 October Attacks,' *The Guardian*, January 18, 2024, https://www.theguardian.com/world/2024/Jan/18/evidence-points-to-systematic-use-of-rape-by-hamas-in-7-october-attacks
40. Williamson, Lucy, 'Israel Gaza: Hamas Raped And Mutilated Women On 7 October,' *BBC*, 5 December 2023, https://www.bbc.com/news/world-middle-east-67629181
41. Hasbara Staff, 'ZAKA: Israeli-Based Volunteer Rescue Organization,' *Hasbara*, Accessed August 10, 2024, https://hasbarafellowships.org/zaka-israeli-based-volunteer-rescue-organization/
42. Goldenberg, Tia and Frankel, Julia, 'How 2 Debunked Accounts Of Sexual Violence On Oct. 7 Fueled A Global Dispute Over Israel-Hamas War,' *Associated Press,* May 22, 2024, https://apnews.com/article/israel-hamas-war-sexual-violence-zaka-ca7905bf9520b1e646f86d72cdf03244# #
43. Ibid.
44. 'JC Reporter, IDF Releases Previously Unseen Footage Showing October 7 Gun Battles,' *The Jewish Chronicle*, October 7, 2024, https://www.thejc.com/news/israel/idf-releases-previously-unseen-footage-showing-october-7-gun-battles-wdb856kb
45. Shaulov, Rone Green, 'Hamas War Crimes: An Elderly Group Gunned Down At A Bus Stop,' *Ynetnews*, October 17, 2023, https://www.ynetnews.com/magazine/article/b1f2eqo11p
46. Zak, Elizabet, 'A Morning Of Kindness Turns To Terror: A Sderot Resident's Story,' *JNS*, November 19, 2023, https://www.jns.org/a-morning-of-kindness-turns-to-terror-a-sderot-residents-story/
47. Kimon, Elisha Ben, 'IDF Probe Of October 7 Sderot Battle: Military Fails To Defend City, Didn't Respond In Real Time,' *Ynetnews*, April 9, 2025, https://www.ynetnews.com/article/skkgb1vrkx?utm_medium=personalized-push&utm_source=taboola
48. Steinberg, Jessica, 'Sderot memorializes the police station that was destroyed on October 7,' *The Times of Israel*, November 24, 2024,
49. Chazan, Guy, 'On Gaza's Doorstep: Israelis Drift Back To Deserted Border Town Of Sderot,' *Financial Times*, April 23, 2024, https://www.ft.com/content/6d5f860f-51e5-46e4-a015-1ac7a2571cd0

50. Williamson, Lucy, 'Israel Gaza: Hamas Raped And Mutilated Women On 7 October,' *BBC*, December 5, 2023, https://www.bbc.com/news/world-middle-east-67629181
51. Bodkin, Henry, 'How seven years of Hamas planning resulted in IDF's Oct 7 failure,' *The Telegraph*, February 27, 2025, https://www.yahoo.com/news/really-happened-october-7-185942283.html
52. Williamson, Lucy, 'Israel Gaza: Hamas Raped And Mutilated Women On 7 October,' *BBC*, December 5, 2023, https://www.bbc.com/news/world-middle-east-67629181
53. 'Summer Goodkind and David Averre, biggest ever criminal investigation,' *Daily Mail*, December 4, 2023.
54. Lisbona, Natalie, 'I Was Raped, Two Held Me Down, There Was Spitting, Screaming . . . I Was A Jewish Doll To Them, To Do Whatever They Wanted': Male Victim Of October 7 Describes Horrific Gang Rape By Hamas And How They Slaughtered People Around Him,' *Daily Mail.com*, July 28, 2024, https://www.dailymail.co.uk/news/article-13675485/Male-victim-October-7-describes-horrific-gang-rape-Hamas.html
55. There is some debate about the exact translation of the word. See *The Atlantic Magazine*'s 'What Hamas Called Its Female Captives, and Why It Matters,' ttps://www.theatlantic.com/ideas/archive/2024/05/israel-hamas-female-captives-sabaya-translation/678505/
56. Estrin, Daniel, et al., 'New Details Emerge About The Hamas-Led Attackers Who Massacred Israelis,' *National Public Radio*, October 27, 2023, https://www.pnpr.org/2023/10/27/1208836319/israel-hamas-islamic-jihad-militants-videos-details
57. McKernan, Bethan, 'Evidence Points To Systematic Use Of Rape And Sexual Violence By Hamas On 7 October Attacks,' *The Guardian*, January 18, 2024, https://www.theguardian.com/world/2024/jan/18/evidence-points-to-systematic-use-of-rape-by-hamas-in-7-october-attacks
58. WelcometotheKibbutzAlumimWebsite,accessedAugust19,2024,https://www.alumim.co.il/ViewPage_mobile.asp?pagesCatID=13738&siteName=Alumim
59. Maddy-Weitzman, Bruce, 'Black Sabbath,' *Tablet*, March 20, 2024, https://www.tabletmag.com/sections/israel-middle-east/articles/black-sabbath-kibbutz-alumim-hamas
60. Paul, Mark 'Who do you mourn for when there is so much evil?,' *The Irish Times*, December 2, 2023, https://www.irishtimes.com/world/middle-east/2023/12/02/who-do-you-mourn-for-when-there-is-so-much-evil/
61. https://mishpacha.com/a-miracle-happened-here/
62. Dumas, Daisy and Davies, Caroline, 'British-Israeli survivor tells of horrific scenes after kibbutz attack,' *The Guardian*, October 10, 2023.
63. Samuels, Andrea, 'Israel At War: 26 Hours In A Bomb Shelter As Death Rained All Around,' *Jerusalem Post*, October 21, 2023, https://www.jpost.com/arab-israeli-conflict/gaza-news/article-769271

64. Yaron, Lee, *10/7 100 Human Stories*, St Martin's Press, New York. 2024, p. 207.
65. Hinshaw, Drew, 'A Foreign Student Saved His Friends from Hamas. Then He Vanished,' *MSN.com*, November 11, 2023.
66. Israel, Yogev, 'The Israeli Alzheimer's Researcher Who Fought Terrorists On October 7,' *Ynet.com,* December 22, 2023, https://www.ynetnews.com/health_science/article/b1t4zcmpp
67. Maddy-Weitzman, Bruce, 'Black Sabbath,' *Tablet*, March 20, 2024, https://www.tabletmag.com/sections/israel-middle-east/articles/black-sabbath-kibbutz-alumim-hamas
68. Grey, Stephen, Lubell, Maayan et al, 'Hunted By Hamas: 27 Hours Of Slaughter And Survival Inside Israel's Kibbutz Be'eri,' *Reuters*, November 3, 2023, https://www.reuters.com/investigates/special-report/israel-palestinians-kibbutz-attack/
69. Anspach, Mark, 'When Pacifists are Victims,' *Bulletin of the Colloquium on Violence and Religion* 78, December 2023, Page 13, Accessed August 31, 2024, https://www.pdcnet.org/covrb/content/covrb_2023_0078_0013_0024
70. Kottasová, Ivana and Izso, Lauren, 'The Close-Knit Kibbutz That Became Home To A Massacre,' *CNN*, October 12, 2023.
71. Ibid.
72. According to first responders, 80% of the recovered bodies showed signs of torture. Some victims were found bound up, decapitated, or with signs of sexual abuse. Source: Poris, Aaron, 'Forensic Accountants Work to Quantify Damage to Kibbutz Be'eri,' *The Media Line*, January 29, 2024, https://themedialine.org/top-stories/forensic-accountants-work-to-quantify-damage-to-kibbutz-beeri/
73. Molana-Allen, Leila, 'Lives Shattered By Oct. 7 Attack, Some Survivors Return To Kibbutz Be'eri,' *PBS News Hours*, November 7, 2023, https://www.pbs.org/newshour/show/lives-shattered-by-oct-7-attack-some-survivors-return-to-kibbutz-beeri
74. Rubin, Shira, and Warrick, Joby, 'Hamas Envisioned Deeper Attacks, Aiming To Provoke An Israeli War,' *Washington Post*, November 12, 2023, NA. Gale Academic OneFile (accessed September 21, 2024). https://link.gale.com/apps/doc/A772549308/AONE?u=anon~e8a92684&sid=googleScholar&xid=d8eee276.
75. Grey, Stephen, Lubell, Maayan et al, 'Hunted By Hamas: 27 Hours Of Slaughter And Survival Inside Israel's Kibbutz Be'eri,' *Reuters*, November 3, 2023, https://www.reuters.com/investigates/special-report/israel-palestinians-kibbutz-attack/
76. Lefkovits, Etgar, 'Be'eri Farmer Who Lost His Wife, Son And Leg On Oct. 7 Returns To His Fields,' *JNS,* April 17, 2024, https://www.jns.org/beeri-farmer-who-lost-his-wife-son-and-leg-on-oct-7-returns-to-his-fields/
77. Ibid.

78. Stephens, Bret, 'Israelis Were Shattered on Oct. 7. Can They Recover?,' *The New York Times*, November 10, 2023, https://go.gale.com/ps/i.do?id=GALE%7CA772206655&sid=googleScholar&v=2.1&it=r&linkaccess=abs&issn=03624331&p=AONE&sw=w&userGroupName=anon%7Ed843a25c&aty=open-web-entry
79. Cortellessa, Eric, 'The Oct. 7 Massacre Revealed a New Hamas Social Media Strategy,' *Reuters*, October 31, 2023.
80. Abraham, Yuval, 'A Gazan Worked In Israeli Kibbutzim For Decades. Then Came October 7,' *+972 magazine*, November 6, 2023, https://www.972mag.com/gaza-workers-israel-kibbutzim-massacres/
81. Poris, Aaron, 'Forensic Accountants Work to Quantify Damage to Kibbutz Be'eri,' *The Media Line*, January 29, 2024, https://themedialine.org/top-stories/forensic-accountants-work-to-quantify-damage-to-kibbutz-beeri/
82. Anspach, Mark, When Pacifists are Victims,' *Bulletin of the Colloquium on Violence and Religion* 78, December 2023, Page 13, Accessed August 31, 2024. https://www.pdcnet.org/covrb/content/covrb_2023_0078_0013_0024
83. Kottasova, Ivana and Izso, Lauren, 'The close-knit kibbutz that became home to a massacre,' *CNN*, October 12, 2023, ttps://www.cnn.com/2023/10/12/middleeast/kibbutz-beeri-israel-war-intl-cmd
84. Hinnant, Lori and McNeil, Sam, '"We Are Officially Hostages." How The Israeli Kibbutz Of Nir Oz Embodied Hamas' Hostage Strategy,' *Associated Press*, December 5, 2023, https://apnews.com/article/israel-hamas-war-news-hostages-0c14750240138853a70e38b0c09ef157. Around 20 Nir Oz residents were killed on Oct. 7, and news of the death of some of them in Gaza has started to trickle in. Those seized from the kibbutz ranged in age from 9 months to 85 years at the time they were taken. All were civilians, and more than half were women and children. All 13 Israeli hostages released in the first exchange on Nov. 24 were from Nir Oz, and they bought the freedom of 39 Palestinian prisoners from Israel.
85. Anspach, Mark, 'When Pacifists are Victims,' *Bulletin of the Colloquium on Violence and Religion* 78, December 2023, Page 13, Accessed August 31, 2024. https://www.pdcnet.org/covrb/content/covrb_2023_0078_0013_0024
86. Ibid.
87. Hinnant, Loir and McNeil, Sam '"We are officially hostages." How The Israeli Kibbutz Of Nir Oz Embodied Hamas' Hostage Strategy,' *Associated Press*, December 5, 2023, https://apnews.com/article/israel-hamas-war-news-hostages-0c14750240138853a70e38b0c09ef157
88. Ali Barakeh, a Hamas official in Beirut, told The Associated Press on Oct. 9 2023. Source; Spirlet, Thibault, 'Hamas says it thought Israel would manage to stop its attack sooner, and couldn't believe how successful it was,' *Business Insider*, October 10, 2023.
89. 'In Harrowing Detail, NYT Reports On Weaponization Of Rape, Sexual Violence On Oct. 7,' *The Times of Israel*, December 29, 2023.

90. The most significant terror attack in terms of casualties per hospital was the attack on the United States embassy in Nairobi, Kenia, in 1998 [1], where Kenyatta National Hospital staff estimated they treated up to 2500 injured on the day of the bombing. Source: Gozlan A, Abuhasira et al., 'October 7th 2023 Mass Casualty Incident In Southern Israel: Lessons For Emergency Preparedness And Management,' *Isr J Health Policy Res*. 2024 Nov 11;13(1):67.
91. Barkan, Noam, 'Inside Israel's Emergency Medical Hotline On Oct. 7,' *JNS*, July 11, 2024.
92. Wen, Leana, 'We Cannot Forget What Happened At Israel's Soroka Hospital,' *Time Magazine*, October 30, 2023, ps://time.com/6329919/israel-soroka-hospital-october-7/
93. In the first 16 hours, the Soroka emergency department treated 680 patients, 120 of whom were critically wounded. As victims started arriving, the hospital discharged at least a hundred patients to make room. They activated staff, many of whom were off because it was a Jewish holiday.
94. Ghert-Zand, Renee, 'Preventative Medicine: After Oct. 7 Mass Casualty Event, Israeli Mds Share Tough Lessons,' *The Times of Israel*, February 16, 2024, https://www.timesofisrael.com/preventative-medicine-after-oct-7-mass-casualty-event-israeli-mds-share-tough-lessons/
95. O'Neill, Brendan, 'A Savage Rupturing Of Our Civilization,' *Spiked*, March 20, 2025.
96. Reed, Kevin, 'Reporter Sarah Wilkinson Arrested By UK Government For Opposition To Gaza Genocide,' *World Socialist Web Site*, August 29, 2024, https://www.wsws.org/en/articles/2024/08/30/fdbr-a30.html
97. Bodkin, Henry, 'How Seven Years Of Hamas Planning Resulted In IDF's Oct 7 Failure,' *The Telegraph*, February 27, 2025, https://www.telegraph.co.uk/world-news/2025/02/27/what-really-happened-october-israel-gaza-war-idf-hamas/
98. 'One year trapped in Gaza by the Israel-Hamas war – CBS News' Marwan al-Ghoul, in his own words,' *CBS*, October 8, 2024, https://www.cbsnews.com/news/israel-hamas-war-one-year-trapped-in-gaza-marwan-al-ghoul-in-his-own-words/
99. Walker, Corey, 'Gaza-Based CBS News Producer Questioned Whether Jews Are "Human," Called Israelis "Zionist Nazi Murderers",' *The Algemeiner*, October 16, 2024, https://www.algemeiner.com/2024/10/16/gaza-based-cbs-news-producer-questioned-whether-jews-are-human-called-israelis-zionist-nazi-murderers/
100. 'EXPOSED: The Terror Ties Of "CBS News", Journalist In Gaza, Marwan Al-Ghoul, Works Closely With The PFLP Terrorist Organization,' *JNS*, July 24, 2024, https://www.jns.org/exposed-the-terror-ties-of-cbs-news-journalist-in-gaza/
101. 'One Year Trapped In Gaza By The Israel-Hamas War — CBS News' Marwan Al-Ghoul, In His Own Words,' *CBS*, October 8, 2024, https://www.cbsnews.

com/news/israel-hamas-war-one-year-trapped-in-gaza-marwan-al-ghoul-in-his-own-words/
102. Looram, Meaghan, 'Photographer's award praised by "Times" same day he's named in lawsuit,' *JNS*, February 23, 2024, https://www.jns.org/photographers-award-praised-by-times-same-day-hes-named-in-lawsuit/,
103. Ibid.
104. Ibid.
105. Brandfon, Fredric, 'Vandals destroyed his tribute to Holocaust survivors — and yet this artist persists,' *Forward,* February 14, 2025, https://forward.com/culture/art/696820/alexsandro-palombo-mural-artist-holocaust-vandalism/
106. 'Defaced mural of Oct. 7 survivor another example of rising antisemitism in Italy,' *Associated Press*, October 7, 2024, https://apnews.com/article/italy-antisemitism-mural-oct7-bbdeecda5a9f98498a9c3ffbebd371fc
107. Mort, Jo-Ann Yair Golan: The IDF General Who Can Revive the Israeli Left,' *The New Republic*, March 3, 2025, https://newrepublic.com/article/191924/yair-golan-idf-general-revive-israeli-left
108. Kelly, Mary Louise, 'For this Israeli general, the horror of Oct. 7 meant a return to the battlefield,' *National Public Radio*, November 7, 2023, https://www.npr.org/2023/11/07/1211329918/for-this-israeli-general-the-horror-of-oct-7-meant-a-return-to-the-battlefield
109. 'Nadejda Spravchikov, 75: Trained Chemist Devotedly Cared For Elderly,' *The Times of Israel*, accessed April 15, 2023, https://www.msn.com/en-us/news/world/nadejda-spravchikov-75-trained-chemist-devotedly-cared-for-elderly/ar-AA1tTNfu
110. Jeffay, John, 'The Resilience Counselor Offering Up Hope Despite Her Own Adversity,' *Israel21c*, January 3, 2024, https://www.israel21c.org/the-resilience-counselor-offering-up-hope-despite-her-own-adversity/
111. Tolub, Gila, 'Spotlight on Esther Marcus: A Pillar of Strength in Times of Crisis,' *ICAR*, December 11, 2024, https://www.icarcollective.org/post/spotlight-on-esther-marcus-a-pillar-of-strength-in-times-of-crisis
112. Marcus, Esther, 'People Ask Me Questions,' *The Times of Israel*, November 15, 2019, https://blogs.timesofisrael.com/people-ask-me-questions/
113. TOI Staff, 'Dana And Carmel Bachar, 48 & 15: Mother And Son Buried Side-By-Side,' *The Times of Israel*, November 5, 2023, https://www.timesofisrael.com/dana-48-carmel-15-bachar-mother-and-son-buried-side-by-side/
114. He said during interviews from his hospital bed after the massacre that if he could, he would wipe out the entire Gaza Strip. Source: 'Kibbutznik Who Lost Wife & Son: "It's 'Mazal' That Massacre Was In Be'eri & Not Gush Etzion,"' Yeshiva World News, December 25, 2024, https://www.theyeshivaworld.com/news/israel-news/2345235/kibbutznik-who-lost-wife-son-its-mazal-that-massacre-was-in-beeri-not-gush-etzion.html
115. 'Israeli pacifists in devastated kibbutz lose faith,' *France 24*, August 11, 2023.

116. TOI Staff, 'Dana and Carmel Bachar, 48 & 15: Mother And Son Buried Side-By-Side,' *The Times of Israel*, November 5, 2023, https://www.timesofisrael.com/dana-48-carmel-15-bachar-mother-and-son-buried-side-by-side/
117. Guertzenstein Forhlich, Raquel, 'Heart of Darkness: Former Gaza Captive Recounts Experience As Hamas Hostage,' *Jerusalem Post*, January 8, 2025.
118. Yang, Luch 'Israeli Woman Held Hostage By Hamas For 55 Days Shares Story Of Survival,' *ABC*, August 28, 2024,https://abc7chicago.com/post/sapir-cohen-israeli-woman-held-hostage-hamas-gaza-shares-story-survival-yeshiva-university-nyc/15238337/
119. Bronznick, Shifra, 'Vivian Silver – We Remember, Jewish Women's Archive,' *JWA*, Accessed April 7, 2025, https://jwa.org/weremember/silver-vivian
120. Ibid.
121. Lapham, Jake, 'Israeli-Canadian peace advocate Vivian Silver confirmed killed in Hamas attack,' *BBC*, November 14, 2023, https://www.bbc.com/news/world-middle-east-67413993
122. Bronznick, Shifra, 'Vivian Silver – We Remember, Jewish Women's Archive,' Accessed April 7, 2025, https://jwa.org/weremember/silver-vivian
123. Teibel, Amy, 'Renowned Canadian-Born Israeli Peace Activist Vivian Silver Is Confirmed Killed In Hamas Attack,' *Associated Press*, November 14, 2023, https://apnews.com/article/vivian-silver-peace-activist-hamas-gaza-israel-canada-aa972990a598d99dea47a8b5abcfb04f
124. Ward, Clarissa, Swails, Bren,; and Clarke, Rachel, 'First on CNN: Father describes how his young daughter Emily Hand survived Hamas captivity,' *CNN*, November 28, 2023. https://www.cnn.com/2023/11/28/middleeast/thomas-hand-emily-hostage-intl/index.html
125. TOI Staff, 'Irish PM Panned For Saying Freed Hostage Child Emily Hand "Found" After She Was "Lost",' *The Times of Israel*, November 26, 2023, https://www.timesofisrael.com/irish-pm-panned-for-saying-freed-hostage-child-emily-hand-found-after-she-was-lost/
126. Ward, Clarissa; Swails, Brent; and Clarke, Rachel, 'First on CNN: Father describes how his young daughter Emily Hand survived Hamas captivity,' *CNN,* November 28, 2023. https://www.cnn.com/2023/11/28/middleeast/thomas-hand-emily-hostage-intl/index.html
127. Danan, Deborah, 'They Are All Hamas,' *The Tablet*, January 24, 2024, https://www.tabletmag.com/sections/israel-middle-east/articles/hamas-palestinians-pogrom-israel
128. Jeffay, John, 'Survivors of Kibbutz Nir Oz massacre speak out,' *Israel21c*, November 16, 2023, https://www.israel21c.org/survivors-of-kibbutz-nir-oz-massacre-speak-out/
129. Tobin, Andrew, 'Children as Young as 10 Took Part in Hamas's Oct. 7 Terror Attack, Survivors Say,' *ZOA*, November 14, 2023.

130. Jeffay, John, 'Survivors of Kibbutz Nir Oz Massacre Speak Out,' *Israel21c*, November 16, 2023, https://www.israel21c.org/survivors-of-kibbutz-nir-oz-massacre-speak-out/
131. TOI Staff, 'Body of hostage Eden Yerushalmi Recovered From Hamas Tunnel In IDF Op,' *The Times of Israel,* December 3, 2023, https://www.timesofisrael.com/taken-captive-eden-yerushalmi-hid-in-car-with-two-dead-friends/
132. Botbol, Amelie, 'I Hope They Shoot Her, I Hope It's Quick,' *Jewish News Syndicate*, January 5, 2024, https://www.jns.org/i-hope-they-shoot-her-i-hope-its-quick/
133. 'Hamas Releases Propaganda Video Showing Executed Hostage Eden Yerushalmi,' *The Times of Israel*, September 2, 2024, https://www.timesofisrael.com/liveblog_entry/hamas-releases-propaganda-video-showing-executed-hostage-eden-yerushalmi/
134. Picheta, Rob, 'Slain Israeli Hostage Held By Hamas In "Inhuman" Conditions Underneath Gaza, Sisters Tell CNN,' *CNN* September 21, 2024, https://www.yahoo.com/news/slain-israeli-hostage-held-hamas-022821674.html
135. Ibid.
136. Ibid.
137. TOI, 'Family of Yarden Bibas Fundraises To Help Him Heal, Memorialize Shiri And The Boys,' *The Times of Israel* , March 16, 2025, https://www.timesofisrael.com/family-of-yarden-bibas-fundraises-to-help-him-heal-memorialize-shiri-and-the-boys/
138. Reed, Kevin, 'Reporter Sarah Wilkinson Arrested By UK Government For Opposition To Gaza Genocide,' World Socialist Web Site, August 29, 2024, https://www.wsws.org/en/articles/2024/08/30/fdbr-a30.html
139. Starr, Michael, 'Anti-Israel Activist Who Praised October 7 Arrested in UK – Report,' *Jerusalem Post*, August 30, 2024, https://www.jpost.com/breaking-news/article-817049

## Chapter 6: The World Takes Note

1. Blinken, Anthony, 'Secretary Antony J. Blinken and Israeli Prime Minister Benjamin Netanyahu After Their Meeting,' *US Department of State*, October 12, 2023.
2. Margolin, Devorah and Levitt, Matthew, 'The Road to October 7: Hamas' Long Game, Clarified,' *CTC Sentinel*, October/November 2023, p. 1.
3. Schenker, Hillel, 'October 7: Black Saturday,' *The Jerusalem Report*, May 27, 2024, p. 28, https://montgomerycollege.idm.oclc.org/login?url=https://www.proquest.com/magazines/october-7-black-saturday/docview/3064134487/se-2.
4. He vowed to wear it until the United Nations condemned Hamas. However, other prominent Israelis criticized this dramatic gesture. Dani Dayan, chairman

of Yad Vashem, emphasized that Jews no longer needed to wear a yellow star because they had a state. Instead, Israelis should don the blue-and-white attire. Source: Samudzi, Zoé, 2024. '"We Are Fighting Nazis": Genocidal Fashionings of Gaza(Ns) After October 7,' *Journal of Genocide Research*, January, 1–9. doi:10.1080/14623528.2024.2305524.

5. Murphy, Paul et al. 'Desert Horror: Music Festival Goers Heard Rockets, Then Gaza Militants Fired On Them And Took Hostages,' *CNN*, October 9, 2023, https://www.cnn.com/2023/10/07/middleeast/israel-gaza-fighting-hamas-attack-music-festival-intl-hnk/index.html
6. Schecter, Anna, 'Israel-Hamas war. Their bodies tell their stories. They're not alive to speak for themselves,' *NBC News*, December 5, 2023, https://www.nbcnews.com/news/world/hamas-rape-israeli-women-oct-7-rcna128221
7. There were 39 times more #freepalestine posts on Facebook than #standwithisrael posts. 'We were surprised not just on the physical fence on October 7,' says Amichai Chikli, Israel's Minister for Diaspora Affairs, 'but also on the digital fence we didn't have.' Source: Cortellessa, Y. Eric and Bergengruen, Vera, 'Inside the Israel-Hamas Information War,' *Time Magazine*, December 22, 2023.
8. Xiao, Mattheew, 'IDF Kills Hamas Terrorist Infamous for Ramallah Lynching of Israeli Soldiers,' *Washington Free Beacon*, October 3, 2024, https://freebeacon.com/latest-news/idf-kills-hamas-terrorist-infamous-for-ramallah-lynching-of-israeli-soldiers/
9. Engel, Richard, and Madani, Doha, '"It's A Massacre": Bodies Of Victims Still Strewn Across Kibbutz Once Home To 700,' *NBC News*, October 11, 2023, https://www.nbcnews.com/news/world/israeli-soldiers-clear-bodies-kibbutz-hamas-attack-rcna119861
10. Molana-Allen, Leila, 'Lives Shattered By October 7 Attack, Some Survivors Return To Kibbutz Be'eri,' *PBS News Hours*, November 7, 2023, https://www.pbs.org/newshour/show/lives-shattered-by-oct-7-attack-some-survivors-return-to-kibbutz-beeri
11. Agmon, Yair and Mevorach, Oriya, *One Day in October – Forty Heroes, Forty Stories*, The Toby Press, 2024, p. 37.
12. Goldenberg, Tia, and Frankel, Julia, 'How Two Debunked Accounts Of Sexual Violence On October 7 Fueled A Global Dispute Over Israel-Hamas War,' *Associated Press*, May 22, 2024, https://apnews.com/article/israel-hamas-war-sexual-violence-zaka-ca7905bf9520b1e646f86d72cdf03244
13. In June 2024 some 41% of West Bankers said they support Hamas, compared to 35% in March and 12% in September. Support for Fatah, Hamas's nemesis and the dominant power in the Palestinian Authority (PA), has decreased since the beginning of the war, dropping to just 17%, compared to 26% in September. Source: Stern, Moran, 'Why Is Hamas' Popularity Soaring Among Palestinians in the West Bank?,' *Washington Institute for Near East Policy*, June 24, 2024, https://www.washingtoninstitute.org/policy-analysis/why-hamas-popularity-soaring-among-palestinians-west-bank

14. Zilberdik, Nan Jacques, 'Never Forget: Pa/Fatah Cheered Hamas' October 7 Massacre, Fatah Bragged About Its Participation In Killing And Stepping On The Heads of Israelis,' *PMW,* October 6, 2024, https://palwatch.org/page/35533
15. Ibid.
16. Glick, Caroline, 'Hamas's deception and our self-deception,' *JNS*, October 13, 2023, https://www.jns.org/hamass-deception-and-our-self-deception/
17. Shragai, Nadav, 'Israel ignored Hamas' rhetoric for years; the Palestinian Authority is just as bad,' *Israel Hayom*, November 13, 2023, https://www.israelhayom.com/2023/11/12/israel-ignored-hamas-rhetoric-for-years-the-palestinian-authority-is-just-as-bad/
18. Zilberdik, Nan Jacques, 'Once Israel comes to an end . . .' – Hamas' or PA's dream?,' *PMW*, October 17, 2023, https://palwatch.org/page/34660
19. Ricardo, Hannie, 'My Daughter Was Killed on October 7; Here Is My Message to the World,' *The Algemeiner,* May 16, 2024, https://www.algemeiner.com/2024/05/16/my-daughter-was-killed-on-october-7-here-is-my-message-to-the-world/
20. 'About 200,000 Israelis Internally Displaced Amid Ongoing Gaza War, Tensions In The North,' *The Times of Israel*, October 22, 2023, https://www.timesofisrael.com/about-200000-israelis-internally-displaced-amid-ongoing-gaza-war-tensions-in-north/
21. Northam, Jackie, 'A Seaside Town Shelters Thousands Of Israeli Evacuees, But Struggles Without Tourists,' *National Public Radio*, February 4, 2024, https://www.npr.org/2024/02/04/1227892139/israel-eilat-tourism-israeli-evacuees-hamas-gaza-war
22. DeRose, Jason, 'Rabbis offer pastoral care for those traumatized by Oct. 7 Hamas attack,' *National Public Radio*, January 30, 2024, https://www.npr.org/2024/01/30/1227578480/rabbis-offer-pastoral-care-for-those-traumatized-by-oct-7-hamas-attack
23. Byman, Daniel and McCaleb, Emma, 'Understanding Hamas's and Hezbollah's Uses of Information Technology,' *CSIS*, July 31, 2023, https://www.csis.org/analysis/understanding-hamass-and-hezbollahs-uses-information-technology
24. Neuman, Scott and Rizkallah, Jawad, 'What Did Hamas Aim To Gain By Its Brazen Attack On Israel? Here's What To Know,' *National Public Radio*, October 12, 2023, https://www.npr.org/2023/10/12/1204881032/hamas-israel-attack-palestinians
25. Kent, Simon, 'Hamas Defies Critics: Says Its Terrorists Upheld "Islamic Values" During Murderous Attack on Israel,' *Breitbart,* January 22, 2024.
26. Neuman, Scott and Rizkallah, Jawad, 'What Did Hamas Aim To Gain By Its Brazen Attack On Israel? Here's What To Know,' *National Public Radio*, October 12, 2023 https://www.npr.org/2023/10/12/1204881032/hamas-israel-attack-palestinians

27. Ibid.
28. ' After he raped her, he took a knife and killed her, murdered her. After he did it, he continued to rape the dead body. The other men around the victim did not seem angry,' Source: Tapper, Jake, Appleton, Kirsten, and Clarke, Rachel, 'Attackers Laughed As They Raped And Murdered A Woman In Israel On October 7, Witness says,' *CNN*, April 10, 2024, https://edition.cnn.com/2024/01/04/middleeast/sexual-assault-october-7-israel-witness-int/index.html
29. 'Hamas' Use Of Sexual Violence Is An All-Too-Common Part Of Modern War – But Not In All Conflicts,' *The Conversation*, December 11, 2023, https://theconversation.com/hamas-use-of-sexual-violence-is-an-all-too-common-part-of-modern-war-but-not-in-all-conflicts-219301. One report concluded that one clear strategy of the attacks was to terrorize the Israeli nation with sadistic sex crimes. The report, authored by Dr Carmit Keller-Halamish and Nega Berger, was sent to the UN for action. Source: 'Hamas's "Sadistic Sex Crimes" On October 7 Set Forth In New Report,' *JNS*, February 24, 2024, https://www.jns.org/hamass-sadistic-sex-crimes-on-oct-7-set-forth-in-new-report/
30. Zilberdik, Nan Jacques, 'Palestinian Authority Leaders Deny October 7 Massacre Took Place,' *Algemeiner*, December 15, 2023.
31. 'This whole [Israeli] outcry and this whole campaign against the Palestinian people is based on a lie, which it took Israel 24 hours to create and formulate properly. They killed their [own] civilians [on October 7], and they committed all these crimes and burned the bodies, and they made up this story.' Source: Zilberdik, Nan Jacques, 'Palestinian Authority Leaders Deny October 7 Massacre Took Place,' *Algemeiner,* December 15, 2023.
32. Ibid.
33. 'Israel: Top EU diplomat legitimizes Hamas terror,' *JNS*, May 9, 2024,
34. Statement by the High Representative for Foreign Affairs of the European Union, Josep Borrell, *Israel Ministry of Foreign Affairs*, September 5, 2024, https://www.gov.il/en/pages/joseph-burrell
35. Becker, Matthias, J., 'Antisemitism Online Since 7 October: European Observations,' *Fathom*, October 2024, accessed June 6, 2024, https://fathomjournal.org/antisemitism-online-since-7-october-european-observations/
36. Becker, Dr Matthias, 'Celebrating Terror: Antisemitism online after the Hamas attacks on Israel Preliminary Results,' *The Decoding Antisemitism Research Team*, 26 October 2023, pp. 8–10. https://decoding-antisemitism.eu Centre for Research on Antisemitism, Technische Universität Berlin, https://api-depositonce.tu-berlin.de/server/api/core/bitstreams/706ba3a6-98d6-46ad-9676-1b7441d32f1b/content
37. Lazaroff, Tovah, 'Scholz: After Holocaust, Germany must stand with Israel against Hamas,' *The Jerusalem Post*, October 17, 2023.

38. In September 2024, Germany's Foreign Minister Annalena Baerbock said. 'Last weekend clearly showed that military action alone will not solve the situation in Gaza,' she said, according to a report in *Bild.* 'Purely military pressure, as we have seen, endangers the lives of the hostages.' Source: Weinthal, Benjamin, 'Why Is Germany Blaming Israel for Hamas's War Against the Jews?,' *Middle East Forum*, September 21, 2024, https://www.meforum.org/middle-east-forum-online/why-is-germany-blaming-israel-for-hamass-war-against-the-jews
39. Ibid.
40. Chaimowizcz, Sascha, 'Alone Again—How Germany Turned Its Back on Jews After October 7,' *MSN*, October 7, 2024, https://www.msn.com/en-us/news/world/alone-again-how-germany-turned-its-back-on-jews-after-october-7/ar-AA1rPsjg?ocid=msedgdhp&pc=U531&cvid=268d633de3c0496095b9e06310a6685c&ei=230
41. Reynolds, Jordon, 'London Police Increase Patrols After Reports Of People Celebrating Israel Attacks,' *The Independent*, October 8, 2023, https://www.independent.co.uk/news/uk/home-news/met-patrols-london-israel-attacks-b2426029.html
42. Davies, Emily Jane and Wolfisz, Fran, 'Palestine Action vandals stole the wrong statue in university raid – grabbing head of CBE-winning professor who played in FA Cup final rather than bust of Israel's first president,' by, *Daily Mail*, November 6, 2024, https://www.dailymail.co.uk/news/article-14048895/Palestine-Action-stole-wrong-statue-university-raid-CBE-professor-FA-Cup-bust-Israels-president.html
43. Central Consistory's vice presidents referenced Jewish Community Protection Service (SPCJ) statistics which indicated that antisemitic incidents in the Republic had increased by 1,000% in 2023 compared to the previous year. That is a tenfold rise – in just one year – in the number of antisemitic incidents. No wonder Jews in France are alarmed. Source: 'Consistory VP: "Jews are beginning to lose hope for a future in France" – interview,' by Michael Starr, *The Jerusalem Post*, September 2, 2024.
44. Fifty-two percent are contemplating leaving France and making Aliyah, go to Israel. Source: '"They Are Death Threats": Kosher Restaurant in France Vandalized With Anti-Israel Graffiti,' *Algemeiner*, September 5, 2024:
45. Marcel de Weerd and Michel Theeboom, representing the Jewish Police Network, expressed concerns over changes they saw in the force. 'There are colleagues who no longer want to protect Jewish targets or events. They discuss "moral dilemmas," and I see a tendency emerging to succumb to them. That would truly mark the beginning of the end. I'm concerned about that,' Theeboom said. Source: Greyman-Kennard, Danielle, 'Dutch Police Refuse To Guard Jewish Sites Over "Moral Dilemmas," officers say,' *The Jerusalem Post*, October 4, 2024, https://www.jpost.com/diaspora/article-823171

46. 'Fringe-Left Groups Express Support for Hamas's Invasion and Brutal Attacks in Israel,' *ADL*, October 12, 2023, https://www.adl.org/resources/article/fringe-left-groups-express-support-hamass-invasion-and-brutal-attacks-israel
47. 'Sarah Silverman Feels "Heartbroken" And "Politically Homeless" As War Rages Between Israelis And Palestinians,' *Forward*, October 19, 2023, https://forward.com/fast-forward/565814/sarah-silverman-podcast-israel-hamas-gaza-war/
48. It is important to note that Black Lives Matter chapters are run independently from the national Black Lives Matter Global Network Foundation, and many are completely unaffiliated. The Black Lives Matter national organization has not yet commented on the current Israel-Hamas war. In a post on October 11, the group wrote: 'When we say Free Palestine, y'all say antisemitic & Hamas. Israel's terrorism created Hamas & Zionism is a betrayal of the peace of Judaism, not those shouting against its genocidal effect on Palestine.' The group's Arizona chapter texted, 'Palestinian freedom fighters are not terrorists.' Source: 'Fringe-Left Groups Express Support for Hamas's Invasion and Brutal Attacks in Israel,' *ADL* Updated October 14, 2023, https://www.adl.org/resources/blog/fringe-left-groups-express-support-hamass-invasion-and-brutal-attacks-israel
49. 'Bay Ridge, Brooklyn Vigil Honors "Beloved Martyrs" Hamas Leader Ismail Haniyeh,' *MEMRI*, #11377, August 11, 2024, https://www.memri.org/tv/bay-ridge-brooklyn-vigil-hamas-leader-ismail-haniyeh-salute-axis-resistance-dismantle-zionist-state
50. 'At Houston, Texas Al-Quds Day Rally Speakers Praise October 7 Hamas Attack, Martyrdom, And Jihad; Add: Hizbullah Leader Nasrallah Highlighted That Martyrdom Is Good, A Goal; Our Leader Khamenei Said That The Cancerous Tumor Of Zionism Will Be Destroyed,' *MEMRI*, Palestinians, United States | Special Dispatch No. 11261, April 8, 2024, https://www.memri.org/reports/houston-texas-al-quds-day-rally-speakers-praise-october-7-hamas-attack-martyrdom-and-jihad
51. 'Philadelphia Rally Against Presidential Debate, Protesters Wave Hamas, Popular Front For The Liberation Of Palestine (PFLP) Flags, Chant: Hamas Leader Yahya Sinwar, You Make Us Proud! The US. Is The Number One Terrorist! Kamala Harris Is A War Criminal! Banner Reads: "Amerika Is The Head Of The Snake",' *MEMRI*, #11393 | 02:17 September 10, 2024 Source: Online Platforms – 'Status Coup News on YouTube' https://www.memri.org/tv/philadelphia-rally-presidential-debate-yahya-sinwar-make-us-proud-banner-amerika-head-snake-hamas-pflp
52. 'Participants In "Flood NYC For Gaza" Rally Wave Flags Of U.S. Designated Terrorist Organizations, Yahya Sinwar; Nerdeen Kiswani Of Within Our Lifetime: A Ceasefire Is Not Enough; If You Stand With Palestinians, You Stand With Palestinian Resistance,' *MEMRI*, #11372 | 02:47, Source: Online

Platforms – 'Various Online Sources,' https://www.memri.org/tv/flood-nyc-for-gaza-flag-us-designated-terror-organizations-yahya-sinwar-nerdeen-kiswani-ceasefire-not-enough-resistance

53. 'Crisis on Campus, Frontline,' *PBS*, Accessed July 21, 2023, https://www.pbs.org/wgbh/frontline/documentary/crisis-on-campus/transcript/
54. Freedman, Eliyahu, 'Jewish Students Say Anti-Israel October 7 Events At Montreal Campuses Set To Celebrate Hamas,' *The Times of Israel*, October 6, 2024, https://www.timesofisrael.com/jewish-students-say-anti-israel-oct-7-events-at-montreal-campuses-set-to-celebrate-hamas/
55. Diker, Dan, 'Hamas' Education of the Ivy League,' *Jerusalem Center for Security and Foreign Affairs* (JCFA), May 1, 2024, https://jcpa.org/hamas-education-of-the-ivy-league/
56. Starr, Michael, 'Columbia Activists Worked With Hamas, Captors Told Rescued Hostage Shlomi Ziv,' *The Jerusalem Post*, March 25, 2025.
57. Greenfield, Daniel, 'Iran is Funding the Pro-Hamas Protests,' *Jihad Watch*, July 18, 2024, https://www.jihadwatch.org/2024/07/iran-is-funding-the-pro-hamas-protests\
58. Guidice, Rachel del, 'Shooting Witness Of Israeli Embassy Staff Says He Saw "Same Thing" In Shooter's Eyes As Columbia Protestors,' *Fox*, May 22, 2025, https://www.yahoo.com/news/shooting-witness-israeli-embassy-staff-230000717.html
59. One example is the beating of a man carrying an Israeli flag in Manhattan. Four men beat Todd Richman after they banged drums close to him. Source: 'Pro-Palestinian Protesters Take To NYC Streets On October 7 Anniversary, College Students Walk Out,' *Daily News*, October 7, 2024, https://www.nydailynews.com/2024/10/07/nyc-pro-palestinian-protests-oct-7-anniversary/
60. 'Amy Schumer and More Jewish Stars Take Aim at TikTok Over Antisemitism,' *Newsweek*, November 1 2023, https://www.newsweek.com/amy-schumer-jewish-tiktok-antisemitism-israel-palestinian-hamas-conflict-1839989
61. In October 2024, a Hamas supporter stabbed six people, severely wounding them. Source: Nick Dole, and Patricia Karvelas, Patricia, 'US Speaker At October 7 Pro-Palestinian Rally In Lakemba Visa Under Review After "Celebration" Comment,' *SABC.net.au,* October 8, 2024, https://www.abc.net.au/news/2024-10-08/pro-palestinian-rally-us-speaker-comment-october-7-visa/104442800
62. 'Steven Spielberg Breaks Silence on Israel-Hamas War: "Never Imagined I Would See Such Unspeakable Barbarity Against Jews",' *USC Shoah Foundation*, Accessed June 16, 2025, https://sfi.usc.edu/pressroom/resources/steven-spielberg-breaks-silence-israel-hamas-war-%E2%80%9Cnever-imagined-i-would-see
63. Rothman, Noah, 'Why Aren't Women's Groups Condemning Hamas?,' *National Review*, November 28, 2023, https://www.nationalreview.com/2023/11/why-arent-womens-groups-condemning-hamas/

64. Uriel-Beeri, Tamar, 'Lipstadt: Only Difference between October 7, Previous Rapes is Jews. World is using "systematic Unawareness" Toward Israeli Victimization, Hamas Sexual Violence, Says Michal Herzog,' *Jerusalem Post*, February 18, 2024, https://montgomerycollege.idm.oclc.org/login?url=https://www.proquest.com/newspapers/lipstadt-only-difference-between-october-7/docview/2928167471/se-2.
65. 'Germany 1938 In Australia 2024: Jewish-Owned Business Defaced With Red Triangles And A Threat, Plus The Nazi Origins Of The Triangle,' *Elder of Zyon*, October 15, 2024, https://elderofziyon.blogspot.com/2024/10/germany-1938-in-australia-2024-jewish.html
66. Lazaroff, Tovah, 'Envoy: UN Is A Dream Come True For Terrorists Seeking To Destroy Israel,' *The Jerusalem Post*, https://www.jpost.com/israel-hamas-war/article-799433May 1, 2024.
67. Ibid.
68. Magid, Jacob, 'Erdan To End Tenure As UN Envoy, Declines Offer To Stay In US As Washington Ambassador,' *The Times of Israel*, May 2024, https://www.timesofisrael.com/erdan-to-end-tenure-as-un-envoy-declines-offer-to-stay-in-us-as-washington-ambassador/
69. 'Gilad Erdan Takes Helm As Global President Of MDA, Enhancing Emergency Response,' *Jerusalem Post*, September 4, 2024, https://afmda.org/news/erdan-takes-helm/
70. Nichols, Michelle, 'At UN, Israeli Former Hostage Appeals For Ceasefire Deal To Go On, Reuters,' February 25, 2025, https://www.reuters.com/world/middle-east/un-israeli-former-hostage-appeals-ceasefire-deal-go-2025-02-25/
71. '"Noa, we're Taking You Home": Helmet Cam Video shows Rescue of Hostage Noa Argamani.' *The Times of Israel*, June 15, 2024, https://montgomerycollege.idm.oclc.org/login?url=https://www.proquest.com/newspapers/noa-we-re-taking-you-home-helmet-cam-video-shows/docview/3068484558/se-2.
72. 'Maariv Online, 'Dressed as an Arab Woman: The Untold Captivity Story Of Noa Argamani – Report,' *The Jerusalem Post*, June 9, 2024.
73. 'Actress? AI? Fixation with Freed Israeli Hostage Noa Argamani Turns into Conspiracy Theories,' *Haaretz*, July 17, 2024.
74. Sarisohn, Hannah. 'Noa Argamani among Hostages Brought on Stage at Trump's Parade,' *The Jerusalem Post*, January 21, 2025, https://www.jpost.com/american-politics/article-838484
75. Doral Website, September 2, 2021, https://doral-llc.com/news/former-israeli-mossad-chief-yossi-cohen-appointed-as-director-at-doral-renewables-llc/
76. 'Former Mossad Chief Threatened ICC Prosecutor Over Probe Into Israel, Report Claims,' *The Times of Israel*, May 28, 2024, https://www.timesofisrael.com/former-mossad-chief-threatened-icc-prosecutor-over-probe-into-israel-report-claims/

77. Ronneburger, Jan-Uwe, 'Germany's Chancellor Scholz Emphasizes Israel as Safe Space for Jews,' *DPA* International (English), November 11, 2023.
78. Von Riegen, Oliver, 'German Chancellor Scholz Warns Israel Against Offensive on Rafah,' *DPA* International (English), May 11, 2024.
79. 'German Chancellor Scholz Calls for Gaza Deal with "Longer-Lasting Ceasefire",' *AFP International Text Wire in English*, March 17, 2024.
80. Thurau, Jens, 'Would Netanyahu be arrested in Germany?,' *DW*, November 22, 2024, https://www.dw.com/en/would-benjamin-netanyahu-be-arrested-in-germany/a-70863500
81. 'Israel-Hamas War: Gaza Reports Many Dead In Hospital Strike,' *DW*, October 18, 2023, https://www.dw.com/en/israel-hamas-war-gaza-reports-many-dead-in-hospital-strike/live-67115875
82. Penna, Dominic, 'Sadiq Khan Criticised Over Call For "Equivalence" In Israel-Hamas Debate,' *The Telegraph*, April 7, 2024, https://www.telegraph.co.uk/politics/2024/05/07/sadiq-khan-criticised-for-calling-for-equivalence-in-israel/
83. Garfinkel, Imogen, '"No Need" For More Gaza Marches If Ceasefire Holds, Says London Mayor,' *The Jewish Chronicle*, January 28, 2025, https://www.thejc.com/news/no-need-gaza-marches-ceasefire-sadiq-khan-cvtsi95a
84. Penna, Dominic, 'Sadiq Khan Criticised Over Call For 'Equivalence' In Israel-Hamas Debate,' *The Telegraph*, July 5, 2024, https://www.telegraph.co.uk/politics/2024/05/07/sadiq-khan-criticised-for-calling-for-equivalence-in-israel/
85. 'London Mayor Says no Room for Hate After Kosher Restaurant's Glass Door Smashed,' *Anadolu Agency : AA*, Oct 09, 2023, https://montgomerycollege.idm.oclc.org/login?url=https://www.proquest.com/wire-feeds/london-mayor-says-no-room-hate-after-kosher/docview/2874635860/se-2.
86. Barnes, Hannah, '"Protecting women is a human rights obligation": Reem Alsalem on sex, gender and violence,' *New Statesman*, March 1, 2024.
87. 'Israeli Forces Deliberately Targeting Palestinian Women in Gaza,' *Tehran: Disco Digital Media,* Inc, April 8, 2024, https://en.mehrnews.com/news/213639/Israeli-forces-deliberately-target-Palestinian-women-in-Gaza
88. 'First Lady Herzog Decries "unforgivable" Silence of Rights Groups Over Hamas Rapes,' *The Times of Israel*, November 22, 2023.
89. Kennedy, Donald, 'Summers and Harvard Science,' *American Association for the Advancement of Science*, 2006–03, Vol. 311 (5766), pp. 1345.
90. Serret, Vivienne, 'University of Florida Suspends Students Arrested In On-Campus Pro-Palestine Protests,' *Miami Herald,* July 10, 2024, https://www.miamiherald.com/news/local/education/article289924594.html
91. Serret, Vivienne, 'University of Florida suspends arrested pro-Palestinian protesters for up to 4 years,' *The Gainesville Sun*, July 10, 2024.
92. 'Florida Issues Strong Penalties to Pro-Hamas Protestors Who Violated Laws,' *Southern Jewish Life Regional* (Online), August 17, 2024.

93. Hanley, Delinda C., 'Pink Floyd's Roger Waters Helps Tear Down the Last Taboo,' *The Washington Report on Middle East Affairs,* September 4, 2017.
94. 'Roger Waters: Israel made Up Stories that Hamas Raped Women and Murdered Babies on October 7,' *Haaretz,* July 3, 2024.
95. Ibid.
96. Coen, Susie. 'Pink Floyd's Roger Waters Says Hamas Massacre "thrown Out of all Proportion",' *Telegraph*, November 7, 2023.
97. Ibid.
98. Friedman, Gabe, 'U2's Bono Changes Lyrics in Tribute to Israeli Music Festival Victims of Hamas Attack,' *Baltimore Jewish Times*, October 20, 2023.
99. 'Roger Waters Faces Argentina, Uruguay Hotel Ban Amid "Anti-Semitism" Row,' *AFP International Text Wire in English*, November 15, 2023.

## Chapter 7: Foreign Powers and the Middle East

1. The US House of Representatives Foreign Affairs Committee reported that in 2011, Qatar pledged $400 million for 'infrastructure,' ultimately used for building terror tunnels to attack Israel. Qatar provided Hamas with over $1.1 billion from 2012 to 2018. Source: Maital, Shlomo, 'Qatar: How it Fed the Beast,' *The Jerusalem Report*, December 25, 2023.
2. After the October 7, 2023, terror attack, when it came to light that Israel had endorsed and aided the Qatari funding of Hamas, PM Netanyahu claimed that he had done this in order 'to prevent a humanitarian disaster' in Gaza – a claim that had no basis. For counter-evidence to the accusations that Gaza had long been suffering from a humanitarian crisis, Source: Carmon, Y., 'The Face Of The "Suffocating Occupation," "Humanitarian Disaster," "Concentration Camp," and "Prison Camp" of Pre-War Gaza – In Pictures and Data (An Answer To António Guterres, Benjamin Netanyahu, Norman Finkelstein, David Cameron, Ron Paul, And Patrick Buchanan),' *MEMRI* Inquiry & Analysis 1742, January 12, 2024.
3. 'Qatar cuts financial aid to Hamas,' *Country Report: Egypt*, September 11, 2023.
4. Ibid.
5. Greenfield, Daniel, 'Iran is Funding the Pro-Hamas Protests,' *Jihad Watch*, July 18, 2024 https://www.jihadwatch.org/2024/07/iran-is-funding-the-pro-hamas-protests
6. In 2019, Iran transferred $42 million to Hamas's military, and an additional $12 million was transferred. in 2020.
7. Bänsch, Arne, 'Report: Hamas and Iran Discussed "Axis of Resistance" at Doha Meeting,' *DPA International (English)*, October 15, 2023.
8. It also referenced a 2022 meeting among senior Hamas leaders discussing defense agreements with Iranian-backed groups, along with documents indicating requests for substantial financial support from Iran.

9. 'Saudi Arabia Pauses Normalization Talks with Israel Amid Ongoing War with Hamas,' *France 24,* October 14, 2023, https://www.france24.com/en/middle-east/20231014-saudi-arabia-pauses-normalisation-talks-with-israel-ami
10. 'Hamas Criticizes Saudi-Funded Channels for "Pro-Israel" Coverage,' *BBC*, September 9, 2024.
11. Marcus, Itamar, 'Abbas' Advisor: Oct. 7 Massacre Was "Legitimate Resistance,"' *Palestinian Media Watch,* March 30, 2025.
12. Ibid.
13. Ibid.
14. An expert from the official PA daily *Al-Hayat Al-Jadida*, June 19, 2025 as reported by Itmar, Marcus, 'PA Condemns Hamas For Murdering Gazans Seeking Food,' *Palestinian Media Watch*, June 26, 2025.
15. Magdy, Mounira,' Israel recalls its ambassadors from Norway and Ireland in response to the recognition of the Palestinian state,' *Arab Canada News*, May 22, 2024.
16. Sforza, Lauren, 'Israel Recalls Ambassadors After Norway, Ireland And Spain Say They'll Recognize Palestinian State,' *The Hill*, May 22, 2024, https://thehill.com/policy/international/4679581-israel-recalls-ambassadors-norway-ireland-spain-palestinian-state/
17. Jeong, Sophie, and Mahmood, Zahid, 'Ireland, Spain and Norway say they will recognize a Palestinian state,' *CNN*, May 23, 2024.
18. Carroll, Rory, and Jones, Sam, 'Ireland, Norway and Spain Formally Recognise Palestine as a State,' *The Guardian,* May 22, 2024.
19. https://www.theguardian.com/world/article/2024/may/22/palestinian-state-recognition-ireland-spain-recognise-palestine 'Israeli Anger as Ireland Recognises Palestine,' *Western Daily Press*, May 23, 2024.
20. 'Irish PM says Israel's actions in Gaza resemble "something approaching revenge"; The Taoiseach Leo Varadkar has said Israel has gone beyond its right to self-defence with its actions in Gaza against Hamas,' *Telegraph Online*, November 3, 2023.
21. Salisbury, Josh, 'Benjamin Netanyahu faces an ICC arrest warrant – which countries would detain him?,' *The Standard*, November 22, 2024.
22. He stated, 'But those affected by the Israeli-Palestinian conflict will only learn that murder, rape, torture, dismemberment, abduction, and holding hostages works.' Source: Bradfield, Philip, 'Israel-Hamas War in Gaza: Ex-Irish Justice Minister Alan Shatter Accuses Irish Foreign Minister Micheal Martin of "Obsessively Demonising" Israel in the First Sitting of New Dail,' *The Belfast News Letter*, December 19, 2024.
23. Lidor, Canaan, 'Spanish minister condemned after ending speech with "river to the sea" call,' *The Times of Israel*, May 23, 2024,
24. 'France says Palestinian Authority makes "unprecedented commitments" to reform ahead of conference on statehood,' by Saskya Vandoorne, Joseph Ataman and Nadeen Ebrahim, *CNN*, June 11, 2025,

https://www.cnn.com/2025/06/10/europe/france-palestinian-authority-reform-commitments-intl

25. '"When Gaza burns, Berlin burns" – suspected arson attack on Berlin high school,' translated for m '„Wenn Gaza brennt, brennt Berlin' – Mutmaßlicher Brandanschlag auf Berliner Gymnasium,' *Welt*, July 15, 2024.
26. A poll carried out by the German public broadcaster ZDF, 61% of respondents saw Israel as the aggressor in the war.
27. 'Hamas and Samidoun banned in Germany,' Press Release, *Federal Ministry of the Interior*, November 2, 2023. https://www.bmi.bund.de/SharedDocs/pressemitteilungen/EN/2023/11/banned-hamas-samidoun.html
28. Ringleben, Franziska, 'Teen riots in Hamburg: Jew haters call for Hitler,' translated from 'Teenager-Randale in Hamburg: Judenhasser ruft nach Hitler,' *Bild*, October 25, 2023
29. UK government: 'No moral equivalence between Israel, a democracy, and Hamas and Lebanese Hezbollah,' *Israel National News*, November 21, 2024, https://www.israelnationalnews.com/flashes/645663
30. 'The UK's Foreign Secretary David Lammy calls destroying Hamas "immoral",' *Elder of Ziyon*, May 21, 2025
31. 'Hungary To Ban Rallies Supporting "Terrorist Organisations", Orban says,' *Reuters*, October 13, 2023, https://www.reuters.com/world/europe/hungary-ban-rallies-supporting-terrorist-organisations-pm-orban-2023-10-13/
32. 'Orban: Hamas flags will not fly in Hungary,' *Caliber*, April 3, 2025, https://caliber.az/en/post/orban-hamas-flags-will-not-fly-in-hungary
33. Harkov, Lahav, 'Ambassador to Czech Republic Hit Jackpot in EU's most Pro-Israel Country,' *The Jerusalem Post*, August 18, 2021.
34. 'Czech Group Asks EU Not to Suspend Association Deal with Israel,' *CTK English-Language News*, January 31, 2025.
35. 'Vucic: Serbia helped supply Israel with arms after Oct. 7, despite European criticism – exclusive,' by Alex Winston, *Jerusalem Post*, June 5, 2025, https://www.jpost.com/international/article-856747
36. Ibid.
37. Ferry Biedermann, 'First ever Indian PM visit to Israel amid booming defense ties,' *CNBC*, June 30 2017, https://www.cnbc.com/2017/06/30/first-ever-indian-pm-visit-to-israel-amid-booming-defense-ties.html?msockid=091098da535c61b5268e8bd9524e60f2
38. India was a notable exclusion from a letter signed by 104 countries, including European and African nations, as well as much of the Global South, that 'condemned' Israel for banning United Nations Secretary-General António Guterres from entering Israeli territory.
39. These include Kenya, Ghana, Democratic Republic of Congo (DRC), Rwanda, Zambia, Togo, Cameroon, Malawi, Gabon, Madagascar
40. Aitken, Peter, 'Argentina's Milei Blasts UN Over Support For COVID Lockdowns, Appeasing "Bloody Dictatorships,"' *Fox News*, September 25, 2024

https://www.foxnews.com/world/argentinas-milei-blasts-un-over-support-covid-lockdowns-appeasing-bloody-dictatorships.amp

41. Ibid.
42. Anonymous, 'Biden Calls Israel's Response in Gaza "over the Top", https://www.timesofisrael.com/white-house-clarifies-biden-spoke-of-israel-when-he-said-gaza-response-over-the-top/
43. 'Biden takes a tougher stance on Israel's "indiscriminate bombing" of Gaza,' *PBS*, December 2, 2023, https://www.pbs.org/newshour/world/biden-takes-a-tougher-stance-on-israels-indiscriminate-bombing-of-gaza
44. Zaanoun, Adel and Rosie Scammell. 'Strikes on Gaza's Rafah as Biden Calls Israel Actions Excessive.' *AFP International Text Wire in English*, February 9, 2024.
45. Since 2021, USAID/West Bank and Gaza has invested over $600 million in economic support funding of the Palestinian people, in addition to the over $2.1 billion in humanitarian assistance since October 7, 2023.
46. Israel Throws Off the Biden Shackles.' *Wall Street Journal*, March 4, 2025.
47. 'CAIR Slams Biden, Praises Trump In Welcoming Hostage Agreement,' *JNS*, January 16, 2025.
48. Ambassador Huckabee's response to the claim that the Arab descendants of people who lived in British-controlled Palestine as 'Palestinians.' 'There isn't such a thing,' he said. 'It's a term that was co-opted by Yasser Arafat in 1962 [sic]. Source: Elbaum, Jack. 'American Jewish Organizations React to Trump's Choice for US Ambassador to Israel,' by Jack Elbaum, *Algemeiner*, November 13, 2024.
49. Tucker, Eric, 'The Justice Department And FBI Announced A New Task Force To Target Hamas Over Oct. 7 Attack,' *Associated Press*, March 17, 2025, https://www.yahoo.com/news/justice-department-fbi-announce-task-191003802.html?fr=sycsrp_catchall
50. The complaint stated that from around 1997 until the date of the complaint, Ismail Haniyeh, Yahya Sinwar, Mohammad Al-Masri, Marwan Issa, Khaled Meshaal, Ali Baraka, and others conspired to provide material support or resources to Hamas, a group designated as a foreign terrorist organization by the US Secretary of State.
51. Walker, Corey, 'US Intel Chief Tulsi Gabbard Declares 'Radical Islamist Terrorism' Most Urgent National Security Threat,' *Algemeiner*, February 25, 2025.
52. Klabin, Nathan, 'Experts warn: Trump's Gaza displacement plan could ignite regional instability,' *The Media Line*, January 29, 2025.
53. 'Israel, US to Continue Cooperation Against Iran's Nuclear Ambitions: ISRAEL US,' *EFE News Service*, March 4, 2025. , https://montgomerycollege.idm.oclc.org/login?url=https://www.proquest.com/wire-feeds/israel-us-continue-cooperation-against-irans/docview/3173309645/se-2.
54. Berman, Lazar, 'In Central Gaza, Where Gunmen Lurk Underground, A Commander Sees A Long Slog Ahead,' *The Times of Israel*,

January 18, 2024, https://www.timesofisrael.com/in-central-gaza-where-gunmen-lurk-underground-a-commander-sees-a-long-slog-ahead

55. When the UN agency began its operations, it addressed the needs of approximately 750,000 Palestinian refugees. Today, about 5.9 million Palestinian refugees in the occupied Palestinian territories of Jordan, Lebanon, and Syria are eligible for UNRWA assistance services. Source: Shabaneh, Ghassan. 'Refugees, International Organizations, and National Identity: The Case of Palestine,' *New Political Science,* vol. 32, no. 2, 2010, pp. 215–16, https://doi.org/10.1080/07393141003722057.
56. Bedein, David, 'UNRWA Involvement in Terror,' *The Jerusalem Report*, November 11, 2024.
57. Lazaroff, Tovah, 'Freeze UNRWA Funds to Gaza Schools Over Hamas Attack Tunnels, Erdan Urges: At Issue were Two Hamas Tunnels found in the Proximity of Two UNRWA Schools this Summer in the Aftermath of the 11-Day Gaza War in May,' *The Jerusalem Post*, August 12, 2021, https://www.jpost.com/arab-israeli-conflict/freeze-unrwa-funds-to-gaza-schools-over-hamas-attack-tunnels-erdan-urges-676504
58. Bassam, Abu Hamad, Zeina Jamaluddine, Sarah Aly, Mohammad Salayma, Yara Asi, Hani Mowafi, Francesco Checchi, Miho Sato, Asli Bali, and Paul Spiegel, 'UNRWA's Work is at Risk again,' *The Lancet* 404, no. 10468, November 30, 2024.
59. 'UPDATED: Evidence Of UNRWA Aid To Hamas On And After October 7th,' *UN Watch*, July 12, 2024, https://unwatch.org/evidence-of-unrwa-aid-to-hamas-on-and-after-october-7th/
60. The IDF released audio recordings of a UNRWA teacher victoriously proclaiming, 'I'm inside with the Jews.' Source: 'We have female hostages. I captured one!,' *Times of Israel*, March 4, 2024.
61. Their schoolbooks are full of antisemitic passages. The walls of their schools are plastered with pictures of dead terrorists — 'martyrs' — whom these children are encouraged to emulate. And in their summer camps, they learn more hatred of Israel, which they are taught has no right to exist. Is it any wonder that some Palestinian 'children,' in their mid-to-late teens, end up engaged in battle alongside adults their fighting against the IDF, by hurling rocks, Molotov cocktails, and fireworks? The IDF soldiers, of course, cannot stop to ask the ages of everyone they are fighting; their task is to neutralize those who are trying to kill them. Source: Bernard, Andrew, 'Human Rights Watch Accuses Israel of "Gunning Down Palestinian Children",' *Algemeiner,* August 28, 2023, https://www.algemeiner.com/2023/08/28/human-rights-watch-accuses-israel-gunning-down-palestinian-children/
62. 'UNRWA Chief Confident He Is On "Right Side Of History",' *AFP*, March 17, 2025, https://www.msn.com/en-us/news/world/unrwa-chief-confident-he-is-on-right-side-of-history/ar-AA1B3MUg?ocid=widgetonlockscreen&cvid=dea987edea284dcc90bcb9e728f6689d&ei=53

63. Orbán, Tamas, 'Conservative MEPs: Are EU Taxpayers Funding Terrorism?,' *European Conservative*, October 31, 2023.
64. 'What You Need to Know About the ICC and the Israel-Hamas War,' *American Jewish Committee*, February 7, 2025, https://www.ajc.org/news/what-you-need-to-know-about-the-icc-and-the-israel-hamas-war
65. Statement of ICC Prosecutor Karim A.A. Khan KC: Applications for arrest warrants in the situation in the State of Palestine, *International Criminal Court*, May 20, 2024, https://www.icc-cpi.int/news/statement-icc-prosecutor-karim-aa-khan-kc-applications-arrest-warrants-situation-state
66. 'Hamas Urges ICC to Hold Israel Accountable Over "crimes" in Gaza,' *Anadolu Agency*, December 25, 2023.
67. 'Prosecutor Karim Khan's attempt to deny the State of Israel the right to defend itself and to ensure the release of hostages held in Gaza must be explicitly rejected.' Source: 'Hamas Welcomes Human Rights Council's Decision to Ban Supply of Weapons to Zionist Entity,' *Yemen News Agency*, April 6, 2024.
68. Ibid.
69. 'The sanctions may include travel and financial restrictions on ICC officials, their families, and anyone materially supporting their initiatives. The first individual affected by these sanctions was ICC Chief Prosecutor Karim Khan. Source: Robbins, James, 'The ICC is Courting Payback,' *Real Clear World*, February 12, 2025, https://www.realclearworld.com/articles/2025/02/12/the_icc_is_courting_payback_1090967.html
70. 'Families of Israeli Captives in Gaza to File Case Against Hamas at ICC,' *Anadolu Agency*, February 14, 2024.
71. Peled, Pamela, 'Former MK says Gaza Should be Split in Two: South for War, North for Peace,' *The Jerusalem Post*, April 26, 2024, https://www.jpost.com/israel-hamas-war/article-798679
72. Keinon, Herb, 'Einat Wilf: Israel's Existential Battle Is Against The Vilifying Of The Collective Jew,' *The Jerusalem Post*, March 21, 2025, https://www.jpost.com/israel-news/article-846864
73. Wilf, Einat, 'Only One Moral End: Hamas Surrenders, Releases All Hostages Unconditionally – Opinion,' *The Jerusalem Post*, September 2, 2024.
74. 'Qatari prime minister says his nation does not "have a war with Israel",' *The Times of Israel*, August 27, 2023.
75. Ibid.
76. 'Qatar's Foreign Minister Visits Iran To Meet Top Officials,' *Al Jazeera*, July 25, 2021.
77. '"We Are All Hamas": Qatari Defense Minister Posts, Then Deletes Message In Support Of Hamas,' *The Jerusalem Post*, April 17, 2025.
78. 'Rachel Goldberg's Battle to Find Her Son Who was Abducted by Hamas: Hersh Goldberg-Polin was Abducted by Hamas at the Supernova Music Festival in Southern Israel. His Mother is Desperate for News about His Welfare,'

*ABC Premium News*, November 28, 2023, https://montgomerycollege.idm.oclc.org/login?url=https://www.proquest.com/wire-feeds/rachel-goldbergs-battle-find-her-son-who-was/docview/2894426249/se-2.

79. Gan, Nectar, 'World Middle East Hersh Goldberg-Polin: The "happy-go-lucky" Israeli-American who became a symbol of Israel's enduring hostage heartbreak,' *CNN* , September 1, 2024, https://www.cnn.com/2024/09/01/middleeast/israel-gaza-hostage-polin-goldberg-profile-intl-hnk/index.html
80. 'Hamas Issues Video Showing Israeli-American Hostage Hersh Goldberg-Polin, Sparking Protests in Israel: Rachel Goldberg and Jon Polin had Assumed they would Never See their Son again – but that Changed when Hamas Released a Hostage Video Featuring a One-Armed Hersh,' *ABC Premium News*, April 25, 2024.
81. Land, Olivia, 'Heartbroken mother of murdered hostage Hersh Goldberg-Polin "begs son for forgiveness" for not being able to save him,' *MSN*, September 2, 2024, https://www.msn.com/en-us/news/world/thousands-line-streets-for-hersh-goldberg-polin-funeral-procession/ar-AA1pRiNV
82. Frantzman, Seth J., 'Iran's President Pezeshkian speaks with Hamas leader, praises Houthis,' *Jerusalem Post*, July 15, 2024.
83. Arguello, Ailin Vilches, 'Iran to Build 1,000 Nuclear Sites if "Enemy" Destroys 100, President Says Amid Reports of Possible Israeli Strike,' *Algemeiner*, February 13, 2025.
84. The Madagascar tomato frog is Dyscophus Antongilii.
85. 'Russia and Iran Sign "Comprehensive Strategic Partnership Agreement", Pledging To Promote "A New Fair And Sustainable Multipolar World Order"; Russian Commentators: The Agreement Formalizes Existing Military Cooperation,' *MEMRI*, January 30, 2025.
86. 'Iran's Supreme Leader, Ayatollah Khamenei, May or May Not Have Died at Age 81,' *Israel Faxx*, December 8, 2020.
87. 'Muslims Awaiting Khamenei's Go-Ahead To Wage War On Israel – Chief Of Staff,' *Iran International*, December 27, 2024:
88. 'Khamenei calls for protesters in US, Europe to "stop" Israeli military in Gaza,' *The Times of Israel*, March 20, 2025:https://www.timesofisrael.com/liveblog_entry/khamenei-calls-for-protesters-in-us-europe-to-stop-israeli-military-in-gaza
89. 'Dearborn Imam: We Should Appreciate Khamenei While He's Alive,' *MEMRI*, November 19, 2024.
90. 'Israel Scorns America's Unprecedented Peace Plan,' *The Economist*, February 7, 2024.
91. 'Saudi Crown Prince Said He Personally "Doesn't Care" About Palestinian Issue,' *Middle East Eye*, September 27, 2024.
92. 'Saudi Arabia willing to make concessions on Palestinians for peace with Israel,' *Reuters*, February 2, 2024.
93. Ibid.

94. 'Saudi Arabia Sees Massive Cultural Shift After Crown Prince's Reforms,' *National Public Radio*, August 7, 2022.
95. Fabian, Emanuel, 'Katz says Israel will renew aid to Gaza via civilian firms to prevent Hamas theft,' *The Times of Israel*, April 16, 2025, https://www.timesofisrael.com/liveblog_entry/katz-says-israel-will-renew-aid-to-gaza-via-civilian-firms-to-prevent-hamas-theft/
96. 'IDF will seize Gaza land permanently until Hamas releases hostages, Katz says,' *The Jerusalem Post*, March 22, 2025, https://www.jpost.com/breaking-news/article-847025
97. ' Prime Minister Jonas Gahr Støre (Labour Party), *Government of Norway website*, October 14, 2021, https://www.regjeringen.no/en/dep/smk/organization-map/prime-minister-jonas-gahr-store/id2877186/
98. 'Norway says Israel Response To Hamas Attack Disproportionate,' *The Times of Israel*, October 29, 2023, https://www.timesofisrael.com/liveblog_entry/norway-says-israel-response-to-hamas-attack-disproportionate/
99. georgegalloway.com
100. Murray, Warren and Jones, Sam, 'George Galloway refuses to debate with Israeli student at Oxford,' *The Guardian*, February 21, 2013, https://www.theguardian.com/politics/2013/feb/21/george-galloway-debate-israeli-oxford.
101. 'Newly-elected British MP Galloway equates Israel-Hamas war to Holocaust,' *The Times of Israel*, March 5, 2024.
102. Greyman-Kennard, Danielle, 'George Galloway, Antisemitic and Demented, Denies October 7 Atrocities Ever Happened,' *The Jerusalem Post*, November 11, 2023.
103. Westrop, Sam, 'SouthAfrica'sTerror-TiedAmbassadorReturnstoWashington,' *Middle East Forum,* December 19, 2024, https://www.meforum.org/fwi/fwi-research/south-africas-terror-tied-ambassador-returns-to-washington
104. Ngcobo, Khayiisile, 'The Expelled Envoy At The Heart Of The Latest US-South Africa Row,' *BBC*, March 17, 2025.
105. Hansler, Jennifer, 'Rubio says South African ambassador "no longer welcome" in US,' CNN, March 15, 2025.
106. Dentlinger, Lindsay, 'Expelled Ambassador To US Ebrahim Rasool Says He Has No Regrets,' *Eyewitness News*, March 17, 2025.
107. Sokol, Sam, 'New US Envoy: Israel's Struggle Against Its Enemies Is A "Battle Between Heaven And Hell",' *The Times of Israel*, April 25, 2025, https://www.timesofisrael.com/new-us-envoy-israels-struggle-against-its-enemies-is-a-battle-between-heaven-and-hell/
108. Visnovsky, Gregory, 'Mike Huckabee, Longtime Israel Supporter, Confirmed As US Ambassador,' *Politico*, April 9, 2025, https://www.politico.com/news/2025/04/09/mike-huckabee-israel-ambassador-032907
109. Bernstein, David, 'Potential Deportee Mohsen Madawi: I Like to Kill Jews [Allegation], *Reason*, May 1, 2025.
110. Ibid.

111. Ibid.
112. Kleiman, Shachar, 'Report Exposes How UNRWA Partners With Hamas, PIJ,' *Israel Hayom*, January 7, 2025, https://www.israelhayom.com/2025/01/07/report-exposes-how-unrwa-partners-with-hamas-pij/
113. 'UNRWA Chief Says He Did Not Know A Suspended Teacher Was Hamas's Leader In Lebanon,' *The Times of Israel*, October 1, 2024, https://www.timesofisrael.com/unrwa-chief-says-he-did-not-know-suspended-employee-was-hamass-leader-in-lebanon/
114. Sewell, Abby, 'Future Looks Dire For UN Palestinian Refugee Agency, Says UNRWA Chief,' *Associated Press*, February 6, 2025, https://apnews.com/article/unrwa-palestinians-israel-ban-philippe-lazzarini-us-funding-trump-gaza-ce33b0fdb0140fd71e2d0f1fd06f7700
115. ' Big answers to big lies: Israel refutes UN's despicable Goldstone Report,' *New York Daily News*, April 9, 2018, https://www.nydailynews.com/2010/02/13/big-answers-to-big-lies-israel-refutes-uns-despicable-goldstone-report/
116. Phillips, Melanie, 'Richard Goldstone Recants. What Price The Israel Witch-Hunt Now?,' *The Spectator*, April 2, 2011.

## Chapter 8: War Aims and Strategies

1. Neuman, Scott, 'What Did Hamas Aim To Gain By Its Brazen Attack On Israel? Here's What To Know,' *National Public Radio*, October 12, 2023, https://www.npr.org/2023/10/12/1204881032/hamas-israel-attack-palestinians
2. Remarks by President Biden on the Terrorist Attacks in Israel,' *The Jerusalem Post*, October 11, 2023, https://www.jpost.com/international/article-767782
3. 'Former Hamas Chief Says He Launched Five Fronts to Support Gaza,' *BBC Monitoring Newsfile*, November 7, 2023. https://montgomerycollege.idm.oclc.org/login?url=https://www.proquest.com/wire-feeds/former-hamas-chief-says-he-launched-five-fronts/docview/2886552067/se-2.
4. 'Hamas Military Commander Mohammed Deif Announces Launch of Operation Al-Aqsa Deluge, Calls On Palestinians In West Bank, Jerusalem, And Israel Proper To Attacks With Guns, Knives, Vehicles,' *MEMRI TV*, #10500, Al-Jazeera Network, October 7, 2023.
5. Elkayam-Levy, Cochav and Cotler, Irwin, 'Kinocide: Hamas Targeting of families is a new crime against humanity,' *The Times of Israel*, May 20, 2024, https://www.timesofisrael.com/kinicide-a-new-crime-against-humanity/
6. Yaron, Lee, *10/7 100 Human Stories*, St Martin's Press, New York, 2024, p. 205.
7. Many of the principles are rooted in Hamas' 1988 Charter and the 2017 General Principles and Policies that encourage any violence that would defeat the Israeli enemy. Source: Lax, Chaim, 'To Understand the IDF and Hamas, Look at Their Military Texts,' *Honest Reporting*, February 13, 2024, https://honestreporting.com/to-understand-the-idf-and-hamas-look-at-their-military-texts/

8. The exact number is still debated. Some thought to have been abducted and held hostage were killed on October 7.
9. Evidence of the kidnappings has come from images taken and published by Hamas both during and after the attack. The data from some of the Israelis' phones showed they were on Palestinian territory. Source: Rousseau, Daphne, 'What We Know About The Hostages Hamas Is Holding,' *AFP International Text Wire in English*, October 14, 2023, https://montgomerycollege.idm.oclc.org/login?url=https://www.proquest.com/wire-feeds/what-we-know-about-hostages-hamas-is-holding/docview/2876910814/se-
10. Hendrix, Steve, Sarah Dadouch, Hajar Harb, Michael Birnbaum, Liz Sly, and Paul Schemm, 'Israel, Hamas Agree To Hostage Exchange Deal,' *The Washington Post*, November 21, 2023.
11. Alkadi, a father of 11 from the Bedouin Arab community, was rescued by IDF soldiers from the 13th Fleet Unit, 401st Brigade, as well as Yalam and Shin Bet fighters, the military said. He was by himself without guards, the officials said. The Israeli military is still trying to piece together why his captors seemingly abandoned him. Source: Land, Olivia, 'IDF Rescues Hamas Hostage And Father Of 11 By Chance After Finding Him Alone In Gaza Tunnel,' *New York Post*, August 27, 2024: https://nypost.com/2024/08/27/world-news/idf-rescues-hostage-from-tunnel-in-southern-gaza/
12. Confino, Jotam, 'Hamas Told To Execute Israeli Hostages If They Fear IDF Are Closing In,' *The Telegraph*, September 3, 2024, https://www.yahoo.com/news/hamas-told-execute-israeli-hostages-094656547.html
13. Elman, R. Amy, 'October 7: Passionate Anti-Zionists, Pornography, and Feminist Impersonators,' *Antisemitism Studies* 8, no. 2, 2024 (accessed December 2, 2024).
14. Blum, Michael, 'Surviving "Hell": The Ordeal of Former Hamas Hostages in Gaza,' *AFP International Text* Wire in English, April 4, 2024.,
15. 'The One Thing Israelis Agree On: Rescuing The Hostages,' *The Economist*, September 4, 2024.
16. Makover-Balikov, Sherry, 'Most Hamas Terrorists Were Drugged, Completely Inhumane, Rescued Hostage Says,' *Jerusalem Post*, January 28, 2025.
17. Dev, Liam and Cohen, Maya, '"The Girls Suffered, But Men Suffer More": Shira Albag Speaks About Liri's Time In Captivity,' *Jerusalem Post*, February 13, 2025.
18. Ibid.
19. Silow-Carroll, Andrew. 'Students and fellow educators on three continents say goodbye to Israeli reservist killed in tunnel blast,' *Jewish Telegraphic Agency*, November 13, 2023, https://www.jta.org/2023/11/13/obituaries/students-and-fellow-educators-on-three-continents-say-goodbye-to-israeli-reservist-killed-in-tunnel-blast
20. Humaid, Maram, and Justin Salhani, 'Analysis: Hamas Has Been Hit Hard By Israel, But Is Not Out In Gaza,' *Al Jazeera*,' January 29, 2025, https://www.

aljazeera.com/news/2025/1/29/analysis-hamas-has-been-hit-hard-by-israel-but-is-not-out-in-gaza

21. Abdulrahim, Raja, 'As War Drags On, Gazans More Willing to Speak Out Against Hamas,' *The New York Times*, June 15, 2024. https://www.nytimes.com/2024/06/15/world/middleeast/hamas-gaza-israel-war.html
22. Many pastors and parishioners support Gazans whom they see as early Christian martyrs. In churches, festive biscuits reading 'Palestinian Lives Matter' and 'What would Jesus say?' were also on sale, stating 'Palestinian Lives Matter.'
23. Allen, Jonathan, 'US immigration agents arrest Palestinian student protester at Columbia University in Trump crackdown,' *Reuters*, March 10, 2025.
24. As of June 2025, 3 hostages killed by friendly fire. 42 bodies were repatriated through military operations. 8 returned in a prisoner exchange deal in 2025. According to Israel, a total of 74 hostages were killed on October 7, 2023, or in Hamas captivity.
25. The data of suicide reveals a mixed picture. According to a government study, approximately 217 Israeli civilians committed suicide from October 2023 until early 2025. This number is no higher compared to rates in earlier years.
26. Byman, Daniel and Aliberti, David, 'What Does Destroying Hamas Mean?,' *CSIS,* December 15, 2023, https://www.csis.org/analysis/what-does-destroying-hamas-mean
27. 'Gaza will be Entirely Destroyed, Israeli Minister Says,' *The Guardian*, May 6, 2025, https://www.theguardian.com/world/2025/may/06/hamas-israel-hunger-war-in-gaza
28. Nissenbaum, Dion, 'Israel Plans to Kill Hamas Leaders Around the World After War,' *The Australian* (Online), December 1, 2023.
29. Melman, Yossi, 'Israel's Targeted Assassinations are a Poor Substitute for a Strategy,' *Haaretz*, May 17, 2023.
30. Davey-Atlee, Florence, '"He was a pious man": The Gaza Neighborhood Shocked To Find Israeli Hostages In Their Midst,' *CNN*, July 19, 2024, https://edition.cnn.com/2024/07/19/middleeast/gaza-neighborhood-israeli-hostages-intl-cmd/index.html.
31. 'Why Accusing Israel of "Genocide" Is Inherently And Purely Antisemitic,' *Elder of Ziyon*, November 17, 2024.
32. 'Gaza in turmoil: Clans emerge as rivals to Hamas's rule,' by Amir Bohbot, *Jerusalem Post*, June 1, 2025, https://www.jpost.com/israel-news/article-856205
33. Ibid.
34. Fabian, Emanuel, 'IAF to dismiss reservists who signed letter demanding prioritization of hostages over war,' *The Times of Israel*, April 10, 2025.
35. DiMarco, Lou, 'Attacking the Heart and Guts: Urban Operations Through the Ages,' IIMG.4plebs.org, accessed June 9, 2025.
36. Fabian, Emanuel, 'In Rafah, IDF Focuses On Tunnels, With Aim Of Destroying Hamas Brigade Within A Month,' *The Times of Israel*, June 19, 2024,

https://www.timesofisrael.com/in-rafah-idf-focuses-on-tunnels-with-aim-of-destroying-hamas-brigade-within-a-month/

37. 'Hamas tunnels under Gaza will be a key battlefield for Israel,' *The Economist*, October 17, 2023.
38. 'More than once a soldier was operating a robot that got stuck inside a tunnel,' complained another officer. 'Now try and go in and retrieve a robot that is 400 metres inside a tunnel complex. It's like running 150 metres where each metre is like crossing a desert for a month. Source: 'Hamas Tunnels Under Gaza Will Be A Key Battlefield For Israel.' *The Economist*, October 17, 2023.
39. Mayer, Gregor and Gaby Mahlberg, 'Israel: Hamas Command Tunnel Found Under UN Aid Agency's HQ in Gaza,' *DPA International* (English), February 11, 2024.
40. Hotter, James and John Paul Rathbone. 'Military Briefing: Has Israel Achieved its War Aims in Gaza?,' *FT. Com* (November 2023).
41. Spencer, John, 'Israel's New Approach to Tunnels: A Paradigm Shift in Underground Warfare,' *Modern War Institute*, December 2, 2024.
42. Roblin, Sebastien, 'How Many Armored Vehicles Has Israel Lost Fighting Hamas?,' *Popular Mechanics*, November 13, 2023, https://www.popularmechanics.com/military/weapons/a45783283/how-many-armored-vehicles-has-israel-lost-fighting-hamas-gaza/
43. Older, non-Trophy-equipped Merkava 4s and 3s remain in reserve units—including Merkava 3s intended for sale to Cyprus and Morocco, which have now been redirected to the newly formed Of Hol ('Phoenix') volunteer reserve tank battalion. Merkava IIBs, relegated to training duties in 2020, have also been seen in combat during Hamas' initial October 7 attack. Source: Roblin, Sebastien, 'How Many Armored Vehicles Has Israel Lost Fighting Hamas?,' *Popular Mechanics*, November 13, 2023, https://www.popularmechanics.com/military/weapons/a45783283/how-many-armored-vehicles-has-israel-lost-fighting-hamas-gaza/
44. Hamas' most capable anti-armor weapons are anti-tank guided missiles (ATGMs), the Russian-origin 9M133 Kornet-E with its large 152-millimeter missile and tandem charges designed to defeat explosive reactive armor. These were effective against Merkava in the 2006 Lebanon conflict. However, during the war with Hamas, these were less effective on Merkavas equipped with the Trophy System.
45. Buncombe, Andrew, 'Israel's "Teddy Bear" Armoured Bulldozer Enters Gaza Amid Fears of Cities being Razed,' *Telegraph. co. uk*, October 31, 2023.
46. Gardner, Frank, 'Reconnaissance By Fire – What Israel's Gaza Raid Tells Us,' *BBC*, October 26 2023, https://www.bbc.com/news/world-middle-east-67226021
47. Baroud, Ramzy, 'Netanyahu's Last Battle: No Victory, Just Slaughter in Rafah,' *Washington Report on Middle East Affairs*, May 2024.

48. Frantzman, Seth, 'How Hamas survived a year of the Israel-Hamas War,' *MSN*, January 19, 2025, https://www.msn.com/en-us/news/world/how-hamas-survived-a-year-of-the-israel-hamas-war/ar-AA1xsPCS
49. Zaanoun, Adel and Phil Hazlewood, 'Hamas Warns Israel Rafah Op may Cause Casualties in "Tens of Thousands",' *AFP International* Text Wire in English, Feb 10, 2024, https://montgomerycollege.idm.oclc.org/login?url=https://www.proquest.com/wire-feeds/hamas-warns-israel-rafah-op-may-cause-casualties/docview/2924183480/se-2.
50. Frantzman, Seth, 'How Hamas survived a year of the Israel-Hamas War,' *MSN*, January 19, 2025, https://www.msn.com/en-us/news/world/how-hamas-survived-a-year-of-the-israel-hamas-war/ar-AA1xsPCS
51. 'IDF Seizes Control of Gaza's Rafah Crossing. Hamas Launches Barrage at Gaza Border Communities. Hostage Confirmed Killed,' *The Jerusalem Post*, May 08, 2024.
52. 'Battles Rage in Rafah as Biden Blames Hamas for Truce Delay,,' *Al Monitor*, June 13, 2024, https://www.al-monitor.com/originals/2024/06/battles-rage-rafah-biden-blames-hamas-truce-delay
53. Fabian, Emanuel, 'IDF declares Hamas's Rafah Brigade defeated; no active cross-border tunnels found,' *The Times of Israel*, September 12, 2024, https://www.timesofisrael.com/idf-declares-hamass-rafah-brigade-defeated-no-active-cross-border-tunnels-found/
54. Baba, Anas, 'Palestinians in Gaza return to find their city in ruins after Israeli troops withdraw,' *National Public Radio*, January 25, 2025, https://www.npr.org/2025/01/25/g-s1-44366/gaza-rafah-ruins-ceasefire
55. Al-Mughrabi, Nidal, 'Israel flattens Rafah ruins; Gazans fear plan to herd them there,' *Reuters*, April 28, 2025.
56. Al-Mughrabi, Nidal and Dan Williams, 'Israel PM Hails Advance into Gaza City as Hamas Fighters Attack from Tunnels,' *Chronicle – Herald*, November 3, 2023.
57. 'Gaza is the "hungriest place on earth", as Israel continues stranglehold on aid,' *United Nations*, May 30, 2025, https://news.un.org/en/story/2025/05/1163861
58. 'PEN America: 'Gravely Alarmed by Destruction and Damage to Hundreds of Culture and Educational Sites in Gaza,' *PEN America*, December 6, 2023.
59. 'I Am Gaza City's Mayor. Our Lives and Culture Are in Rubble,' by Yahya R. Sarraj, *New York Times*, December 24, 2023, https://www.nytimes.com/2023/12/24/opinion/gaza-city-palestine-war.html
60. Halpern, Micah, 'Operation Gideon's Chariots: A Powerful Name For A Powerful Gaza Op. – Opinion,' *Jerusalem Post*, May 20, 2025, https://www.jpost.com/opinion/article-854559
61. Shoval, Lilach, 'Operation Gideon's Chariots begins: IDF Launches Major Ground Offensive Across Gaza,' *Israel Hayom*, May 18, 2025.

62. Fabian, Emanuel, 'IDF Says It Is "Seizing Strategic Areas" As It Launches First Stages Of Major New Gaza Offensive Dubbed "Gideon's Chariots",' *The Times of Israel*, May 16, 2025, https://www.timesofisrael.com/liveblog_entry/idf-says-it-has-launched-first-stages-of-new-major-gaza-offensive-dubbed-gideons-chariots/
63. Neumann, Neomi, 'Will Israel's New "Chariots" Plan Trample or Strengthen Hamas? Policy Analysis,' *PolicyWatch* 4038, May 14, 2025, https://www.washingtoninstitute.org/policy-analysis/will-israels-new-chariots-plan-trample-or-strengthen-hamas
64. 'Seven European Countries Condemn Operation "Gideon's Chariots" Ahead Of Its Start,' *The Jerusalem Post*, May 16, 2025, https://www.jpost.com/breaking-news/article-854278
65. 'IDF kills Bibas family kidnappers, hostage video producer in Gaza,' *Jerusalem Post*, April 7, 2025.
66. Merlin, Ohad, 'Hamas Pledges To Execute, Amputate Gazans Accused Of "Treason," "Theft",' *The Jerusalem Post*, May 4, 2025, https://www.jpost.com/breaking-news/article-852578
67. Jordan, Eliana, 'Ex-Hamas Leader Says October 7 Massacres Were "Completely Within Our Strategy",' *Jewish Chronicle*, October 14, 2023, https://www.thejc.com/news/israel/ex-hamas-leader-says-october-7-massacres-were-completely-within-our-strategy-f6t97ujm
68. Cook, Ellie, 'One of Israel's Biggest Targets Is Still on The Loose,' *Newsweek,* October 22, 2024, https://www.newsweek.com/israel-hamas-war-gaza-strip-khaled-meshaal-yahya-sinwar-1972101
69. 'Hostage rescued from Gaza in daring raid after 326 days in Hamas captivity,' *Ha Yom*, August 27, 2024, https://www.israelhayom.com/2024/08/27/qaid-farhan-alkadi/
70. Cohen, Shimon, 'Nobel Prize winner: We Are Only Encouraging More Abductions,' *Israel National News*, January 27, 2025.
71. Ibid.
72. Marcelo, Philip, 'What To Know About Mahmoud Khalil, The Columbia Protester Arrested By ICE And Facing Deportation,' *Associated Press*, March 11, 2025, https://apnews.com/article/columbia-university-mahmoud-khalil-ice-440828980a4ee7bf4ddcf3d123e02b3e
73. Neumeiser, Larry, 'Columbia University Student Says His Detention Is Indicative Of Anti-Palestinian Racism In US,' *Associated Press*, March 18, 2025, https://apnews.com/article/columbia-university-mahmoud-khalil-ice-arrests-cebf66ac78ace72647891c16ed43ac1a
74. 'Rubio: State Dept Reviewing Columbia Protesters' Visas,' *News Max*, May 8, 2025, https://www.newsmax.com/politics/palestine-protest-visa/2025/05/08/id/1210092/
75. 'Bugged out: Mahmoud Khalil says feds' claim that bedbugs drove him from NJ to Louisiana lockup is bogus,' *MSN*, March 18, 2025, https://www.msn.com/

en-us/news/us/bugged-out-mahmoud-khalil-says-feds-claim-that-bedbugs-drove-him-from-nj-to-louisiana-lockup-is-bogus/ar-AA1Bbt4z

76. Ashkenazi, Eli, 'Father Of Woman Killed At Nova Festival Commits Suicide After Devastating Loss,' *The Jerusalem Post*, March 4, 2025, https://www.jpost.com/israel-news/article-844656
77. Derrick, Kossy, 'Journalist Confirmed Sophia Bongart's Father, Vladislav Bongart, Has Committed Suicide,' *Kossyderrick Ent*, February 23, 2025, https://www.kossyderrickent.com/photo-journalist-confirmed-sophia-bongarts-father-vladislav-bongart-has-committed-suicide/
78. Reynolds, James, 'Tragedy As Israeli Father Of Woman, 21, Murdered In Hamas NOVA Massacre Kills Himself After Being Consumed By "Heavy Guilt" For Not Saving Her,' *Daily Mail*, March 5, 2025, https://www.dailymail.co.uk/news/article-14463519/Tragedy-Israeli-father-woman-21-murdered-Hamas-NOVA-massacre-kills-consumed-heavy-guilt-not-saving-her.html
79. Davey-Attlee, Florence, '"He Was A Pious Man": The Gaza Neighborhood Shocked To Find Israeli Hostages In Their Midst,' *CNN*, July 19, 2024, https://www.yahoo.com/news/pious-man-gaza-neighborhood-shocked-111141983.html
80. Hass, Saar, '*Al Jazeera* Journalist, Physician Father Held Hostages, Palestinians Say, *YNET*, June 9, 2024, https://www.ynetnews.com/article/rjwzufmr0
81. Fabian, Emanuel, 'DF Confirms Abdallah Aljamal, Hamas Terrorist And News Contributor, Was Holding 3 Hostages In His Home In Nuseirat Alongside His Family,' *MSN*, June 6, 2024, https://www.msn.com/en-us/news/world/idf-confirms-abdallah-aljamal-was-holding-3-hostages-in-his-home-in-nuseirat-alongside-his-family/ar-BB1nUuwc
82. 'Who Is Fawzia Amin Sido? Yazidi Sex Slave Recounts ISIS Horror, Claims She Was Forced To Eat Babies,' *The Week*, October 20, 2024, https://www.theweek.in/news/world/2024/10/20/who-is-fawzi-amin-sido-yazidi-sex-slave-recounts-isis-horror-claims-she-was-forced-to-eat-babies.html
83. 'Fawzia Amin Sido Should Never Have Spent a Decade in Captivity,' *Nadias Initiative*, originally published by *Time Magazine*, October 8, 2024, https://www.nadiasinitiative.org/news/fawzia-amin-sido-should-never-have-spent-a-decade-in-captivity
84. 'Fawzia Amin Sido Taken as ISIS Slave at Age 11 and Held by Hamas for 10 Years is Rescued by Israeli Troops in Gaza,' *Homeland Security Today*,' October 8, 2024, https://www.hstoday.us/subject-matter-areas/counterterrorism/fawzia-amin-sido-taken-as-isis-slave-at-age-11-and-held-by-hamas-for-10-years-is-rescued-by-israeli-troops-in-gaza/
85. Spencer, John, 'Israel's New Approach to Tunnels: A Paradigm Shift in Underground Warfare,' *Institute of Modern War*, West Point, p. 1 December 2, 2024, https://mwi.westpoint.edu/israels-new-approach-to-tunnels-a-paradigm-shift-in-underground-warfare/A
86. Weiss, Farley, 'No other alternative to the moral war Israel wages,' *Cleveland Jewish News*, June 8, 2025, https://www.clevelandjewishnews.com/jns/

no-other-alternative-to-the-moral-war-israel-wages/article_341d2ec8-b3e2-5190-8d6e-92367ede79d9.html

87. '"Commanded the Kidnappings": Israel Eliminates Terrorist Implicated in Kidnapping and Murders of Bibas Family and American Citizens,' *FDD*, April 5, 2025, https://www.fdd.org/analysis/2025/04/05/commanded-the-kidnappings-israel-kills-terrorist-implicated-in-kidnapping-and-murders-of-bibas-family-and-american-citizen
88. 'Terrorist Who Oversaw Abduction Of Bibas Family Killed By IDF,' *The Jewish Chronicle*, April 6, 2025, https://www.thejc.com/news/israel/terrorist-who-oversaw-abduction-of-bibas-family-killed-by-idf-yukuzz7t
89. '"Commanded the Kidnappings": Israel Eliminates Terrorist Implicated in Kidnapping and Murders of Bibas Family and American Citizens,' *FDD*, April 5, 2025, https://www.fdd.org/analysis/2025/04/05/commanded-the-kidnappings-israel-kills-terrorist-implicated-in-kidnapping-and-murders-of-bibas-family-and-american-citizen
90. Berman, Lazar, 'Body Of Slain Chabad Rabbi Found In UAE; Israel Condemns "Antisemitic Act Of Terror",' *The Times of Israel*, November 24, 2024:https://www.timesofisrael.com/body-of-slain-chabad-rabbi-found-in-uae-israel-condemns-antisemitic-act-of-terror/amp/
91. 'Rabbi who went missing in UAE has been murdered, says Israel; Zvi Kogan, 28, who ran a kosher supermarket in Dubai, was found dead in Abu Dhabi after his abandoned car was discovered,' *Telegraph Online*, November 24, 2024.
92. '3 People Sentenced To Death In The Killing Of Rabbi Zvi Kogan In The United Arab Emirates,' *CBS News*, March 31, 2025, https://www.cbsnews.com/news/rabbi-zvi-kogan-death-sentences-united-arab-emirates/
93. Jaspal, R., 'Antisemitism and Anti-Zionism in Iran: The Effects of Identity, Threat, and Political Trust,' *Contemporary Jewry*, 35(3), (2015). 211–213. https://doi.org/10.1007/s12397-015-9133-6
94. '3 People Sentenced To Death In Killing Of Rabbi Zvi Kogan In The United Arab Emirates,' *CBS News*, March 31, 2025, https://www.cbsnews.com/news/rabbi-zvi-kogan-death-sentences-united-arab-emirates/

## Chapter 9: Afterward – Vivisection

1. Meckler, Laura, and Susan Svrluga, 'Pro-Hamas messages intensify on college campuses,' *Washington Post*, November 10, 2024.
2. Spencer, Robert, 'They entered Gaza alive, but today they are leaving in coffins! Our fighters are the ones who memorized the Quran!,' *Jihad Watch*, February 23, 2025.
3. 'Hamas publishes "Victory Anthem" after ceasefire agreement,' *Yemen News Agency*, January 19, 2025, https://www.saba.ye/en/news3426038.htm
4. Peisner, David, 'Fergie Chambers Is Heir to One of America's Richest Families – and Determined to See the U.S. Fall,' *Rolling Stone*, March 24, 2024,

https://www.rollingstone.com/culture/culture-features/fergie-chambers-cox-enterprises-heir-overthrow-us-1234983156/

5. Sullivan, Helen, 'What we know about the attack in Colorado,' *BBC*, June 3, 2025, https://www.bbc.com/news/articles/c74n3122pgpo
6. 'Boulder, CO Firebomber Mohamed Sabry Soliman Recorded Video Before Attack Declaring: Jihad Is More Beloved to Me Than My Mother, Wife, and Children; Allah Is Greater Than the Zionists and America,' *MEMRI,* June 3, 2025.
7. Simons, Jake Wallis, 'Greta's blind eye to murder,' *The Telegraph*, June 10, 2025, https://www.telegraph.co.uk/news/2025/06/10/goodbye-greta-at-least-israel-knows-how-to-deport-people/
8. Davies, Maia, 'British-Israeli hostage says scars show "hope" ahead of surgery,' BBC News, March 2, 2025.
9. Hennessey, Ted, 'Freed Hostage Emily Damari Says Scars show 'freedom' as She Undergoes Surgery,' *Press Association*, March 2, 2025.
10. Confino, Jotam, "Dr Hamas' Sewed My Nerves Together, Says Freed Hostage,' *The Hamas*, March 2, 2025, https://www.yahoo.com/news/dr-hamas-sewed-nerves-together-195513280.html?fr=sycsrp_catchall
11. Prinsely, Jane, 'Widely reported 50 Nova suicides story "not correct" says Israeli psychologist,' *The Jewish Chronicle*, April 25, 2024, https://www.thejc.com/news/israel/nova-suicide-figure-50-israel-health-ministry-not-correct-survivors-help-mental-health-xzvlidnc
12. Agmon, Yair and Mevorach, Oriya, *One Day in October – Forty Heroes, Forty Stories*, The Toby Press, 2024, p. 167.
13. Ibid.
14. Ibid., p. 139.
15. Tenoria, Rich, 'Documentary On October 7 Supernova Festival Massacre Makes US Debut,' *The Times of Israel*, February 23, 2024, https://www.timesofisrael.com/documentary-on-october-7-supernova-festival-massacre-makes-us-debut/?__cf_chl_tk=9r2XyQ5xrUsnYK7FYlSyi2Vmi-4W13ui9vL1Ouj5I8vU-1723301684-0.0.1.1-3945
16. https://www.msn.com/en-us/news/world/new-york-artist-inspired-by-his-eight-months-as-a-hostage-of-hamas/vi-AA1FxBlZ?ocid=msedgntp&pc=HCTS&cvid=8f70a185cbb6431daa6eec8179eda7be&ei=11#details
17. Steinberg, Jessica, 'Andrey Kozlov Drew In Hamas Captivity. Now He's Painting His Story,' *The Times of Israel*, May 19, 2025. https://www.msn.com/en-us/news/world/andrey-kozlov-drew-in-hamas-captivity-now-he-s-painting-his-story/ar-AA1F4hwE?ocid=BingNewsVerp
18. Stanley, Tim, 'Israel's Ambassador to the U.K., Tzipi Hotovely, was recently interviewed: "Israeli ambassador: The two-state solution is over. We are no longer willing to jeopardize our security",' *Telegraph*, June 1, 2025, https://www.telegraph.co.uk/news/2025/06/01/israeli-ambassador-interview-two-state-solution/

19. Saleman, Yaron, 'Light unto the Nations Through Arms Sales: Israel's Arms Diplomacy Goals, Achievements, and Limitations,' *Contemporary Review of the Middle East*, Volume 12, Issue 2, p. 1. https://doi.org/10.1177/23477989251318874
20. Barsky, Anna, 'Foreign Barbarians And Assimilation: Hamas Deeply Concerned About Gazans Emigrating, Doc. Reveals,' *Jerusalem Post*, February 7, 2025.
21. Al-Mughrabi, 'Hamas-led Groups Execute Four For Looting Aid Trucks Amid Some Gaza Dissent,' *Reuters,* May 26, 2025.
22. Agmon, Yair and Mevorach, Oriya, *One Day in October – Forty Heroes, Forty Stories*, The Toby Press, 2024, p. 21.
23. Ibid., p. 13.
24. Ibid., p. 237.
25. Herb. Jeremy, Oren Liebermann, Lauren Kent and Alex Marquardt, 'They Came From Thousands Of Miles Apart To DC And Found Love. Then Tragedy Struck,' *CNN*, May 22, 2025.
26. 'Anti-Israel group that helped incite Columbia library takeover praises DC shooter: "an act of solidarity and love",' by Kate Sheehy, *New York Post*, May 23, 2025.
27. Peisner, David, 'Fergie Chambers Is Heir to One of America's Richest Families– and Determined to See the U.S. Fall,' *Rolling Stone*, March 24, 2024. https://www.rollingstone.com/culture/culture-features/fergie-chambers-cox-enterprises-heir-overthrow-us-1234983156/
28. Ibid.
29. Kennedy, Dana, 'Communist Cable TV Heir Giving $24K Payout From NYC BLM Protest To Anti-Israel Causes To Spite "Chief Pig" Eric Adams,' *New York Post*, January 9, 2024, https://nypost.com/2024/01/09/news/cable-tv-heir-giving-24k-nypd-payout-to-palestinian-causes/
30. McPhee, Michele, 'Heir to Cox Family Fortune: "I Chant Death to America Every Day" (Exclusive),' *Los Angeles Magazine*, October 27, 2023, https://lamag.com/crimeinla/cox-family-heir-james-fergie-chambers-funding-palestine-action-in-exclusive-funding-palestinian-action-us
31. Adler, Dan, 'The Life and Times of Fergie Chambers,' *Vanity Fair*, May 2024, https://www.vanityfair.com/news/story/fergie-chambers?srsltid=AfmBOoo9iM3qurn8SCpdwpgM7Fv3Ae_SDHJAkqrvVoGPhcwEXOssg-Tt
32. 'Greta Thunberg: A year to Change the World,' *PBS*, Accessed June 15, 2025, https://www.pbs.org/show/greta-thunberg-year-change-world/
33. 'Greta Thunberg to world leaders: "How Dare You? You Have Stolen My Dreams And My Childhood",' *Guardian News*, Accessed June 15, 2025, https://www.youtube.com/watch?v=TMrtLsQbaok
34. 'Climate activist Greta Thunberg arrested at pro-Palestinian protest in Denmark,' *AFP*, September 4, 2024.
35. 'Climate activist Greta Thunberg arrested at Eurovision pro-Palestinian protest,' *Jerusalem Post*, May 11, 2024.

36. Jaffe-Hoffman, Maayan, 'Greta Thunberg Slams COP28 Climate Deal And Israel, Waves Palestinian Flag,' *Jerusalem Post*, December 17, 2023.
37. O'Neill, Brendan, 'Greta Thunberg's moral siege of Israel,' *Spiked*, May 7, 2025:
38. '"Hope Greta and her friends can swim!" Lindsey Graham writes regarding Gaza "Freedom Flotilla,"' *Jerusalem Post*, June 2, 2025.
39. Heller, Mathilda, 'Undercover agents, no-fly zones: Israel prepares for pro-Palestinian protests at Eurovision, *Jerusalem Post*, May 13, 2025.
40. Ibid.
41. Confino, Jotam, 'British Protesters Try to Storm Stage During Israel's Eurovision Performance,' Yahoo.com May 18, 2025, https://www.yahoo.com/news/british-protesters-try-storm-stage-150140223.html?fr=yhssrp_catchall
42. Brown, Hanna, 'Austria's Eurovision winner says he hopes Israel will be excluded next year,' *Jerusalem Post*, May 22, 2025.
43. 'Eurovision Cuts Israel From Official 2025 Album Reel,' *JNS*, May 25, 2025, https://www.jns.org/eurovision-cuts-israel-from-official-2025-album-reel/
44. *All Israel News* Staff, 'One of the evilest crimes in history': British historian Andrew Roberts on Hamas Oct 7 massacre, "This is a book of evidence about a massacre," Roberts tells Christian journalist Paul Calvert,' *All Israel News*, April 19, 2025.
45. Ibid.
46. Bejamin Ferencz (1920–2023), *United States Holocaust Memorial Museum*, Accessed May 23, 2025, https://www.ushmm.org/information/press/in-memoriam/benjamin-ferencz


## Appendix A: Glossary


1. Lieutenant Colonel Antulio J. Echevarria II, US Army, 'Clausewitz's Center Of Gravity It's Not What We Thought,' *Naval War College Review*, Winter 2003, Vol. LVI, No. 1, http://www.au.af.mil/au/awc/awcgate/navy/art4-w03.htm.


## Appendix B: Orders of Battle


1. IDF Editorial Team Sayeret Matkal, *IDF Homepage*, Accessed June 1, 2025, https://www.idf.il/en/mini-sites/our-corps-units-brigades/elite-units/sayeret-matkal/


## Appendix D: Assassinations – 'Dead Men Walking'


1. 'Hamas leader Ismail Haniyeh assassinated in Iran,' *The Washington Post Videos*, July 31, 2024.
2. 'Most Wanted: The Hamas Leaders on Israel's Radar,' *France24*, November 3, 2023, https://www.france24.com/en/middle-east/20231103-most-wanted-the-hamas-leaders-on-israel-s-radar

3. Hudson, John, and Birnbaum. Michael, 'Iran says Hamas leader's killing in Tehran will not go unanswered,' *Washington Post*, September 24, 2024.
4. Mackinnon, Mark, 'Hamas Leader Yahya Sinwar Killed in Gaza, Israel Confirms: Israel Confirmed the Death of Sinwar, Who Ordered Last Year's Shock Invasion of Israel, After Examining Forensic Evidence,' *The Globe and Mail*, October 17, 2024, https://www.theglobeandmail.com/world/article-hamas-leader-sinwar-death/
5. 'Mohammed Deif, The Elusive Architect of Hamas's October 7 Attacks on Israel,' *France 24*, October 19, 2023.
6. Raghavan, Sudarsan, 'Mohammed Deif, the Shadowy Figure Who Heads Hama's Military Wing,' *The Washington Post*, August 3, 2014, https://www.washingtonpost.com/world/middle_east/mohammed-deif-the-shadowy-figure-who-heads-hamass-military-wing/2014/08/02/ed68c46e-1a85-11e4-85b6-c1451e622637_story.html
7. Fatima Al-Kassab, 'What To Know About The Elusive Hamas Military Commander Behind The Attack On Israel,' *National Public Radio,* October 13, 2023, https://www.npr.org/2023/10/13/1205448988/hamas-military-mohammed-deif-gaza-israel
8. Seibt, Sebastian, 'Mohammed Deif, the Elusive Architect of Hamas's October 7 Attacks on Israel,' *France 24*, October 10, 2023, https://www.france24.com/en/middle-east/20231010-mohammed-deif-the-elusive-architect-of-hamas-s-attack-on-israel
9. Daou, Marc, 'Most Wanted: The Hamas Leaders on Israel's Radar,' *France 24*, November 3, 2023, https://www.france24.com/en/middle-east/20231103-most-wanted-the-hamas-leaders-on-israel-s-radar
10. 'Abu Ubeida Announces Martyrdom of Chief of Staff Mohammed Deif during Al-Aqsa Flood,' *Yemen News Agency*, January 30, 2025.
11. Flemming, Tessa, 'Israel Says it's "Assessing" Air Strike on Hamas' Deputy Military Commander Marwan Issa. Here's what we Know: For Years, Hamas' Marwan Issa Evaded the Public Eye, Becoming One of Israel's "Most Wanted" Men,' *ABC Premium News*, March 12, 2024.
12. 'Most Wanted: The Hamas Leaders on Israel's Radar,' *France 24*, January 3, 2024, 2023.https://www.france24.com/en/middle-east/20231103-most-wanted-the-hamas-leaders-on-israel-s-radar
13. Rumpf-Whitten, Sarah, 'Israel Kills Hamas Commander Who Led Heinous Oct. 7 Attack On Kibbutz Nir Oz Killed In Drone Attack,' *IDF*, December 31, 2024, https://www.foxnews.com/world/israel-kills-hamas-commander-who-led-heinous-oct-7-attack-kibbutz-nir-oz-killed-drone-attack-idf?msockid=091098da535c61b5268e8bd9524e60f2
14. 'First Female Member Of Hamas' Political Bureau Killed In Gaza,' *Middle East Monitor*, October 19, 2023 https://www.middleeastmonitor.com/20231019-first-female-member-of-hamas-political-bureau-killed-in-gaza/